The Essential Jewish Stories

THE
ESSENTIAL
JEWISH STORIES

Collected, Annotated,
and Retold by
Seymour Rossel

Preface by
Henry Roubicek

Rossel Books
Dallas, Texas

Rossel Books
6523 Genstar Lane
Dallas, Texas 75252
www.rossel.net

Dedicated to

Susan C. Bass
who inspires us with her courage
& Jerold Morton Bass, *z"l*
for memory that continues to inspire
SR

Contents

❧ FAITH ❧

❧ REFERENCES ❧

Preface

Torah defines the righteous not as those who have succeeded, but who have persevered. I spent years trying to understand that proclamation. Thanks to Seymour Rossel, I think I got it. *The Essential Jewish Stories* takes readers on a journey befitting a community to which religion is important and must endure. Rabbi Rossel's humor, both endless and enchanting, centers on the relationships of Judaism to the individual Jew and the community. Additionally, he prepares us for the critical range of religious teachings with the wittiness that is characteristic of the consummate storyteller: Religious oppressors are revealed. Those who challenge the justice of a harsh decree are exposed. Mystical attempts to hurry the coming of the Messiah are divulged. Then, there is humble charity that always eclipses power and wealth. He leaves nothing out.

With that said, stories in this compilation avoid unimportant sidebars that keep readers from feeling frustrated and lost. Instead, Rossel skillfully uses the power of brevity to dispense God, Torah, Israel, and Faith as spiritual landscapes dotted with legions of lessons so simple and profound and told so brilliantly that any story familiar to the reader will unfold as fresh and pristine. This renewed gist of Jewish narratives blended with unmatched verbal artistry creates a distinctive kind of storytelling ownership that can only belong to Seymour Rossel.

Like Torah, Rossel's collection is not as much about learning as it is transformation. Perhaps Rebbe Nachman of Breslov holds the most precise take on Seymour Rossel's reason for us reading *The Essential Jewish Stories*: "If you are not a better person tomorrow than you are today, what need have you for tomorrow?" Growing up in a home with Holocaust survivors taught me about the strength that comes with tomorrow. I learned about perseverance and this elusive thing called truth. Still, I felt incomplete. I felt an insatiable desire to engage in meaningful discourse about the truth that fuels Jewish thought.

After years of reflection, I had a revelation, one that transformed me more movingly than merely into a life with enough sense to know that spreading a layer of schmaltz on rye may be the invention of a chosen people but should not be the chosen snack for those who are fond of their arteries. It was that I survived challenging episodes in my life—at times so grueling that to revisit them is incomprehensible—just like those belonging to my Jewish ancestors. What I needed is what every Jew eventually requires: The chance to be nourished with the warmth and soul of Jewish thought. It is my friend, Seymour Rossel, who supplies that nourishment by telling the stories that must be told to furnish us with wisdom to learn the essential messages found in these essential stories about persistence and pride, wisdom and wit, forgiveness and faith, and indeed about becoming a better person with every tomorrow.

And truth? No one has ever provided me with a satisfactory definition. However, it is in this striking anthology of Jewish narratives where truth may be lurking more visibly than any other place, because Seymour Rossel's persona is captured permanently in the words of an old Chasidic proverb: "What's truer than truth? The story."

Dr. Henry Roubicek
Professor of Communication Studies,
University of Houston Downtown,
author of *So, What's Your Story:
Discovering the Story in You*

Introduction

An old man felt compelled to enter the palace if only once before he died, if only to stand in the throne room to admire the king and all his hosts. To his dismay, he found guards stationed at the palace gate blocking the way. Day after day he returned to sit beside the gate, waiting. A year passed and then years. Finally, he approached the captain of the guards to express his frustration. "Will I ever be permitted to enter the palace?"

"*You?*" the captain asked, incredulous. "Don't you know? We guard this gate to prevent anyone but you from entering. You yourself have always been welcome."

Jewish stories guard the gate to the throne room. You yourself are always welcome to enter.

This collection of Jewish stories grew organically. I began teaching in Jewish afternoon schools in my teens and soon discovered that my students not only enjoyed stories but also remembered them. As a camp counselor, I learned the kind of stories best for campfires as distinguished from the kind best for launching discussions. Before long, I was able to help others learn to use stories in diverse settings. Throughout my career in writing, teaching, and publishing, I scrutinized Jewish stories as jewelers evaluate diamonds beneath a loupe—one beautiful specimen after another, each unique and each potentially the centerpiece of a stunning setting.

As a congregational rabbi, the stories I had collected through the years gained another dimension. Through sermons, adult education, and rabbinic counseling, I could see how individuals I knew intimately responded to the stories. The stories effected moral and spiritual change, as they opened new visions and understandings. I felt especially rewarded when I heard congregants telling one another stories I had introduced to them—using the stories with their own children, bring the stories to bear as examples in their own conversations, making the stories part of their everyday lives.

Of course, this was always my purpose in collecting, adapting, and retelling the stories. Certainly, this was also the purpose of those throughout the generations who had told the stories before me. We all trust the stories to do their work which is ultimately our work: to communicate. The Hebrew national poet, Chaim Nachman Bialik, once wrote, "Some say that what was truly given at Mount Sinai was style." And the Jewish style consists of communicating the deepest truths and most hidden meanings through stories.

Nearly fifty years into my life as a Jewish teacher and raconteur, two of my four children have themselves undertaken to become rabbis. Like any father, I wish to leave them a personal legacy. There may perhaps be some estate more earthly that I will also pass on to them, but there will surely be no estate more heavenly than this collection of Jewish lore. As I share it with them, I share it with you, too.

The remaining question stands like an elephant in the room: *What sets this treasury apart from other collections?* The first answer must be that I have re-imagined and rewritten every story. It is only natural that each new generation should make the traditions of the past vital to the present. I have tried to ensure that these stories speak to us, to people of our time; that they address themselves to issues of our time. Perhaps, they will help build a future generation which will then re-imagine and rewrite these stories once again.

The second answer is that I have attempted to track down the sources of these legends, anecdotes, stories, and sayings. By and large, these are not original creations, but the "coin of the realm." Those who wish to study further may wish to consult the earlier versions I consulted—many in English translation, most standard Jewish tellings, and at times the first recorded telling.

The third answer is that I have arranged these stories according to Jewish themes and provided indices that point to when the stories may be used to their best advantage. One index arranges the stories according to Jewish holy days, while another arranges them according to the Jewish values they convey, and yet another arranges them by periods according to notable characters—the people they portray and also the people who related them.

I wish I could list all those who have aided me in my search for the stories that stand guard over the gates of Jewish wisdom. I owe thanks to many whose names you would recognize and not a few whose names you might not know but who have made enormous contributions through their teaching and good works. The best I can do in this brief introduction is just to say thank you to them, one and all, for their help and guidance.

Being a Jew means inheriting a vast treasure chest of tradition that has been amassed by the Jewish people over thousands of years. Even choosing to become a Jew gives one the rights to this inheritance. But inheriting it does not automatically open it.

Nor is this treasure available to Jews alone. Many Jewish values can be equally claimed by members of Judaism's sister religions, Christianity and Islam. Christian and Muslim teachers can avail themselves of the Jewish treasure at will. It is equally their legacy and this book may be of some value to them in this regard.

My prayer is that I have made these stories accessible and made teaching and telling them interesting and appealing through my adaptations. Surely, my collection is idiosyncratic. After all, it is my collection. The challenge for you is to make it your own, to tell the stories in your own way, to place in your vocabulary those stories you find most pertinent to you and your setting, and to add whatever stories you collect on your own as you become the collector and the teller.

The choice is now in your hands. You can sit every day outside the palace, fearful of the guards, wishing that you could enter the throne room and behold the king and all his hosts just once in your lifetime, or you can discover for yourself that the guards are there not to prevent you, but to insure that you yourself enter the palace meant for you.

I

GOD

1
Creation

1. Blueprint

🕮 Rabbi Oshaya taught: When a human king builds a palace, he does not build it with his skill alone. The king employs a builder. Moreover, the builder does not build it out of his own imagination. The builder consults a blueprint—a plan and diagram—to know how to arrange the chambers and the doors of the palace. In the same way, God as both king and builder consulted the Torah and then created the world.

[Midrash Genesis Rabbah 1:1]

2. Creation and the Watch

🕮 Imagine you are walking down a quiet road and you notice a watch on the ground. You pick it up, but since you have never seen a watch before, it is a mystery to you. At first, you admire the gold back and the white face with its small black figures and its two black hands. How fascinating it is that someone thought of making it. But when you hear it ticking, you open it up to see where the noise is coming from. Then you behold a complex of gears and wheels whirring and turning, moving in steady patterns. And you wonder, "How does it all work?" So you study it, using magnifying glasses and microscopes. And you begin to understand how it works, and to see that the one who created the watch must have been very wise and very learned.

In the same way, we discovered our world. At first, we saw only the surface: We came to love the trees and the flowers, the waters flowing down to the oceans, the great mountains and the mighty thunderclouds. But then, we began to study these things and found that they were even more wonderful on the inside! We still do not understand exactly how everything operates, what makes the world go on being the way it is, but we keep musing and experi-

1

menting. In the meantime we can easily see that the Creator of this world was far wiser than the wisest human being, for God above is the greatest of all mysteries.

[Rossel, *When a Jew Prays*]

3. The Emperor and the Sun

Rabbi Joshua was visiting with the emperor, when the emperor asked, "Tell me, wise sage, does the world have a ruler?"

Rabbi Joshua answered, "Surely God is the ruler of the world."

"And who created heaven and earth?" the emperor asked.

Rabbi Joshua answered, "In the Torah it is written, 'In the beginning God created heaven and earth.'"

Then the emperor asked, "Why is God not like the emperor of Rome? God should be seen twice a year so that people may know God and worship their ruler."

"The Torah teaches that God is too powerful for people to see. As God has said, 'No person shall see Me and live.'"

"Nevertheless," the emperor insisted, "if you do not show God to me, I will not believe there truly is a God."

Rabbi Joshua took the emperor out into the garden. It was noon, and the sun was high in the sky. Rabbi Joshua said, "Now look into the sun, and you will see God."

The emperor tried to look into the sun, but as he did, he was forced to cover his eyes to keep them from burning. "I cannot look into the sun," he said.

"Listen to yourself," said Rabbi Joshua. "If you cannot look into the sun, which is just one of God's creations, then how can you expect to look at God?"

[Yalkut, *Ki Tisa*, #394; B. Talmud, *Chulin* 59b-60a; also *Sefer HaAggadah*]

4. Should We Have Been Created?

For two-and-a-half years, the schools of Shammai and Hillel debated the issue, Should human beings have been created?

The school of Shammai took the position that it would have been better for humans not to have been created.

The school of Hillel opposed them, saying, "It is better that we have been created."

In the end, both schools agreed: "It would have been better for human beings not to have been created, but since we are here, let us search our ways."

And what does it mean, "let us search our ways"? A person must ask: "If I am not for myself, who will be for me? And if I am only for myself, what am I? And if not now, when?"

[B. Talmud, *Eruvin* 13b; Mishnah *Avot* 1:14]

5. Adam's Heritage

Rabbi Meir used to say: When God decided to create Adam out of dust, God gathered the dust from the four corners of the earth. Therefore, the people of one country can never claim, "The first human was made of our dust!" while people of another country claim, "No, of the dust of our soil!"

Our Rabbis taught: Adam was created alone for the sake of both the righteous and the wicked: The righteous cannot claim: "Ours is a righteous heritage." And the wicked cannot say: "Ours is an evil heritage."

Our Rabbis taught: Adam was created alone for the sake of peace among families: So that no family could say to another, "Ours is the finer lineage."

Our Rabbis taught: Adam was created as a single being to glorify the Supreme Sovereign of Sovereigns, the Holy One, the Blessed. For when human beings mint many coins from one mold, the coins are all alike; but God fashions all human beings in the mold of the first human, and not one resembles another. Therefore, it is said: "How manifold are Your works, O God" (Psalms 92:6).

[B. Talmud *Sanhedrin* 38a; see also Mishnah *Sanhedrin* 4:5]

The notion of preventing any one family from claiming superior lineage is also the subject of a modern Jewish parlor story. Rabbi Stephen Wise was attending a formal dinner when one of the very proper ladies seated nearby leaned close and confided, "Can you imagine, Rabbi, my ancestors were present at the signing of the Mayflower Compact!" Not to be outdone, Rabbi Wise riposted: "Yes, dear lady, but my ancestors were present at Sinai making the covenant with God!"

6. One Life

Human beings were first created as a single individual to teach the lesson that whoever destroys one life, Scripture accounts it as though a whole world had been destroyed; and whoever saves one life, Scripture accounts it as though a whole world had been saved.

[Mishnah *Sanhedrin* 4:5]

7. I Have Designed a Palace

God created human beings with loving care. First, God created food for them and only then did God create humankind.

Nevertheless, the angels complained, using the words of the Psalms: "What are humans, that You have regard for them?" (Psalms 8:5). "This trouble," they pressed, "for what purpose have You created it?"

God replied, "I have designed a palace and filled it with all things good. But what pleasure have I in this palace full of goodly things with no guests?"

The angels replied, "Sovereign of the Universe! Do what pleases You."

[*Midrash Genesis Rabbah* 8:6]

8. In Praise of God

When creation was complete, God asked the angels, "What do you think of the world I have created?"

The angels replied: "All is very good, as You have said. But there is one thing in the world above that is missing in the world below."

"What is that?" asked God.

"It is the sound of praise," the angels replied. "Here in heaven we sing Your praise from morning to evening, how can it be that the world below should not do the same?"

Then, so the sages say, God created earth's music—the twittering of birds, the whispering of wind, the murmuring of waters, the rustling of leaves. And God inclined the hearts of Adam and Eve and their children forever to learn from nature's melodies how to sing the praises of God.

[adapted from Certner, *101 Jewish Stories*]

Jewish legend has it that God creates a new host of angels each day to form the heavenly choir which disappears at day's end.

9. The Shamir

It is said that the wise King Solomon knew all the secrets of nature and could speak the languages of animals and birds.

Once, as the curtain of evening drew across the sky, an eagle landed beside the king and said, "You seem troubled, O King. What bothers you?"

The king answered, "I am trying to solve a mystery: God commanded that I build a Temple to be God's house on earth. But God also commanded that, since metal is used to make weapons, no metal should strike the stones of the Temple, a house dedicated to peace. How can the stones be cut from the hills without iron axes? How can the stones be shaped without hammer and chisel? Still, there must be a way, for God would not command me to do the impossible."

"Indeed," the eagle said, "God has created a way to cut and shape stone without metal. But the secret is in the Garden of Eden."

"Then the secret is useless," Solomon sighed, "for God has commanded that no man or woman may ever return to the Garden of Eden."

The eagle flapped its wings. "Yet, God allows me to fly in and out of the Garden of Eden whenever I please. I will go now and bring you the secret."

Days passed. Then, at last, the eagle appeared with a nest in its talons. "Here is the secret," said the eagle, gently placing the nest on the ground at Solomon's feet.

Solomon looked into the nest. It was filled with tiny worms, each the size of a grain of barley. He had never seen the like of them. As he watched, they wriggled and slithered. "What creature is this?" Solomon inquired.

"This is the shamir," said the eagle. "The shamir eats rock. These little creatures were created by God to help you build the Temple. They can cut and trim the stones so that you do not have to use any metal."

Solomon thanked the eagle, adding: "People say I am wise, but truly there is greater wisdom in even the least of God's creatures."

[B. Talmud _Sotah_ 48b; Yalkut _First Kings_ #182 (which cites _Midrash Psalms_ 78:11); also _Sefer HaAggadah_]

According to a saying in the Mishnah: "Ten things were created on the eve of Sabbath in the twilight: the mouth of the earth [_which swallowed Korach and his companions_]; the mouth of the well [_named after Miriam, this well accompanied the Israelites in their wandering through the wilderness_]; the mouth of the ass [_which spoke to Balaam_]; the rainbow [_destined to be the sign of the covenant with Noah_]; the manna [_the food provided by God for the Israelites in their forty years of wandering_]; the rod of Moses [_used to perform wonders_]; the shamir [_which cleaved rock as easily and noiselessly as leafing through a book_]; and the writing on the tablets [_of the Ten Commandments_]; some say, also the destroying spirits ['_demons' or 'inclinations to do evil'_]; the grave of Moses [_who was buried by God in an unknowable place_]; the ram of our father Abraham [_caught in the thicket to be sacrificed instead of Isaac_]; and others say, the tongs of tongs [_the tongs with which the first tongs were forged_]" (_Avot_ 5:9).

10. The Lowly Spider

🐾 Before David became king, he was accustomed to sit on the roof of his house enjoying the warm afternoons. Once, as he sat, he saw a spider spinning a web. As the spider spun, the sunshine caught the white wetness of the web and caused it to shine. David shook his head and said, "O God, what a strange creature you made! This spider has no real use. It wastes its time and all its efforts. It spins a web but makes no clothing. And in the end, all that is left is just a sticky mess."

But God answered, "Do not think that any of My creatures is useless. The time will come when you may need even the spider."

Later, when King Saul had grown angry at David and was trying to kill him, David ran away and hid in a cave. But Saul was not far behind. Saul searched one cave after another, looking for David.

But God called on a spider, and the spider spun a web that covered the opening of the cave in which David was hiding. Saul soon reached that cave, but, seeing the web, he thought, "Surely, David could not have entered this cave, for he would have broken the web if he had tried to go in." So Saul passed by the cave.

When David awoke, he went to the opening of the cave and saw what the spider had done. "Spider, O spider," David said, "you have saved my life. Blessed is your Creator; blessed are you!"

[*Alphabet of Ben Sira*; also *Sefer HaAggadah*. Similar to "Androcles and the Lion" in *Aesop's Fables*. In Scottish tradition, a closely-related tale is told of King Bruce.]

11. How God Protected the Sheep

The sheep complained to God, saying, "O Creator of the Universe, You have created many evil creatures who pursue me to slay me. To the ram you gave horns, to the deer you gave speed, to the chameleon you gave the ability to change colors and blend with its background. But You have given me no defense."

God asked the sheep, "What shall I do to help you? Would you like sharp teeth so that you might bite your attackers? Or fierce claws in place of your soft hooves?"

The sheep replied: "I don't want sharp teeth or vicious claws like a beast of prey. I haven't the fierce nature to use such things."

God asked: "Would you like poisoned fangs?"

The sheep shivered. "Poison? No! It frightens me and everyone hates the snakes and spiders that have it. But You have created me as a likeable creature, gentle and mild, as I like to be."

So the Holy One, the Blessed, said: "I will grow great horns from your forehead."

But the sheep answered: "O God, You have given horns to my mate, the ram. And all day long the rams batter one another, showing off. Shall I grow prideful like the rams or as fierce as some wild buffalo? I would rather be helpless than cruel."

God smiled and said: "You please me because you wish to remain as I created you, gentle and kind. But I will not leave you without protection. See, I have given you a coat of thick wool, white and soft as snow. Go now, and show it to Adam. He will love you for it. He will take your coat each year to make clothing and blankets for himself and all his kin. So he will keep you close and protect you from all your enemies."

From that day to this, the sheep have had their shepherd; and the shepherd has protected the sheep.

[adapted from Certner, *101 Jewish Stories*]

12. The Lie and His Partner

🐾 Now let me tell you about the Lie. The Lie was just lying around one day when the word reached him that God was about to bring a great flood upon the earth. A fox brought him the news, a clever fox who thought to himself, I may need the Lie some day, and if I do him a favor now, surely he will do me a favor or two later.

This was not the way Noah wanted it. Noah well understood what God wanted. The world had gone wrong—it was a false place where you could not trust your neighbor and where the finest art in the land was the art of lying.

When God told Noah to build the ark, Noah sent the word far and wide. He set down the rule: Only pairs would do. Cattle came two by two according to their kind, flamingos and zebras came in pairs, elephants and birds came in couples; and along with the animals came others who needed to be saved. Truth and Justice came hand in hand. Love and Friendship came as a pair. And Noah and his wife greeted them all and watched over their loading from the top of the ramp.

Then Noah noticed a shadowy figure between the giraffes and the hyenas, sneaking up the ramp, trying to steal aboard. "Hold on," he called, "and let me see who you are." As he stood before the figure he saw a beautiful lady, her long hair reaching to her waist in curls, dressed in a splendid gown. But Noah had not been born yesterday. He could tell a clever disguise when he saw one. Reaching up with his hand, he tore the wig from the Lie's head and revealed beneath it a haggard old man so wretched and ugly that it was difficult to look him straight in the eye.

"Be gone," Noah said. "I know who you are, and why you have come. This time you will not succeed. I have been commanded to save two of everything, but there is only one of you—and, in the whole world, I do not think you will find any one or any thing reprehensible enough to become your partner!"

The Lie snarled and turned back. But he wasted not a moment. He cajoled and coaxed and promised and pleaded, and tried to convince every creature to give up its rightful spouse and espouse him instead. But the Lie was such a terrible beggar that no one would take him.

No one that is, but one. As the Lie came to the edge of a forest, he saw a creature sneaking among the bushes lighting a forest fire. She bent low and breathed life into the flames, and smiled as the wood began to burn. "This one will surely be my partner," the Lie said to himself, and he followed her as she fled the scene of her crime.

"Stop," he cried, but the creature, thinking she had been discovered, only ran faster. "Stop," he said again, "I'm your friend!"

"Friend?" she said, turning. "Who are you?"

"It's me," he cried, "the Lie. Now tell me, friend, who are you?" But he had only to look into her empty eye sockets and to see the wrinkled skin gathered around her face in folds to know who this was: he had found Wickedness herself!

"I love you," he cried. "Marry me. For a flood is coming to destroy the world, and we must go in pairs on the ark built by Noah to be saved."

"Surely you are lying," said Wickedness. "After all, you are the Lie. Can you be trusted to tell the truth?"

"Forget truth," he said. "It does not sound well on your lips, and it frightens me. But trust me this once—for I am desperate— so desperate that anything you ask of me I will grant you in return for this marriage."

Wickedness did not hesitate. She knew what she wanted, for she knew well the fruits of lying. "Let this be our covenant," she said. "I will marry you, and, in return, you will promise to give me all that is gained by lying, now and forever."

The Lie had little choice. The sky was already filled with clouds and growing dark. "So be it," he cried above the thunder. "Now hurry, my bride, let us run to the ark that Noah has filled."

So it was in the last moment before Noah threw the ramp overboard, the Lie and Wickedness scurried onto the safety of the ark. Noah wanted to keep them off, but for the sake of Righteousness and Valor, for the sake of Courage and Honor, and for the sake of Mercy and Forbearing, he admitted them.

You may have wondered why the world after the flood was not one hundred percent better than it was before. Now you know the reason. And you know this, too: To this very day, wherever the Lie is told, Wickedness flourishes in the bargain. So it has been; so it will ever be—until the Day of Judgment, when the world is made anew.

[*Midrash Psalms* 7:11; *Yalkut Noach*; also in *Sefer HaAggadah*]

13a. Natural Light

🕮 Once upon a time a cruel pasha ruled the land of Israel. He heard that Jewish learning was flourishing in the holy town of Safed. "How can we keep the Jews from studying their Torah?" he asked his advisers. And they recommended that he forbid the people of Safed from kindling any lights after dark.

All day long the people of Safed worked and it was only in the evening, when the darkness kept them from working, that they had time to teach their children the Torah. But now, oil lamps and candles were forbidden. What would they do? It was the children who had the idea.

They went down into the valley when twilight came and gathered all the fireflies they could find, collecting them in jars and pitchers and boxes. When they had a great many, they climbed the hill back to the town and went to the synagogue. They closed the door and released the little insects.

Lo and behold! Instead of flying away, the fireflies buzzed above the benches, giving light for the people to study by.

A watchman of the pasha came and reported that the Jews were disobeying the pasha's order; they had lit the lights of the synagogue to continue their studies. Guards came and gathered around the synagogue, but when they opened the door, they could only stare at the astonishing scene. No light had been lit but it was as light as daytime in the synagogue; and the people studied Torah by the light of myriads of fireflies.

The guards told the pasha what they had witnessed. He shrugged his shoulders and said, "Go and tell the Jewish elders and their rabbi. They can light their homes, their houses of study, and their synagogue however they wish. I can struggle against the Jews, but who am I to struggle against nature?"

When the Jews heard, they rejoiced, for they knew it was not nature that the pasha was struggling against, it was the light of God.

[adapted from Certner, *101 Jewish Stories*]

13b. Natural Light

🕮 During the Holocaust, the Nazis prevented the Jews from lighting candles in the Lodz Ghetto. They had two reasons: Lights might provide targets for Allied pilots on their bomb raids. And, they were also pleased at the prospect that the lack of light at night would provide additional hardship for the Jews.

In 1944, on the eve of Rosh Hashanah, Jews gathered for prayer in the small apartment of Rabbi Melech Roitbart on Deburska Street. They could not light the candles of the festival, so the darkness entered their souls, and filled their hearts with every reminder of their troubles. But when the cantor began to chant the *Barchu*, the traditional Jewish call to prayer, a sudden buzzing noise distracted the congregation. Then, all watched in amazement as thousands of fireflies came in through the windows. All at once, their light brightened the rooms, and the people knew that the Holy One, the Blessed, was with them, lighting their prayers and lightening their burdens.

Before long, the light was seen and the Gestapo arrived with their local henchmen. They rushed into the apartment with guns drawn, yelling, "Jews, extinguish the lights, and we won't shoot."

This was the moment of the second miracle, as the fireflies scattered, swarming around the Germans and the traitors who served them. Every one of them was blinded by the fireflies' light. Every one of them swatted helplessly at the air, trying to scatter the swarms of fireflies.

In this moment, the Gestapo officer suddenly understood what was happening and it seemed to him that the swarms of fireflies marked the beginning of the end for his people. The God of the Jews, who had been silent for so long, was silent no longer. The officer ordered his men to retreat and the Jews finished their prayers in peace.

When Rabbi Mordechai, one of the few survivors of the Lodz Ghetto, told the story of the miracle of the fireflies, he always added that the events of that night put a glow in the souls of the worshipers. Sometimes, though, Rabbi Mordechai would say that there were no fireflies at all. There was a certain Reb Yoel who was rumored to be one of the hidden righteous, the thirty-six people in every generation whose merit sustains the world from God's wrath. It was well-known that Reb Yoel, a simple wagon driver, somehow remained alive through all the deportations and all the murderous actions of the Nazis in Lodz. Day after day, this simple soul went from house to house, encouraging Jews not to lose hope, comforting them, and strengthening their spirits. Rabbi

Mordechai swore that a great light surrounded Reb Yoel wherever he went, and on the eve of Rosh Hashanah, when Reb Yoel entered the apartment, it seemed in the eyes of those gathered in prayer that a mountain of fireflies had suddenly appeared.

[adapted from a tale in the Israel Folktale Archives (File 2361) as related in Hebrew by Chaim Dov Armon in 1960]

Both versions of "Natural Light" deal with persecution. In both, the light of the fireflies is an indication of God's favor. Version "B," collected by the Israel Folktale Archives, incorporates elements of another Jewish legend: that in every generation there are thirty-six "hidden" saints upon whom the world's continued existence depends.

14. Reflections

In the beginning there was God. God spoke and a spark appeared. And God immediately recognized it for the beauty it could become. So God chiseled at its rough surface until God had carved a face of it. In the face of the spark, God saw the reflection of the Eternal shining out mysteriously and God saw that it was good. God affirmed it. And having affirmed it, God again carved a face, this one beside the first. Now the first face reflected the second; and the second, the first; and both reflected the remainder of the rough surface and the entire spark reflected the Eternal God. So God carved again, affirming it by recreating it.

When all the faces of the spark were carved like a diamond, God had reached the inside of the spark and began to carve outward again. And the splinters and shavings that gathered about the place God was carving, falling in God's lap, each reflected the light of the other and of the spark of which only the inside remained, and of God. And God reaffirmed each reflection by carving a face for it and then another and then another until only the insides of the clippings remained. Then God carved the inner faces, the inner reflections, until the inner too was all carved away and only the outer remained, a sparkling reflection of the inner and the former outer and of the Eternal and of the mother gem, the spark that seemingly no longer existed, but which was present in every shadow of every reflection.

God's world is suspension in suspension, tension in tension, noise in noise, silence in silence, and light in light. Adrift, as we all are, like the clippings our light emanates from one another and reflects the way we reflect our Creator.

[Rossel, based on two Jewish mystic ideas: that all creation begins in a *pintele*, a single point of light; and that the restoration of the world (*tikkun olam*) depends on redeeming the scattered sparks of God's light.]

2

Heaven and Earth

1. Elijah and Rabbi Joshua

Once the prophet Elijah agreed to grant Rabbi Joshua ben Levi a wish. Joshua wished to accompany Elijah on his wanderings through the world. Elijah agreed, but on one condition: No matter how odd or strange the rabbi might think Elijah's actions were, Joshua was to ask for no explanation. If he asked, Elijah said, they would have to part company.

The first night they came to the house of a poor couple whose only possession was a cow. The man and wife welcomed the two weary wanderers, fed them, and insisted that the two sleep in the cottage's only bed, while the man and his wife made a pallet on the floor. The next morning, Elijah prayed that the couple's cow might die; and, before they left the house, the cow was dead. Rabbi Joshua thought to himself, "Is this the way God rewards kindness to us?" But, remembering his promise, he said nothing.

That night they came to the house of a wealthy man. After much begging, the man agreed to let the two wanderers sleep in his barn. Being stingy, he offered them no food. The next morning, the rich man ordered his servants to repair a breach in the wall around his property. But before the servants reached the place, Elijah prayed, and the wall was miraculously rebuilt. "Is this the way God rewards a lack of hospitality?" Rabbi Joshua wondered. But, again, he said nothing.

The next day they reached a magnificent synagogue. The seats were made of silver and gold, but the people there seemed to have hearts of stone. No one offered to feed them, and it was only with diligent begging that they were allowed to remain in the synagogue overnight, sleeping on the hard benches. The next morning, Elijah blessed the congregation, praying that they would all become leaders. Rabbi Joshua was astonished; he kept his silence, but with great reluctance.

14

In the next town, the synagogue was a simple, wooden one; but the congregation had genuine regard for the two wayfarers. They invited the men to dine, and offered them a choice of homes in which to spend the night. The next morning, Elijah prayed that God choose any one of the congregation to be its leader.

This was too much for the good rabbi. He could hold his peace no longer. He demanded an explanation for Elijah's strange prayers and God's equally strange responses.

"Now we must go our separate ways," said Elijah, "for you have broken your promise. But before we part, I shall explain what you have seen, and how little you have understood.

"As for the congregation of the rich synagogue, I prayed they might all become leaders, for a multiplicity of leaders brings a multiplicity of strong opinions and disputes. That congregation will destroy itself. As for the congregation that offered us warm hospitality, I prayed they might have only one leader. With one to guide them, success will follow their every undertaking.

"As for the couple who gave us their bed and shared with us their last crumbs of bread, I prayed their cow might die, for I knew that on that very day the wife was to be stricken deathly ill by decree of Heaven, and, because of my prayer, the cow was taken instead of her.

"And as for the rich man, I rebuilt his wall for him. Once more, there was a reason you could not know. Beneath the broken section of the rich man's wall, there is a vast treasure which his servants would surely have found while making the repairs. Now, the miser will never know what wealth his hospitality might have brought him.

"Learn from this," Elijah concluded, "if you see an evil person prosper, it is not always to his advantage; and if you see a righteous person suffer in need and in distress, do not imagine that God is unjust." The next moment, Rabbi Joshua found himself back in his own house, in his own room.

[B. Talmud *Sanhedrin* 98a; also in a variant form in Gaster, *Sefer Ha-Maasiyot* and in an adulterated form in the Koran]

Elijah and Rabbi Joshua did not occupy the same space in time. Elijah lived in the ninth century, BCE; Joshua ben Levi was active in the first half of the third century, CE. By the time of Rabbi Joshua, legend held that Elijah (destined to announce the coming of the Messiah) had never died (*see* Second

Kings 2:1-11). Elijah wanders the earth, serving as God's agent here and there, rewarding good and punishing evil.

2. Clowns

🐌 Many Sages of Talmud and Midrash had poetic souls. They used to say that they were visited by "the heavenly academy," as if to say that Heaven is a parallel world to Earth. (When modern folk speak of "parallel worlds," we call them fantasists, science fiction writers, or physicists.) Since the Sages met in Houses of Study here on earth, those who died must be meeting in Houses of Study in Heaven.

At other times, the Sages spoke of hearing a *Bat Kol*, literally, an "echo." This heavenly voice expressed God's opinion, ruling on a point of law or providing some heavenly advice A *Bat Kol* might call to a single Sage or it might interrupt a discussion.

From time to time, too, the Sages found themselves face-to-face with the prophet Elijah, who never died, but was taken to Heaven in a chariot of fire. Elijah might appear anywhere: disguised as a beggar, as a stranger, or even as a non-Jew. It was said that Elijah wandered the world endlessly, helping people with advice or blessings—all the while waiting for the right moment to announce the coming of the Messiah. The Sages often encountered Elijah in the marketplace, the outdoor mall of villages, towns, and cities.

Rabbi Baruka of Chuza often shopped in the marketplace of Lapet. One day, he saw Elijah there. The rabbi asked Elijah, "Is there anyone here in this marketplace that will have an honored place in the world to come?"

Elijah pointed to two men. "These two," he said, "will share in the world to come."

Rabbi Baruka went to the two men and asked them, "What do you do for a living?"

They said, "We are clowns. When we see folks who are sad, we perform to cheer them. And when we see people quarreling, we use our arts to make peace between them."

[B. Talmud *Taanit.* 22a]

3. Torah Is Not in Heaven

🐍 Our sages taught: "In the Torah, God gave us all the laws we need. Since the time of the Torah, people have had to settle arguments between themselves."

The students asked: "How do we know this?"

The sages answered: "From the story of Rabbi Eliezer and the oven of Achnai."

In the time of Rabbi Eliezer, a new kind of oven was invented. Old ovens were made of bricks or clay. The new oven was made like a layer cake, with coils of clay separated by layers of sand. The whole oven was then covered over by cement. It was called the Achnai oven. Some say that it was called this because the name of the inventor was Achnai. Some say that it was called Achnai because *achnai* means "snake," and the clay seemed coiled like a snake ready to strike. But some say it was called Achnai because the rabbis encircled it with many arguments as if a snake had wrapped itself around the oven.

The problem was, would the oven be kosher, ritually acceptable, if it were used for meat and a drop of milk fell on it? If it was ruled that the oven was no longer kosher, then it would have to be replaced. But if it was ruled that the oven was still kosher, then it could still be used. Rabbi Eliezer argued that the oven would always be kosher. It could not be spoiled since it was not made of one piece and so it was not one thing. The rest of the rabbis argued that the cement that covered the oven made it all one piece and so it would no longer be kosher if any part of it was spoiled. Rabbi Eliezer argued fiercely, but the rabbis would not agree with him.

The rabbis were sitting on the benches near the walls of the house of study in Lydda. A small stream ran nearby. And the trees shaded the rabbis from the sun. It was a beautiful day, but Rabbi Eliezer paid no attention to the sunshine and the breeze. He argued and argued until it was clear that he could not win.

Then he turned to all the other rabbis and said, "I will prove to you that I am right and you are wrong. If I am right, let this carob tree move."

As sudden as a flash of lightning, the carob tree jumped from the ground and flew across the stream. And just as suddenly, it planted itself on the other bank of the stream. The rabbis were amazed. They could hardly believe their eyes. For a moment, they sat quietly, lost in thought.

At last, one rabbi stood and said, "Carob trees do not know the law. You can't prove that you are right by asking a carob tree to move."

Rabbi Eliezer would not give up. "If I am right," he said, "let the stream flow backward."

As the rabbis watched, the water in the stream came to a complete stop. Then the water began to run uphill toward the mountains of Judea.

A rabbi stood and said, "Streams do not know the law. You can't prove you are right by asking a stream to flow backward."

Rabbi Eliezer refused to give up. "If I am right," he said, "let the walls of the house of study fall."

The brick walls of the house of study began to tremble. The rabbis jumped from their seats and started to run for safety.

"Wait," cried Rabbi Joshua, pointing to the walls. "You walls have no right to make laws for Israel! You must stand and not fall."

Listening to Rabbi Joshua, the walls refused to fall. But because Rabbi Eliezer had asked them to fall, the walls leaned a little. And, from that day on, the walls of the house of study at Lydda always leaned over the rabbis when they sat outdoors on their benches.

When they saw that it was safe, the rabbis took their seats again. One of them asked, "Rabbi Eliezer, why not give up and admit that you are beaten?"

Rabbi Eliezer crossed his arms and spoke again. "I can prove that I am correct." Then he raised his voice and cried out, "If I am right, let heaven say so."

In a deep and rolling thunder, a *Bat Kol*, an echo came from the distant hills and filled the heavens with sound. "Rabbi Eliezer knows the law. Why do you argue with him?"

Now Rabbi Joshua stood again. "God has told us in the Torah, 'Torah is not in heaven.' We Jews pay no attention to voices from the sky because long ago the Torah told us, 'The majority rules.' When we rabbis argue about a law, we take a vote to see who wins."

Then the rabbis voted. Rabbi Eliezer cast one vote for his argument. All the other rabbis voted against him. Rabbi Eliezer lost the argument. Thus the rabbis taught us that we must not rely on trees or streams or walls or even heaven itself to settle our arguments; we must settle them ourselves.

[B. Talmud *Baba Metzia*, 59a-b; also *Sefer HaAggadah*]

The Talmud includes this addendum to this story: One of the sages later asked the prophet Elijah what God thought of the rabbis' decision. Elijah replied, "God laughed and said, 'My children have overruled me.'"

4. Every Four Generations

It is said that God created human beings because God loves stories. And no people has a prouder heritage of telling stories than the Jews. Indeed, the first great work was bringing together all the finest stories of the ancient world and reworking them into the Torah, the Five Books of Moses. When that was accomplished, our stories became a Tree of Life for us.

But our stories continued to multiply. After the Torah came the prophets and the kings; then the stories of Ruth and Esther and Job and Daniel, and all the writings of wisdom. It seemed like a never-ending fountain. Until suddenly the fountain became a trickle, and then the trickle stopped.

For six hundred years after the Bible was complete, no new legends were set down in writing. This was the time of the Oral Law, when legends and teachings were given by word of mouth, from earlier generations of sages to be memorized by their students. Everyone knows that this is so, but not everyone knows the real reason. In that, there is a legend.

It happened in the moment that the Great Assembly, sitting in its meeting house, declared that the Bible was complete—no new Writing could be added to it, no further word of the Prophets could be included in it.

Suddenly, a chill came upon the meeting house—ice formed on the walls and icicles dangled above the Ark.

Though it was summer outside; inside the sages shivered. And, just as they began to whisper to one another in confusion, an angel appeared, robed in snow. The angel's face was like the light of the sun—so you could barely look upon it for fear of being blinded.

The angel stood in the center of the meeting house and began to speak. "You have dared to break the law of heaven! Not since Moses struck the rock instead of speaking to it has such a thing happened in Israel. Only heaven may close the books of heaven's teachings. You have declared the end, but only heaven knows the end of things!

"What you have done is truly sad," the angel continued, "yet, the law of earth has been given to the Great Assembly, and by your own decision, the Bible is now truly closed—though Heaven did not declare it so. Now, the written word of heaven's law must remain closed until six hundred years have passed. If you try to open the books again by recording so much as a single new legend, your bones will turn to ice—ice as chilling as that which now clings to the walls of your meeting house and hangs from its ceiling."

As suddenly as it had appeared, the angel departed and the ice melted and dripped, as if the walls themselves were weeping. And the falling drops were salty and bitter, like the tears of mourning when a loved one dies.

As the tears became a stream, and the stream threatened to swamp the Holy Ark, another angel appeared. Again, the angel's face was sunlight, but its velvet robe was every color of the rainbow—or was it a rainbow that was thrown across its shoulders like a prayer shawl?

When the angel spoke, it was to say "An argument has taken place in heaven. While it is true that heaven's decree cannot be rescinded, yet it has been declared that a heavenly reward will be given for the silence that heaven has imposed.

"When the legends told in the next six hundred years are written down at last, Israel will find that the legends have been transformed. If before, the legends were seen in one light, each will now be seen in lights as numerous as heaven's stars.

"In turn, there will come six hundred more years of silence with the same reward at the end of it. For each time the legends are again recorded, they will be filled with a myriad of meanings such as only heaven could ordain."

Now, the light in the meeting hall grew dim. When the sages looked up. the angel was gone and the sea of tears departed with it. But they remembered the angel's words. They told this story, and the words of the angel came true. Counting from that time to this, every six hundred years the Jewish soul has found new expression in writing down its stories.

And, you should know, no riches of story have been seen in our midst for nearly six hundred years. So, it is here in our lives, here in our days, that the time has come to write down all we have learned. And every word we write will be like a diamond with six hundred facets. Every story we tell will be like another star lighting heaven's sky.

[based on *Midrash Numbers Rabbah* 14:4; see also B. Talmud *Temurah* 14b]

The process of creation assumes that we human beings are always more adept than we seem. For example, it was well-known to music lovers that Rachmaninoff had huge hands and his music was written for fingers that could span many keys. At the end of one inspiring performance of a Rachmaninoff concerto, someone praising the pianist noticed that he, unlike Rachmaninoff, had very small hands. "How do you manage to play so fluidly on the piano with those short fingers?" the amazed person blurted out. "Is that what you imagine?" the pianist asked in return, "Do you think that I play the piano with my fingers?"

5. Where Is Paradise?

A rabbi once fell asleep and dreamed that he went to paradise. There, to his surprise, he saw all the sages gathered—Moses, Miriam, Aaron, Deborah, Hillel, Beruriah, Akiva, and Solomon—and they were arguing about a problem from the Talmud.

He was amazed. When he saw an angel, he said, "This is the very same thing that the sages were doing on earth! Can this really be paradise?"

The angel said, "You human beings are really quite a foolish kind. You cannot even tell what you see when you see it. You dream of paradise and think the sages are in it. The truth is just the opposite. Paradise is in the sages."

[tale of Rabbi Moshe Teitelbaum in Buber, *Later Masters*, pp. 189-190]

6. The Baal Shem Tov at the Curtain

While we sleep and rest, God takes our souls to heaven, only to return them to us, refreshed and renewed each morning. In all the world, though, there was one soul that never rested. This was the soul of the founder of Chasidism, the great Rabbi Israel Baal Shem Tov. Every night, his soul went to heaven with the others, but his soul constantly sought to move upward through the heavens. His soul was seeking to reunite with God and, with each passing night, it drew a little closer to the heavenly throne.

Now, in front of God's throne there is a curtain of woven light. Imprinted on this curtain are perfect images of all things on earth. In this way, God sees things only the way they should be, only the way they could be.

It is said that one night, the restless soul of the Baal Shem arrived at that final curtain. The Baal Shem's soul knew that if he pressed on, if he passed through that curtain, he would forever be removed from the struggles of the world. He would become the perfect Baal Shem Tov and would dwell forever united with God. This was what the soul had been yearning for during all those nights of seeking. His hand reached up to part the curtain.

But, just at that last moment, down below on earth—so far down below—the wife of the Baal Shem Tov turned in their bed and her hand gently brushed his cheek. With a start, the soul of the Baal Shem Tov realized that true perfection is not in heaven to be reached, but on earth to be realized. The Baal Shem awoke and whispered a prayer of thanks to God for safely restoring his soul.

[adapted from Levin, *The Golden Mountain*, p. 135]

7. We Are All Travelers

🐟 Among the followers of Rabbi Israel Baal Shem Tov was a Jewish farmer from a small village near Mezeritch. The Baal Shem Tov loved such rural Jews, holding them in high esteem for their wholesomeness, their integrity, and their unequivocal faith in God. So whenever this particular farmer came to spend a Sabbath with his *rebbe*, his teacher and mentor, the Baal Shem Tov welcomed him with true affection.

At the end of one Sabbath visit, the Baal Shem Tov made a request of the farmer, saying, "As you travel home, please stop by Mezeritch to give my regards to one of my closest and most illustrious disciples, the scholarly and pious Rabbi Dov Baer."

The farmer was overjoyed to be given this honor by his beloved *rebbe*. He hurried to Mezeritch and asked if anyone knew the whereabouts of the great Rabbi Dov Baer. To his chagrin, no one seemed to know of a "great Rabbi Dov Baer," even though the town was famed for its scholars and mystics. But, in the end, someone suggested that the farmer try a certain "Reb Baer," an poor teacher who held his one-room schoolhouse on the edge of town.

When the farmer approached the place to which he was directed, he found it was an alley in the poorest section of town. Both sides of a muddy path were blocked from the light of the sun by row upon row of dilapidated wooden hovels, one leaning upon the other for support. Soon, though, he found the one-room "schoolhouse," a tumbled-down hut with broken windowpanes. If it was possible, the hut's inside was even more pathetic than the outside. A man of middle-age sat on a block of wood, at a "table" that was nothing more than a rough plank set up other blocks of wood. Around the table, rows of studying children sat on "benches" that were also made of rickety planks and blocks.

Nevertheless, the farmer saw something in the teacher's face, some hint of greatness, that made him believe that he had indeed found his man.

Rabbi Dov Baer offered a kind greeting to his visitor, but he begged for forgiveness, saying, "Perhaps, it would be better—if you can—to return later when the students are finished studying?"

The farmer returned that evening and things had changed. The simple classroom furniture had been turned into rickety beds for the children who were boarding with the rabbi. And Rabbi Dov Baer sat upon one lone block of wood, reading a book by the light of a single candle.

The farmer gave his words of greeting from the Baal Shem Tov, and Rabbi Baer thanked him and invited him to sit, pointing to a nearby table-turned-bed. Suddenly, the farmer could contain himself no longer. He very nearly yelled as he spoke out against this poverty: "Rabbi Dov Baer, how can you live like this? I myself am far from wealthy, but at least in my home I have the basic necessities—some chairs, a table, beds for my children..."

The rabbi was very calm. "Is that so?" he asked. "Then why don't I see your furniture? How do you manage without it?"

"What do you mean?" the farmer asked. "Do you think I take my furniture everywhere I go? Listen, when I travel, I make do with what's available. But at home—a person's home is a different matter altogether!"

"We are all travelers in this world," said Rabbi Dov Baer gently. "At home? Oh yes... At home, it is a different matter altogether...."

[adapted from a story by Rabbi Yosef Yitzchak of Lubavitch]

8. Rabbi Simeon's Recipe

At Sinai the Children of Israel made a covenant with God. Our covenant pledge was *na'aseh v'nish'ma.* "We will do and we will hear." *We will do*—meaning, we will do the *mitzvot*, the "commandments" of God. *We will hear*—meaning, we will listen to God's teachings. In return for our pledge, God promised to dwell among us and to treat us as God's chosen people. To bind God to the people Israel, Torah was passed from heaven to earth. The covenant is our agreement; the Torah is our written contract.

Rabbi Simeon bar Yochai compared this to a recipe: Take two ships. Bind them together with ropes and cords. Build a palace on them. Now, as long as the two ships remain lashed together, the palace will stand; but if the ships drift apart, then the palace will collapse.

The two ships are heaven and earth. The cords and ropes are the covenant. The palace is the Torah, a glorious "home" we share with God. So long as we do God's will and heed God's teachings, the ships remain lashed together and the palace is safe. Then, God dwells close to us and we feel chosen—special—because we have the palace, the Torah and the covenant. But when we forget or turn away from God, the ships are washed apart by the waves. Earth drifts away from heaven. The palace of Torah splits and shatters. Then, God seems far away and we forget how "chosen" we are.

[*Sifre Deuteronomy* 144a]

~⚜ 3 ⚜~
God and Humanity

1. Where Is God's Dwelling?

⚜ The Kotzker *rebbe* confronted his students, asking, "Where is the dwelling of God?"

The students were prompt with their answer. "*Rebbe*, is it not true that the whole world is full of God's glory?"

The Kotzker sighed. "In truth," he said. "God only dwells where we let God in."

[Buber, *Later Masters*, p. 277]

2. What Shall I Worship?

⚜ Abraham's father, Terach, was a maker of idols. Abraham watched his father making the idols out of wood and stone. People came and bought Terach's idols. Abraham knew that the people worshiped them. "How foolish they are," thought Abraham. "These idols are not gods, they are just dolls my father makes."

One night, Abraham noticed how the stars filled the sky. Abraham thought, "The stars shine like sparkling diamonds! Surely, it is the stars who are the real gods. They are far greater than idols of wood and stone. I will worship them."

All night, Abraham prayed to the stars. But at dawn, the stars faded and sun's light washed them away. Then Abraham thought, "Why worship those little lights when I could worship the mighty sun?" All day, Abraham prayed to the sun but, as the day ended, the sun turned red and fell from the sky. "The sun is no god," Abraham thought.

That night, the moon appeared. "Why did I not see this at once?" Abraham wondered. "Surely, the moon is a god. I will worship the moon." But the moon also disappeared. So Abraham thought, "Stars and moon, sea and sun—all these come and go. Just as my father creates idols, there must be One who creates all

25

things in the heavens and on the earth. I will worship the One God, the One who is the Creator of all things."

[Rossel, _Storybook Haggadah_; based on Jellinek, _Bet ha-Midrash_, 2:118-196]

A well-known story tells how Terach once left young Abraham in charge of his idol shop. When Terach returned, he found all the idols broken except the largest. Abraham placed a broom in the hand of the standing idol. Terach clapped his hands to his face and exclaimed, "My son, what have you done?" Abraham replied, "Father, I did nothing. The big idol grew angry, grabbed the broom, and destroyed all the other idols." Terach said, "Abraham, you know that no idol could do such a thing. They are only wood and metal." To which Abraham replied, "If that is the case, why should people bow down to them, sacrifice to them, and worship them?" (_Midrash Genesis Rabbah_ 38:12). No one knows the actual profession of Abraham's father. The rabbis simply identified Terach as "before Abraham" and, therefore, an idolater.

3. Seeing God

🐾 Tolstoy tells a story about a cobbler named Martin who despaired of life and yearned to see God. In a dream one night, Martin learned that he would see God the very next day.

He began his day on the alert, ready to catch a glimpse of the Almighty, but he was distracted when he encountered a needy family. They were cold and desperate, in need of food and coats, so Martin took them in and cared for them. The day passed as he tended to their needs, and suddenly, as he was lying down to sleep, he realized that he had forgotten to look for God.

Again that night he heard a voice promising that, if he only remained vigilant, he would see God the next day. But the next day, the same thing happened, he was again distracted by people in need, and he again turned his kindly face toward them instead of watching for God.

The third night, in total despair, he apologized to God and asked to die. Instead, he fell asleep and dreamed that he saw the people he had helped walking by. As they passed, he heard the voice again, saying, "Martin, be assured. You _have_ seen God's face. It is in the face of all you helped."

[adapted from a parable by Leo Tolstoy]

4. Hillel's Image

🖎 When the day's study was over, the students of the School of Hillel left the academy with their master, still asking him questions about the day's lesson. After a few minutes, Hillel excused himself. This made the students curious, since Hillel usually loved to tarry and exchange words with them. "Where are you going?" they asked.

Hillel said, "I am running to fulfill a *mitzvah*."

They said, "Then let us help you."

"This commandment I will fulfill on my own," Hillel replied with a wry smile. "I am going to take a bath."

The students asked, "Is that a *mitzvah*?"

"Yes," he answered. "Look at the statues erected by the Romans. They make statues of their kings which they set up in the theaters and in the circuses. The men who wash the images and keep them clean are paid to honor the kings. I am created in the image of the Ruler of the universe. Shall I not honor that image by keeping it clean?"

[*Midrash Leviticus Rabbah* 34:3]

5. Shechinah

🖎 For our Sages, God could be both far and near. As the Creator of the heavens and the earth, God was distant, far beyond the created world. When they spoke of God in this way, the Sages would called God, *HaMakom*, "The Place," indicating that God was not in the world but the world was in God, therefore God was "The Place" of the world.

At the same time, they felt God near them, close by, protecting them, even as a mother protects her young. When they spoke of God in this way, the Sages called God, *Shechinah*, the "Presence," saying that God is "present" to us in our world. Both *HaMakom* and *Shechinah* are human conceptions, so the Sages assigned them human attributes, saying that *HaMakom* was the masculine side of God and *Shechinah* was God's feminine side. Of course, the Sages worshiped the One God. The two names they used were just expressions of their feelings.

When is the experience of the nearness of the *Shechinah* most acute?

Rabbi Chalafta ben Dosa taught: When ten people sit together and study the Torah, the *Shechinah* sits with them. We
prove this since ten people are necessary for a *minyan* for public
prayer and Scripture teaches "God attends the congregation of
the godly" (Psalms 82:1). Can we show that the *Shechinah* is also
present in the company of five people? Yes, for five people are required to speak of a group and Scripture records "God has
founded God's group upon the earth" (Amos 9:6). Can we show
that the *Shechinah* is also present in the company of three people?
Yes, for three judges are required for a court and Scripture asserts
"God judges among the judges" (Psalms 82:1). Can we show that
the *Shechinah* is also present in the company of two people? Yes,
for Scripture declares "Then they that revered God spoke one with
the other ..." (Malachi 3:16). And can we show that the *Shechinah*
is also present even with only one person? Yes, because God avers:
"In every place where I cause My name to be remembered, I will
come to you and I will bless you" (Exodus 20:24).

[Mishnah *Avot* 3:6]

The sages developed the art of quoting—in or out of context—a verse,
half a verse, or even a few words of Scripture as "proof" of a law or a teaching.
Rabbi Chalafta assembled five elegant "proof texts" to demonstrate that the
Shechinah is present whenever and wherever we would expect to find God—
in prayer, in fellowship, in the law court, in dialogue, and in contemplation.

6. The Bargain

🐟 When Jacob and Esau were young, they made a bargain. Esau
said, "I will take everything this world gives, and you can have everything God gives." Jacob readily agreed, but Esau thought, "I
have outsmarted Jacob. I have taken everything that is really important. All he can hope for is a good place in heaven."

Many years later, Jacob returned from his journeys. He had
two wives and many children. He had servants and cattle. He had
silver and gold. Then Esau said to him, "You have cheated on our
bargain. I was supposed to get everything in this world, and you
were supposed to get only the things of heaven."

Jacob replied, "I have not cheated you. None of what I have
belongs to me. Everything belongs to God. Yet God allows me to
use these things as I need them."

[*Tanna devei Eliyahu*, 19; also *Sefer HaAggadah*]

7. Why Moses Stuttered

The characters of the Bible are not perfect. Jacob limped, Isaac was very nearly blind, and Moses stuttered. At the burning bush, Moses complained to God that someone else should be sent to Pharaoh, someone who would be a better spokesperson, someone who did not stutter. God replied that Moses was chosen to lead the Jewish people, but his brother Aaron would serve as his spokesperson.

The rabbis wondered, Why did Moses stutter? So, they added this tale to the many legends of Moses:

Pharaoh's daughter loved Moses as her own son. She kept him close, never allowing him to leave the royal palace. Pharaoh also kissed and hugged the child, and Moses would play with Pharaoh's crown and put it on his own head.

The magicians of Egypt complained to the Pharaoh, "We fear this little one, who grabs your crown and dons it. One day, he may take your kingdom from you."

Pharaoh asked, "What shall I do?"

Some of the magicians replied, "Have the boy put to death." Others said, "Burn the child alive." But one magician advised otherwise: "Perhaps, the child is too young to know what he is doing. Why not test him? Place before him a shiny gold piece and a burning coal. If the boy reaches for the gold, he is dangerous and you should slay him. But if he reaches for the coal, he is no danger to you, for he has no understanding. Then you may leave him play as he will."

Pharaoh sent for the gold and the coal. As any child would, Moses ignored the white ash of the coal and put forth his hand to grab the glittering gold. In that instant, the angel Gabriel descended from heaven and shoved the boy's hand to the burning coal. Not only did Moses seize the lump of coal, he also brought his hand still holding the fiery lump to his mouth, whereupon he burned his tongue.

God had saved Moses' life. But from that day on, the rabbis said, Moses was "slow of speech and slow of tongue."

[Midrash Exodus Rabbah 1:26]

8. Let My People Go

🐚 Rabbi Chiya bar Abba said: Moses and Aaron arrived on the day of the week when Pharaoh received ambassadors who wished to pay him honors and bring him gifts. At the end of the day, Moses and Aaron were still waiting. Finally, Pharaoh's servants informed him: "There are still two old men at the gate." Pharaoh commanded, "Let them enter."

When they stood before his throne, Pharaoh looked at them, expecting they would offer him a gift or bring greetings from some distant kingdom. But they did not greet him. At last, Pharaoh demanded, "Who are you?" They replied, "We are the ambassadors of *Adonai*, the God of the Israelites."

"What do you want?" he asked. They replied: "*Adonai* commands: 'Let My people go!'"

Pharaoh became angry. "Has your God not the sense to send me a gift so that you do not come to me with mere words? Who is this '*Adonai*'? I do not know your God and I will not let Israel go."

Moses and Aaron turned to leave, but Pharaoh wished to mock them further: "Stay awhile. I will search my records." He called for the list of every nation and its gods. As the long scroll was unrolled, he read the names of the gods of Moab, Ammon, Zidon, and all the seventy nations of the world. He said, "You see, I have searched for your God's name in my archives but I have not found it."

Rabbi Levi said: It was then that Moses and Aaron berated Pharaoh: "Idiot! Do you think the dead are found with the living, or the living with the dead? Our God is living, whereas the gods in your list are dead."

Pharaoh refused to be bested. "Is your God young or old? How many cities has *Adonai* captured? How many provinces has *Adonai* subdued? How long is it since *Adonai* ascended your throne?" They answered, "God's strength and might fill the universe. Before the world was created God existed and God will be when the world ends. God fashioned you and gave you the breath of life."

Pharaoh laughed and said, "From the first, you have spoken nothing but lies. For, behold, I am Pharaoh, the Lord of the Universe. I have created 'myself and the Nile,' as it is written on the walls of my palace. As for your *Adonai*, I do not know who this God of yours is."

They replied, "Soon enough, you shall know."

[*Midrash Exodus Rabbah* 5:14; *Tanchuma* 95a]

The four-letter Hebrew name of God is never pronounced by Jews. This forbearance has persisted so long that the true pronunciation of the four-letter name seems to be lost. Wherever the four-letter name appears, the word *Adonai*, meaning "My Liege" or "My Master," is spoken as a substitute.

9. God's Power

Our rabbis taught: As the Children of Israel crossed through the Sea of Reeds, Pharaoh commanded his army of chariots to follow them. At first, the horses of Pharaoh's army were afraid to go forward. They saw the towering walls of water on either side and refused to move. So God worked a miracle. All the waves of the sea shaped themselves to look like charging horses. Following the watery herd, Pharaoh's horses charged into the sea.

Suddenly, the soldiers riding in the chariots were afraid. They cried to their horses, "Yesterday we had to drag you to the Nile just to give you water to drink. Now you are dragging us into the midst of the sea." But the horses could not be stopped.

Pharaoh, however, could not go forward. His horse saw only walls of water and refused to budge. Pharaoh could but watch his six hundred chariots charge into the dry path in the sea's midst.

When the Egyptian chariots had gone halfway, the earth beneath them turned to mud. Their wheels were trapped. Their horses grew exhausted trying to pull the chariots free. All at once, the walls on either side toppled, and the sea rushed together, trapping horses, chariots, and Egyptians.

Pharaoh's heart grew soft in agonizing despair. At long last, after plagues and defeat, Pharaoh comprehended God's power.

[*Midrash Exodus Rabbah* 23:14; *Midrash Song of Songs Rabbah* 1:9, #6]

10. Enough for Just a Day

The students of Rabbi Simeon ben Yochai asked, "Why did God give the Children of Israel enough manna for only one day at a time? Why not provide them enough for a whole year so that they could gather it once and eat it all year long?"

Rabbi Simeon explained: There was once a king who had a child. He decided to give his child an allowance. When the king gave his child enough money for a whole year, the child visited the king only once a year. So the king gave enough money for only a single day. In that way, the child came to visit every day. God gave the Israelites manna every day to teach them and us that we must turn our hearts to God daily.

[B. Talmud *Yoma* 76a; also *Sefer HaAggadah*]

In Exodus (16:15), the Israelites encountered manna (*mahn*, in Hebrew) for the first time and asked one another, *Mahn hu?*, meaning "What is it?" This is a pun since the real word for "what" in Hebrew is *mah*, not *mahn*. Nevertheless, this is the Bible's explanation for how manna got its name.

In legend, manna was one of the ten things created in the twilight before the first Sabbath (see page 7). It was called "angel's bread" because it was supposedly prepared by the angels for the sustenance of the righteous in heaven. There was no need to cook the manna; it fell ready to eat. And it tasted like any food that the Israelites wanted to taste. To children it tasted like goat's milk, to teenagers it tasted like bread, to adults it tasted like honey, and the sick and feeble thought it tasted like cakes of barley steeped in oil and honey. Manna gave off such a wondrous fragrance that the Israelite women wore it as a perfume (B. Talmud *Yoma* 75a).

The Bible relates that a small portion of manna was placed in a jar and stored alongside the Ark of the Covenant. When the prophet Jeremiah later exhorted the poor folk of Israel to study Torah, they asked, "If we study Torah, how shall we sustain ourselves?" He brought forth the jar from the Temple and showed them the manna, reminding them that God had fed the Israelites for forty years on nothing more than this. If they had faith, they, too, would be fed by God (Mechilta *VaYisa* 6).

11. Your People, Good or Evil

Reb Berechiah preached:

A king rented a vineyard to a tenant. When the vineyard produced fine grapes and good wine the king would say: "How wondrous is the wine of my vineyard!" But when the grapes were poor and the wine was inferior, the king would say to the tenant, "How rancid is the wine of your vineyard!" The tenant corrected the king, saying, "Good wine or rancid, the vineyard belongs to you."

In the same way, when the Israelites were righteous, God said to Moses, "I will send you to Pharaoh that he may let My people go." But after the Israelites committed the sin of the golden calf, God said, "Go, get yourself down, for your people have corrupted themselves!" But Moses responded, "You call the Israelites Yours when they are good, but mine when they are sinful? But good or bad, O God, the Israelites are Yours!"

[Midrash Ecclesiastes Rabbah 6:9; Midrash Exodus Rabbah 43:7]

12. Martin Elbingrod

In his book, *Jewish Prayer*, Louis Jacobs quotes a tombstone found in an English village that conveys (in somewhat ironic manner) what may well be the ultimate sermon:

Here lies Martin Elbingrod,
Have mercy on my soul, Lord God.
As I would do were I Lord God,
And you were Martin Elbingrod.

[Louis Jacobs, *Jewish Prayer*]

13. Israel and the Nations

Let not the nations of the earth say that God favored Israel and neglected them. Whatever benefit God bestowed on Israel was likewise given to other nations. Solomon was a great king; Nebuchadnezzar was likewise a great king. David was wealthy; Haman was also wealthy. Moses was a revered prophet; so, too, was Balaam. But see how the people of Israel used their gifts and how the people of other nations abused their gifts.

Solomon employed his wisdom in building the Temple, composing hymns of praise to God, and writing books of the Bible. Nebuchadnezzar used his gifts to amass greater wealth, to revel in luxury and excess, and to oppress other nations.

David used his wealth to build up Jerusalem and all Israel for the glory of God. Haman offered his wealth to have a nation destroyed.

Moses, humble and righteous, lived his whole life for the good of others, ever standing in the breach between a sinning people and an offended God. Balaam was ready to curse a people he did not know though they had offered him no provocation.

Moreover, the prophets, though they were sent to preach to Israel, always showed concern and compassion for the welfare of other nations. God's spirit was granted to non-Israelites and, even so, they were often found wanting.

[Midrash Numbers Rabbah 20:2]

14. Placing God First

There is an interesting history to the letters and gifts that King Merodach-baladan sent to King Hezekiah (see Isaiah 39).

King Merodach-baladan was a heathen who worshiped the sun. He was accustomed to sleep regularly up to a certain hour of the day. But one time, an eclipse of the sun darkened the sky at the hour when he normally arose; and the king overslept. When he awoke, he was incensed at his courtiers for allowing this to happen. When they pleaded that the sun had been eclipsed and the darkness kept them from awakening him, he grew even more angry. "What god is greater than my god, the sun," he demanded, "What god can impede the sun's progress?"

His courtiers replied, "The God of King Hezekiah is greater than your god. For the Israelites say their God created the world and all that is in it, the heavens and all that is them, even sun, moon, and stars." Immediately King Merodach-baladan dictated a letter to King Hezekiah inquiring about his God and the source of his God's power. He began the letter with a formal greeting: "Peace to Hezekiah, Peace to the God of Hezekiah, and Peace to Jerusalem." To insure a reply, he instructed his courtiers to deliver the letter with many fine gifts.

Now the messengers entrusted with the letter and the gifts had gone but a short distance when King Merodach-baladan had misgivings. "All the honor," he thought, "that I now bestow on Hezekiah is only because of his great God, and yet I addressed the letter to him, with peace to him first, and only after that, peace to his God." He was so distraught at this grievous error that he himself ran after the messengers, brought them back, tore up the original letter, and dictated another one which began: "Peace to the Great God of Hezekiah, Peace to Hezekiah, and Peace to Jerusalem."

When God saw what King Merodach-baladan had done, the Eternal decreed a reward for him. It was decided that three of his descendants—Nebuchadnezzar, Avilmerodach, and Belshazzar—should each reign over extensive kingdoms.

[*Midrash Esther Rabbah* 10]

The Chaldean King Merodach-baladan waged a successful war ©. 710 BCE) against the might of the Assyrians who had conquered Babylonia only a short time before (728). The Chaldeans were cousins of the Israelites. They were part of a larger kinship group called Arameans. The principal language of this group was Aramaic which eventually replaced Hebrew as the spoken tongue of the Israelites in Canaan. The Bible states that Abraham was born in "Ur of the Chaldeans" (Genesis 11:28) and that the Israelites were descended from a "fugitive Aramean"—intending either Abraham or his father Terach (Deuteronomy 26:5).

15. Making Marriages

In the days of the Second Temple, sages were often sent to Rome to serve as negotiators. The Romans were curious about Jewish beliefs and the texts record many conversations about religion. When Rabbi Yose ben Chalafta visited Rome, a Roman princess asked him, "How long did it take your God to create the world?" He answered, "Six days."

"If so," she said, "What has your God been doing since then?"

Rabbi Yose said, "Since Creation, the Holy One has been busy arranging weddings—matching the soul of a man to the soul of a woman, over and again."

The princess laughed. She said, "If that is all God does, I can do better. In no time at all, I can arrange a thousand weddings."

Rabbi Yose replied, "Matchmaking may be a trivial thing in your eyes; but for the Holy One, it is as awesome an act as splitting the Red Sea."

When the rabbi left, the princess lined up a thousand of her male servants and a thousand of her maid servants in two rows facing each other, saying, "You shall each marry the person opposite you." Thereby, she arranged a thousand weddings in a single night.

The next morning, though, her servants were lined up, waiting at the door of her chamber. One man's head was bloodied, one woman's eye was swollen, one man's shoulder was dislocated, one woman's leg was broken. There were cuts and bruises, and moans and groans, all down the line. She asked, "What happened to you?" And the answers were all the same. One said, "I don't want *that* woman," and another said, "I don't want *that* man."

The princess sent a messenger, asking Rabbi Yose to come. When he arrived, she said, "You were correct. Arranging a wedding—making the right match—is as difficult as parting the Red Sea."

[*Midrash Leviticus Rabbah* 8:1]

16. The Parable of the Bountiful Tree

The Dead Sea Scrolls contain many works well-known to us and some otherwise entirely unknown. Though a few of the manuscripts are well preserved and nearly complete, most are fragments. From one group of fragments, scholars have pieced together the following transcription (with missing or damaged pieces noted by the use of an ellipsis, and guesses at words indicated by a question mark):

> [Folio 1 Column 2]
>
> Please consider this, you who are wise: If a man has a fine tree, which grows high, all the way to heaven (...) (...) of the soil, and it produces succulent fruit every year with the autumn rains and the spring rains, (...) and in thirst, will he not (...) and guard it (...) to multiply the boughs (?) of (...) from its shoot, to increase (...) and its mass of branches (...)
>
> [Folio 2 Column 1]
>
> (...) your God (...) your hearts (...) (...) with a willing spirit. (...) Shall God establish (...) from your hand? When you rebel, (...) your intentions, will God not confront you, reprove you and reply to your complaint? (...) As for God, God's dwelling is in heaven, and God's kingdom embraces the lands; in the seas (...) in them, and (...)

What follows is my reworking of the parable.

Let the wise take note: If you own a fine tree, which grows high, all the way to heaven, with roots that reach deep and drink the fine waters below the earth and reside in the warmth of the soil... If you own a fine tree which produces succulent fruit every year, benefitting from the autumn rains and the spring rains... If you own such a tree, will you not watch over it and guard it—even in times of drought—so that the tree will stand strong and you can plant saplings from its shoots and branches to increase your yield—so that your precious tree will become a grove of precious trees?

You are like the tree, with your feet on the ground and your head reaching up into the heavens. If you faithfully do as your God commands, with all your heart and with a full and willing spirit, will God not look over you and protect you, establishing the works of your hands? And, if you should rebel, will God not confront you, reprove you, and reply to your complaint? For you are a treasure to God, even as the tree is a treasure to you. You must be tended—in good times and bad—even as you tend the tree.

And think not that you are different from all other things in God's creation. As for God, God's dwelling is in the heavens and God's kingdom embraces the earth. God plants in the seas, in the land, and in the skies; and wherever God plants, God's tender mercies are over all God creates.

[adapted by Rossel from Dead Sea Scroll 4Q302a]

17. Learning to Walk

A disciple once asked the Baal Shem Tov: "Why is it that one who senses that God is close experiences moments of interruption and remoteness? Why does God sometimes seem so far away?"

The Baal Shem Tov explained: "When a parent starts to teach a child to walk, the parent stands in front of the child and holds both hands on either side of the child, so that the child cannot fall, and the child comes toward the parent between the parent's hands. But the moment the child is close to the parent, the parent moves away a little, and holds both hands farther apart, and the parent does this over and over, so that the child may learn to walk."

[Buber, *Early Masters*, p. 65]

18. Golem

Amid the persecution, the disease, and the poverty of the Middle Ages, a legend was born that circulated among the Jews of Italy, Germany, and Eastern Europe. It was a legend of hope emanating from a people short on hope at a time when death was always too close at hand. Babies struggled to survive, all too many succumbing to infant diseases, passing fevers, and outright starvation. Men and women were taken before their time, their lives shortened by conflicts of nations that little interested them; by epidemics, bad medicines, lack of medicines; and even by riots arising from the ignorance and prejudice of their neighbors. Life was tenuous; death was familiar. In such a time, magic and magical protection possessed a healing quality.

From ancient times, the Jewish mystics taught the doctrine of the thirty-two paths: that God created the entire universe with nothing except the 22 letters of the Hebrew alphabet and the 10 basic numbers.

The Talmud itself recorded that, by linking together the right combinations of numbers and letters, the righteous could, if they so desired, create an entire world. It was even said that the Babylonian sage Rabbah once created a man and sent him to Rabbi Zeira. Zeira spoke to the man, but when the man did not answer, Zeira said to him, "You are not one of the sages! Return to your dust" (B. Talmud *Sanhedrin* 65b).

So when the medieval sage, Rabbi Judah Lowe of Prague sensed that his community was in danger, he took two of his servants and went deep into the forest to a clearing beside a river.

Together, the three shaped mud from the riverbank into the likeness of a man. Then Rabbi Lowe carved three letters into the forehead of the clay figure—*alef, mem*, and *tav*—the letters that make up the word called, "the seal of God," the word *Emet*, "Truth." The clay figure started to glow with a fiery redness that surprised the rabbi and his servants. Hair began to grow on it, and fingernails and toenails. But still the creature was not alive.

The rabbi slowly circled the figure while his two servants brought water from the stream. As the water was poured into the figure's mouth, the redness disappeared and the clay took on the color of skin. But still the creature was not alive.

Now the rabbi took out a parchment he had prepared. On the parchment was written the name of God. Rabbi Judah Lowe placed the parchment on the tongue of the clay figure and its fingers twitched, it eyes opened, and its legs moved. Rabbi Lowe commanded it to rise and the creature rose up from the muddy riverbank. Four figures—three men and the Golem—walked back from the banks of the River Moldau, through the dense forest, toward the City of Prague.

The danger the rabbi had sensed soon became a reality. Rabbi Lowe sent the Golem to stand between the rioting peasants with their sticks and clubs and the entry to the Jewish Quarter. Some versions of the legend say that just the sight of this mighty creature was enough to stop the rioting peasants. Other versions speak of a great battle in which the peasants were routed and scattered by the Golem alone.

Some say that, because the Golem was created by human magic, it was unable to speak. Other say that it could speak, though it was usually as silent as a good servant. One version of the legend says that the Golem wanted to study Torah and dreamed of one day being counted in the *minyan* like a normal person. Another version says that the Golem kept growing from day to day so that, eventually, it became a great burden on the entire community just to find enough food for it. In any case, the Golem became inconvenient once the danger had passed and the Rabbi knew that the time had come for it to depart.

Rabbi Lowe had given much thought to this question even before creating the Golem. So one night he lovingly approached the great bulk as it slept and he reached up to its forehead where the three letter word, the seal of God, the word *Emet*, "Truth," was written. Tenderly, the Rabbi erased the first letter, *alef*, leaving behind the two other letters—*mem* and *tav*—so that now the word on the forehead of the Golem read *Meit*, meaning "the dead one."

In this way, so the legend concludes, the Golem of Prague returned to the dust from which it was created.

[adapted from Rappoport, *Folklore of the Jews*, pp. 195-203]

The Golem legend persists in the collective imagination. Frankenstein's monster probably owes a debt to this oft-told tale. Likewise, the Jewish savant and science fiction writer, Isaac Asimov, may have had the Golem in mind when he penned his famous three laws of robotics. The Jewish creators of Superman, Joe Shuster and Jerry Siegel, may also have been aware of the tale of how the mighty Golem saved the Jews of Prague.

19. Someone Always Sees

There was a drought. Farmers plowed, praying for rain. But no rain fell that year. The land was dry and bare, not a blade of grass to hold it in place. Then, one day in November of 1933, a strong wind blew up a dust storm and dust and topsoil swirled high into the air in a huge black cloud. More dust storms followed. The next May, one dust storm lasted two days, sucking soil upward from the Great Plains. Enormous clouds of black, choking debris blew across the prairies, falling like a black blizzard on the people of Chicago. And the storm kept moving, dumping dust and dirt. A few days later, it reached Buffalo, Boston, New York City, and Washington, D.C. That winter, dust clouds mixed with rain clouds; and red snow fell on New England.

Things went from bad to worse. Farmers sought other work to earn money to send back to their families. Thousands were on the road when one of the worst dust storms turned day into night. The travelers pulled hats down over their heads, covered their mouths with handkerchiefs, leaned into the wind, and tried to keep moving. At times, they could barely make out the road before them. That was the April day in 1935 they called, "Black Sunday."

There was no crop again that year. Now many farmers packed up their families and abandoned their farms forever. Now there was little or no business in the shops in the small villages and towns of that vast part of America that people were calling "the dust bowl." Many family stores closed and some of the store owners were Jews. That is why the brother of my grandmother, the man we all called "Uncle Joe," was on the road in the Texas panhandle heading for Los Angeles, half-a-continent away.

Uncle Joe was on foot, like others who had lost everything and had left nearly everything behind. Of course, he still had his Jewish soul. He trusted that God would watch out for him. And, just as he was asking for God's help, an old battered automobile came down the road, going in his direction. He waved and the driver stopped and leaned out the window.

"Where are you headed?" the driver asked.

"West to California," Uncle Joe said.

"Long walk," the driver said. "And the dust storms keep blowing. I'm not going that far, but I am going West a way,"

"Can I ride with you?" Uncle Joe asked.

The driver said, "You can ride with me if you will help me."

Uncle Joe said, "I don't drive." But the driver said, "That's okay. Just climb in." So Uncle Joe settled into the passenger's seat, happy to rest his feet a while.

After they had gone a short way, the driver pulled the car to the side of the road and stopped. "See that apple tree over there?" he asked. "I know the fellow who owns it, but he never gives me any apples. I'm going to take a few for myself. You keep watch and, if you see someone coming, yell out, 'Someone sees!'"

Uncle Joe nodded, not saying a word. The driver got out of the car and looked around. When he saw that no one was nearby, he ran across the road to the apple tree. But just as he was about to steal the first apple, Uncle Joe yelled out, "Someone sees!"

The driver panicked. He raced back to the car, jumped in behind the wheel, and sped away.

After they had gone a short distance, the driver spied a patch where some farmer had planted a few onions to help feed his family. The driver stopped the car again, and said, "You keep watch, and if you see someone coming, yell out, 'Someone sees!'"

He got out of the car and looked around. When he thought there was no one in sight, he climbed over the fence and stepped into the onion patch. But as soon as he had taken hold of the first onion, Uncle Joe yelled out, "Someone sees!"

Again the driver raced back to the car and drove off quickly. But then he looked around and saw that no one was following.

"There was no one watching," he complained to Uncle Joe. "Why did you yell out, 'Someone sees!'?"

Uncle Joe shrugged his shoulders and, from the depths of his Jewish soul, he told the driver, "Someone always sees."

[Rossel, based on a teaching in Bunim, *Ethics from Sinai*]

20. The Doubtful Message

The emperor sent a message to a rabbi who lived in a town at the edge of the kingdom, far from the capital. The messenger traveled many days. At last, he knocked on the rabbi's door. The rabbi himself opened it.

"I bring you a letter from the emperor," the messenger announced in his most stately voice.

"A letter from the emperor? For me?," the rabbi asked with suspicion. "Do you expect me to believe that the emperor of all the kingdom knows that I exist? The emperor has never sent a letter to Reb Yankel, the mayor. He never sent a letter to Reb Moishe, who collects the taxes. Does he know that *they* exist? And, if he does not know them, why should the emperor know me?"

The messenger shrugged his shoulders. "All I know is that I was sent to deliver this letter."

The rabbi began talking to himself out loud. "The emperor lives far away. He has endless stores of treasures. He has his palace and his court. Could it be that some small thing I have said has reached his ears? But, even then, the distance is so great, why should he wait for the answer to a question? Why should the emperor send a letter to me?"

The messenger said, "Maybe the emperor is pleased with you. Why ask me, I am only a messenger. Do you want the letter?"

The rabbi thought deeply, scratching at his beard. "Aha," he said, "I have it. This is a trick. Someone paid you to trick me."

"This no trick," the messenger said. "I have traveled many days to deliver this letter to you."

"I think it is a trick," the rabbi went on, "and I will prove it to you. Tell me, who gave you this letter? Did the emperor hand it to you and say, 'Go far away to a distant town and deliver this to Rabbi Yosef?'"

The messenger was shocked by this. "Do you really think that I am permitted to see the emperor? When the emperor wishes to send a letter, he gives a command. His adviser hands the letter to a runner. The runner comes and hands the letter to me. I take the letter and deliver it. That is how it is done."

"Aha," said the rabbi. "So you admit that you did not receive this letter from the emperor himself. So, tell me this, my dear messenger, have you ever been in the emperor's presence? Have you ever seen the emperor face to face?"

Again, the messenger was taken aback. "I am only a messenger. I am not a member of the royal family. I am not permitted to look upon the emperor!"

"Aha," said the rabbi. "So you can not be sure that there is an emperor. And you expect me to take your word for it?"

Did the messenger begin to wonder? But, no, he just stood at the rabbi's door, with the letter still in his hand.

The rabbi went on: "Perhaps there is an emperor and perhaps not. If there is an emperor, perhaps he sent this letter, perhaps he did not? Now, if he did not send this letter, the emperor will praise us for finding the trickster who is posing as the emperor and sending letters in his name. But imagine if there is no emperor at all. Then everyone in the kingdom will praise us for revealing the truth. So, let me get my coat and hat. We will go together to the emperor's city and together we will get to the bottom of this mystery."

Lo and behold! The messenger found himself on the long road with the letter still in his pocket and the rabbi walking along beside him, mumbling and humming. The distance was great, but the rabbi did not seem to mind and the messenger was used to walking great distances. In this way, they arrived outside the palace.

Many soldiers stood guard at the gateway to the palace. Most of them were dressed alike, but one was festooned with feathers and ribbons. "My, my," the rabbi said, "I have never seen such a costume before." He went right up to the fancy soldier, and spoke to him.

"I see by your uniform that you are something special," the rabbi said. "What is your occupation?"

"I am the captain of the guards," the man replied with pride. "I serve the emperor."

"What emperor would that be?" asked the rabbi.

"Why, it is the only emperor, the one who rules over us all, the one who is served by all who live here."

"Tell me," the rabbi pressed on, "have you ever seen this emperor? Do you know what he looks like?"

"I am only a captain of the guards. I have never seen the emperor, but I suppose he looks like a man."

"Aha!" the rabbi cried, throwing a finger into the air. "You say you serve someone you have never seen and never will see. Are all soldiers as foolish as you? How about the general, do you have a general?"

"Of course, I have a general," the captain said. "He is standing right there."

And, so he was. And the general's uniform was even grander than the captain's. So the rabbi went over to the general and questioned him. Surely, he would have seen the emperor. But, no, the general had never seen the emperor either. So the rabbi questioned a few more soldiers. But none of them had ever seen the emperor. Everyone, it seemed, was serving an invisible king.

Finally, the rabbi turned his attention back to the messenger. "Do you see now?" he asked. "Imagine how foolish people can be. Whatever they are told, they believe. They are told that there is an emperor and they do not ask to see him. And, when they do not see him, do they ask why? And if they do not ask why, how can they ever hope to know the truth? They just go on with their foolish lives, serving a king they do not know and cannot see."

The messenger was exhausted. He shrugged his shoulders. Maybe the rabbi was right and maybe the rabbi was wrong. The messenger knew only one thing for certain. In his pocket there was a letter that he was supposed to deliver. If only he could deliver it, he could go home to his wife and children.

The messenger reached into his pocket, took out the letter with its royal seal, and said, "Rabbi, do you want this letter?"

The rabbi laughed. He said, "My dear messenger, since you have gone to so much trouble, I may as well read the message."

[adapted from a tale of Rabbi Nachman of Bratslav]

This tale is typical of the many enigmatic stories told by Rabbi Nachman of Bratslav (1772–1811), a great grandson of the Baal Shem Tov. During Nachman's lifetime, a core group of disciples formed around him, calling him a *tzaddik*, a "righteous one." He demanded their personal devotion. All doubts, he preached, will be answered when the Messiah arrives. In the meanwhile, it is a Jew's sacred duty to phrase the important questions (*kushiyot*, literally, the "difficulties"). In a most unlikely development, the ranks of his followers continued to swell after his death. No new *tzaddik* was chosen to lead his flock. Instead, his messianic hopes, his belief in his own role in the bringing of the Messiah, and the body of his teachings have sustained the Bratslaver Chasidim to the present day.

21. The Imperial Message

The emperor—on the day of his coronation—has sent a message to you alone. Yes, before the assembled spectators awaiting his coronation—the inner court and all the princes—before all these he delivered his message.

He commanded the messenger to come close and he whispered the message in his ear. So much store did he put by its exact words that he ordered the messenger to whisper it back into his ear again. Then, with a nod, he confirmed it to be right. The messenger immediately set out on his journey.

A powerful, a mighty man, now pushing with his left arm, now with his right, the messenger cleaves a way for himself through the throng. The crowd moves back as he approaches. The way is made easier for him than for any other. But the multitudes are so vast, their numbers have no end.

If he could reach the open fields how fast he would fly, and, soon, doubtless you would hear the welcome hammering of his fists on your door. But instead, see how he wears out his strength in vain. Still he is making his way through the chambers of the innermost palace, never will he get to the end of them.

What is more, if he succeeded in that, little would be gained. He must next fight his way down the stair. And if he succeeded in that, little would be gained, for the courtyard is filled with people awaiting news of the emperor.

And, if he succeeded in reaching the outermost gate—but that never will happen—the imperial capital would lie before him, the center of the world, full to bursting with the citizens of the kingdom.

Nobody could fight his way through here, even with a message from an emperor. But you sit at your window when evening falls and dream the message to yourself.

[adapted from Kafka, *Parables*]

22. Two *Yods*

🐾 When I was a little boy and the teacher had just taught me to read Hebrew, he once showed me two little letters—they seemed like square dots in the prayer book—and he said, "Urele, you see these two letters side by side? That's the monogram of God's Name, and whenever you see these two square dots side by side, you must pronounce *Adonai*, the Name of God, at that spot, even if it is not written in full."

I continued reading with my teacher until we came to a colon. It also consisted of two square dots, only instead of being side by side, they were one above the other. I imagined that this must also be the monogram of God's Name and so I pronounced *Adonai* at this spot.

But my teacher told me:

"No, no, Urele, those two dots do not stand for *Adonai*. Only where there are two sitting nicely side by side, where the one looks on the other as an equal—only there is the Name of God: where one is under the other and the other is raised above his neighbor—there God's Name cannot be found."

[adapted from Langer, *Nine Gates*, p. 110]

II

TORAH

1

Law and Torah

1. Not a Bird Twittered

🕊 Rabbi Abbahu remembered hearing this teaching from Rabbi Yochanan:

When God gave the Torah no bird twittered; no fowl flew; no ox lowed; none of the *Ofanim* angels stirred a wing; the *Serafim* angels did not say "Holy, Holy"; the sea did not roar; the creatures spoke not; the whole world was hushed into breathless silence.

Only then did the voice go forth, saying, "I am *Adonai* your God."

So it is written: "These words *Adonai* spoke unto all your assembly... with a great voice..." (Deuteronomy 5:19). And what does Torah mean when it says, "All your assembly"? It was not just the Children of Israel. In that moment, all of Creation held its breath waiting to hear "these words."

[*Midrash Exodus Rabbah* 29:9]

The Bible maintains that, at Sinai, God's voice so terrified the Children of Israel that they beseeched Moses to listen to God's commands in their stead. The rabbinic commentary debates just how much the people heard before they panicked. Was it the first sentence as Rabbi Yochanan states above or only the first word *Anochi* ("I")? One sage avers that the Israelites actually heard only the first letter of the first word, the letter *aleph*, and that alone was more than they could endure. Ironically, the letter *aleph* in Hebrew has no sound of its own; it is silent!

2. The Torah Dance

🕊 Rabbi Joshua ben Levi taught: When Moses went up to heaven to receive the Torah, the angels asked: "Holy One, why should a mortal man be in the heavens amongst us?"

Now Rabbi Joshua ben Levi was one of the great storytellers of ancient Israel. He was so famous for his stories that people began

49

telling stories about him: about how he once talked with the angel of death, about the time he traveled with the prophet Elijah, about the time he spoke with the Messiah. I would share them all with you, but we are celebrating the holiday of Simchat Torah when we rejoice at the giving of the Torah, so I will tell you Rabbi Joshua's tale about the Torah dance.

Adonai our God, the Holy One, the Blessed, called Moses to Mount Sinai to receive the Torah. Moses went up the mountain. The Children of Israel watched as he climbed higher and higher until they lost sight of him when he entered the cloud that covered the mountaintop. And Moses was on the mountain in the cloud for forty days and forty nights.

What the people did not know was that during those forty days and forty nights, Moses was taken up to God's holy palace in heaven. At least, that is the way that Rabbi Joshua tells the story. Now, in God's palace, Moses was surrounded by angels and all of them treated Moses like a stranger. He was like a new kid at school. No one knew him, no one knew quite what to make of him. And none wanted to talk to him, either. The angels in heaven considered themselves better than human beings and even dared to ask God, "Holy One, Creator of all, what is this human being doing here in heaven?"

God replied, "Moses has come to heaven to learn My Torah."

That *really* bothered the angels. They murmured and whispered amongst themselves. They even argued with God. They asked, "Will You give the Torah to a being of flesh and blood, even though You know that human beings are lower than the angels? Will You give the Torah to a human being, even though You know that human beings are far from perfect, that they make mistakes, that they do evil in their world?"

But God said, "That is what I am doing. I have brought my servant Moses to heaven to teach him the Torah so that he can teach it to the people of Israel, so that the people of Israel can teach it to the nations of the earth. I am giving My Torah to every human being on the earth."

The angels pressed: "Holy One, Creator of all, the Torah is very precious. You kept it beside Your throne for nine hundred and seventy four generations even before the world was created. Shall You now give Your precious Torah to creatures who are only a little better than beasts? Let the Torah remain in heaven where we angels sing to You every morning, praise Your name every afternoon, and speak of Your greatness every evening. Why send the Torah away?"

Then God said, "I will let Moses answer you. "

But Moses pleaded with God, saying, "I am afraid of Your angels. Their breath is fire and their bodies are light. They blind me with their glory and they can destroy me with a single word from their lips."

God said, "Take hold of My throne. As long as you hold on to it, you can look at the angels and not be blinded by their light. As long as you hold on to it, you can listen to the angels' words without being harmed by their fire."

Moses took hold of God's golden throne. Now Moses turned to God and asked, "What is written in this Torah You are going to teach me?"

God said, "It is written that 'I am *Adonai* your God who brought you out of the land of Egypt to be your God.'"

Then Moses turned to the angels and asked them, "Did you go down into Egypt? Were any of you angels ever slaves to the Pharaoh?"

The angels responded: "No. None of us was ever a slave in Egypt. None of us ever served Pharaoh. We have only served God."

Moses smiled and said, "Then, you do not need the Torah." And, it seemed to Moses that as he spoke these words, the angels' light was not quite as bright as before.

Moses turned to God again and asked, "What else is written in Your Torah?"

God said, "It is written that 'You shall not lie and use God's name to swear that your lie is true."

Moses turned to the angels and asked, "Do you ever lie? Do you ever use God's name vainly, without telling the truth?"

The angels responded: "We never make promises; and we only use God's name to praise God."

Moses said, "Then you have no need of this command." And, as he said these words, Moses thought that the angels' fiery breath was just a little cooler.

Moses asked God again, "What is written in Your Torah?"

God said, "It is written that 'You should keep the Sabbath day to make it holy.'"

Moses asked the angels, "Do you work?" When they said, "No," Moses said, "Then what is a day of rest to you? Down on earth, we work all week and we need a day of rest." And the angels' light and fire diminished again.

And so it went. Moses asked God what is written in the Torah and God answered, "Honor your father and mother." Moses asked the angels, "Do you have a father or a mother?" Of course, God created the angels, so none of them had either a father or a mother. Moses asked God what is written and God answered, "You shall not murder and you shall not steal." Moses asked the angels, "Do you have murders or stealing among the angels?" But they knew nothing about evil, so they knew nothing about murdering or stealing.

You can imagine what happened. The light of the angels grew dimmer and the fire of their breath was reduced to smoke. And, though he was unaware of it, Moses' face gave off more and more light until it was brighter even than the faces of the angels. And his breath began to smoke until his own words were like the fires of heaven.

Now that Moses was more like them, the angels began to like Moses. The more they listened, the more they realized he was right. God's Torah was needed in the world below. It would be more precious to human beings than it ever would be in heaven.

Moses let go of the golden throne and stood close to the angels. God watched approvingly as each angel whispered a gift into Moses' ears. One taught him a prayer for the morning. Another taught him how to praise God in the afternoon. Another whispered a tune for evening prayers. Another taught him the words to say when he took the Torah from the ark. And one whispered to Moses, "Celebrate the Torah every year as we do: by marching and dancing with it. On Simchat Torah, circle seven times around the people, carrying the scrolls in a dance of joy to rejoice for God's gift."

At the end of the forty days and forty nights, God said to Moses, "The time has come for you to return to the earth, to teach the Torah to the people of Israel so that they can teach the Torah to the nations of the world."

Moses was sad to leave the angels and the angels were sad to see him go. But Moses brought a little of the angel's brilliance and a touch of the angel's fire down the mountain. And Moses took the precious gift God had given, the teachings of the Torah. And Moses taught us how to rejoice in God's teachings, to dance the angels' dance.

Rabbi Joshua ben Levi finished telling the story and he turned to everyone listening and said, "Know this: When we dance with the Torah here on earth, the angels in heaven dance with us. For the Torah was given to all on earth and one day, perhaps soon, all will dance its jubilant dance together."

[Rossel, based on B. Talmud *Shabbat* 88b-89a]

3. Who Will Be My Surety?

🐍 Moses went up Mount Sinai and the people of Israel waited below for him to return. They were anxious. They wondered what God would command Moses. When they saw Moses coming down the mountain, they eagerly surrounded him; but, they could see from his face that he was perplexed.

"What has happened?" they asked.

Moses said, "God wishes to give us a most wonderful gift, a precious thing."

Excitedly, the people asked, "What is this gift?"

"It is called the Torah," Moses said. "In its words the light of truth shines like pearls in the dark oceans. In the Torah there are stories which teach us how God wishes us to live. There are laws in it which teach us how to dwell peacefully with our neighbors. The Torah will enable us to live in freedom so that we will never be slaves again."

The people remembered being slaves to Pharaoh in Egypt. They had no wish to be slaves again. They thirsted for freedom. They hungered for peace. Truly, they thought, God's Torah must be a great gift.

"All this is good news, Moses. Then, why are you unhappy?" the people asked.

Moses sat upon a rock at the foot of the mountain. "God will not give us this gift of Torah unless we promise something in return. We must offer God a surety."

Then the people too were uneasy. "What have we to offer God in exchange for such a precious gift?" one asked another. "A gift like this is worth empires, and we are a poor people in the desert. How can we ever aspire to possess the gift of Torah?"

Then the women of Israel approached Moses and said, "We have bracelets with rubies and rings with diamonds. We have precious necklaces and pins. We will give them all to God in exchange for the Torah."

So Moses went up the mountain again and spoke with God. But when he returned, he was still sad.

"God has said that the Torah is more precious than all the jewels and gems in the world. The words of Torah shine so bright that they will light our souls. Not even a thousand diamonds can do that!"

All night long the people thought and when the sun came up they had an idea. "We will offer God our great leaders, Moses and Aaron, as surety for the Torah. Surely God will accept the loyalty of Moses and Aaron in exchange for this wonderful gift."

So Moses went up Mount Sinai again. But again he returned with bad news.

"God has spoken and told me that Aaron and I cannot be offered as surety. We already belong to God; we have already pledged our loyalty to God."

Now, in the camp of the Israelites there was an elder known for his great wisdom. When this wise man heard Moses' words, he rose and spoke to the people.

"The Torah is God's most precious possession. In return, we must offer God our most precious possession. If we could choose only one thing in all the world to be our own, would we choose precious jewels? No. Would we choose an honored leader? No. Would we choose money? No. What would we choose if we had only one choice?—our children!"

Then the people cried out, "Yes! We will offer our children as surety for the Torah. If God will give us the Torah, we will teach it faithfully to our children. And our children will teach it to their children. What could be a better surety?"

So Moses went up the mountain again to speak with God. And when he came down, he was carrying the Tablets of the Law, the Torah which God had given him.

Moses stood before all the people of Israel and said, "God has given us the Torah. Our children will be God's surety. For God has said that all people are God's children, and the children of all people are precious to God."

Then the people of Israel thanked God by studying the Torah, and they have kept their promise by teaching the Torah to their children from that day until this.

[*Midrash Song of Songs Rabbah* 1:23]

4. Why Moses Dropped the Tablets of the Law

🕮 Moses came down from Mount Sinai carrying the tablets of the law. As he drew near enough to see the people worshiping the golden calf, he said to himself: "It would be terrible for me to present them with these commandments now! For the tablets prohibit them from worshiping idols on pain of death. If I give them the tablets now, they will all suffer God's wrath."

At once, Moses turned to take the tablets of the law back to heaven. But the seventy elders of Israel had caught sight of him and ran toward him, trying to wrest the tablets from his grasp. Miraculously, Moses was stronger than all seventy of them, resisting their every attempt, while keeping his firm grip on the tablets despite their great weight.

Just then, however, the writing on the tablets caught fire of its own accord, swirling upward to heaven in a column of smoke. Suddenly, Moses felt the great weight of the stones—for while the writing was on them, they had carried their own weight, but as the writing disappeared the stones reverted to their full sixty *seahs* of weight in his arms. Now Moses asked himself, "How can I give the tablets to the people without the writing that was on them? Will they believe me when I tell them what was written thereon?"

At once, without consulting God, Moses summoned all his strength and threw the tablets to the rocks below, shattering them to pieces. And God thanked Moses for breaking the tablets.

[adapted from J. Talmud *Taanit* 4.68c; *Avot deRabbi Natan* 2,11; B. Talmud *Shabbat* 87a; *Midrash Song of Songs Rabbah* 19:3 and 46:3; B. Talmud *Pesachim* 87b; *Pirke deRabbi Eliezer* 46; Targum Yerushalmi *Exodus* 32.19; B. Talmud *Baba Batra* 14b]

The disappearance of the writing from the tablets is described in Pseudo-Philo (12.5), where it is said: "And Moses looked upon the tablets of the law, and saw that they were unwritten, and he hastened and broke them."

5. God Gives the Law Again

🕮 "If the first tablets had not been broken, Israel would never have forgotten the Torah." [B. Talmud *Eruvin* 54a]

The first set of two tablets were the work of God, but the second set of tablets was crafted by human labor. So we see that God dealt with Israel like the king who took to himself a wife, drawing up the *ketubah*, the marriage contract, with his own hand.

One day the king noticed his wife at a party, dancing and singing with the servants. He was outraged by her unworthy conduct, so he sent her away and told her not to return. But the man who had given the bride away at the wedding came before the king and said, "Sire, surely you knew, even before you wed, the nature of your bride. She was raised among servants, and it is only natural that she should dance and sing with them."

Thereupon, the king allowed himself to be appeased, saying to the man: "Take paper and have a scribe draw up a new *ketubah*, and seal it with my seal, so that it is signed in my own hand."

It was likewise with the Israelites and God. When the Israelites worshiped the golden calf, Moses spoke on their behalf, saying, "Adonai, surely You knew, even before You chose these people, that, in bringing them out of Egypt, You were raising them up from a land of idolaters?" God answered, "I see it is your wish, Moses, that I forgive them. Well, then, I shall do so. Now, bring to Me two tablets on which I may write the words that were written on the first."

[Tosefta *Baba Kamma* 7:4]

6. The Fox and the Fish

🕮 The great prophet of the Arab peoples, Mohammed, called the Jews "the People of the Book," *Am ha-Sefer*. But even the Romans, hundreds of years before Mohammed, knew that the Torah was the Jews' lifeblood.

The Romans, attempting to eliminate the Jewish religion, issued an edict forbidding the Jews from teaching and studying the Torah, the Five Books of Moses. Anyone caught teaching it, the Romans decreed, would be put to death. Rabbi Akiva kept on teaching the Torah. A man came to him and asked, "Do you not know that you will suffer death if you continue teaching the Torah?" Rabbi Akiva replied with this story:

Once, a hungry fox came to the edge of a stream and, seeing a school of fish swimming in the center of the stream, the fox decided to trick one of the fish and then catch it for his supper. He called to an old and large grandfather fish, "Come over here, I have an important thing to tell you."

The grandfather fish came swimming near the fox, keeping just out of the fox's reach. "What is it?" he asked.

The fox smiled and said, "A fisherman is coming this way. He will catch you and eat you for his supper if you do not escape quickly." The fox paused to lick his shiny fur, then continued, "If you will come out of the water, I will take you downstream far from the fisherman's net."

"No, thank you," said the old fish. "In the water, I can swim and perhaps escape the net, but out of the water I have no protection, and I will surely die." He swam away from the hungry fox.

So you see, Akiva concluded, as long as the Jewish people continue to study the Torah, they may still live; but the Jewish people without the Torah is like a fish without water—they would surely perish. The Torah's words are "our life and the length of our days, and we should study them day and night" (Deuteronomy 30:20).

[B. Talmud *Berachot* 61b; Rossel, *When a Jew Prays*]

It is uncertain whether Hadrian's decree outlawing the study of Torah came before or after the Bar Kochba Rebellion, but it fell as a heavy blow upon a people already suffering under rapacious Roman governors. At some point, probably in the persecutions just after the rebellion, Akiva and nine other leading rabbis, were martyred. Nevertheless, if the Jews could not match the military prowess of Rome, neither could the Romans quench the spiritual fire of the Jews.

7. City Guards

Resh Lakish taught: Rabbi Judah the Prince sent Rabbis Chiya, Ammi, and Assi to all the small cities of the Land of Israel. In each city, they established schools and provided teachers for the children. Rabbi Judah said: "The whole world depends on the breath of schoolchildren. It is more important for children to study than for the Temple to be rebuilt."

Resh Lakish taught: When the rabbis came to a place where they found no teachers, they would say, "Bring us the guardians of your city." When the people brought forward the soldiers who stood by the city gates, the rabbis would say, "You have brought us men of war. In the end, they may even destroy your city. Now bring us the guardians of your city."

The people would inquire, "Who, then, are the real guardians of our city?"

The rabbis answered, "The teachers of Torah, for they teach the love of God. So it is said, 'If God does not guard the city, it little matters if the watchmen stay awake'" (Psalm 127:1).

[B. Talmud *Shabbat* 119b; J. Talmud *Chagigah* 76c.]

8. Akiva Studies Torah

Akiva was forty years old and he could neither read nor write. One day, standing by a hill, he noticed a jet of water springing from a rock above him. He asked his friend, "Who opened up this stone to let the water out?"

His friend laughed. "Akiva, don't you know that water wears away stone?"

Akiva thought, "If soft water can break hard stone, then the words of Torah can break through my hard head." He determined to study the Torah.

How did he begin? He sat in a class with children. He took hold of one end of a writing tablet and a child took hold of the other. The teacher wrote down *alef* and *bet* for Akiva, and he learned them. The teacher wrote the whole alphabet for him, and he learned it. The teacher gave him a book of Torah, and he learned it. He studied until he learned the whole Torah.

Then he went where the older students studied with the great teachers Rabbi Eliezer and Rabbi Joshua. They explained a law to him, and he learned the law. Why was this law made? What good did this law do? When he knew the law well, he returned to his teachers and said, "Teach me another law." He did this for twelve years until the teachers had no more to teach him.

One day, Akiva explained a law to Rabbi Eliezer. Rabbi Joshua said, "We have trained this student well, although we hardly paid him any attention. Now he will be a greater teacher than either of us."

Rabbi Eliezer was puzzled. How had Akiva gained so much wisdom in such a short time?

Another rabbi, Simeon, explained by comparing Akiva with a stonecutter hacking away at a mountain. First, Akiva climbed to the top of the mountain and sat down. (That was like learning to read a single letter.) Then Akiva took out his pick and began to chip small stones from the mountain. (That was like learning the alphabet.)

Then some fellows happened by and asked Akiva, "What are you doing?"

He answered, "I am going to hack away at this mountain until I move it all."

The fellows were amazed. "Can you do such a thing?"

"Yes," Akiva replied.

Akiva chipped away at the small stones until he came to a big boulder. (That was like learning a single law.) Then he took a piece of iron and wedged it under the boulder. He pried the boulder loose and sent it rolling off the mountain. (That was when he explained the law to Rabbi Eliezer.) Soon Akiva came to an even bigger boulder. He looked at the boulder and spoke to it, saying, "Your place is not here but there." Then he used his piece of iron to move even that boulder. (That was like using the teachings of Rabbi Eliezer and Rabbi Joshua to explain more laws.)

Rabbi Simeon concluded, "Akiva studied Torah the way a stonecutter cuts away a mountain. As it is written in the Book of Job: 'He goes to work upon the flinty rocks, he turns up mountains by the roots, he carves out channels through rock, and his eye sees every precious thing.' This explains how Akiva ben Joseph went from being our student to becoming our teacher."

[Avot deRabbi Natan 6; Avot deRabbi Natan (version B) 12]

9. Solomon and the Snake

The snake was thirsty. It raised its head from the coil of its body and looked around. A man was coming its way, and the man was carrying a pitcher. At once, the snake conceived a plan. As the man came closer, the snake began to slither and moan. The man bent over and said, "Why are you moaning like that?"

"I am so thirsty," said the snake. "What do you have in your pitcher?"

"Milk," the man answered.

"Give me some milk," the snake said, "and I will show you where money is buried—enough money to make you rich."

So the man placed the pitcher of milk on the ground and the snake drank from it. When the snake had slaked his thirst, the man said, "Now show me the money."

"Follow me," said the snake, slithering toward a large rock near the road. "The money is buried under this rock." And, sure enough, when the man moved the rock and dug into the soft earth, he found a bag of golden coins. He took the bag and leaning close to the ground, he began to tie it around his neck.

Suddenly, the snake leaped up and coiled itself around the man's neck.

"What are you doing?" the man asked.

"I am going to kill you because you are stealing my money," the snake said, tightening its body around the man's neck.

"Stop," the man said. "You said you would trade me the money for the milk I gave you."

"No," said the snake. "I said only that I would show you the money."

"Stop!" the man said. "You have treated me unfairly, and you must come with me to the court of wise King Solomon. He will decide who is right."

Lo, the snake was so sure of his case, and so enamored of his plan, that he decided to humor the man. In a little while, snake and man came before King Solomon. The king was in his court, sitting on his throne, holding his staff, and judging one case after another. At once, Solomon saw that the snake was tightly wound around the man's neck and that the man was trembling with fear. "Present your case," he said to the man.

Quickly, the man recounted his tale: how the snake had been thirsty, how he had given the snake milk, how the snake had promised money, and how the snake had tricked him. Then the snake told his story in which he, of course, was the innocent victim.

"I will judge this case," Solomon said to the snake, "But, first, you must get down off the man so that you and he may stand as equals in my court."

Reluctantly, the snake obeyed. It slithered off the man and coiled itself on the floor, sending its head high into the air. Then Solomon said, "Now, snake, tell me, what do you seek?"

"Only what is written in the Torah," the snake answered. "God commanded snakes, 'You shall attack human beings.' I want to obey God by killing this man."

Then the king turned to the man, saying, "It is also written in the Torah that God commanded human beings to kill snakes." And with that said, Solomon handed his staff to the man who struck the snake on the head and killed it.

[*Tanchuma Buber*, Introduction, p. 157; also *Sefer HaAggadah*; with many medieval variants, especially in Sephardic folklore]

10. Paradise

🐚 Once there was a man of the mountains who knew nothing of the way of people who lived in towns. Year after year, high on his mountain, he sowed wheat. And whatever wheat he reaped, he ate it raw, as grain.

One day he visited the town below the mountain. The people welcomed him and set before him a loaf of bread. He asked, "What is this?" and they explained that it was food to eat. He ate the bread and liked it. He asked, "Of what is this bread made?" They said, "It is made of wheat."

With dinner, they served him cakes of flour mixed with oil. He ate these, too, and liked them. He asked, "Of what do you make these cakes?" They said, "The cakes are made of wheat."

Then they served a dessert fit for a king. It was light, flaky dough flavored with oil and honey, calculated to melt in the mouth. He ate this, too, and he liked it. Once more he asked, "Of what do you make this confection?" And they answered, "We make it from wheat."

Then the man said, "In truth, I have always had all of these at my command, because I eat the one thing that makes them all: wheat!" And he returned to his mountain to sow his wheat and eat the raw grain.

Now, what are those grains but the *Peshat*, the simplest level of knowing the Torah? And what is the bread but the *Remez*, the Torah expanded through teaching? And what are the cakes but the *Derash*, the Torah enjoyed by adding stories and examples? And what is that dessert but the *Sod*, the sweetness of Torah produced by the teacher who knows its secrets? Learn the Torah in all its ways and you achieve what is spelled out by the initials of the four methods, *PaRDeS*, "paradise."

The hapless mountain man thought it was enough to eat just the raw grains of wheat, to stop at *Peshat*! He had found "paradise," but because he had no training, he lost it as quickly as he had found it. So it is with those who stop short when they think they know enough. How sad it is when they remain ignorant of the never ending delights, the "paradise," that teachers and sages and wise companions can help them find in the Torah.

[Zohar *Shemot* Section 2, Page 176a-b]

11. Buying Torah

🕮 Hillel and Shevna were brothers. Shevna became a merchant, earned his fortune, and lived a life of luxury. But Hillel studied Torah and he hardly ever had a spare coin in his pocket. All the same, it was Hillel who became famous throughout Israel. People came from near and far to listen to him teach.

One day, Shevna came to Hillel and said, "Why should I be rich and you be poor? Even as we are brothers, let us be partners. We can share our profits."

Hillel shook his head. He loved his brother, and did not want to hurt his feelings. But, in his heart, Hillel knew the answer that heaven would give to Shevna. "You cannot buy Torah," he said. "You could give me all your wealth and still I could not share with you a word of Torah. The only way for you to share in the world of Torah is to study it yourself."

[B. Talmud *Sotah* 21a; also in *Sefer HaAggadah*]

12. Gold or Torah

🕮 A student of Rabbi Simeon ben Yochai left the academy and went to sea. When the student returned, he brought with him a chest of gold. Rabbi Simeon asked, "How did you become so wealthy?"

The student said, "I acted the merchant. I traded this for that: a small thing for a thing slightly larger, then a larger thing for a thing even larger. In the end, I had traded so many times that I had a chest filled with golden coins."

"It is good," Rabbi Simeon said. But he was soon to change his mind.

When the other students saw the chest of gold, they grew jealous. They came to Rabbi Simeon and said, "Let us all go to sea so all of us might return with gold."

Rabbi Simeon said, "Forget this idea. Come along with me to the house of study." But the students no longer wished to study Torah. Rabbi Simeon would say, "The law teaches us this," and the students would say, "When can we go down to the sea?" and "When can we leave to seek our fortunes?"

At last, Rabbi Simeon said, "You do not need to leave the Land of Israel to become wealthy. I will take you to a place where there is more gold than anyone can carry."

They followed him to a valley near Mount Meron. There they watched as the rabbi began to pray. They heard him say, "Valley, O valley, fill up with coins of gold." All at once, the olives disappeared on the olive trees, and gold coins hung where every olive had been. The water in the streams stopped flowing, and the riverbeds were filled with golden coins instead of pebbles. Gold coins rolled down from the top of Mount Meron until the floor of the valley was paved with gold from one end to the other. Gold coins gathered in small heaps around the sandals of the students. Gold glittered at the tops of every bush.

"Is it gold you want?" asked Rabbi Simeon. "Here is more gold than anyone can carry. You can take as much of it as you wish."

The students yelped with joy. Laughing and singing, they gathered gold, filling every pouch and pocket and hand until they could carry no more. When they had enough, they came back to the rabbi to thank him.

The rabbi told them: "You may not wish to thank me for this. Look around. You have gathered as many gold coins as you can carry, and there is still gold everywhere."

The students looked, and it was so.

Then Rabbi Simeon said: "It is the same with Torah. You can take as much of the riches of Torah as you can carry, and there will always be more Torah than any one person can take. Yet there is a difference between the gold coins and the Torah. When you have finished spending the coins, you will have nothing left. When you die, you will not take gold coins with you to the next world. But with Torah, you can teach all you want, and you will still have all you have learned. And when you die, you will be able to take your learning with you to the next world. It is up to you to choose. Which would you rather have, Torah or gold?"

In the end, every student dropped the gold coins. Water returned to the stream. Olives returned to the olive trees. And the floor of the valley was green with grass and dotted with flowers. And Rabbi Simeon smiled at his students, saying, "You have chosen wisely."

[_Midrash Exodus Rabbah_ 52:3; also _Sefer HaAggadah_]

13. The Space Between

Each letter of the Torah scroll hides a profound mystery. Even more sublime mysteries are contained in the vowels (which are known, but do not appear in the scroll of the Torah). And still more sublime mysteries are in the annotations (pronunciations and variations which cannot be adduced from the writing on the Torah scroll, but must be memorized).

But the most sublime mysteries of all lie submerged in the sea of white which surrounds the letters on all sides. No one is able to unravel this mystery, none can fathom it. So infinite is the mystery of the white space of the parchment that the combined efforts of all the human beings in the entire world would be incapable of deciphering it. No vessel is fit to receive it. Only in the world to come will this mystery be understood. Then shall be read not what is written in the Torah, but what is not written: the white which encompasses, surrounds, and binds the letters.

In this fashion, each of us is like the letters of the Torah. Our personalities are like the vowels which are not written. Our values are like the annotations which must be memorized and handed down from generation to generation. The infinite mystery is in the space between us. Not in what we say when we speak to one another, but in the fact that we are able to say anything at all to one another. Not in what we pass on from generation to generation, but in the fact that one generation can impart anything at all to the next. Only in the world to come will the mystery of the space between us be understood.

[Rossel, based on Buber, _Early Masters_, p. 232]

2
Mitzvot
Commandments

1. All Your Heart, All Your Soul, and All Your Might

The Romans decreed that Torah should not be taught in the Land of Israel, but Rabbi Akiva continued to teach. The Romans placed him in a prison. But even there, he continued to teach. He smuggled out answers to difficult questions of law. His students would dress up as beggars and walk beneath his prison window. Rabbi Akiva would whisper teachings to them, or toss them scraps of parchment with teachings written on them. To every visitor that the Romans permitted him, Rabbi Akiva taught Torah.

The rest is not pleasant. One night the soldiers came for him and took him from his cell. All night they tortured the rabbi; but when the dawn came and with it the time to recite the *Shema*, Rabbi Akiva did so.

The Roman officer in charge was astounded. "What are you?" he asked Rabbi Akiva. "Are you a magician? Can you feel no pain?"

Rabbi Akiva answered, "All my life I have waited to do this *mitzvah* properly. In the Torah, it is written, 'You shall love Adonai Your God with all your heart, with all your soul, and with all your might.' I have always loved God with all my heart and all my might; and now—because you are torturing me—I can love God with all my soul, too." Then, repeating the words of the *Shema* prayer, Rabbi Akiva died.

Some claim that the Roman officer in charge, having witnessed the great bravery of Rabbi Akiva, later converted to Judaism. No one knows. But the teachings of Rabbi Akiva live on.

[J. Talmud *Berachot* 14b]

2. Feeding All Alike

🐟 Rabbi Judah the Prince had a storehouse that he kept filled with grain. Once, during a year of famine, he told his servants: "Open the storehouse to all those who have studied—whether they have studied Bible or Mishnah; whether they are students of *halachah* ("law") or *aggadah* ("legend"). But if "common folk" come for food, be quick to bar the doors." His instructions were soon known and students came for grain to feed themselves and their families. But those who worked in common professions—the bricklayers, the water carriers, the wood carriers, the sandal makers, the blacksmiths, and the beggars—they and their families went hungry.

Rabbi Jonathan ben Amram saw what was happening and took pity on the common folk. He put on the clothes of a blacksmith. He darkened his hands and his cheeks, as if he had just come from leaning over the smoky fires of a forge. In this disguise, he pushed his way in to Rabbi Judah's courtyard, where the rabbi sat and studied in the afternoon, and he called out, "Master, give me food."

Rabbi Judah looked up and what he saw was a blacksmith. "My son, have you studied the Bible?" he asked.

The "blacksmith" shook his head.

"Have you studied the Mishnah?"

He shook his head again. "I have not studied," he said, "not Bible, not Mishnah. I have not studied *halachah* and I have not studied *aggadah*."

"If you have not studied," Rabbi Judah asked, "how can I give you food?"

Jonathan the "blacksmith" said, "You take pity on your dog and on your cat. Neither of them go hungry. Feed me, then, even as God feeds the beasts and the birds."

Rabbi Judah was a kind man, and the words of the blacksmith reached to his heart. "Go to the storehouse and take grain, " he said. But, after the blacksmith went away, Rabbi Judah was angry at himself. "Woe is me," he said, "that I have given my grain to a person without learning!"

Then his son Simeon said, "Father, hear me. I do not think you have given your grain to a blacksmith at all. I think that "blacksmith" was your own pupil, Rabbi Jonathan ben Amram!"

Rabbi Judah sent for Jonathan. "Why have you done this thing? I offered grain to all my students. Why did you come as a blacksmith and not a student?"

Jonathan replied, "You taught me Bible and Mishnah. You taught me the *halachah* and the *aggadah*. You taught me the verse that says, 'without food, there can be no Torah.' Tell me, my dear teacher, if the common folk have no food to eat, will they turn their hearts to the study of Torah? No. If they see a rabbi feeding his students while their children go hungry, they will say, 'The rabbis study the laws of God, but they do not honor them. God commands them to feed the needy, but they feed only themselves.'"

Rabbi Judah listened and tears came to his eyes and ran down his cheeks. "You speak the truth," he said. "I was thinking like the father of a family. My students are my children. So I told my servants, 'Feed only my students and turn away all others.' But in a time of famine, all of us must be one family, helping one another. The one who has more, must give more; and even the poor must give to those who are poorer."

Rabbi Judah sent for the servants who stood guard over his storehouse of grain. He commanded them, saying, "Open wide the gates and let all who are hungry come and take the grain they need for their daily bread. Tell all who receive grain to bless God and to bless the wise 'blacksmith,' Rabbi Jonathan ben Amram."

[B. Talmud *Baba Batra* 8a]

The story mentions two formative types of rabbinic learning. The word for Jewish law is *halachah*, from the Hebrew root meaning "to go" or "to walk." Though translated as "law," better translations would be "the way" or the "the path." While many rabbis became experts in *halachah*, others were equally well-known for their skills in *aggadah*, "legend" or "lore."

3. The Lost Bracelet

Rabbi Samuel was visiting Rome when the queen lost her bracelet. Rabbi Samuel had been standing by the side of the road waiting for the queen and all her servants to pass by. He saw the bracelet drop from her hand and he picked it up. He started walking toward the palace to return the bracelet.

But even before he came close to the palace, he heard a crier going about the city making an announcement. (Nowadays, we have announcers on radio and television, we have signs that can be changed to announce traffic and weather, we have microphones and amplifiers, and we have enormous sound systems with loud-speakers. Of course, the town crier, who went from place to place yelling out decrees and important announcements, he was the original "loud speaker.")

So Rabbi Samuel stopped to listen to the crier, who announced, "Whoever returns the queen's bracelet in thirty days will be given a great reward, but if someone is found with the bracelet after thirty days, his head shall be cut off."

Rabbi Samuel made his decision. For thirty days, he waited. On the thirty-first day, he went to the palace and returned the bracelet to the queen.

She asked, "When did you find my bracelet?"

He said, "Immediately after you lost it."

She said, "Did you not hear the message of the crier?"

He answered, "I heard it."

"Then why did you not return my bracelet at once, before the thirty days were up?"

Rabbi Samuel replied: "If I returned the bracelet at once, you would think that I was returning it because I fear you. But the real reason that I am returning the bracelet is because I fear God."

Hearing this, the queen forgave Rabbi Samuel, and said: "Blessed be the God of the Jews."

[Mishnah *Baba Metzia* 2:5]

4. Keeping the Commandments

🐾 Every Jew is obligated to observe only those of the 613 *mitzvot* ("commandments") of the Torah as are possible. Of course, no one can be considered perfect unless he or she has performed all 613. But who has ever done this? Even Moses, the greatest of the prophets, did not perform them all. For Moses, as for us, four obstacles must be overcome.

First, there is the case of complete prevention. Take, for example, the commandments intended only for priests. Only priests can perform certain *mitzvot* and yet these precepts are included in the 613. Then, again, some are special laws for Levites; and some are laws forbidden for priests and Levites but binding upon Israelites. Yet these *mitzvot* are likewise included in the 613.

Second, there are impossible cases. How can a couple observe the commandment to circumcise a son if there is no son born to them?

Third, there are conditional cases. Many *mitzvot* concern the maintenance and the practice of the Temple. Today, there is no Temple, but should, God willing, there be a Temple in the future, Jews will again be required to maintain it and perform its rituals.

Fourth, there are exceptional cases. Some of the *mitzvot* can only be performed in the land of Israel. If a Jew lives in Israel, he or she is expected to perform them. But Jews living outside the land are not required to perform them. They are exempted from these *mitzvot*.

Therefore, every Jew is obligated to observe only those of the 613 *mitzvot* of the Torah as are possible. Any that are not performed because of insurmountable obstacles, will be counted to a Jew as if he or she had actually performed them.

But, miracle of miracles, the Holy One, the Blessed, has given the law for God's faithful servants, the nation of Israel, and as a nation it is always accounted for them as if they were keeping the whole law.

Compare this to a king who once wrote to his subjects, saying, "Behold, I command you to prepare for war against the enemy: raise the walls higher, collect arms, and store up food and water;" and those that were builders took care of preparing the walls, those that were armorers took care of preparing the weapons, those who were farmers took care of preparing the stores of food, and those who were water carriers took care of preparing the stores of water. Each, according to his ability, did all that was required, and all taken together fulfilled the king's command.

[*Kitzur Shulchan Aruch*, p. 6, cols. 1-2]

The number of *mitzvot* in the Torah is not literally 613, as becomes clear in the next story. Nevertheless, the philosopher-sage, Moses Maimonides (1135–1204), combed the Five Books of Moses to isolate exactly 613 *mitzvot*. This gave rise to a controversy that lasted for nearly 300 years! To be fair, the so-called "Maimonidean Controversy" extended also to his greater effort, the attempt to isolate from the entire Talmud only those decisions of the rabbis which were authoritative and binding; and it extended also into philosophical and theological problems, some of which were apparent before the time of Maimonides: How should a Jew understand the anthropomorphism in the Bible? How should a Jew understand the concept of the resurrection of the body? Should Jewish leadership be a matter of hierarchy and descent or a matter of intellect and wisdom? Following the example of Maimonides, other sages wrote codes of law, though no two lists of the 613 *mitzvot* ever agreed. The Torah itself mentions no such number and makes no claim to any absolute number; nor do any of the books of the Prophets or the Writings.

5. Six Hundred and Thirteen to One

Rabbi Simlai was preaching a sermon. He began, "There are six hundred and thirteen commandments in the Torah." He asked, "Why this number?"

And he answered his own question, explaining: The positive commandments number two hundred and forty-eight, "the number of the members of the human body"—meaning that our whole bodies should be used in God's service. The negative commandments number three hundred and sixty-five, "the number of days in the solar year"—meaning that we should spend every day of the year struggling to turn our evil impulses to good use.

Although Rabbi Simlai was preaching, not counting, Jewish scholars used this number as a kind of shorthand. The number 613 when formed in Hebrew letters is pronounced *Taryag*. And "*Taryag mitzvot*" has become an expression for "all the commandments of Torah."

Rabbi Simlai was not finished with his sermon, though. That day, he was not trying to tell us that there are so many commandments that our heads should spin. He wanted to show that the commandments given by God were a lot *like* God, too. Here is what he taught:

Rabbi Simlai said, "King David came and summarized all six hundred and thirteen commandments in eleven (Psalm 15). Then came the prophet Isaiah, who condensed all six hundred and thirteen commandments into six (Isaiah 33:15-16).

"Then Micah came and reduced all six hundred and thirteen commandments to three, as it is written, 'It has been told to you, O mortal, what is good, and what Adonai requires of you: only to do justly, to love mercy, and to walk humbly before your God' (Micah 6:8).

"Then came Isaiah again and reduced them to two commandments, as it is said, 'Thus says Adonai, Keep justice and do righteousness' (Isaiah 56:1).

"Then came Amos, who summarized all six hundred and thirteen commandments in one command, as it is said, 'For thus says Adonai to the House of Israel: Seek Me and live'" (Amos 5:4).

But Rabbi Nachman ben Isaac interrupted, saying, "People might think that Amos intends to speak of two commandments—'Seek Me' by observing the whole Torah and 'live.'"

"If so," Rabbi Simlai ended his sermon, "then, it is the prophet Habakkuk who came and summarized all six hundred and thirteen commandments in one commandment, as it is said, 'But the righteous shall live by faith'" (Habakkuk 2:4).

One God. One commandment. "Live by faith."

[B. Talmud *Makkot* 23b-24a]

3
Tradition

1. Memory—The Forest

It is said that the Baal Shem Tov, the great Rabbi Israel ben Eliezer, was a true seer. A man once sought him out for a minor complaint, but the Baal Shem saw the Angel of Death hovering over the man's shoulder. So he spoke of the need to cast off wretchedness, the need to shatter and destroy evil thoughts. All the time, he was not talking to the man, but to that other, removing the evil from it, saving the man.

Now whenever the Baal Shem Tov had a vision that misfortune was about to visit his children, the Chasidim, he had a certain custom. He instructed his driver to take him to the edge of the forest. There he had the driver wait.

The Baal Shem walked deep into the forest, into the glades where the sun did not reach, where cool entered the soul. And, in the midst of the forest, the Baal Shem found a particular clearing, a sun-lit alcove like a purified heart in the midst of a dark world. Then the Baal Shem Tov gathered sticks and gathered, too, his full strength for the task ahead. He lit a fire and he uttered a prayer.

And when he finished praying, the miracle was accomplished. And, in this way, the misfortune was averted.

Time passed. The Baal Shem died and was buried with the honor and reverence befitting a great teacher. His student, the Maggid of Mezeritch, took his place. The Maggid, too, had visions and knew when trouble loomed. Then he, too, would drive to the forest's edge, instruct the driver to wait for him, and make his way deep into the coolness, to find that same clearing. Alas, the Maggid did not know the secret of gathering the sticks and lighting the fire. All the same, when he spoke the prayer, the miracle was accomplished, and the danger to the Jews was averted.

In time came the turn of the Sassover *Rebbe* to take the place of the Baal Shem and the Maggid of Mezeritch. The Sassover had no visions, nevertheless he could sense the approach of danger. When he did, he too made the journey deep into the forest. He would find the sunlit alcove and sit in it, and meditate. He knew nothing of the gathering of the sticks, or of the fire, or of the prayer. And yet, when he arose from his meditation, the miracle was accomplished and the danger was averted.

A while later, it fell to Israel of Rizhin to lead the Chasidim, his children, his students. He had no visions, nor did he sense oncoming danger, but he had an uncanny ear and could hear the rumble of disaster approaching. He did not know the proper prayer, he had no instruction regarding the fire, and he did not know the location of the clearing within the forest. But he gathered up his inner strength, sat in his chair, placed his head in his hands and said: "I do not know what the Baal Shem Tov did, or the words spoken by the Maggid of Mezeritch. Nor do I know the place where the Sassover sought You in the forest. All I can do is tell this story, and this must be sufficient."

And it was.

[Buber, *Later Masters*, pp. 92-93]

2. Moses and Akiva

🕮 Rabbi Judah remembered a story that he heard from the great sage Rav: When Moses arrived in heaven, he saw God decorating some letters of the Torah with little crowns. Moses asked, "Why do You decorate these letters? And, if decoration is important, why not decorate every letter?"

God answered, "After many generations, a great teacher will come to Israel. His name will be Akiva ben Joseph. When he sees these crowns, he will discover their meaning and he will teach My people many wondrous things about each and every little crown."

"Ruler of the universe," Moses pled, "allow me to see this great teacher."

God replied: "Turn around." When Moses turned he found himself standing behind the last bench of students in the house of study. Rabbi Akiva was teaching. All the students listened intently. Their faces were beatific. At times, hearing a particularly poignant point of law from the master, they even sighed. But Moses was dismayed to discover that he could not fathom the meaning of Akiva's teachings. Moses' heart grew heavy with sadness.

Then, one of the students asked Rabbi Akiva, "Master, where did you learn these teachings?"

Akiva answered, "These were the laws given by God to Moses at Mount Sinai."

Moses was immediately cheered. Turning around again, he asked God, "O Holy One, if You have such a great teacher as this Akiva, why did You choose to give the Torah through me and not through him?"

God replied, "You were the right teacher for your generation; he is the right teacher for his generation."

[B. Talmud *Menachot* 29b]

3. Temple Windows

In the Bible, it is written, "For the [Temple] Solomon made windows, broad and narrow" (First Kings 6:4).

Rabbi Avin the Levite explained: When we make openings for windows, we make the openings broad on the inside and narrow on the outside. Why? So that the windows may draw in the greatest amount of light.

But Solomon commanded that the windows in the Temple should be made with broad openings on the outside and narrow ones on the inside. Why? So that light would flow out from the Temple to illumine the world.

[Tanchuma *Behaalotcha* #2; Yalkut *First Kings* #182]

4. Show Bread Secrets

The House of Garmu served the Holy Temple in Jerusalem as its official bakers. They fashioned the twelve "show breads"—the loaves that were displayed on the golden table from one Shabbat to the next, then were eaten by the Temple priests as sacrifices.

Now, the twelve loaves were made from four quarts of flour. Each loaf was the thickness of only half an inch. But the loaves were twenty-eight inches long and twelve inches wide, with decorations baked into each corner. Taking them out of the oven without breaking them was the first great secret known only to the bakers of the House of Garmu.

The twelve loaves also stayed fresh. They were baked on Friday before Shabbat—sometimes on the Wednesday before—yet they were fresh enough to eat even ten days later! What did the bakers put into the loaves to keep them fresh so long? This was the second great secret known only to the bakers of the House of Garmu.

The Sages fretted about these secrets. What if something bad were to happen to the House of Garmu? How would the Jewish people of the future bake the show breads then? But, no matter how often they were asked, the bakers of Garmu stubbornly refused to reveal their secrets.

The Sages insisted that the show breads belonged to God because God twice in the Torah commanded that they be baked (Exodus 25:30; Leviticus 24:5-9). Therefore, the sages commanded the House of Garmu to teach their secrets to God's people. Even then, the House of Garmu remained silent.

Then the Sages heard of another family of Jewish bakers in Egypt. It was said their breads were praised by every Jew of Alexandria. So the Sages brought the Egyptian bakers to Jerusalem to take the place of the bakers of the House of Garmu. The news spread throughout the Jewish world, "The House of Garmu has been fired!"

As it turned out, the Sages were not as wise about baking as they were about studying Torah. The bakers from Alexandria did their best, but they could not get their loaves out of the oven without breaking them; and, worse, their loaves molded and spoiled in just a few short days. And, all the while, the bakers of Garmu watched and waited.

The Sages discussed their problem. Some said, "Give the bakers of Alexandria time. By trial and error, they will learn how to keep the loaves fresh and how to remove them from the oven without breaking them. As they learn, we will learn the secrets. Then, we will teach the secrets to the Jewish bakers of the future." But others said, "We sages have always taught, 'Serve God with your best.' And, as we have learned, every moment is the most important moment and every generation is the most important generation. We must offer to God the best show breads we can, now." In the end, the Sages all agreed, "Let the House of Garmu return to their work."

But the House of Garmu refused to return. The Sages sent a message, saying, "If you return, we will double your salary." The House of Garmu still refused. The Sages sent another message, saying, "If you return, we will never ask for your secrets again." Only then did the House of Garmu agree to return.

The Sages inquired, "Why is the House of Garmu so stubborn? Why do you refuse to reveal your secrets?"

The bakers of Garmu replied, "Our fathers taught us that Temples are buildings; and buildings can be destroyed. If God's Temple in Jerusalem were ever destroyed—may God forbid it!—our secrets might land in the hands of those who worship idols. Such a thing may never be allowed to happen. We bakers of Garmu are servants of the Holy One alone."

Then the Sages blessed them, saying, "What you have done is good. The name of the House of Garmu shall be remembered always by the people of Israel for a blessing." And so it is: The name of Garmu will ever be remembered; and the secrets of Garmu will ever remain a mystery.

[Tosefta *Yoma* 2:5; 3:11; B. Talmud *Yoma* 38a]

5. The Magic Ring (Version 1)—Melchizedek Avoids a Trap

Saladin had very little money left in his treasury. What he had not spent on costly wars, he had given to the mosque and to the poor. As he pondered ways to raise funds, he recalled a certain Jew of Alexandria, Egypt, a wealthy merchant named Melchizedek. Saladin did not wish to be seen taking money by force, but he thought that, if he could find a clever way to back Melchizedek into a corner, then the wealthy Jew would offer to buy his way out of the corner.

So Saladin invited Melchizedek to his palace for a feast. During the meal, he said, "Melchizedek, my friend, you are known throughout the world for your wisdom. Tell me, then, what is the true way of God? There are three great religions—Judaism, Christianity, and Islam—which is the true one?"

Melchizedek knew that Saladin was putting him in a tight spot. How could he answer such a question truthfully without insulting the Sultan? So Melchizedek answered, "Yours is an excellent question, my lord. I can only answer it with a story."

It was known to all that the Obiad family had a treasured possession, a precious ring. In each generation, before his death, the father would choose one of his sons and give him the ring. After the father died, the son possessing the father's ring would become the new head of the Obiad family. And thus it continued from one generation to the next.

But after many generations, the ring came into the hand of a father who had three sons and loved all of them equally. All three were models of obedience, virtue, and worthiness. And no one of the three was better than the other two. The father decided not to decide. He called for a master craftsman to make two exact copies of the precious ring, and he gave a ring to each son.

When the father died, each son came and showed his ring, saying that this was the proof that he would be the next head of the Obiad family. Jewelers were called to inspect the rings, but the craftsman had taken great care, and no one could say for certain which ring was the true one. To this day, no one knows.

And the same is true for Judaism, Christianity, and Islam. The peoples who are faithful to each of them claim that they are the true heirs of God's truth. But even a careful inspection of each will fail to tell us which is the true religion. To this day, no one knows.

When Melchizedek finished his story, Saladin said, "My friend, you have true wisdom. I thought I might trap you by my question and that you might try to buy your way out of my trap. But, in truth, you have trapped me by your story." Then Saladin went on, saying, "Therefore, you leave me no choice. Tell me, would you be willing to loan me the money I need?"

Melchizedek smiled and said, "The honor would be mine, My sultan."

So Melchizedek made the loan and Saladin repaid him in full; and the Sultan and the wealthy Jew remained friends as long as they lived.

[Giovanni Boccaccio, *The Decameron*, day 1, tale 3]

Giovanni Boccaccio (1313–1375) portrayed Jewish characters in two stories of *The Decameron*, basing them on personal acquaintances among the Jewish merchants of Naples. A Jewish "magic ring" story first appeared around 1550. (A second version is given in the chapter on "Friendship.")

6. Jerusalem

🐚 In 1903, the British offered the leaders of the new Zionist movement an immediate solution for "the Jewish question." A Jewish "homeland" could be established in Uganda, Africa. Theodor Herzl and other Zionist leaders felt hard-pressed at that moment. Pogroms, anti-Jewish riots, had broken out in Eastern Europe and innocent Jews were being abused, tortured, raped, and slaughtered. Herzl and his inner circle refused to give up the struggle for a Jewish homeland in the land of Israel, but they thought that a temporary transfer of Eastern European Jews to Uganda might serve two very important purposes: It would rescue the many Jews being threatened by the pogroms and it would strengthen the relations between the Zionist movement and the British, which might speed the day when the British would agree to a Jewish state in the Holy Land.

In August 1903, Herzl presented "the Uganda Plan" to the Sixth Zionist Congress. The delegates from Eastern Europe—the Jews most in need of rescue—vehemently rejected the plan and stormed out of the Congress. The issue threatened to destroy the Zionist movement. The efforts of Herzl to hold the movement together were a great strain on his already weak heart and he died before the Seventh Zionist Congress in 1905.

In those days, the most famous Zionist in Great Britain was the brilliant young chemist of Manchester University, Chaim Weizmann. When the Seventh Zionist Congress defeated the Uganda Plan, the former Prime Minister of Britain, Arthur Balfour, invited Weizmann to come and explain the Jewish decision to him. Why were the Zionists opposed to rescuing their people and establishing a Jewish homeland in Africa?

"Just suppose," Weizmann said to Balfour, "I were to offer you the city of Paris instead of the city of London. Would you accept Paris?"

Balfour said, "Dr. Weizmann, London is our capital."

"Jerusalem is our capital," Weizmann replied. "It was our capital when London was a marsh."

On that day, Arthur Balfour glimpsed the Zionist dream. Over the next dozen years, as the two men became friends, Weizmann constantly urged Balfour to help the Zionist cause. In 1917, as Foreign Secretary of Great Britain, Lord Balfour was pleased to issue what became known as "The Balfour Declaration," a letter to the British Jewish leader Lord Walter Rothschild, promising Great Britain's support for the establishment of a Jewish homeland in the Land of Israel. Weizmann would soon have his capital again, and he was also destined to become the first president of the new State of Israel.

[adapted from Weizmann, *Trial and Error*; with historical detail from Rossel, *Israel*]

7. The Jewish Melody

☙ The Zionist leader and writer, Hayim Greenberg, was a master of many languages. He spoke Russian, Yiddish, English, and Hebrew; and wrote essays in Yiddish, English, and Hebrew. He was devoted to teaching Hebrew to all Jews, not just those who lived in the new State of Israel. As head of the Department of Education and Culture of the Jewish Agency Executive in America, he encouraged Jews in the United States to set up "Hebrew schools."

He said, "[Hebrew is,] first of all, a sort of "social cement," a bridge or social medium of contact between Jews in Israel and Jews abroad ... If [the Jew] does not know to their deepest sounding, and in their context of spiritual tensions, such Hebrew expressions as *mitzvah, averah, geulah, tikkun, tumah, yirah, ahavah, tzedakah, chesed, mesirut nefesh, kiddush hashem, devekut, teshuvah*, he cannot carry a part in that choir that gives voice, consciously or not, to what I have called "the Jewish melody."

[Hayim Greenberg, from an address given at the World Zionist Congress, August 1951]

Until modern times, Hebrew was considered a "holy tongue," used only in prayer and study. But leaders of the *Haskalah* (the Jewish Enlightenment movement) and idealistic Zionists argued for Hebrew as a "national" language to express Jewish values. Here are the most common translations for the terms on Greenberg's list: *mitzvah* ("commandment," but also "good deed" or "favor"), *averah* ("sin"), *geulah* ("redemption," also "salvation"), *tikkun* ("repair [of the world]"), *tumah* ("integrity"), *yirah* ("fear, as in "awe"), *ahavah* ("love"), *tzedakah* ("charity," but also "righteousness"), *chesed* ("benevolence," but also "mercy" and "piousness"), *mesirut nefesh* ("risking one's life" on behalf of an ideal or another person), *kiddush hashem* ("martyrdom," literally, "sanctifying God's Name"), *devekut* ("clinging," as in "faithfulness to God"), and *teshuvah* ("repentance," but also "turning" or "returning").

8. The Treasure

🕮 The story is told of a poor man named Israel who lived in a small town in the very corner of the kingdom. Israel had a dream, and it kept returning—the same dream—night after night. In his dream, he saw the capital city and the palace where the king lived. And, before the palace gate, he saw a drawbridge.

Now, in his dream, he went to that drawbridge and at the junction where the drawbridge and the palace gate came together, under the bridge's stone foundation, he saw a certain spot of open earth. Here he dug and dug until he found a treasure! It was a treasure of enormous wealth.

In the end, he could not resist the recurrent dream. One day, he set out on the long journey. After many trials and tribulations, he came to the capital and to the palace—and, just as in his dream, there was the drawbridge. And there was the palace gate. And there was the open spot of earth where he was meant to dig. All was as in his dream—all, that is, except for one thing.

All along the drawbridge, guards were posted. How would he, a poor Jew, get to the open spot of earth to dig? Surely, the soldiers would stop him. And, if he found a treasure, surely they would confiscate it.

Day after day he returned to the drawbridge and waited for an opportunity. In time, he made friends with the captain of the guards. When, at last, he saw that no opportunity would ever present itself, he decided to confide in the captain. He described his dream to the captain.

"Strange," the captain said. "For I have had a very similar dream. It came many nights and each time it was the same.

"In my dream," the captain continued, "I had to travel a long distance to a small town in the very corner of the kingdom. There I searched, looking for the house of a certain Jew named Israel. And when I found this house, I went to the fireplace and there, in the open earth before the hearth, I dug and dug until I reached an enormous box. And when the box was opened, there was a great treasure inside—diamonds, emeralds, rubies, and pearls the size of your fist."

"What a strange dream," said Israel to the captain.

But Israel took the message of the captain's dream to heart. He packed his belongings and put the spade across his shoulder and made the long journey home. He faced many trials and tribulations on his way, but when he reached his house he did not pause an instant. He proceeded to the spot of open earth before his fireplace and he dug until he reached the heavy wooden box buried deep in the ground. He lifted the lid of the box, and—behold— there was the treasure. There were diamonds, emeralds, rubies, and pearls the size of your fist.

It was altogether too much treasure for any one person; and, at once, Israel sent a small fortune to the captain of the guards. Then he began to share his treasure with all in need.

After all is said and done, the treasure is always at home— within reach. You are Israel. The treasure is the treasure of Israel. And there is more than enough for all to share.

[adapted from a tale of Simcha Bunam in Buber, *Later Masters*, pp. 245-6; a far older version is found in the *1001 Tales of the Arabian Nights* ©.950- 1050)]

4

Students and Teachers

1. Study or Doing?

Once Rabbi Tarfon and the Sages gathered in the upper chamber of the house of Nitzah in Lydda. The question was raised, "Which is greater? Study or doing?"

Rabbi Tarfon said, "Doing is greater."

Rabbi Akiva said, "Study is greater."

When the discussion was over, the sages agreed: "Study is greater, because study leads to doing."

[B. Talmud *Kiddushin* 40b]

2. Whoever Would Teach Him

When the rich man died, the heavenly court asked him: "Why did you not spend more time studying?"

He answered, "I was worried about my possessions and my property, so I spent my time taking care of it."

Then the court said, "Were you more wealthy than Rabbi Eleazar, whose father promised him a thousand cities and a fleet of a thousand ships? Still, every day Eleazar threw a bag of flour over his shoulder and went from town to town and from province to province to study Torah. Using the flour as payment for his lessons, he learned from anyone willing to teach him.

[B. Talmud *Yoma* 35b]

3. The Cave and the World

As they walked along a Roman road, Rabbi Judah said to Rabbi Simeon, "The Romans are a grand nation. Throughout our land, they pave the streets, construct bridges, and build baths."

Rabbi Simeon said, "No, the Romans are a selfish people. Whatever they make, they make for themselves. They pave roads so their armies can pass more easily. They construct bridges just to collect tolls from the poor. And they build baths just to pamper themselves."

A man nearby overheard the words of Rabbi Simeon and repeated them to others. Soon the Roman emperor himself heard Rabbi Simeon's words. "No one should speak this way about Rome. I shall have this man put to death for what he said," the emperor decreed. "Send soldiers to seize him."

Rabbi Simeon was warned that the Romans were coming to arrest him. He thought, "If I hide alone the Romans will torture my wife and child until they tell where I am hidden. I will take my son and hide with him to keep him safe. And to keep my wife safe, I will not let her know where I am hidden."

So Rabbi Simeon and his son found a cave in the hills and hid in it. The entrance to the cave was covered by thorns and vines. Yet from the small entrance, the cave opened up to a huge open space. Miraculously, Simeon and his son found a small spring of water in the cave and, beside it, a carob tree full of fruit. It was all they needed for food and drink. All day every day, they studied the Torah. When it was time for prayer each put on a *tallit* ("prayer shawl") and prayed. They took care of their robes, wearing them as little as possible, so they would not fray. In this way, they passed twelve years in the cave.

In those days, there was a custom in Rome: When a Roman emperor died, all decrees of death against his enemies were forgiven. At the end of twelve years, the Roman emperor died. Now it was safe for Rabbi Simeon and his son to come out of hiding. But where were they hidden? No one knew. His friends did not know. His wife did not know. How could they be found?

A stranger came to Rabbi Simeon's wife. "I have a plan for finding your husband and your son," he said. "I have decided they must be hiding in a cave somewhere in the hills of Judea. I will go through the hills calling out to them until I am heard. Do not worry, I will find them for you."

Then the stranger went from hilltop to hilltop, crying out at every stop, "Who will tell Rabbi Simeon that the emperor is dead and his decree has been set aside?"

Rabbi Simeon's wife was puzzled. "Who could this stranger be?" she asked Rabbi Judah.

Rabbi Judah said, "Do not be afraid. This can be none other than the wandering Jew—the prophet Elijah—who goes from place to place, providing help wherever it is needed."

Inside the cave, Rabbi Simeon's son heard the words echoing from a hilltop, "Who will tell Rabbi Simeon that the emperor is dead?" He ran to his father. "Wonderful news, my father," he cried. "The emperor is dead. We can leave the cave and return home!"

They put their robes over their loin cloths and made ready to leave the cave. As they cut through the vines at the cave's entrance, they were blinded by sunlight. They stood still until they could see and then set off on their way. For the first time in twelve years, they saw farmers plowing the fields.

"What are they doing?" asked Rabbi Simeon. "Why do they waste their time plowing the earth when they could be studying Torah. I shall teach them a lesson they will not soon forget." He raised his eyes to the heavens and pointed to the fields. With that, lightning struck where his finger pointed, and the field burned as the farmers ran to safety.

They walked a little more, and they saw men gathering olives from a grove of olive trees.

"What are they doing?" asked Rabbi Simeon. "Why are they not studying Torah?" He pointed to the olive trees, and lightning struck them, setting the trees ablaze, sending the men scurrying off in all directions.

Suddenly, the stranger whose words had called them from their cave, stood before them. "What are you doing, Rabbi Simeon?" he inquired. "God has sent me to ask you, 'Have you come out to destroy My world?' God says, 'Return to your cave, and study the Torah again until you understand its words!'"

Then Rabbi Simeon and his son returned to the cave and studied the Torah for another twelve months. At the end of the twelve months, they heard a voice calling to them, saying, "Leave your cave. Let us see if you have learned to love both Torah and the world."

Rabbi Simeon and his son left the cave. This time, when they saw men picking olives from the olive trees, Rabbi Simeon said,

"Blessed are those who make oil for the lamps of the house of study." And when they saw farmers in the fields, Rabbi Simeon said, "Blessed are those who help God to feed the hungry."

[B. Talmud *Shabbat* 33b; also *Sefer HaAggadah*]

4. Yochanan and the Digger of Wells

A digger of wells once noticed Rabbi Yochanan ben Zakkai walking by. "Ho, there, Rabbi," he called out. "Did you know that I am as important as you?"

"How is that?" Yochanan asked.

"You see," the well-digger said, mopping the sweat from his brow with a cloth, "it is because my work is as important to our community as yours. When you tell a man or woman to go to the ritual baths and cleanse themselves, its is I who provide the water for them."

"You may be as important as I," said Yochanan, "but you would be a nearer equal if you would study Torah as cheerfully as you brag."

[*Midrash Ecclesiastes Rabbah* 4:17]

Jewish law requires that the water for a *mikvah*, a "ritual bath," must be fresh, running water. Water from a well is not used for this purpose (though the Bible permitted it) because the rabbis enacted a requirement that *mikvah* water should not be "drawn," that is, placed into any kind of vessel or receptacle prior to its use in the ritual bath. Hence, the well-digger's brag is false bravado. Rabbi Yochanan implies that the well-digger would know this, if only he had studied.

5. Early and Late

Let no person say inwardly, "I have studied Torah and Mishnah today, and tomorrow I do not need to study. I have done good deeds today, tomorrow I need do none. I have given charity today, tomorrow I need not give charity."

Let a person rather reflect and realize that soon enough death arrives. Let a person lift eyes heavenward and say, "Who created this universe?" For heaven and earth, sun and moon, stars and planets, early and late do the bidding of God who created them. So, too, should you early and late study the words of Torah, and ever seek to do the will of your Creator, as it is written, "Let us continue to know *Adonai*" (Hosea 6:3).

[*Tanna devei Eliyahu*, p. 195]

6. Parables

🐟 In what way did Solomon's wisdom enhance the glory of God? Solomon made "handles" for the Torah. And what were the "handles?" Parables!

Rabbi Nachman took up a parable, saying: Imagine a maze-like palace with many halls and many doors. Whoever entered the palace was lost in an instant and could not find the way out. Along came a clever fellow who tied a coil of rope to the entrance, so that whoever entered could take the loose end of the rope and feel free to explore the palace, knowing that, in the end, it would only be necessary to follow the rope back to the entrance. Solomon was this clever fellow. Until he arose no one was able to find their way through the words of the Torah, but Solomon attached the parable at the entrance to Torah and soon all began to comprehend God's words.

Again, Rabbi Nachman took up a parable, saying: Imagine a thicket of reeds which no one could penetrate, till one clever man came and took a scythe and cut down some of the reeds making a path. Then all began to enter through the path that had been cut. Solomon was this clever man. By means of parables, Solomon cut a path through the Torah that many could follow.

Then Rabbi Yose took up a parable, saying: Imagine a huge basket full of fruit, but without any handle, so that it could not be lifted. Along came a clever man and attached handles to it. From then on, the basket could be carried by the handles. Solomon was that clever man. Before Solomon applied parables to the Torah, no one could properly understand it. But by means of the parables, the words of the Torah could be lifted and carried, so even the simplest person could comprehend the Torah.

Then Rabbi Shila took up a parable, saying: Imagine a jug filled to the brim with hot water, but with no handle by which to carry it. Along came a clever man and attached a handle to the jug. Solomon was that clever man. After he applied the parable, the white-hot words of Torah could be taken from one end of the earth to another.

Then Rabbi Chanina took up a parable, saying: Imagine a deep well full of cold, sweet, refreshing water, but none could drink from the well. Along came a clever man who tied rope to rope and cord to cord until the water could be drawn, pail by pail, from the well. Solomon was that clever man. He tied parable to parable and example to example, until the inmost words of Torah came to the surface where all could drink them in and thereby gain health and healing.

Our sages taught: Lo, the parable is deceptive. Those who take it lightly are woefully mistaken, for by means of the parable all can master the teachings of the Torah. If a king loses a gem from his crown at night, it does not require an army to find it, only a wick for his oil lamp. A wick—it seems a petty thing, but do not take it lightly. The parable is a wick for finding concealed gems, since by means of the parable the true meaning of the words of the Torah may be revealed.

[Midrash Song of Songs Rabbah 1:8]

7. The Perfect Story

There was once a storyteller—What a storyteller! When she spoke, simple speech became eloquent, ordinary days turned miraculous. At entertaining, at amusing, at enlightening, at pleasing, at prodding, at stirring, the storyteller never failed.

Most amazing of all was that no matter what story she told, it always seemed the perfect story for that moment. One day I asked her the secret of her success; and, since she is my friend—and since she knew that I tell a story here and there—she said to me, "To tell you how it is that I always have the right story, I will tell you a story." And this is the story she told me:

A king once sent his son to an academy far away. There the prince studied the many arts of the nobility. At one of these, he excelled: archery. In only five years, the master archer taught the prince all he knew—the secrets of feathering the arrow, bending the bow, aiming, judging the wind and the distance, stance and balance, and unerring release.

When the five years were up, the prince mounted his steed and began his long journey home. He stopped to rest his horse, to eat, and to sleep at a local inn. After a satisfying meal, he took a brisk walk; and came to a barn.

He stopped to stare at the barn for it piqued his interest greatly. All along its side targets were painted. And in the very center of each target, a single arrow had been driven straight and true. Whoever the archer had been, he had hit dead center without ever sending as much as one arrow astray!

The prince was astonished. Who among the people of this small town could possibly be such an expert marksman? And, if such a one was about, was he not the master of all masters of archery?

Now the prince stopped every villager. "Where is your master archer?" he would ask. But no one in town knew of any archer. At last, in desperation, he sat before the barn and stared at the targets. A boy came along, and the prince stopped him. "Do you know who has been taking practice here on the side of the barn?" the prince asked.

"I have," said the boy.

"*You?*" the prince insisted. For before him he saw nothing but a common ruffian, a churl. It set his royal blood afire to think that this skipjack could be a great archer. But the prince so loved his art, if there was something left to learn, he was determined to learn it. "Show me," he said to the boy.

"Sure," the lad said affably. "Come along."

Together they stood opposite the barn as, from a fair distance, the boy took aim and loosed an arrow from his bow. It sailed through the air and struck with a thud at a spot away from any of the targets. The prince was confused.

Nor did his confusion abate when the boy ran into the barn, emerging a moment later with a brush and a can of paint. But all became clear when the boy painted a solid circle around the arrow he had just shot, and, following that, painted two more circles around the dot to form a target.

"That's how it's done," said the boy. "First I shoot at the wall. Then, I draw the target."

"And now you know," my friend, the storyteller, said, "why I always have the right story for each and every occasion!"

[adapted from a story of the Maggid of Dubno (various sources); also in Ausubel, *Treasury*, p. 4, where it is said to have been told to Elijah the Vilna Gaon]

8. The Rooster Prince

The prince of a distant land went mad. His madness took a strange form—he was convinced that he was a rooster. Under this hallucination, he went without clothing, roosted under a table in the Great Hall, and ate only such food as roosters eat.

The king sought the help of physicians, astrologers, magicians, even quacks of all kinds. With no prospect of a cure from any of these, he offered a great reward to anyone in the kingdom who could cure the prince.

Many came forward, many tried. None succeeded. Time passed and the boy still rose with the sun and crowed every morning.

One day a self-proclaimed healer came forward, and said, "If you let me do as I will, I think I can cure the prince."

The king, who had long since lost hope, agreed.

The healer proceeded to shed his clothing and join the prince under the table.

"Who do you think you are?" demanded the prince.

"A rooster like you," answered the healer. "I've come to keep you company."

For a while, the prince was suspicious. In time, though, his attitude changed. He began to accept the man at his word. True enough, he looked exactly like a naked man. Still, just like the prince, he ate rooster food, preened all day, and rose early to the task of crowing. He must be a rooster.

This led to a degree of affection and trust. The prince and the healer became friends.

One day the healer put on a shirt. The prince was taken aback.

"Why in the world are you doing that?" he cried. "Don't you know that roosters never wear clothing? Only human beings wear clothes."

The healer pacified his friend, saying, "I will share a truth with you: though a rooster may dress like a human being, he remains a rooster. How can the way we dress matter? What is there to be afraid of? And, the truth is, we'll be warmer this way."

The prince thought about this and nodded. "It makes sense. I admit that I've been a bit chilly of late." The next day both dressed as human beings.

More time passed. Their friendship deepened. The day came when the healer called for food from the royal kitchen—the kind of food that humans eat.

The prince was perplexed. "You call yourself a rooster when you not only dress like a man but eat like one, too?"

The healer said, "Trust me a little, my friend. Have I let you down so far? Who says you can't remain a rooster even though you eat like a human being? In fact, you could eat at a table, as humans do, and still… a rooster is a rooster and does not stop being one, any more than a human being stops being a human being."

The prince became calmer, and the healer continued: "Since you are a rooster, why be afraid that you'll turn into something else because of what you do? Stay what you are, by all means, but if you can, why not live in the human world since it is so much more comfortable for the both of us? Think about it."

The prince considered this advice. "You're right! We can remain what we are no matter what we do!"

In this way it came about that the prince took up his former life. He lived in the human world, and—rooster though he remained to the end of his days—forever after he acted like a prince.

[a tale of Rabbi Nachman of Bratslav (various sources); a slightly variant version appears in Wiesel, *Souls on Fire*, pp. 170-171]

A patient who had been incarcerated for many years in a mental hospital was healthy and seemingly functional, but for one idiosyncrasy. Instead of speaking English, the patient spoke what is known as "word salad." He seemed always to be trying to express himself, but the syllables and words did not add up to language. Many psychologists and psychiatrists had tried to help him through the years, but none had succeeded.

Along came a brash new intern. He sat across from the patient and listened for a while until he was able to reproduce some of the unintelligible patterns of the patient's speech. Happening to hear what he thought to be the inflection of a question, the intern spoke a few syllables of "word salad" back to the patient.

The patient was startled. He tilted his head and seemed to consider what to do. Then he launched into another long spate of gibberish, ending again with a seeming question. The intern responded with a long spate of gibberish of his own, gesticulating with his hands and nodding with his head. The bizarre dialogues continued whenever the intern was able to break away from his duties. Slowly, the intern introduced a word or two of English into the mix, but the patient continued to answer in babble.

One day, the intern sat before the patient and asked, "How are you feeling?" The patient answered, "I have been feeling better ever since I met you." There were many more exchanges in gibberish, but after another few days, an entire conversation took place entirely in English. Within a short time, the patient was released and went on to find a job and become a useful member of the community.

The intern became the famous psychologist, Milton Erickson (1901-1980). From time to time, he would receive a post card from the former patient, written entirely in "word salad." He would draft a return post card of his own entirely in "word salad," closing with a single sentence in English: "I'm glad to hear that things are going so well for you, my friend" (paraphrased from a story related to the author by Rabbi Jack Bloom).

9. Seven Stars of David

One of my favorite students proudly informed me that she had applied and been accepted to a rabbinic school. From time to time, during her career at the seminary, she would drop in to chat with me. During one such visit, she told me this story:

In her senior year, a professor who seemed to like her very much said, "Laura, how do you think you will do on my examination?" Laura replied, "I won't have any trouble with your examination. You will ask only ten questions and they are—" and she proceeded to name all ten questions!

The professor was stunned. "You know exactly the questions I'm going to ask! You have even told them to me in the order that I plan to ask them! Did you break into my office or hack into my computer?"

Laura said, "No. I just know you; so I know what you would ask on a final examination."

The professor said, "That's hardly a feasible explanation. I'm afraid that you and I will have to have a little talk with the dean."

The dean listened to the professor. Turning to Laura, he asked, "Is this true? Do you actually know the questions?"

Laura said, "Of course I know the questions. I attended the course and I listened to the lectures."

The dean replied, "Many students did. But I am certain that not many know the questions and the order in which they will be asked. You must have cheated in some way. And, unless you can prove otherwise, I will have to bar you from taking the examination and bar you from graduating and being ordained. The school cannot countenance dishonesty."

Laura said, "If you want proof that I knew, possibly before the professor did, what his questions on the final exam would be, send someone to my room to fetch my notebook with the notes I took in class.

"You will see that I have marked certain notes with stars of David. The ten questions that the professor is going to ask are the only ones marked with seven stars of David.

"You will also see that I placed numbers—from 1 to 10—beside those ten questions. Because he has a habit of asking only ten questions on his examinations, I selected ten notes to label with seven stars. Those were the things he emphasized throughout the term and, again, in his summary session at the end of the term."

So they sent the dean's secretary to get that notebook and they found that Laura had marked some notes with one star of David, some with two, some with three, some with four, some with five, and some with six. But only ten were marked with seven stars of David. And the ten questions were scattered on different pages and numbered out of sequence, just as she had described.

The dean conferred with the professor, after which he said to Laura, "You need not take the final exam. You really listened and you really heard everything your professor was teaching."

Laura went on to become a rabbi. Her congregation is fortunate to have acquired such a good listener. Even when she was my student, I knew she was remarkable. She paid attention to more than what was being said. She sensed the things that I thought were important, anticipated the questions I was going to ask. You may have a friend like that, someone who knows you well enough to complete the sentences you begin. Or you might be like Laura, able to complete someone else's thoughts.

Our facial expression, our eyes, the way we hold our bodies, the way we move our hands, the way we move our heads, the way we breathe, even the way we flex our muscles—all of this discloses a lot of information to the student prepared to receive it.

[Rossel, adapted from a case study by Milton Erickson]

10. Expert Mechanic

The ship was just out of an expensive overhauling in dry dock and a cargo of fresh fruit had been loaded. Suddenly, it was discovered that the boilers would not fire up. The ship's mechanics labored for an entire day, but they could not find the problem. The captain called the ship's owner and told him the bad news.

"If we do not get underway quickly," the captain said, "the cargo will rot, and we will not only lose the profit of the journey, but the cost of the fruit, as well."

The ship's owner was perturbed. "What can we do?" he asked.

The captain said he had heard of a certain mechanic on the dock who was known to be an expert. "But," he added, "this man is very expensive."

"How expensive could he be?" asked the ship's owner. "Get him."

The captain called the expert mechanic. On board the ship, the mechanic looked at the boilers and nodded. He walked halfway down the boiler room, ran his hand along a pipe, then took a wrench from his tool kit and tapped the pipe one time. Immediately the boilers sprang to life. Within the hour, the ship was underway.

Two days later the ship's owner received an invoice from the mechanic. He could hardly believe his eyes. The bill was for one thousand dollars!

He was so shocked that he sent a letter to the mechanic asking him to itemize the bill. Two days later, he received the itemization.

It said, "One dollar for tapping. Nine hundred and ninety-nine dollars for knowing where to tap."

[American folktale, often cited as a story about Henry Ford and the famous engineer, Charles Steinmetz]

11. The Messiah in Your Classroom

Being a Jewish teacher is an awesome responsibility. You must teach each lesson as if the world depended upon it. And, you know, it may.

The time will come when the Messiah will appear. Naturally, before the Messiah becomes the great leader of destiny, the

Messiah will be a child attending some religious school, being taught by some religious school teacher.

Nor is it only the Messiah who has the potential to change the world. Some teacher first taught Albert Einstein that we are all our brothers' keepers. Some teacher explained to Dr. Jonas Salk the Jewish value of choosing life. Some teacher first quoted "Love your neighbor as yourself" to Henrietta Szold. And some teacher inspired Golda Meir to love her homeland. Some teacher encouraged a boy named David Green to join a youth group in Russia and he grew up to become David Ben-Gurion.

No wonder Judaism considers teaching such an awesome responsibility.

[Rossel]

12. The Full Barrel

Our Rabbis taught: A person who goes to honor a government official, goes with hands filled with gifts and returns empty-handed; but God is not that way. A person who goes to honor the Holy One, the Blessed, goes empty-handed and returns full.

With human beings, only an empty barrel gets filled. Once it is full, it can receive no more. But with God, the full barrel, too, is filled. If you have heard old teachings, you hear new teachings. If you have heard old stories, you hear new stories. Only if you turn your heart away—then, perhaps, you will hear no more.

When your barrel is full—full of stories, full of teachings—God continues to fill it and the barrel overflows. You feel the need to teach, you yearn to teach, your heart breaks because you have to teach. Your barrel is full and still filling. You must teach because you are "filled-full," "full-filled," "fulfilled." You teach and so you learn: We teach best as the barrel overflows.

[Pesikta Rabbati *Shuvah Ish Shalom* p. 185a; B. Talmud *Berachot* 40a; developed from a suggestion by Rabbi Fred Davidow]

13. The Perfect Lesson

It is said that the great Rabbi Israel of the Chasidim, the Baal Shem Tov, could teach the perfect lesson. On Friday evenings, when the Sabbath service was over, he would sit in a large room. At one end of the room, a table was set. On it, were two enormous candelabra. Between them was an open book, the mystic composition, *Sefer Yetzira*, "The Book of Creation."

Any Chasid with a problem that week, would come into his large room and stand in front of the table. Then, the Baal Shem Tov would speak to the group. And every person's problem would be solved.

One Sabbath eve, as the Chasidim left the presence of the Baal Shem Tov, one turned to another and said, "I'm surprised that you and the others stayed tonight. After all, the Baal Shem Tov was speaking only to me."

"To you?" asked the other. "That's not possible. Everything the Baal Shem Tov said was directed to me alone."

A third Chasid, overhearing this conversation, interrupted. "Put aside your argument. You are both mistaken. The Baal Shem Tov was speaking only to me."

Then a fourth Chasid spoke up, saying the same thing; and a fifth; and a sixth; and so on. Finally, all fell silent, for they realized what had truly happened.

[Buber, *Early Masters*, p. 55]

5

Wisdom

1. Good Advice

Along the road one day came a grandfather and his young grandson leading a donkey by the reins. The trio painted a colorful picture as they moved along, the donkey's head bobbing up and down in time to their steps. All was well until they met a stranger. "Hello there," she said to them. "Why do you walk and not ride? Donkeys are made for riding."

The grandfather and his grandson agreed that this was good advice and they thanked the stranger as they climbed up on the donkey's back.

But when they came closer to the town, they noticed people along the road pointing to them and whispering to one another. Soon one fellow stopped them. "Such a small donkey," he said, shaking his head from side to side. "The two of you are too great a burden upon its back. Are you not ashamed? It's cruelty to treat an animal in such a way."

Immediately the grandfather and grandson saw the wisdom in the man's words, and the boy slipped off the donkey's back to walk along beside.

They had not gone very far in this fashion when they were met by a peddler pushing his cart before him. "Why do you force that boy to walk while you ride?" the peddler asked the old man. "Don't you think that you weigh too much for that poor donkey's back? Why tire the boy and the donkey when you could walk?"

The grandson looked at his grandfather. They shrugged their shoulders as if to say, What's to be done? For they saw the sense in the peddler's words. It was true that the old man was the heavier burden, though not as heavy as the both of them had been together. Still, the old man could walk and the boy could ride. So the old man climbed down from the donkey's back and placed his grandson there instead.

In this way they proceeded again toward the town. But all too soon they were stopped by the call of a farmer standing by the roadside with his friend.

"You, boy," the farmer cried out, "have you no respect for your elders? It's a disgrace for you to ride and make that poor old man walk."

The farmer turned to his friend and still speaking loudly enough for the boy to hear, he said, "Imagine a strong young boy like that making an old man walk while he rides!"

Again the boy climbed down from the donkey's back, for he felt the sting of truth in the farmer's words. But what was to be done now? No matter whom they listened to, someone was not pleased. And all the advice they had got was good advice. It was no good to lead the donkey with no one riding. It was no good for both to ride. It was no good for the grandfather to ride alone. It was no good for the grandson to ride alone. Only one choice was left. With a sigh, the grandfather and his grandson heaved the donkey up on to their backs and continued on their way.

[Yiddish/European folktale retold by Rossel]

2. Three Men

Three men—two of them wise and one of them foolish—were thrown into a dungeon black as night. There were no windows and no light. Every day food and utensils were lowered to the men.

But the great darkness robbed the foolish man of the little sense he had. He forgot even how to use the utensils to bring the food to his mouth. One of the wise men instructed him in the use of fork and knife, but by the next day, the fool had forgotten what he had been taught. The sage, a patient man, went on teaching the same lesson, day after day.

Meanwhile, the other sage sat in silence, paying no attention to the fool. Once the patient sage asked him, "Why do you not help to instruct our poor foolish friend? Perhaps *you* could teach him in a way that would help him remember what he learned from day to day."

The quiet sage said, "Pay attention: You take infinite pains to teach him and yet you never achieve your goal. Each day, the darkness destroys your work. On the other hand, I am contemplating how we can bore a hole through the wall so that light and sun can enter. Then, all three of us will be able to see things clearly."

[attributed to Rabbi Simcha Bunam in Buber, Later Masters, p.247]

Rabbi Simcha Bunam (1765–1827) once offered this formula: "God's works are a mystery; reason is light; therefore, reason is greater than works."

3. Three Pieces of Knowledge

A bird-catcher caught an unusual bird. As soon as it was caught, it demonstrated its superior intellect by speaking to him. "Set me free," the bird chirped. "If you do, I will give you three pieces of invaluable knowledge."

"How do I know that you will not take off and leave me standing here and looking stupid?" asked the bird-catcher.

"Very well," the bird said. "I will trust you. I will give you the three pieces of knowledge first, if you will give me your solemn promise to let me go."

The bird-catcher promised.

"The first teaching," the bird said, "is never regret what has already happened. The second teaching is: Do not believe what sounds too good to be true. The third teaching is: Never attempt to attain what is beyond your ability to attain."

The bird-catcher had the bird repeat the three teachings, then he let the bird go, as he had promised. With a quick beating of her wings, the bird flew to the top of a high tree and began to mock the bird-catcher in the most sarcastic tones. "What a fool and simpleton you are! You did not know you were holding a treasure beyond your wildest imagination! Only two days past, I swallowed an enormous pearl. And had you cut me up to eat me, no doubt you would have become a very wealthy bird-catcher! Pity, pity, poor you!"

The bird-catcher was angry beyond words. He caught hold of the tree and began climbing. The bird merely walked to and fro on the highest branch calling out, "Pity you" and "What a simpleton."

Three-quarters of the way up the tree, the bird-catcher at last took hold of a branch that could not possibly bear his weight. With a snap, the branch and the bird-catcher plummeted to the forest floor. Injured and out of breath, he could not move. The bird calmly flew to the lower branches of the tree and shook its head at him.

"Fool and simpleton! Only a few moments ago, I gave you good wisdom. You forgot it at once. I advised you, first, that you should never regret what has already happened. But, no, you ignored that advice and regretted letting me go. I advised you, second, not to believe what sounds too good to be true. Anyone can tell you that swallowing a large pearl would have choked me to death; nevertheless, you swallowed my lie—hook, line, and sinker. And I advised you, third, never to attempt to attain what is beyond your ability to attain. Even you should have known that it was impossible for you to climb to the top of the tree; but, no, in your anger you reached too high.

"Because you did not heed the wisdom I gave you in return for my freedom, you lie broken and suffering on the ground. Fortunately for me, among human beings, you are typical. Give them good advice and they plunge headlong into foolishness." And, with that, the bird laughed as it flew away.

[adapted from Ausubel, *Treasury*, p. 628]

4. Three Sabbaths

On the Sabbath, the rabbi of Chelm always had a word of wisdom for his congregation. His inspiration came from the sun and the sky, from the breeze and the river, from the bushes and the trees. As he grew older, though, the things that used to inspire him lost much of their luster. He found himself running out of ideas. A rabbi with nothing to say? The thought was too awful for words. There was nothing he could even say about saying nothing!

So he found himself one Shabbat, as he entered the synagogue, trying to imagine what he would utter when the time came for him to preach. Just then, though, he had an idea. He rose to speak to the people of Chelm.

"My friends, wise people of Chelm," he said, " do you know what it is that I mean to say to you today?"

As if they had one voice, the people responded enthusiastically, "No, great rabbi, we do not know!"

He shook his head sadly, asking, "How can I speak in the face of such ignorance?" And he spoke not another word. He sat down.

After a moment of shock, the congregation continued the Sabbath prayers.

The whole next week was equally uninspiring. The rabbi still had nothing to say. Instead, he had another idea. He stood when his moment came.

"My friends, wise people of Chelm," he said, "do you have any idea what I mean to say to you today?"

The people were ready with the answer they thought the rabbi was seeking. "We do, great rabbi, we do!"

"If so," the rabbi said, "that is wonderful. Now there is no need for me to preach." With that, he sat, free from having to speak for another week.

Much to the rabbi's dismay, however, the third week was also uninspiring. In his whole life, nothing like this had ever happened. Three weeks with nothing to say. And, now, as he approached the synagogue, he saw that a large crowd had gathered. He had never seen such attendance at the synagogue. There were many people he did not even recognize! He turned to his assistant, and asked, "Why are there so many today?"

The assistant said, "Rabbi, did you not know, everywhere people are buzzing with curiosity. They are sure that today you are going to deliver your greatest message ever! They have come from miles around!"

"I see," the rabbi said, curious himself to know what he would say.

When the time came, he rose to his feet before the huge congregation. "My friends," he said, "do you have any idea what it is that I mean to say to you today?"

There was no unanimity this time. Some called out, "Yes, great rabbi, we do!" while others cried, "No, great rabbi, we do not know!"

"What a blessing!" said the rabbi. "Let those who know tell those who do not know." And with that, he resumed his seat.

[Sufi tale, adapted by Rossel]

5. Cause and Effect

🔖 A sage was walking along the road when suddenly a man fell from a rooftop and landed on the sage's neck. The man who fell was unhurt, but the sage had to be taken to the hospital. His students came to visit him, and asked, "What can we learn from what happened to you?"

The sage answered, "We learn from this that you must not rely on the inevitability of cause and effect. One thing does not always follow another in the way we expect. Look, that man fell from the roof, but my neck was broken! Give up theoretical questions such as: `If a man falls from a roof, will his neck be broken?'"

[adapted from Shah, *Pleasantries of the Incredible Mulla Nasrudin*, p. 26]

6. Like This Day ...

When the northern kingdom of Israel was conquered by Assyria, the people of Israel were led away in chains into slavery, never to be seen again. Thereafter, they were called "the ten lost tribes."

The sages, wanting to know if the ten lost tribes would ever return to the land of Israel, searched the Bible for a verse that would foretell the future. In the last book of the Torah, the Book of Deuteronomy, they believed they found it. There it is written, "God ... will cast them into another land, like this day" (29:27).

Rabbi Akiva said: "Like this day" means that the ten lost tribes will never return, for "this day" happens only once. It never comes again.

But Rabbi Eliezer disagreed, saying: "Like this day" shows that the sun comes up and goes down and returns again. In the same way, the sun went down on the ten lost tribes, and now they are in darkness. In the days to come, they will return with the light.

The sages recorded both opinions. Until this very day, the legend ends, our people wait to see which rabbi was right.

[B. Talmud *Sanhedrin* 110b; Yalkut *Nitzavim* #940]

7. Seventy Years Was But a Dream

Rabbi Yochanan was reading the Book of Psalms with his students when they came to the verse: "When the Holy One brought back those who returned to Zion, we were like those who dream" (126:1). Yochanan told his students: "When the First Temple was destroyed, the people were taken to Babylonia. Seventy years passed like a dream. Then God brought us back to the Land of Israel."

One student inquired, "Can a person really dream for seventy years?"

Rabbi Yochanan laughed. "Not just any person. But once there was a holy man named Choni who asked the very same question you are asking. The sages say that it was God who answered. So let me tell you his story."

And this is the story that Rabbi Yochanan told:

It was a lovely day and Choni went out walking. He crossed a small stream, and saw an old man planting a carob tree. Choni was puzzled. He scratched his beard and asked, "Old man, don't you know that it takes seventy years for a carob tree to bear fruit?"

The old man said, "I am old, but I am not a fool. Of course, I know that it will take seventy years for this tree to grow and bear fruit."

"But you are old," Choni pressed. "Why not plant a pomegranate tree or a date palm? You might live long enough to eat the fruit of those trees. Why should you plant a carob tree, knowing you will not live long enough to eat its fruit?"

The old man replied, "When I came into this world, I found fully-grown carob trees waiting for me. So I am planting this carob tree for my children."

Choni left the old man and continued walking. Suddenly, he felt very tired. He sat down in the shade to rest and fell fast asleep. As he slept, plants grew up around him, hiding him from sight. Farmers came and plowed the fields nearby, but they never saw him. Shepherds led their flocks nearby, but they did not notice him. Years went by, and the bushes and trees grew thick around him. His beard reached his belly and kept on growing. Seventy years passed while Choni slept and dreamed.

One day, the breeze blew through the branches and a leaf tickled Choni's cheek. He stretched his arms and rubbed the sleep from his eyes. "I must have dozed off," he thought. Looking down, he saw that his beard ended at his knees. "I have been sleeping a long time," he thought. Looking around, he saw trees on every side of him. "I must have slept a very long time," he thought.

Choni made a path through the trees and walked back toward the stream. He saw a man there gathering carobs from a tree.

"This is the same tree I watched the old man plant," Choni thought. He asked the man: "Are you the one who planted this tree?"

The man smiled. "Old one," he said to Choni, "don't you know it takes seventy years for a carob tree to bear fruit? I am gathering carob from a tree my grandfather planted."

"Can it be?" Choni wondered. "Have I truly slept for seventy years?"

He went home, but the town had changed, and his house was gone. He asked a woman, "Do you know the son of Choni the Circle Maker?" She answered, "Choni's son died long ago, but his grandson still lives."

Then Choni said: "I am Choni the Circle Maker."

The old woman laughed. "If you are Choni," she said, "then I am Queen Esther, and today is Purim."

Choni went through the whole town. To everyone he met, he announced, "I am Choni the Circle Maker." None believed him.

Looking for a place to rest, he found the house of study and entered it. There he heard the teachers telling the pupils, "In the old days, when there was a hard lesson to learn, our fathers would ask Choni the Circle Maker to explain it." Then Choni called out, "But I am Choni!" The students laughed, and the teachers shook their heads. No one would believe him.

So Choni crossed the stream once more and sat down beneath the carob tree. He recalled the old man's words: "When I came into this world, I found fully grown carob trees waiting for me. So I am planting this carob tree for my children." Suddenly, these words seemed very wise. Choni thought, "When I came into this world, I found wisdom waiting for me. Still, I studied and taught so there would be wisdom for my children. Each of us has only one lifetime in this world, but together with our children and grandchildren we can share many lives."

Whereupon, Choni turned his face to the heavens and spoke to God: "I have learned the meaning of my life. Now my time is over and the time of my grandchildren has come." And Choni smiled and fell asleep forever.

[B. Talmud *Taanit* 23a; also in *Sefer HaAggadah*]

Choni the Circle Maker is often called "the Rip Van Winkle" of the Talmud. The story of how he came to be known as "the Circle Maker" is given in the chapter on "Merit." Though this story is told in matter-of-fact terms in the Talmud, it is a Jewish version of a popular ancient legend. Diogenes Laertius tells a similar story about the miracle worker, Epimenides of Knossos (sixth century, BCE), and another version appears in the Fourth Book of Baruch, an apocryphal work. In *The Antiquities of the Jews,* the historian Josephus suggests that the historical Choni actually died as a martyr.

8. Alexander and the Rabbis

Our rabbis taught: Alexander the Great conquered much of the known world. Then, he wanted to explore the world of the unknown. On one journey, he caught fish from a spring. He salted the fish to preserve them so he could eat them later. So doing, he noticed that the fish gave off a heavenly odor. He thought, "Could it be that this spring is one of the four that comes forth from the Garden of Eden?" He scooped up some of the water and drank deeply. Suddenly, he felt tired and fell asleep beneath a willow beside the spring.

In his dream, he imagined that he followed the spring to its beginning at the gate to the Garden of Eden. He called out, "Open the gate for me." From inside a voice called back, "This is the gate of the King, the Holy One; only the righteous may enter" (Psalms 118:20). Alexander replied, "I, too, am a king. If you will not let me enter, send out a souvenir so that all may know I reached the Garden." The gate opened a crack and something was tossed out. It rolled to the feet of Alexander. He reached down to pick it up, blew the dust from it, and found—much to his amazement—it was a human eyeball!

Suddenly he awoke from his dream. He shook himself to clear his head, and he looked down. Behold! At his feet was a human eyeball. He picked it and blew the dust from it, even as he had in his dream. But this time he covered it with a cloth and threw it into a corner in his purse.

On his return to the Holy Land, he called on the rabbis. He told them of the stream, of how he dreamed of the gate of Eden, and of the gift he was given. Then he reached into his purse, pulled out the wadded cloth, and opened it. "What do you make of this?" he asked them.

They told Alexander to bring a scale and set the eyeball in one side. "Now put gold and silver on the other side," they said. Alexander did as the rabbis instructed. Behold! No matter how much gold and silver he placed on the scale, it never tipped at all. The eyeball was always heavier.

The rabbis said, "Now, place some dust over the eyeball." And, behold! As soon as the eyeball was covered with dust, the scale tipped and the silver and gold was heavier.

"What does this mean?" Alexander asked.

The rabbis explained: "This is the message of the Garden of Eden: The human eye is never satisfied. No matter how much it possesses, it still wants whatever it sees. But, an end comes to wanting when we die, when we see no more, and dirt is piled over us. Only then, does the human eye stop wanting."

[B. Talmud *Tamid* 32b]

9. Mercy and Justice

🐟 In the Bible and in the prayer book, God's name often appears as *Adonai Eloheinu* ("Our Ruler Our God"). A Midrash tells us that the reason the name *Adonai* always precedes the name *Eloheinu* is because *Adonai* stands for God's mercy, while *Eloheinu* stands for God's justice. We like to think of God as a God of mercy, first.

The Midrash goes on to tell about a king who had a new drinking glass. Two drinks were brought to the king. One was a wine so hot that the king was afraid that if he poured it into his new glass, the glass would shatter from the sudden heat. But the other wine was ice cold; and the king knew that cold, too, could crack the glass. So the king poured both drinks at once into his new glass and the glass was saved.

Mercy, the Midrash tells us, is like the hot drink and Justice like the cold one. When God wished to create the world, God considered first what to do. If God made it only of Justice then even when human beings sinned by mistake, God would be forced to punish them. But if God filled the world with Mercy alone, human beings would never stop sinning, knowing that God would forgive them no matter what they did. So God wisely chose to use an equal measure of both Mercy and Justice, and thus the world survived.

[*Midrash Genesis Rabbah* 12:15, as told by Rossel in *When a Jew Prays*]

10. Two Pockets

🐾 Rabbi Simcha Bunam instructed his disciples: You should always wear a garment with two pockets. In your right pocket, you should carry a piece of paper with the words, "The world was created for my sake." In your left pocket, you should carry a piece of paper with the words, "I am but dust and ashes."

When you feel high and mighty, you can reach into your left pocket and remind yourself, "I am but dust and ashes" and so regain your humility. When the world seems too great a burden to bear, you can reach into your right pocket and remind yourself, "The world was created for my sake."

[Buber, *Later Masters*, pp. 249-250]

A similar story was told of the captain of a ship. His junior officers noticed that, from time to time, he would reach in the left pocket of his jacket, take out a slip of paper, and read it. At other times, he would take a piece of paper from the right pocket of his jacket and read it. They became convinced that the secret to the captain's success was contained on these two slips of paper. When the captain died, they immediately went to his jacket and pulled out the two slips of paper. Each piece of paper had only one word written on it. From the right pocket came the word, "Starboard." And from the left pocket came the word, "Port."

11. Reb Naftali's Secret

🐾 One of Reb Naftali's students wanted to know why the rabbi always wore white trousers. The rabbi said, "That is one thing I cannot tell you. It is a great secret."

Hearing the word "secret" only made the fellow more curious. He pestered the rabbi time and again. At last, the rabbi wearied of this and said, "It is a great secret that can only be told to someone who fasts for six straight days."

The young fellow was so curious that he actually managed a six-day fast. After that, he turned up again.

Reb Naftali said, "Okay, so now I will tell you. But you have to promise me that you will not betray the secret to anybody so long as you live."

The student promised and Reb Naftali led him off into a room. From that room, he led the student to a second room. From that room, he led the student to a third room. Then the rabbi went back to each room to be certain that the doors were well closed so that no one could overhear what he was about to reveal to the student. By now, the student was transfixed. A guarded secret. For him alone. From the great rabbi. It was too much to be believed.

Now Reb Naftali appeared intent. He bent down to the student and whispered in his ear. "Know this: The reason I wear white cloth trousers is because they are the cheapest trousers."

"That's all?" the student cried in agony. "That is the secret I fasted six days to hear? Why make such a secret of that?"

Reb Naftali replied, "If people learned my secret, they would want this sort of trousers, too, and in no time white cloth trousers would be more expensive. I would not get them so cheaply after that.... Now, don't forget your promise. Do not tell anyone, so long as you live!"

[adapted from Langer, *Nine Gates*, p. 76]

12. Bellows

🐾 One day, after the Maggid of Dubno had spoken at length, a skeptic came up and asked him a question, "Why do your words not enter my heart and burn in me?" The Maggid told him this story:

A man from a large city went to visit relatives in a backwater *shtetl*. While there, he witnessed a crowd of people blowing on a flame to make it larger. "Why go to all this trouble?" he asked them, "when you could use a bellows." But they had never heard of a bellows. So he took leather and wood and he made a large bellows for them. He pumped it to show them how it took in air gently and sent air out forcefully.

A while later, his relatives sent him a message, saying, "Your bellows are useless." So the city man made the trek back to the *shtetl* to see what had gone wrong. He pumped the bellows and found them to be in good working order. He took the bellows over to a pile of wood that they wanted to turn into a fire. Then he said, "Where are the coals to make a spark?"

They stared at him. "We need to have fire in order to make fire?" they asked.

"Foolish people," the city man said. "If you have no spark of fire to begin with, the bellows cannot make a fire."

The Maggid told the skeptic, "I am a bellows for the heart. If your heart had even a spark of fire, the bellows would fan it into a

flame. But in a heart that has no spark, the bellows can have no effect."

[adapted from *Parables of the Preacher of Dubno* (Yiddish)]

13. I Myself

Rabbi Chanoch told the story of a man who had a hard time
remembering things. At night, the man hated to go to bed because he knew that, on awakening, he would face the gravest difficulties in finding the clothes he had taken off only the night
before. Determined to break this vicious cycle, one evening the
man took a pad of paper and, as he undressed, he wrote down
where he put everything. The next morning, he picked up the pad
and was very pleased with himself. Following his own instructions
to himself, he found his cap, his trousers, his shirt, and all his
other clothing—each item precisely where it had been left and
where he had recorded leaving it.

And that left the man more troubled than ever before. For he
realized that, in making the list on the pad, he had omitted the
most important item. "Where shall I look to find myself?" he wondered anxiously. "Where in the world did I leave me?" And, no
matter how hard he looked, this search was in vain.

"So it is with us," the rabbi concluded.

[Buber, *Later Masters*, p. 314]

14. The Eyeglasses and the Talmud

The old rabbi left the room. He was gone only a minute. But
when he returned, he suddenly discovered that his eyeglasses were
missing. Could it be that they were in the pages of the book he was
just reading? He picked up the book and shook it. No, no eyeglasses fell out. Somewhere else on the desk, then? He riffled
through the many papers and books on the desk, but no eyeglasses appeared. He was certain that he had left them right here
in this room, so he searched from wall to wall, from one end to the
other. There were no eyeglasses anywhere.

"Well," he said to himself, "there is a reason that I study the
Talmud. So I will seek my eyeglasses by applying talmudic logic."

"Let us take up the question of the eyeglasses," he began,
"Perhaps someone who needed glasses took them, or else they

may have been taken by someone who does not need eyeglasses. If it was someone who needed eyeglasses, he would need eyeglasses to see my eyeglasses, so he already has eyeglasses and would not need mine. And, if it was someone who does not need eyeglasses, my eyeglasses could be of no possible use to him. Therefore, my eyeglasses were not taken by one who needs eyeglasses and they were also not taken by someone who does not need eyeglasses. So, I am making some progress.

"Let us take up the question of the eyeglasses again. They could have been taken by someone who planned to sell them for profit. In that case, he must either sell them to someone who needs eyeglasses or to someone who does not need eyeglasses. Again," he thought, "talmudic logic brings us to the point: One who needs eyeglasses already has eyeglasses and would not want mine; and one who does not need eyeglasses would certainly not wish to buy them. More progress!

"Let us then take up the question of the eyeglasses again. It can only be someone who has eyeglasses if he has lost his eyeglasses. Or it could be someone who has eyeglasses and has absentmindedly pushed them up on his head, where he has forgotten all about them. In that case, the someone could only be ... me."

The rabbi reached up to his head and lowered his eyeglasses onto his nose. "Praised be the Holy One," he said aloud. "If I had not been trained in talmudic logic, I would never have found my eyeglasses!"

[adapted from Ausubel, *Treasury*, pp. 4-5]

15. It Was Obvious

🐿 A Talmud scholar went to Vilna and was returning home by train. When he took a seat, he looked around and saw a young man sitting beside him. When the conductor came by, he heard the young man say he was headed for the same *shtetl* as the scholar. That was odd. "Who could it be and why is he traveling to my little village?" the scholar wondered. He began to reason.

"The young man looks a modern type, not a peasant and not a farmer. He is obviously a Jew, or he would not be coming to such a small place inhabited only by Jews. And he is smoking a cigar, so he must have a little money."

"Aha," he said. "He must be coming to the wedding of our town doctor. But no," he thought, "that is more than a month from now. Surely a young man like this would not hang around our *shtetl* with nothing to do for a whole month!"

So he went on reasoning. "Perhaps he is courting a young woman. But who, in our town, could that be? It could not be Joseph the tailor's daughter, Eva. She's too old for him. Could it be Yentl, the daughter of the money-lender? But, no. She would be a good catch because of her money, but she would not be to the liking of a well-dressed young man from Vilna. Poor thing, even the cows turn away and hide their eyes when she passes! And there are no other eligible young women in our *shtetl*. No," he thought, "He is definitely not coming to court a young woman." So he went on reasoning.

"Aha," he said to himself. "He is coming because of our merchant, Yaakov, who is going bankrupt. Could he be a lawyer that Yaakov hired? No, not that. Yaakov would never communicate all his business affairs to a stranger, even a lawyer! Could he be one of the people to whom Yaakov owes money? No, not that! Look, he has not a worry in the world; and the creditors of Yaakov the merchant would be biting their nails. So, it has nothing to do with Yaakov the merchant and his bankruptcy." So he went on reasoning.

"So, who could he be? Could he be the son of Esther, Chaim Cohen's wife? But no. They were married only ten years ago and this young man looks about twenty-five years old." But, suddenly, everything was clear. "Aha," he said. "He is surely the son of Chaim's older brother Yankl who was married in the old wooden synagogue a full thirty years ago. Let's see. Yankl and his wife moved to Vilna twenty-four years ago and they took with them their one-year-old son named Aryeh. So this is Aryeh Cohen! And I also heard from Chaim that the boy studied medicine. So this is Dr. Cohen."

At last, he turned to the young man and spoke out loud for the first time. "Dr. Cohen," he said, "would you mind if I open the window to get a little fresh air?"

"Of course," the young man said. "But, tell me, how did you know that I am Dr. Cohen?"

The Talmudist waved his hand in the air. "It was obvious," he said.

[adapted from Ausubel, *Treasury*, pp. 7-8]

16. Foolish Haman

🕮 Haman came and tried to destroy the Jewish people in Persia. The people were saved by Mordecai and Esther. And it came to pass that Haman was destroyed.

Our sages told the story of a certain bird:

A bird made its nest at the edge of the sea, and the waves came and swept the nest away. What did the bird do? It took sand in its beak and threw the sand into the sea. Then it took water into its beak and threw the water on the sand. Over and over, it kept doing this.

Another bird came and said, "What are you doing?" And the first bird replied, "I will not leave this place until I turn the sea into dry land and the dry land into sea."

The other bird said, "You are the biggest fool in the world. With all your work, you cannot change sand to sea, or sea to sand."

Our sages taught: So it was with Haman. For Haman could no more destroy God's people than a bird could change the sea into dry land or the dry land into the sea. And so the Jews lived, and Haman died.

[*Midrash Esther Rabbah* 7:10; also in *Sefer HaAggadah*]

17. God Provides

🕮 A beggar came to the door of Rava, asking for a meal. The teacher asked him, "What do you usually eat?"

The beggar answered, "Bread and chicken, figs and dates, olives and pickles are my food. For drink, I take a fine wine. For dessert, I eat cakes bathed in honey."

"It is very costly to feed you!" Rava remarked. "If you eat like that every night, the whole community can hardly afford to give you food."

The beggar shook his head. "I do not eat the food of the community. I eat the food God provides for everyone. Is it not true, my master, that God provides all food?"

Just then, Rava's sister came to the door. He had not seen her in many years. He greeted her and kissed her. Then he asked her what she was carrying. "I have brought you many fine things to eat," she said. "In my bag are dates and figs, pickles and olives, and a chicken fit for a king."

Rava turned to the beggar. "You are right," he laughed. "God does provide. Come in and share our meal."

[B. Talmud *Ketubot* 67b; also *Sefer HaAggadah*]

In Psalms (107:8-9), it is written: "Let them praise *Adonai* for steadfast love and wondrous deeds for humankind; for God has satisfied the thirsty, filled the hungry with all good things." And Isaiah (55:1-2) prophesies: "Ho, all who are thirsty, come for water, even if you have no money; come, buy food and eat: buy food without money, wine and milk without cost. Why do you spend money for what is not bread, your earnings for what does not satisfy? Give heed to Me, and you shall eat choice food and enjoy the richest viands."

18. Honest Words

Rabbi Chaim of Zans went out one day to interview "strangers on the street."

He stopped a woman who was unknown to him and asked: "Tell me the truth: If you found a purse full of ducats in the road, would you return the purse to its owner?"

"Rabbi," she said, "if I knew the owner, I would not hesitate a moment. I would return the purse at once."

The rabbi thought: "Her answer was too quick."

He stopped a second stranger, asking the same question.

This time the answer came, "Only a fool would return it! When fortune smiles, should we question? No, I would keep it and thank my good luck. That is, as long as I was certain that no one saw me pick it up."

The rabbi thought: "Even here in Zans, we still have wicked people."

Rabbi Chaim stopped a third person, asking the same question.

"Rabbi," the third stranger said, "I cannot say now what I would do then. Let's say that I was very poor and my family was destitute. Then my *yetzer hara*, that evil urge in us all, might conquer my *yetzer tov*, my inclination to do what is right. I might want to do good. I might know the proper thing to do. And I still might keep the purse for myself. Or, perhaps, I would pray to God for the strength to resist the *yetzer hara*. With God's help, I might return the purse. But, who can say now, what he or she will do then?"

"These are honest words, bravely spoken" said the rabbi. "You, my friend, are a true sage."

[Buber, *Later Masters*, p. 212]

Of course, any sage looking for an honest man makes one think of Diogenes. When the melodramatic Greek was not carrying a lantern, it is said that he spent most of his time chilling in a barrel outside the city of Corinth. Once Alexander the Great came to see him and, respecting the philosopher, offered him any gift. Diogenes scowled and said, "What you have taken away, you can never give me." Alexander was puzzled. "What is that?" he asked. Diogenes answered, "You are blocking my sunlight."

19. Buber

As a young man, studying in Jerusalem, I encountered Martin Buber. It came about in this way: my classmates and I were assigned to read *I and Thou*, Buber's masterwork, and I was preparing for class with a close friend. Try as we might, there was a passage in the book that neither of us could comprehend. We argued for nearly an hour over its interpretation, at the end of which time, my friend looked at me mockingly and said, "Well, Buber is here in Jerusalem. Why don't we just ask him?"

He obviously intended to put an end to our discussion, but the idea appealed to me. I realized the chances of arranging such a meeting were remote. But I determined to try.

Perhaps it was the idea of two young people from the Diaspora trying to fathom the depths of *I and Thou* that was amusing to Dr. Buber. Or perhaps it was his own guiding principle that "All real living is meeting" that turned the trick. Whatever the case, without undue formality, and to my utter astonishment, Dr. Buber's secretary set an appointment for us with the scholar for a week later.

My friend and I sat with Martin Buber for half an hour. He first checked whether we could speak Hebrew (which we both could, though haltingly). Next, he asked about our backgrounds and where we were studying. Only then did he inquire about the problematic passage which had prompted our visit. We read the paragraph to him and he sat back in his chair and contemplated it in silence. Then he asked what we thought it meant.

When each of us had expounded the meaning we individually gleaned from the passage, he smiled. He said, *Ken, ken*—"yes" twice.

Now, in the Hebrew language, this doubling of a word may be taken in one of two ways. The doubling may lend emphasis, so that his phrase would mean, "Absolutely." Or it could simply be one "yes" for each of us, inferring that each of us was correct. Dr. Buber went on to say that we had both glimpsed the actual meaning. Then, in a minute's time, he explained the passage.

I have no recollection of the exact passage or of our two interpretations of it. I no longer recall the explanation the great professor gave. I remember no detail of the room in which we sat. But I see eyes speaking eloquently. I hear comforting tones. And I recall the feeling that his presence somehow encompassed us, that Martin Buber was concerned with us—with me—with two students he had never seen before and would, no doubt, never see again. All too soon, then, our encounter was over.

A few years later, when I heard the news of Dr. Buber's death, I felt a sense of personal loss. Yet, I could not bring myself to feel depressed. My memory of Dr. Buber was too vivid. Ever since, when I read a passage in his work, I can close my eyes and ask my questions and seek my understanding without fear that he would be judgmental.

And, when I think I understand the meaning of a passage correctly, I can hear again his voice, saying, "Yes. Yes."

Today, one "yes" is definitely for me, but, if you remember my story and share it, the other "yes" is my gift to you.

[Rossel]

20. Maimonides and the Blind Man

The Sultan Saladin, a friend of the Jews, loved his court physician Maimonides and honored him above all his other advisors. The Muslim physicians at court were naturally envious of Maimonides and their envy eventually turned toward venomous. "Why should a Jew be worthy to be the chief physician to the Sultan?" they asked one another in whispers.

Out of this came their desire to influence the Sultan against Maimonides. One of them would disagree with a prescription of the Jewish doctor. Another would ask, "Is this Maimonides really so great as his reputation?" But Saladin brushed them aside for a long while, until at last, he said to them, "If you are convinced that he is not a great doctor, test his skill and see for yourself."

One day, all the physicians presented themselves at court and one said to the Sultan, "O Mighty Saladin, tomorrow morning we will perform a miracle. Your Islamic doctors will restore the sight of a man who has been blind from birth." Saladin turned to Maimonides and asked, "Is such a thing possible?" Maimonides thought the matter over, before replying, "Your majesty, it is not possible. If a person has been blind from birth, his vision cannot be restored."

The Sultan sensed that this was the test that the other doctors had prepared for Maimonides. He was intrigued. "Let us witness this great miracle on the morrow," he commanded.

The next morning all the physicians returned to the court. The boastful doctor brought a man who was obviously blind. He asked him, "Have you been blind since birth?"

The man replied, "It is so, my lord. Since the day I was born, I have been unable to see."

The doctor bowed before the Sultan, but he spoke to the entire court, "You have heard his words." From his doctor's purse, he removed a container, and spread a salve on the eyelids of the blind man.

Suddenly, the blind man opened his eyes. He squinted at the light in the room, then cried out: "Allah be praised, I can see! I can see!" At this, even the Sultan applauded. But Maimonides did not applaud. And, as the applause faded, everyone, including the Sultan, turned to the Jewish physician.

Maimonides stood and removed a red kerchief from his pocket. He waved it before the eyes of the man who had been blind. He said, "I am glad that you have received the precious gift of sight. But, let us test your gift. Tell me, what is the color of this kerchief?"

"Why, it is red," the blind man said.

Maimonides nodded. He turned to the Sultan and said: "Your majesty, this man claims he has been blind since birth. But someone blind from birth could not possibly know one color from another. If he knows my kerchief is red, it can only be that he has seen red before."

Then the Sultan laughed. He looked at the other physicians of his court and said, "Is this the best that you could do to test the great rabbi and doctor? Leave off your jealousy and accept the fact. My physician, Maimonides, is the greatest physician of our time."

[Iraqi Jewish folktale; also in Certner, *101 Jewish Stories*]

21. My Driver

🐝 The Maggid of Dubno traveled far and wide, speaking to Jews in city after city. One day, his driver said to him, "Rabbi, I have heard you make the same speech so many times that I could make it word for word."

The Maggid smiled.

"And," the driver said, "I have watched in every town as we enter and as you speak, and even when you leave, the city does you great honor."

The Maggid smiled.

"I wonder," the driver said, "is it a crime to wish to feel like a famous rabbi? Even though I cannot read or write, I can speak. Would it be so terrible if, when we come to the next town, we pretended that you were the driver and I was the rabbi?"

The Maggid took an impish delight in the plan. He said, "I would not mind so much. It might be fun for me to pretend to be your driver. But if the people in the town discover our little ruse, they may grow angry at us both."

The driver was enthusiastic. He said, "Let me worry about that, Rabbi."

So the Maggid of Dubno traded clothing with his driver. He sat in the front of the coach and headed the horses for the next town. As they entered the Jewish section, he called out (as his driver always did), "Make way for the Maggid of Dubno! Make way for the rabbi!"

Just as always, the people gathered beside the road to greet the famous Maggid. When they reached the synagogue, the Maggid climbed down and opened the coach door for the "rabbi." As a driver should, the Maggid walked behind as they entered the synagogue. Many men of the town had already gathered, and more crowded in as the "rabbi" was greeted with handshakes and drink and morsels of tasty food. The women's gallery was also filled to overflowing, with all the women peeking through the curtain to get a glimpse of the well-known Maggid.

Then the leaders of the synagogue called on the "rabbi" to speak. The Maggid listened in amazement. It was true! His driver knew all his stories and all the things that he would say. For a moment, the Maggid thought he was listening to himself! At the end of the speech, the congregation applauded the "rabbi" and all the local students of Torah surrounded him.

The local students were filled with the usual questions and the "rabbi" was answering each of them as the Maggid would, when suddenly there came a question that even the Maggid had never heard before.

"Oy," the Maggid said to himself. And he feared that the truth would now come out and the town would be angry at the trick played by the Maggid and his driver.

But the driver acting the Maggid did not seem at all hesitant. He spoke in a loud, clear voice. "What a question," he said, "I would answer it immediately. But it is such a simple question that even my driver can answer it." Then, with a flourish of his hand, he motioned to the Maggid dressed as the driver, saying, "Driver, please answer the question."

The Maggid smiled.

[adapted from *Parables of the Preacher of Dubno* (Yiddish)]

22. *Rebbe,* Pray for Me

The Chasidim tell about a man who came to see the great rabbi of Kotzk, to ask the *rebbe* to pray for him.

"Very well," the *rebbe* said, "and what shall I ask of God?"

"Pray that my son may become a learned man," said the Chasid.

"No," replied the *rebbe*. "Pray instead that you will become a learned man. Then you will educate your son and your prayer will come true for you and for your son."

[Buber, *Later Masters,* p.284]

23. Motivation

⚜ Motivationally, man is a strange, if not bizarre creature: he is the only known organism to arise in the morning before he is awake, work all day without resting, continue his activities after diurnal; and even crepuscular organisms have retired to rest, and then take narcotics to induce an inadequate period of troubled sleep. But lest we decry man's motivational mechanisms, we should point out that without them we would not have the steam engine, the electric light, the automobile, Beethoven's *Fifth Symphony*, Leonardo da Vinci's undigested "Last Supper," gastric ulcers, coronary thrombosis, and clinical psychologists. Indeed, we might as well regard this aggregate as the human motivational syndrome.

[H. F. Harlow, "Motivation as a Factor in the Acquisition of New Responses," 1953)]

24. The Sea Horse Seeks a Fortune

⚜ Once upon a time, a sea horse set off to seek his fortune. He traveled only a short distance, when he chanced upon an eel. "Where are you hurrying?" the eel asked.

"I'm going to seek my fortune," the sea horse answered.

"I have just the thing you need," said the eel. "Look at this lovely flipper. Put this on your tail and seek your fortune at twice the speed! And I will sell it to you for just four pieces of eight."

The sea horse bought the flipper, put it on, and found that the eel was right. He was able to speed through the water twice as fast as before. At that speed, it was not long before he met a sponge.

"What's your hurry?" the sponge asked.

"I'm going to seek my fortune," the sea horse answered.

"Lucky you," the sponge said. "For only four pieces of eight, I can sell you this slightly used inkjet. It used to belong to a spinster squid who squirted it only on Sundays. Put it on and try it out. It will take you places five times as fast."

The sea horse gave the inkjet a trial run and, it was true! He could travel five times as fast. He paid the sponge and thanked her. Then off he went, a veritable speed demon. He was going so fast that he ran smack dab into the side of a shark.

The shark shook himself and stared at the sea horse. "Wherever are you going at such a clip?" the shark asked.

"I'm going to seek my fortune," the sea horse replied.

"Really?" the shark asked with a large, toothy grin. "Well, you are in luck. I know a short cut and I would be glad to share it with you. Just swim in here." And the shark pointed to his open mouth. "Take my word for it. This will save you a lot of time."

So the sea horse jetted right into the shark's mouth, nor was the sea horse ever seen again. And the moral of this story is, as the Talmud says, "If you don't know where you are going, any road will get you there."

[folktale, adapted by Rossel]

25. Sharing the Cheese

When a woman selling cheeses in the marketplace turned her back for just an instant, a cat knocked a quarter wheel of cheese to the ground and a dog picked it up in his teeth and made for a grove of trees just past the end of the town. Needless to say, the cat was hard on the dog's tail, at some times more literally than at others, hissing and yowling all the way to the trees.

The ensuing argument took on talmudic proportions as the cat claimed the cheese for its own and the dog, baring its teeth, dared her to take it. The problem boiled down to this: the dog was not at liberty to eat the cheese, for any letting-down of his guard would surely result in the worst of injuries from the incensed feline. And the feline was in no position to eat the cheese, which, for the moment at least, was in the firm possession of the dog.

Enter the fox. "Why should the two of you argue? I can cut the cheese into two halves and you can each prosper from your theft."

Now, it is the way of the animal kingdom to always allow a fox to do something crafty, in order to teach us—those paying close attention—some lesson or other. This case was no exception. The dog and the cat decided to trust the fox.

For his part, the fox cut the cheese in two, but not as he promised. Instead, he purposely made one "half" larger than the other.

"There," he said, "you can now each have half of the cheese." But the cat and the dog complained bitterly: One half was too large; one half, too small.

"No problem," said the fox. He cut the larger half down a bit in size and devoured the extra cheese that had been cut away. "Now," he said, "you can each have your equal portion."

But, clearly, the fox had now made the larger portion smaller than the small portion had originally been, so that the two portions were again unequal. This fact was duly pointed out to him by both the cat and the dog.

"No problem," the fox said. He cut the larger of the two pieces down a bit in size and ate the extra cheese he had cut away. Of course, he had once again made the two portions unequal. And, as the cat and dog continued to complain about the fox's sloppy cutting job, the fox continued to lop off pieces and eat them so that, in a short time, he had eaten all but two tidbits. "Silly to argue any further," he said to his two companions. "Why don't you each take your share?"

The cat and the dog looked at the two tiny pieces that remained. Finally, they realized that, as they quarreled, the fox had robbed them of their cheese. At that juncture, dignity prevailed, and both walked away with their tails between their legs, leaving the two morsels for the fox to finish. Which he did.

[Yiddish/European folktale; adapted from Ausubel, *Treasury*, pp. 626-627]

26. Sharpening the Axe

Once upon a time, two men were chopping wood. One man worked all day, took no breaks, and stopped for lunch only briefly. The other man took numerous breaks throughout the day, and even enjoyed a nap after lunch. At day's end, the fellow who had worked continuously was upset to find that the "break-taker" had chopped far more wood than he had. "I simply don't understand it," said the first guy. "Every time I looked up, there you were, sitting down." The other fellow replied, "Well, I guess you didn't notice... Every time I took a break, I sharpened my ax."

[adapted from an anecdote told by Dale Carnegie]

27. Students

Rabbi Nachman ben Isaac said: Why are the words of the Torah compared to a tree, as it is said, "It is a tree of life to them that hold fast to it" (Proverbs 3:18)? This is to teach you just as that a chip of wood can set aflame a great tree, so young students can sharpen the minds of great scholars. For which reason, Rabbi

Chanina said: "Much Torah have I learned from my teachers, more from my colleagues, but from my students most of all."

[B. Talmud *Taanit* 7a; *also see* B. Talmud *Makkot* 10a]

28. What My Father Did

🐾 Many are the stories told of Herschel Ostropolier, a poor man with a rich Jewish sense of humor. For example:

Herschel stopped at an inn one night. The innkeeper was away, so he dealt with the innkeeper's wife. "Please bring me some food to eat, for I am famished," he said.

The woman saw before her a poor man, dressed in rags, and thought, "There's a good chance I will feed him and never get paid." To Herschel she said, "I have nothing left in the kitchen."

"No food whatever?" he asked. Then he narrowed his eyes and stared a meaningful look at the woman. "In that case, I shall have to do what my father did!"

The woman could tell a threat when she heard one. "What did your father do?" she asked.

"Never you mind," Herschel said, clenching his fists. "My father did what my father did."

The woman was agitated. After all, her husband was away. And who knows what kind of father this poor fellow had. Any moment, she might find out. It was all too much. "Sit here," she said, pointing to the chair at the head of the table. "I will see what is in the kitchen." One by one, she brought out trays of food. And, one by one, Herschel consumed them.

When the eating was finished, Herschel thanked her, saying, "Not since last Passover have I had such a feast!"

"Look," the innkeeper's wife said, "now that you have been fed. If it is not too much trouble, could you tell me, what would your father do?"

"Oh, my father," Herschel said, "Whenever there was nothing for supper, my father would go to bed without it."

[Yiddish folktale; also in Ausubel, *Treasury*, p. 313]

It is said that a rich man once offered Herschel one ruble if he could tell a lie without thinking about it. "What do you mean one ruble?" Herschel immediately asked. "You just said two rubles."

29. Two Measures of Fine Wheat

Husham was a nice boy, but he never quite got things right. Send him for milk, he returned with bread. Send him for bread, he brought back water. There was no telling where his mind was, but it was not in this world.

On this day, his mother was too busy with the other children to go to the miller. Reluctantly, she called Husham and said, "You must listen closely for once. Go to the miller and bring home two measures of fine wheat." Husham nodded. But his mother knew him. "Where are you going?" she asked him. "To the miller," he said. "Very good. And what will you bring back?" Husham looked a little puzzled. "Listen closely," she said in her most patient voice. "Bring back two measures of fine wheat." Husham nodded. She asked, "What will you bring back?" Husham answered, "Fine wheat. Two measures of fine wheat." His mother patted him on the head and said, "Keep repeating that all the way to the miller's shop."

Husham went down the road saying, "Fine wheat. Two measures." He said it over and over.

He happened past a field where a farmer had just finished plowing; and the farmer overheard him saying, "Two measures. Two measures."

The farmer grew very angry. "Don't make fun of me!" he cried. "Do you think that this whole field will give me only two measures of wheat?"

Husham shrugged. He was trying to remember his errand. But the farmer said, "Stop saying, 'two measures,' and bring me luck by saying, 'You will have an abundant harvest.'"

"You will have an abundant harvest," Husham called out as he ran away from the angry farmer. Then he kept on repeating, "Abundant harvest, abundant harvest."

He came to the town square. How could he know that all the people were busy chasing a plague of mice out of the town?

"Abundant harvest," Husham repeated.

"Are you crazy?" the people asked. "Do you think we should have more mice! an abundance of mice? How dare you?" They stopped chasing the mice and chased him, saying, "Away with the cursed thing!"

So he ran away, repeating over and over, "Away with the cursed thing!"

He passed mourners carrying a coffin to the cemetery. "Away with the cursed thing," Husham was heard to say. The mourners turned and said, "Hush! It is terrible to speak of the dead in such a way! You should say, 'Grant him eternal rest.'"

Husham walked away repeating, "Grant him eternal rest." Until, that is, he came upon a butcher leading a calf to slaughter. "Stupid child!" the butcher said. "Who cares about eternal rest for a calf? Better you should say, 'That's how a victim is led to slaughter.'"

Husham repeated, "That's how a victim is led to slaughter." But he chanced on a wedding party and the guests all screamed at him, "Stop saying 'That's how a victim is led to slaughter'! You will upset the bride and groom. Join the rest of us and say, 'Bliss will come to the house.'"

Husham went away repeating "Bliss will come to the house." Until, that is, he passed a bunch of people trying to put out a house fire. When they heard him say "Bliss will come to the house," they turned on him and said, "Idiot! Say something useful like 'May God keep the wind from blowing!'"

"May God keep the wind from blowing," he repeated. And he was saying it over and over when he came to the miller's shop beside the windmill. Just his luck, that day there was no breeze at all and the windmill blades were sitting dead still. Husham got out one more, "May God keep the wind from blowing," before the miller grabbed him by the shoulders and gave him a good shake.

"Fool," the miller said. "I need the wind to blow. I pray for the wind to blow. All day I have been waiting for the wind to blow."

Husham said, "I know I am not smart, but I really do not know what to say. And everyone keeps telling me something new to say. And, besides, I cannot remember what I am doing here in the first place."

The miller calmed down. He said, "Tell me, why did you say, `May God keep the wind from blowing?'"

"A house was burning," said the boy, "so the people were angry when I said: 'Bliss will come to the house.'"

"Who told you to say: 'Bliss will come to the house'?"

"The people at the wedding. They told me to stop saying, 'That's how a victim is led to slaughter.'"

"Who told you to say: `That's how a victim is led to slaughter?"

"The butcher who told me we should not say of a calf, `Grant him eternal rest."'

"And who told you to say: 'Grant him eternal rest?"'

"The people at the funeral who told me not to say `Away with the cursed thing!"'

"Who told you to say: 'Away with the cursed thing?"'

"The people chasing away the mice. They said not to say: 'Abundant harvest.'"

"Who told you to say, 'Abundant harvest?"'

"A farmer who was angry when I said, 'Two measures...'"

"Two measures of what?" the miller asked.

"Fine wheat," said Husham without thinking.

"Praise God," the miller said. He turned and scooped out two measures of fine wheat. "Now listen," he said to Husham seriously, "on the way home, you are to say not a word. Do you understand?"

Husham nodded. He took the bag of fine wheat and started for home. And, as he walked, he repeated over and over, "Not a word. Not a word."

[Baghdadi Jewish folktale; collected by Eliyahu Chayim Agassi (Hebrew)]

The Husham stories are the Iraqi Jewish equivalent to the Eastern European stories of the wise men of Chelm and the adventures of Herschel Ostropolier.

30. Wisdom Brightens the Face

A Roman princess saw Rabbi Judah bar Ilai and noticed that his face was glowing. She said, "Old man, you have eaten so many pigs that their oil shows on your skin."

"I have not eaten any pigs," said Rabbi Judah.

"Then you must be flushed with happiness because you are a money lender who has made a vast fortune," she said.

"I am not a money lender," responded Rabbi Judah.

"Then you must be all aglow because you have drunk too much wine," she said.

"I drink wine on the Sabbath, when it is required," said Rabbi Judah, "and the four cups of wine that I must drink at Passover always make me feel weak for weeks."

The princess asked, "Then why does your face shine with such a glow?"

Rabbi Judah answered, "This is the glow of the teachers of Torah. As the wise Solomon used to say, 'It is wisdom that brightens the face'" (Ecclesiastes 8:1).

[J. Talmud *Shabbat* 8:1, 11a; B. Talmud *Nedarim* 49b; *Midrash Ecclesiastes Rabbah* 8:1; also in *Sefer HaAggadah*]

31. True and False

It used to be that Truth walked about the streets of Jerusalem as naked as the day he was born. In those days, the people greeted him kindly, saluted him, and made much of him. For it was a time in which truth was respected and beloved for his own sake; and his walking about that way was nothing more than the simple statement that he was revealed and there was no reason for him to hide.

But it was not too long before people were scandalized by him. Whoever saw Truth approaching hid in a doorway, hoping that Truth would pass without a murmur; or they would cross the street to avoid having to talk to him or greet him. Now when Truth approached a house, its doors were closed to him, and the people could be seen quickly bolting the shutters of their windows. Love of Truth had departed even from the holy City of David. It was a sad time for Truth.

One day, Truth packed a few belongings in a sack and wandered out into the countryside, hoping to meet people there who would respect and honor his presence. But it was not to be. No matter where he traveled, he found that he had been eclipsed by his nemesis, the Lie.

But it chanced one day that Truth, as he brooded and journeyed, met Parable along the way. Parable was decked out in his very best, gaily gotten up, wearing a brand new pair of Levis, a western shirt, a ten-gallon Stetson hat—the works! Parable said to Truth, "Brother, what is wrong with you? Why do you look so downhearted and dismayed? Why do you walk about this way, naked and depressed? Don't you know it's a sin to let the world get you down?"

Truth said, "It's all right for you to speak that way. People like you. When they see you, they don't run away in shame. But everything goes wrong for me. I am so old, so decrepit, that people shun me and refuse to face up to me."

But Parable said, "How could that be? You and I are the same age. If it were a matter of age, people would avoid me, too. Yet the older I grow, the more people find me attractive. Brother, you and I went to the same school, but I have learned a few things since then that you have failed to see.

"Let me tell you a secret regarding people," Parable went on. "The people of this world do not like things to be bare and plain—naked, as you are. People like you to dress up in natty clothing. They like their friends to be fancy and even a little artificial. So I'll tell you what I'll do for you. You come home with me, and I will find you some fine clothes to wear. You'll soon see how quickly people will take to you again."

So Truth followed Parable home. And, a little while later, Truth emerged in designer jeans, fashionable shoes, and smelling of expensive cologne, too. He was all decked out in Parable's clothing.

Lo and behold! Suddenly people were talking to him again. Instead of running away when Truth approached, people stayed and greeted him with a hearty, "Shalom, y'all."

And ever since that time, Truth and Parable may be seen together, companions, loved and respected by all!

[adapted from *Parables of the Preacher of Dubno* (Yiddish)]

32. You Must Ask Questions

🐾 A man was walking with his grandson along the road when his son looked up at him and asked, "Grandpa, why does the sunshine look yellow?"

His grandfather answered, "That's a very good question, my boy, a very good question. I don't know the answer, but the question is excellent."

They walked a little while longer and the boy looked up again and asked, "Grandpa, what makes the sky blue?"

His grandfather answered, "I really don't know. But that's a wonderful question."

They went on walking, and pretty soon the child asked, "Grandpa, why is grass green?"

Again, the grandfather said, "That's a very good question, my boy. I don't know the answer, but the question is very good."

Now the boy sensed that he was causing his grandfather some discomfort, so he looked up and said, "Grandpa, I'm sorry that I am asking such hard questions."

The grandfather replied, "Tut, tut, my boy, that's quite all right. If you don't ask, you will never learn."

[based on a story told by Rabbi Manuel Gold]

III
ISRAEL

.

1
Community

1. Serving Me

🐚 Ben Zoma was famous for his wisdom. Once he was walking with his students when he saw a group of people gathered on the Temple Mount. He said, "Blessed be God who created all these people to serve me."

His students asked, "How do these people serve you."

Ben Zoma explained, "Imagine the labors that our ancestor Adam had to carry out before he had bread to eat! He plowed, he sowed, he reaped, he bound the sheaves, he threshed, he winnowed, he picked out the ears of grain, he ground them, he sifted the flour, he kneaded, he baked, and, only then, at last, he ate. But I wake up and find all these things have been done for me.

"And imagine how many labors our ancestor Adam had to carry out before he obtained a garment to wear. He had to shear, wash the wool, comb it, spin it, weave it, and, only then, at last, he could put on his clothing. But I wake up and find all these things have been done for me."

[B. Talmud *Berachot* 58a; J. Talmud *Berachot* 13c]

2. Minyan

🐚 Rabbi Acha, who lived in the time of the Talmud, explained the *minyan* (the quorum of ten required for public worship) in this way:

If rich men make a crown for a king, and a poor man comes and gives his share toward the making of it, what does the king say? "Shall I refuse to accept the crown because of this poor man?" The king immediately accepts the crown and sets it on his head.

In the same way, if there are ten good souls standing in prayer and a person who has sinned joins them, what does the Holy One,

131

the Blessed, say? "Shall I refuse to accept their prayer because of this sinner?" No. All the prayers are accepted.

[*Midrash Lamentations Rabbah* 3:3; Rossel, *When a Jew Prays*]

3. A Place of Torah

❦ Rabbi Yose ben Kisma was out walking one day and a man came up to greet him. The man said, "Rabbi, tell me where you are from." Rabbi Yose replied, "I come from a great city of sages and scribes."

The man said, "My city needs a good rabbi. If you will come to my city and be our rabbi, I will give you a thousand thousand *dinar*s, precious stones, and pearls, too."

Rabbi Yose said, "If you were to give me all the silver and gold and precious stones and pearls in the world, I would not dwell anywhere but in a place where Torah dwells—a place where there are other scholars, other scribes, and other sages; where Houses of Study can be found at every turn."

The man rejoined: "But, Rabbi, in our place you would become rich."

Rabbi Yose replied, "Do you not know, my friend, that when we die neither silver nor gold, nor precious stones, nor pearls will go with us, but from this world to the next we will take only the Torah we study and the good deeds we do."

[Mishnah *Avot* 6:9]

4. Nazirites

❦ After the destruction of the Second Temple, many people took vows to become Nazirites, denying themselves both wine and meat. Rabbi Joshua asked them why. They said, "How can we eat meat now that the Temple has been destroyed? It was the Temple that made meat holy through the acts of sacrifice to God. And how can we drink wine, for wine was also made holy through the Temple rituals."

Rabbi Joshua said, "In that case, how can you eat bread, since bread was made holy through the grain sacrifices at the Temple?"

They answered, "Perhaps we shall live on fruit."

Rabbi Joshua said, "In that case, you cannot eat fruit, since offerings of fruit were brought to the Temple on Shavuot, and there can be no more offerings of fruit."

They answered, "Perhaps we can manage only on fruits that were not sacrificed in the Temple ritual."

Rabbi Joshua pressed them harder. "In that case, you may drink no water, for water was used in the Temple service."

Then they were silent.

But Rabbi Joshua added, "Not to mourn at all is impossible, for it is true that the Temple has been destroyed. But to mourn overmuch is also not appropriate for us. It is a dictum of the rabbis that no requirement can be imposed that a majority of our people cannot endure."

[B. Talmud *Baba Batra* 60b]

Nazirites not only refrained from wine and meat. They swore on oath that they would not cut their hair, imbibe strong drink, or touch a corpse. The rabbis of the Talmud discouraged the taking of Nazirite vows since abstinence and asceticism were against the spirit of Judaism.

5. Trees and Iron

On the third day, God created the trees, starting with the mighty cedars. In turn, God created the trees that shade and those that flower and those that produce fruit and nuts. Now, seeing that they were created first, the cedars said to the redwoods, "We shall be the greatest trees on earth. We shall grow in the Lebanon. And King Solomon will use our wood to build the Temple in Jerusalem." And the cedars shot upward and their branches and leaves spread outward like a crown.

The lowly bush complained to God, "The cedars and the other tall trees create so much shade with their leaves and branches that barely any sunlight filters through to us. We shall always be small and scraggly."

God said, "I have created all things with a purpose. In the time to come, I will set a blaze in you that will do you no harm, just so that I can call My servant Moses to turn aside and look at you. In that moment, you will be the most important plant in the history of the world." And so the bush was satisfied that it would never grow tall and never get all the sunlight it wanted, but it would be rewarded for remaining small and scraggly.

In the meanwhile, God saw that the cedars were puffed up with pride; and God said, "I despise pride, for in the shadow of pride come other sins like jealousy and mastery and hatred and prejudice." So God created iron. When the trees saw the mountains of iron appearing, they began to tremble; and some even began to weep. There was fear in the tallest of them and terror in the smallest of them. Even the cedars complained, saying, "We thought we were created to be the tallest of all beings, but now, You have created iron and iron can be shaped to make the heads of axes and the axes can be used to cut us down and destroy us."

God answered saying, "You are right to fear the iron. But this will be the way of life on earth: No matter how big or proud a thing grows, there will always be something else that can bring it down. But the largest and even the smallest beings can protect themselves by sticking together. If no tree gives wood for the handle of the axe, no axe can be made to cut you down. Therefore, make sure that all trees realize there is security in unity."

The trees were satisfied. If they refused to give wood the iron could not harm them. But, soon human beings were created; and men came to tempt the smaller trees, saying, "Give us just a branch and we will cut down those huge trees that block your sunlight." At first, the smaller trees refused, but the humans persisted, saying, "Why should those trees grow tall and you remain small? We can help you, if you will only help us. Just a branch or two is all we need."

In the end, as everyone knows, one tree gave one branch to one man; and that was one branch too many. The man created one axe and cut down one tree; and the wood from that tree made handles for many axes that cut down many trees.

If only we could find a way to remain unified—without contending about who is tallest and who is smallest, without debating who is strongest and who is weakest—then we would stand strong and firm against all who would do us harm. What we require is faith and trust. Faith that God is with us when we are good; and trust that God created each and every one of us—from the mighty cedar to the lowly bush—for some special purpose.

[*Midrash Genesis Rabbah* 5:9]

6. The Dark Synagogue

🐾 In a mountain village in Europe many centuries ago, there was a nobleman who wondered what legacy he might be able to leave for his townspeople. At last he decided to build a synagogue.

None of the local folk saw the plans for the building until it was finished. When the people entered for the first time they marveled at its beauty and detail. Then someone asked, "Where are the lamps? How will it be lighted?" The nobleman pointed to brackets which were on every wall of the synagogue. Then he gave each family a lamp to bring with them every time they came to the synagogue. "Each time you are not here," he said, "your place within the synagogue will be unlit. This will be a reminder that, whenever you fail to attend, especially when the community needs you, some part of God's house will be dark."

[based on a story told by Rabbi Lawrence "Jake" Jackofsky]

7. Blind

❧ Rabbi Yose ben Chalafta would tell this story: He was walking along a path through a forest. It was night, and there was no moon to brighten the skies. Through the trees, he could see tiny pinpoints of light, the scattered stars. In his hand, he held a lantern to light the road ahead. From time to time, he passed other people walking. Most of them also carried a lantern. This made him think. From above, the earth would look much like the sky: The ground would be as black as the heaven at night, and each lantern would be a pinpoint of light, an earthly star.

Just then he approached a traveler different from all the others. From the way the man held his head—high, with his eyes facing directly forward—and from the way he walked—probing the ground with his staff—Rabbi Yose knew that the man was blind. So he was surprised to see that this man also carried a lit lantern.

"*Shalom aleichem*," he called out, "peace be with you."

"*Aleichem shalom*, peace be with you, too," the man replied.

"Tell me, sir," said Yose. "Is it true that you are blind and cannot see?"

"It is true."

Yose went on, "Is it true that you cannot see during the day and you cannot see at night?"

"It is true."

"So it makes no difference to you whether it is day or night?" asked Yose.

"No difference," the man answered.

"Then, tell me, kind sir, why do you bother to carry a lantern?"

The blind man smiled. "You ask questions like a teacher," he said. "Are you a teacher?"

"I am," replied Rabbi Yose.

"With all your wisdom, can you not guess why a blind man should carry a lantern at night?"

"I cannot," Rabbi Yose answered. "Pray, tell me."

"As long as I have my lantern, people can see me and see the road, too. So they can save me from vines, thorns, and holes. If I did not carry my lantern at night, and if you did not carry your lantern, then both of us would be blind."

[B. Talmud *Megilah* 24b; also in *Sefer HaAggadah*]

8. Singing Stories

🎵 As the High Holy Days approached, Rabbi Chaim would tell his stories to the congregation using a tune that turned the souls of the listeners back toward God. He would sing this story:

A fellow lost his way in a dense forest. After a while, a second fellow also lost his way. Then the two chanced to meet.

The first fellow asked, "Can you help me find my way out of the forest?"

The second fellow answered, "I cannot, but I can show you the ways that I have tried without success. After that, you and I together can seek to find the true way."

The Rabbi concluded his story by saying: O my beloved Jews, we are all lost together; and the most any of us know are the ways that have not worked, the paths that we took in error. But if we listen to one another, we can avoid taking false paths others have tried. After that, we can seek together to find the true way."

With that, the rabbi singing stopped; and a soulful silence enveloped the synagogue, the town, the country, the world, and the universe.

[Buber, *Later Masters*, p. 213]

9. Three Great Men

🎵 The king wanted quiet at night, so he put the town under a curfew. He instructed his soldiers to imprison anyone out and about after midnight. Two nights later, just before midnight, a soldier on patrol accosted three men laughing and yelling at one another, victims of their own carousing.

He demanded, "Do you know that the king has placed a curfew on the town? If you are out after midnight, I will arrest you."

"Ho!" said the first man. "Why should I fear? No one would dare arrest me. All people rich and poor, weak and mighty, tip their hats to me!"

The second man stuck a finger in the air and pointed at the sky. He said, "I, too, have nothing to fear. From lowest to highest, the children of the poor and the children of the rich—even the king's own son—obey me and do as I instruct. No one would dare arrest me."

The third man gave an exaggerated wink at his inebriated compatriots. Then he glared at the soldier and said, "You would not dare arrest me, for certain! The king would not be the king without me. If I were arrested, the king might as well don pauper's rags!"

The soldier was no fool. The men must be important, but they could not be allowed to roam about after midnight. He reasoned with them: "Why should I cause you trouble? And why should you bring trouble upon me? My job is to get you off the streets after midnight, but there is food and drink and comfortable beds back at the guardhouse. Why not rest at the king's expense and allow the king's guards to comfort you for the night?"

No sooner were they in sight of the beds, the three men fell upon them and slept. During the night, though, rumors that three noble guests snored in the guardhouse spread through the ranks of the soldiers. Pretty soon, word reached the back halls of the palace and, by the next morning, the king knew. "Have the three noblemen brought to me," he commanded.

So it came to pass that the three, a bit more sober than they had been the night before, were brought before the king. The king asked the first, "Did you tell my soldier that everyone, including kings, must tip their hats in your presence?" The man bowed low and said: "It is true, your Majesty, for I am a barber."

The king asked the second, "Did you claim that my son and all the sons of the land must always obey your orders?" The man bowed low and said, "Yes, your Majesty, for I am a teacher."

The king turned to the last man. "Did you tell my soldier that, but for you, I would be no king and I would wear no royal robes?" The third man bowed low and whispered, "That is true, you Highness, for I am your tailor."

There was a moment of silence in the throne room. Then the king chuckled and laughed. All the nobles chuckled and laughed, too. "Far be it from me," the king said, "to punish the three most important people in my kingdom? But I adjure you: Drink less and be off the streets before midnight!"

[adapted from Certner, *101 Jewish Stories*]

10. Justice in Chelm

🐾 The town shoemaker of Chelm cheated everyone. In the end, he was brought to justice and the rabbi pronounced on him Chelm's most severe punishment. The shoemaker would be expelled from Chelm, never to return.

At once, there was an outcry. "What is the problem?" the rabbi asked. Mottel the Mayor stepped forward, "Rabbi, if the shoemaker is sent into exile, everyone in Chelm will suffer! He is our only shoemaker. Before long our shoes will wear out and we will have no one to repair them. And who will cobble new shoes for our children?"

"You are right," the rabbi said. "But justice must be served."

There was silence as the wise men of Chelm considered what to do. At last, Berel the Blacksmith spoke up. "It is true that Chelm has only one shoemaker, but it is equally true that we have two tailors."

"Excellent!" said the rabbi, "Then, this is my final judgment: Let one tailor be expelled from Chelm, never to return!"

And the wise people of Chelm all nodded their approval.

[adapted from Simon, *Wise Men of Helm*]

This, of course, is the legendary Chelm, not to be confused with the actual Chelm, which was a Jewish city of great learning in Poland. As the legend of Chelm usually begins, an angel is sent to earth to collect all the foolish souls in the world so that the world may be at last free of foolishness. Having collected all the foolish souls and put them in a bag, the angel slings the bag across his shoulders and starts back to heaven. But the angel is caught in a sudden downdraft and falls into the branches of a tree on a high hill. The bag rips open and all the foolish souls roll down the hill into the city of Chelm where they inhabit the "wise men of Chelm" to this day.

11. Stone Soup

🐌 Yehudah's daughter was finally getting married: You know, the *eldest* one of his five daughters. The one with the *strange* grin. The one who kept knocking things over *whenever* she moved. The *last* to find a man.

Now this was a cause for a celebration! This was a reason to invite the whole town! This was a moment when the father of the bride needed to have a little cash on hand, enough to buy food and drink for everyone. Unfortunately, when it comes to a father who has five daughters, I can tell you, there is never any cash on hand.

Yehudah went to see the rabbi. "You know I have no money," he said. "But I need to make a wedding feast for my daughter, Yentl."

"Yentl—getting married? Now this is good news!" said the rabbi, clapping a hand on Yehudah's shoulder. "No, this is great news!" he said, squeezing Yehudah's hand. Unfortunately, there is bad news, too. Winter was harder than usual and there is no money left in the charity fund."

"Rabbi," said Yehudah, hanging his head. "What can I do?"

For a time, the rabbi caressed his sidecurls and stroked his beard. Then, his face brightened. "Find the largest cooking pot in town. Fill it with water. Invite everyone! I will provide the feast!"

"O Rabbi," Yehudah said, "You are no rabbi. You are a worker of miracles!"

The day of the wedding feast came at last. Everyone, including a few people from the next village, turned out for the celebration. Watching the crowd gathering, Yehudah had a moment of doubt. Could the rabbi really produce enough food for this many people?

In the middle of the town square stood the largest cooking pot you have ever seen and it was filled with water. The rabbi instructed, "Build a fire under the pot." The fire was built. The pot commenced to groan and the water slowly came to a simmer. Suddenly, the water was boiling and roiling, sending steam into the air and little spurts of water, too, as bubbles rose to the top and burst. People approached the pot and sniffed it. Their faces changed. Disappointment crossed their brows. The word was passed, "The meal is nothing but boiling water!" Tension was brewing. People began to sneer. There was anger and resentment. "We have been tricked! There is no feast!"

Now the rabbi stepped forward. He held up his hand and showed the people a single, round, clean, polished stone. "My dear friends," the rabbi said, "Have no fear. I have brought this wedding gift for Yentl." He looked up at the stone still raised above his head. "Have you ever seen one like it? This is the finest soup stone for miles around."

"Soup stone?" they asked one another, "What is a soup stone?"

The rabbi called for silence. "I will demonstrate for you how the soup stone works," he said. The rabbi dropped the stone into the boiling water. He watched and waited. Minutes passed and then he called for a spoon. He tasted the soup. "It needs salt," he said, "and a bit of barley."

He handed the spoon to Mirele, saying, "Please, taste it to see if I am right." She dipped the spoon and tasted. "The rabbi is right. Salt and barley."

So the miracle began. Mirele said, "I live less than a minute from here. Give me a minute or two. I will be back with salt and barley."

True to her word, salt and barley were thrown in the pot only a few minutes later. The rabbi waited a minute, tasted the soup again, and said, "I'm not sure." He handed the spoon to Yitzchak, saying, "Tell me what you think."

Yitzchak tasted the soup. "Rabbi, the soup needs potatoes and some vegetables. Yes, and a bit of butter would be nice."

One neighbor said, "I have some potatoes in my root cellar. I'll be back in a minute." Another offered vegetables; and yet another said, "I'll fetch some butter."

When all these had been added, the rabbi tasted the soup again. "It is good," he said. "The stone has not failed us. But for a wedding, some chicken broth and chunks of meat would do it well."

Berel the butcher offered to fetch some meat. And Feivel the tailor remembered some boiled chicken that would cook to perfection if it were added. They went off in separate directions and soon returned, each with his offering.

As Berel threw in the meat, he called out in a loud voice, "Soup stone, do your thing!" Not to be outdone, Feivel threw in the chicken, meat and bones alike, crying, "Soup stone, do not fail!"

Imagine! By now, others had left and returned with more potatoes, with turnips, carrots, and beans. As they threw each new ingredient into the pot, they cried out, "Soup stone, do your thing!" And the wedding guests watched and applauded.

Soon there was no need for the rabbi to dip in the spoon to taste the soup. Every nose knew that the soup was ready. The fine smell wafted in the air with the steam from the pot. Bowls were produced and the wedding feast was served.

The spirit of love was in the air. The innkeeper rolled out a barrel of wine. Everyone toasted the bride and groom. Everyone toasted the rabbi. But the most enthusiastic toast of the day came when the rabbi put the spoon into the bottom of the nearly empty pot and produced the soup stone. "A blessing for the soup stone," the people cried, raising their glasses.

The rabbi wiped the stone carefully, brought it to Yentl the bride, and placed it on her lap. Then, he glanced up to Heaven, winked, and called out, "My dear Jews, let the dancing begin!"

[Yiddish/European folktale, adapted by Rossel]

12. Fisherman and King

The story is told of a king who loved to collect taxes. Year after year, his storehouses filled to overflowing. Finally, the king's subjects had no more money with which to pay their taxes. So the king turned to collecting taxes in payments of wheat or barley, of rice or oats; of goats and chickens; or in merchandise and goods.

It happened once that a drought lingered in the land and no crops grew. Nevertheless, like clockwork, the king's tax collectors demanded payment for the king.

The people gathered for a meeting. "What can we do?" they asked one another. "Who will go to the king to plead our case?" But all were afraid, save for one old man. "Let me go to plead with the king," he said. "I am too old to fear death."

The old man came to the palace gates and called out, "I have come to deliver a message from the people to our king." And when he was taken to the king, he said, "Your Majesty, the people love you. But they are starving and dying of thirst from the drought. You have taken everything from them in taxes, but you have given them nothing in return. Now you must help your people if your kingdom is to survive."

The king scowled. "This is the message my people have sent? Go back and tell them not to be lazy. If they work a little harder, they will have food for themselves and money to pay their taxes."

In this way, the old man knew that the king would never listen to reason. Still, he had not come all this way empty-headed. He had a plan.

"Your Majesty," the old man said, "all my life I have been a fisherman on the king's lake. Now my days are nearly done. I beg you, grant me a small favor? Take a short ride with me in my boat. Let all see that I am the king's friend."

The king was pleased by this humble suggestion. "To this I agree," he said. "It is a pleasant day. Why not take an outing on my lake?"

But the king's guards grew suspicious when they saw the old man's boat. There was only enough room in it for two. But the king said, "Never mind, I can take care of myself," and he climbed into the little boat.

The old man rowed as the king sat in the bow. Soon they reached the center of the lake. It was then that the old man rummaged under his seat and brought out a little drill. Without a word, he began drilling a hole in the bottom of the boat.

The king's eyes grew wide and round. He screamed out, "Stop what you are doing! We shall be drowned!"

The fisherman paused to answer: "You have nothing to fear, your Majesty. I am boring the hole only on my side of the boat, only beneath the seat I am sitting on."

The king stared at the fisherman. Something like a glimmer of light flashed in his eyes. "Put down the drill," he said. "I see what you mean. We are one kingdom, just as this is one boat. The drought is like a hole, swallowing up my people, and I was foolish enough to think it would not swallow me. But what is a king without people? Quickly now, row me back to shore so that I may fix the hole in my kingdom before my people are lost."

[Rossel based on *Midrash Leviticus Rabbah* 4:6]

2
Leadership

1. The Ruling Powers

🔹 Rabban Gamaliel said: "Be mindful of the ruling powers, for they bring no one near them except for their own advantage; they seem to be friends when it profits them; but they will not stand by a person in distress."

Joseph ben Joseph Nachmias explained the words of Gamaliel with this story:

A king once promoted one of his officers to captain of the king's guards. Each day the king would rise from his throne when the captain entered the throne room. The king would embrace the captain and kiss him on the neck. Then, one day, the king ordered that the captain be beheaded.

Afterward, the king bragged that he used to kiss the very spot on the captain's neck where the sword would land when his head was cut off.

People say, "Do not think the lion is smiling when the lion bares its teeth; it only shows its teeth to devour." As with lions, so too with kings.

[Nachmias, *Commentary on Avot* 2:3]

Joseph ben Joseph Nachmias lived in Spain in the first half of the fourteenth century. It is possible that he was still alive to witness his commentary become reality in the famous case of the court Jew, Don Samuel ben Meir ha-Levi Abulafia, treasurer to King Pedro the Cruel. Pedro permitted Don Samuel to construct the magnificent synagogue of Toledo (1357) but, soon thereafter, Don Samuel fell from favor and was thrown in prison where he languished until his death. Not much had changed since Rabban Gamaliel made his statement in reference to the Roman rulers.

2. Jeremiah and Moses

🔹 When the armies of Babylon came to destroy Jerusalem and the Children of Israel, God said to the angels, "Babylon is mighty,

143

Jerusalem will be lost to flames. Even My Temple will be reduced to ruins. But My people cannot be destroyed."

The angels said, "Can the Temple be destroyed? Can human beings devastate the place where God dwells?"

God answered, "I promised that I would always dwell with the Children of Israel. Soon, Babylon will capture the people and take them from the land. I must go where the Children of Israel go. So My Presence shall leave the Temple and, when it is departed, the Babylonians will destroy the Temple. When the Israelites return to build a new Temple, My Presence shall return with them."

The angels began to weep. "See now, how the city burns and the people suffer!"

God said, "The time for weeping is come. In this day, the Temple will be destroyed."

Early in the morning, God's voice came to the prophet Jeremiah: "Go and teach the Children of Israel how to weep for the Temple. Cry out to Moses. Let the greatest prophet of My people weep for the end of Jerusalem."

Jeremiah replied, "O God, no one knows where you buried Moses."

God said, "Call out from the banks of the river Jordan. Moses will hear your cry."

Jeremiah went and cried out, "Moses, O Moses, you are needed on this day." And as Jeremiah cried, he heard the echo of his own voice coming back from the hills on the other side of the river.

Then Jeremiah heard another voice like an echo, but this time it was the voice of Moses saying, "Why am I needed on this day, more than on any other?"

Jeremiah answered, "God has called you to Jerusalem."

So Moses went to the angels and found them weeping. He asked, "Why am I needed on this day, more than on any other?"

"Do you not know? On this day the Temple will be destroyed."

Then Moses grabbed the sleeve of his robe and ripped it. Tears filled his eyes. He called to the spirits of Abraham and Sarah; Isaac and Rebecca; Rachel, Leah, and Jacob. "Rise up and go with me to Jerusalem. On this day, the Temple is dying. We must be there." And together they went, their heads bent in sorrow, weeping and mourning, to the gates of the Temple.

God saw that Jeremiah and Moses and all the great fathers and mothers of the Jewish people had gathered at the gate of the Temple. And God said to the angels, "Now I can leave the Temple and let it die. The Children of Israel will hear words of comfort from their leaders. And they will remember the Jewish past, so they can dream of a Jewish future."

[*Midrash Lamentations Rabbah* proem 24; Yalkut *Lamentations* #996; also in *Sefer HaAggadah*]

3. Leadership

🔖 Being a leader is more than just an honor. The fate of the community rests on its leaders. The rabbis explained this with a parable:

One day, the serpent's tail said to its head, "How much longer will you move first? I want to go first."

The head said, "Go!" So the tail went ahead. Now, when it came to a water hole, the tail flung the serpent's head into the water. When it encountered fire, the tail flung the serpent's head into the fire. And when the tail came to thorns, it flung the serpent's head into their midst. What caused these misfortunes to befall the serpent?

It all came about because the serpent allowed its head to follow its tail.

In the same way, when the rank and file follow the guidance of wise leaders, the leaders counsel together knowing that God is in their presence, and God respects what they decree. But when the leaders are not wise, they allow themselves to follow the rank and file, so they inevitably share in the misfortunes that follow.

[*Midrash Deuteronomy Rabbah* 1:10]

4. Hillel and Shammai

🔖 There were two great teachers of Torah in Jerusalem. One was Hillel, and the other was Shammai. Both formed schools for their many students. Both were very busy. Yet it was said that Hillel was always ready to take time to help anyone. So our sages loved to tell stories about Hillel's kindness and patience.

Once a non-Jew came to Shammai and asked, "How many Torahs do the Jews believe in?"

Shammai answered, "Jews believe in two Torahs: the Written Torah that is in the Five Books of Moses and the Spoken Torah that explains and amplifies the Written Torah."

The non-Jew said, "I can trust what is written down, but how do I know I can trust what is spoken? I will become your student if you promise to teach me only your Written Torah."

This angered Shammai. "How can you be my student if you will not trust what I say?" he asked. "Be gone. And do not return to my school."

The same fellow came to see Hillel and asked the same question, "How many Torahs do the Jews believe in?" And Hillel answered in the same way. Then the non-Jew said, "I will become your student if you promise to teach me only your Written Torah." And Hillel agreed.

On the first day, Hillel taught the non-Jew the Hebrew alphabet from its beginning: "*alef, bet, gimel, dalet*," and so on. But on the second day, Hillel taught the alphabet backwards: "*tav, shin, reish, koof*," and so on.

The non-Jew said, "Hold! Yesterday, you taught me that the alphabet begins with *alef* and today you say it begins with *tav*. Which is correct?"

"Now you see," replied Hillel, "that you must trust me even when it comes to what is written. So you must also learn to trust me when it comes to the Spoken Torah."

In this way, Hillel gained a student.

Another time, a non-Jew came to Shammai and said, "I wish to study with you if you can teach me the whole Torah, all of it, while I stand on one foot."

Shammai took a ruler from his desk and shook it at the fellow. "Be gone," he yelled out. "And do not return to my school with any more of your silliness."

The same fellow came to see Hillel and made the same request, "Teach me the whole Torah while I stand on one foot."

Hillel replied, "What is hateful to you, do not do to another. This is the whole Torah, all of it. Now, go and study it."

In this way, Hillel gained another student.

It happened again. This time, a non-Jew came to Shammai and said, "I will study with you if you make me the High Priest of your Temple." Shammai took his ruler and chased the man away.

This time, Hillel smiled. "Come and study with me," he offered. "But first, answer a question for me."

The non-Jew asked, "What question shall I answer?"

Hillel said, "Would you like to live in a country where the king did not know the laws of the country?"

The fellow shook his head. "A king should know the laws so he can be fair."

"That is a good answer," said Hillel. "If you wish to become the High Priest of the Temple, you must first learn the laws of the Temple."

The fellow nodded. "That makes sense," he agreed.

Then Hillel taught the non-Jew the laws of the Temple, adding, "And the High Priest can come only from one born to the family of Aaron."

"Then I could never be the High Priest!" said the non-Jew.

"Not the High Priest," answered Hillel, "but, see what a wonderful student of Torah you are! You understand the laws even as I teach them."

Then the fellow smiled at Hillel, saying, "O gentle master, may you be blessed! I came to you to gain glory for myself, but you have taught me the spirit of Jewish study."

In this way, Hillel gained another student.

There came a time, the sages said, when these three fellows met on their way to Hillel's house of study. Each of them told his story—how he put his request to Shammai and then to Hillel. And all three said, "If we had listened to Shammai, we would never have become converts, but Hillel's gentleness turned us to the ways of Torah."

[B. Talmud *Makkot* 23b-24a; B. Talmud *Shabbat* 31a]

5. A New Rabbi

The Jews of Nikolsburg were a proud crowd. The reason was obvious. The rabbi of the synagogue of Nikolsburg was also the chief rabbi of all of Moravia, an important land with a long Jewish history. Nikolsburg, the pride of Moravia, was a city of peddlers, haulers, and traders. In Nikolsburg, Jews grew grapes for wine and turned plums into a jam coveted far and wide. The finest students of Torah came to the *yeshivot* of Nikolsburg from backwater cities like Vienna and Brno. It had been this way since the fourteenth

century; and, four hundred years later, the proud Jews of Nikolsburg had every reason to believe that it would always be this way.

Therefore, choosing a new rabbi for the Nikolsburg synagogue was always a job that the town elders dreaded. So much
rested on their shoulders. Not only did the candidate have to live
up to the highest standards, the new rabbi had to be even better
than that. Not only did the new rabbi have to set an example for
the Jewish community of Nikolsburg, he would make vital decisions on behalf of the Jews of Moravia. Choosing a new rabbi was
an awesome task.

Would the new rabbi command the respect of the country by
possessing a deep fount of learning in Talmud and Torah? But,
what if he was a great scholar who could not relate to peddlers and
traders? Or would the new rabbi command the respect of the Jews
by his warmth and his wit? And, if he did, would he have the learning in Talmud and Torah that would enable him to be wise in making judgments? Should the new rabbi be stern and commanding, a
towering figure who would rule the Jewish community by his stat-
ure? Yet, what if he was so officious and overbearing that he could
not relate to the congregation? Can you imagine what it would be
like to have to find a new rabbi for Nikolsburg—especially if the
last rabbi, or the rabbi before the last, had been particularly beloved and had led the country, the town, and the synagogue
through many a crisis, minor or major, making many a wise decision, and endearing himself to so many in the congregation?

Such was the dilemma of the elders of the Nikolsburg synagogue as they sought their new rabbi. They interviewed many candidates. Some were brilliant young folk, fresh from studies in the
academies. They interviewed rabbis from villages all around. They
spoke with friends and relatives in many places, asking how this
rabbi behaved and what they thought of rabbi so-and-so. The more
they interviewed, the more confusing and difficult the choice became. One candidate was championed by some but not much
liked by others; another was liked by everyone but not by the Jews
of his present synagogue. No matter which way the elders turned
in their search, they soon discovered that what they really wanted
was their old beloved rabbi. Alas, he had departed for the academy
on high.

In the end, a decision had to be made. For one thing, Moravia could not be without a chief rabbi for long, and, for another thing, it was July and the High Holy Days were approaching. Among all the candidates, there was one whose name came up time and again. And, as fate would have it, this Rabbi Shmelke (his name was Samuel Horowitz) had been born in Nikolsburg. He had left home to study with the great Rabbi Dov Baer, who had himself been a student of the Baal Shem Tov. But—even though Rabbi Shmelke was a student of Chasidism, even though he revered the mystical teachings of Dov Baer and the Baal Shem Tov—he did not hold with the drinking and dancing ways of the new Chasidic rabbis. This was his special appeal: that he still held to the traditional ways of older rabbis and yet breathed the life of the new movement that was taking hold of the Jewish world of eastern Europe. Pretty soon, all the elders were satisfied that they had made a fine choice. They had found a new leader who would continue the proud tradition of the rabbis of Nikolsburg.

Rabbi Shmelke was pleased to be called to serve his birthplace, the famous Nikolsburg. In a month or so, he and his family, his books and his belongings, arrived in town. The elders set about to welcome them. There was dinner after dinner in the homes of rich merchants and wine growers. There were celebrations at the synagogue and meetings to all hours of the night. There was much the elders had to explain to the new rabbi and much that they wanted to ask him about himself and about the way he wanted to do things. And, everywhere, he was advised and warned, "Make changes slowly. Let the congregation come to know you. Get used to us and let us get used to you before you try too many new ideas."

Rabbi Shmelke, though, was a man of the inner self. He spoke little and nodded often. That was his way. Soon, the advice stopped coming and the community waited. But the new rabbi seldom spoke.

Now, there was a longstanding tradition in the synagogue of Nikolsburg. So one day, the head elder took Rabbi Shmelke to the back of the synagogue and showed him a table that held a large book. "This," he said, "is the book of the rabbis of Nikolsburg. From first to last, every rabbi that has led our synagogue has written in this book. Every rabbi has chosen some law or *mitzvah*, some rule or regulation, especially important to him. He wrote the regulation in this book where everyone in the congregation could read it. And, from first to last, the Jews of Nikolsburg have been especially careful to observe that *mitzvah*, that law, that rule, in honor of our rabbi."

Rabbi Shmelke glanced at the book, turned a few pages, and nodded. The elder shrugged and thought to himself, "Now, it is up to him to decide what is important."

But day after day, curious folk would pass before the table at the back of the synagogue to look at the book of the rabbis. And, day after day, the pages were open to the name of Rabbi Shmelke, but there was nothing written beneath it. Day after day, Rabbi Shmelke watched people pass the book with his eagle eyes and saw them sigh or shrug or simply shuffle on. He watched in silence, but he wrote nothing in the book.

The elders whispered among themselves. Had they made a wise choice? Was Rabbi Shmelke equal to the task? When would finally take his place in the long chain of tradition of rabbis of this synagogue? And, what would happen if he did not? What would people think?

Worse still, the Jews of Nikolsburg were dismayed. When would this rabbi let them know what he wanted? When would he make his true self known to them? What was he waiting for? And why was he watching them so intently? It was almost embarrassing to visit the empty pages day after day.

Just before the High Holy Days, the elders of the synagogue came to Rabbi Shmelke as a group. "There is no time for further delay," they said to him. "The pages of Rabbi Shmelke cannot remain empty any longer. Everyone knows the custom and everyone is waiting for you to give us a rule that we can obey in your honor."

But when they left the rabbi's study, they were no more satisfied than they had been when they arrived. For the rabbi had said only two words: "I understand." And still his pages in the book were blank.

Only when the Jews of Nikolsburg gathered for Rosh Hashanah, when everyone was seated, before the sun had set, the rabbi left his seat and walked back to the book. For breathless moments, the congregation watched as he wrote. No one dared move. No one even whispered. Finally, the rabbi stopped writing and returned to his seat, directing the prayers to begin.

All through the evening service, the people had to hold their curiosity in check. Not even those closest to the book could really see what was written there. They would just have to wait. Everyone wondered what special observance this new rabbi thought most important. The tension mounted until, at long last, the prayers were over and the time came for people to file out of the sanctuary.

One by one, they passed the open pages of the book of the rabbis of the synagogue of Nikolsburg, and, one by one, they stared at the pages and realized what the new rabbi had written. For there, on the pages of Rabbi Shmelke, in the book of the rabbis, were the words of the Ten Commandments.

[Rossel, based on Buber, *Early Masters*, p. 184]

6. Satan and Israel

🐚 Young Israel—the boy who would grow up to be the Baal Shem Tov—started out as a teacher's apprentice. His first duty each morning was to go from door to door collecting the children to escort through the forest to the study house. As the children gathered and as they walked, Israel would sing. Some of his songs were prayers, some were stories, some were wordless, and some sounded like the voices of the birds and animals of the forest.

Looking down from heaven, Satan could see where this was heading. This carefree singer was destined to spread love and joy and devotion in the world. So Satan set out to do his job—that is, to find a way to destroy the great man while he was yet in his youth. Unfortunately for Satan, the hosts of Heaven loved to hear young Israel and the schoolchildren sing every morning. Let Satan do his worst, Heaven was on the side of Israel.

One morning, as Israel and the children were passing through the woods, Satan took the shape of a werewolf, raised up on his hind legs, and terrified the children. They screamed and ran in every direction. Israel patiently rounded them up and safely saw them home. But many of the children were now afraid of the woods and afraid of meeting the werewolf again. They anxiously told one another that there was danger of being eaten alive.

The parents, of course, did not believe their children had seen a werewolf. They knew that the new teacher's apprentice, young Israel, loved to tell stories. They convinced themselves that Israel had told a frightening tale. The next morning, every door was closed to Israel. No one would allow a child to go with him to the study house.

For days, Israel went from house to house, promising each parent that he would protect the children, persuading each child that it was safe to go with him. With great effort, he regained their trust. Yet Israel knew that more would be necessary. He would also have to face the evil that had risen up in the forest. And he would have to face that evil while keeping the children together and protecting them.

So he told the children a story: An old wizard lives at the edge of the forest, he said. The wizard has lived there since before there was a village; but no one is afraid of the old wizard any longer, for his magic is all dried up. Still, the last trick the old wizard can manage, Israel said, is to send an evil image shaped like a bear or a wolf out into the forest. Of course, it is only an image, only a picture in the air, nothing to fear. In fact, Israel assured the children, if you are brave, you can walk right through the picture!

The next morning, Israel and the children paraded into the forest singing a "brave" song. Suddenly, Satan appeared before them—again, in the shape of a huge werewolf standing on its hind legs. The wolf's evil teeth were menacing; the raised claws had sharp, pointed nails. The effect was the same as it had been before, but this time no child was frightened.

Satan was angry and threatened the children with every flick of his tail and every flash of his eyes, but—just as young Israel had guessed—the werewolf had no real power over innocent children. So Satan focused all his evil and all his menace on young Israel himself.

Just then, Israel stepped forward and thrust his hand deep into the werewolf's chest. When his hand came out, in it was the beating heart of Satan!

Everything stopped and everyone stood as if frozen in time—the children, the werewolf, even the breeze that had been rustling the trees—nothing stirred. Israel lowered his hand to put the heart on the ground, but the earth cried, "Have pity. The heart of

Satan is too evil for me to swallow." Israel tried to set the heart in the crook of a tree, but the tree bent back, pleading, "Mercy! My boughs would be torn asunder." The air wanted nothing to do with it; and even though they were a great distance from the ocean, the ocean roared: "Do not think to send it to me—I would spew it up and vomit it back at you."

Israel held the beating heart up to offer it to heaven, but the hosts of Heaven said, "Return it to Satan. The time has not come for evil to be destroyed on the earth, though you were created to help destroy it."

Israel raised himself to his full height. He spoke out in a thundering voice. "I will return this heart to Satan, if Satan will promise us peace." And a thundering voice echoed in wretched anger: "So be it."

Just as suddenly as everything had stopped, the heart disappeared from young Israel's hands. The werewolf evaporated like smoke. The children came to life singing and walking along as though nothing had happened. Israel smiled, joined their song, and led them to the house of study.

The next day, the news spread that an old forgotten wizard who lived at the forest's edge had died. When Israel heard, he knew that Satan would keep the bargain.

[adapted from Buber, *Early Masters*, pp. 36-37]

The word *satan* comes from a Hebrew verb meaning "to oppose" or "to obstruct." Satan makes his appearance as an angel with some evident permanence in the books of Job, Zechariah, and Second Chronicles. In Zechariah, Satan is a prosecutor in the heavenly court. In the Book of Job, it is Satan who accuses Job but God who tests Job. And in Chronicles, Satan is blamed for King David's unfortunate decision to take a census. In the Bible, then, Satan is neither a "fallen angel" nor an angel in rebellion. Satan's close association with evil evolved in later legend.

3
Judging and Justice

1. What Justice Requires

Once a beggar borrowed a sum of money from a wealthy merchant, promising to repay the loan at the end of two weeks. Two weeks passed, and another two weeks, but the beggar did not repay his debt. To the rich man it was a small sum; but to the beggar who could not raise it, it was a fortune.

At last the wealthy merchant found the beggar in the marketplace and demanded, "Have you my money to return?" But the beggar answered, "No."

"In that case," said the rich man, "You must come with me before the court and the judge will decide what shall be done with you."

At once, the townspeople knew what had happened—for gossip in a small town is like water in a sponge, in an instant every space is filled with it. As the rich man pulled the poor man toward the courtroom, the whole town gathered to march behind the dismal duo.

"Come and judge a case of law," the wealthy merchant called out to the judge. So the judge donned his black hat and robe and sat behind his table.

The courtroom was full of townspeople. Everyone listened as the merchant told of the loan and the broken agreement. Then they heard the beggar tell of how he had been unable to raise enough money to repay his debt.

Suddenly the courtroom was alive with whispers. "The merchant does not need this money." "He has enough money without it." "It is such a small amount that the rich man will not miss it at all." "Why does he not forget the money and count it as charity?"

But the judge called out, "Silence!" and a hush spread over the crowded room.

154

"Now I will pronounce the verdict," said the judge. "This beggar must return the money he owes immediately. That is justice; and that is what justice requires."

The people were dismayed. But, before they could begin to murmur again, something even more surprising happened. The judge stood, took off his black judge's hat, and turned it upside down. "Now," he said, "I will collect charity from you people. Reach into your pockets and help this poor man pay what he owes our rich neighbor. That is mercy; and that is what mercy requires."

[Yiddish/European folktale]

2. Helping Hand

☙ Once Rabbi Samuel was having some difficulty boarding a ferry boat. A fellow came and offered him a helping hand. When both were safely aboard, Rabbi Samuel asked the fellow why he happened to be traveling on this ferry. The man replied, "I am headed for the court because I have a case for the judge." Then Samuel said, "I am sorry to hear that. Normally, I would have judged your case. But, because you offered me your hand to help me board the boat, I am forbidden to be your judge."

[B. Talmud *Ketubot* 105b]

3. Buying a Donkey

☙ Rabbi Simeon ben Shetach went to the marketplace to buy a donkey. When he saw one he liked, he asked the Arab for the price and paid for it. Then he led the donkey home. His students came for their lesson, and they saw the new donkey. "It looks like a fine animal," they said. And they examined it closely.

Excitedly, they came running into Simeon's house. "Master," they said to him, "look what we found tied around the donkey's neck." They showed Simeon a little bag on a string. They opened the bag and inside was a beautiful jewel. "You thought you were buying just a donkey," they said. "But you have bought a jewel worth ten times the price of the donkey. Surely, God has given you this gift as a reward for all your learning."

Simeon said, "I bought only the donkey. I did not buy the jewel."

"But Master," the students said, "if you buy a field and a treasure is buried in the field, then the treasure belongs to you. So, too, if you buy a donkey and a jewel happens to be tied around the donkey's neck, the jewel belongs to you. That is the law as you yourself taught us."

"You are correct," said Simeon. "That is the law. But when it comes to helping others, the law is only the least we can do. We have to learn to go beyond the law in order to increase peace in the world."

So Simeon returned the jewel to the Arab in the marketplace. From that time on, the Arab was heard to say, "Blessed be the God of Simeon ben Shetach."

[*Midrash Deuteronomy Rabbah* 3:3; also in *Sefer HaAggadah*]

4. Body and Soul

🍃 Antoninus said to Rabbi Judah HaNasi, "It seems to me that, after death, it would be easy for the body and the soul to free themselves from Heaven's judgment. For example, the body can plead, 'The soul alone has sinned. Ever since the day it left me, look, I lie in the grave like a mute stone.' Likewise, the soul can plead, 'The body has sinned. Ever since the day I departed from it, look, I fly about in the air like a bird.'"

Thereupon, Rabbi Judah offered a parable to explain why this is not possible:

A mortal king owned a beautiful orchard which yielded luscious figs. The king appointed two watchmen—one lame and the other blind—to guard it and keep anyone from eating his figs. Once, though, the lame watchman said to the blind one, "I see some fine figs have already grown in the orchard. If you put me on your shoulder, we can pick the figs and eat them."

The lame man climbed up on the shoulders of the blind man. Together, they picked figs and ate them. After a while, the king returned to his orchard and inquired, "Where are those early figs?"

The blind man replied, "Why accuse me? Have I eyes to see with?"

The lame man replied, "How can you accuse me? Have I legs to walk with?"

What did the king do? He had his soldiers place the lame man upon the shoulders of the blind one. Then he judged them together, as though they were one. So will the Holy One bring the soul, toss it inside the body, and judge the two together, as is written, "God shall call to the heavens from above, and to the earth, that God's people may be judged" (Psalms 50:4). "God shall call to the heavens from above"—that is, call for the soul; "and to the earth"—that is, call for the body; "that God's people may be judged'—that is, together.

Body and soul are one; and neither can escape what the other does, for neither can do anything without the other.

[B. Talmud *Sanhedrin* 91a-b; also see *Midrash Leviticus Rabbah* 4:5]

In the second century CE, relations with imperial Rome improved greatly and the Roman emperors showed a sincere interest in Jewish thought. It was even said that "Antoninus" would be resurrected in the time of the Messiah as the first "righteous proselyte" (J. Talmud *Megilah* 3:2, 74a). But it is never quite clear which of the Antonine emperors is intended. Some scholars suggest that, at times, it is the emperor Marcus Aurelius, though the name used throughout is always "Antoninus."

5. The Most Precious Gift

Ardavan, the king of Parthia, sent a costly pearl to Rav with a message, saying, "Send me something equally precious in return for this pearl." In return, Rav sent a *mezuzah* to Ardavan.

Ardavan sent back a message to Rav, saying, "I sent you something so valuable that it could not be bought by anyone but a king, and you have sent me something that every Jew has, and anyone can buy."

This time, Rav wrote a message for the king: "O King of Parthia, what I have sent you is worth much more than what you sent me. You have sent me a pearl that I must guard day and night; I have sent you a *mezuzah* that will guard you at your going out and at your coming in."

[*Midrash Genesis Rabbah* 35:3; J. Talmud *Peah* 1:1 15d; also in *Sefer HaAggadah*]

King Ardavan V of Parthia ruled in the first quarter of the third century, CE. He is mentioned several times in the Talmud. When the sage Rav heard of his death, he lamented, "The bond has been sundered" (B. Talmud *Avodah Zara* 10b–11a). In the Jerusalem Talmud's version, Rabbi Judah HaNasi is cited as the Jewish sage but the dates for Judah and Ardavan do not match.

6. Two Witnesses

A case of murder came before the rabbinic court. Jewish law states that a person can be convicted of murder only if there are two witnesses to the act.

Two witnesses testified at the trial. Both told the same story: "We saw the accused person running after the victim with a sword in his hand. The victim fled into a shop and the accused murderer ran in after him. We ran into the shop a moment later and found the victim dead on the floor. In the accused man's hand was the sword, still dripping blood."

Nevertheless, the murderer was set free because the witnesses had not actually seen the murder take place and so they could not be absolutely positive that the accused man had truly committed the crime.

[Tosefta *Sanhedrin* 7:3]

7. The Mystery of Manasseh

Rav Ashi was once teaching a lesson in the Mishnah and came to a mention of the Jewish king, Manasseh. Manasseh, he told the students, had turned to idolatry. The hour of the lesson was up, however, before he could describe the situation in the days of Manasseh.

"Tomorrow," he said in closing, "we will speak further of this 'wise' king."

Now, in truth, the sages knew that Manasseh was wise, but Rav Ashi spoke the word "wise" in a sarcastic tone, as if to say that Manasseh could not have been very wise if he worshiped idols.

That night, in a dream, Manasseh came to Rav Ashi.

"Do you honestly judge me to be ignorant?" Manasseh asked. Then the king posed some difficult questions of Jewish law and when Ashi could not reply, Manasseh himself answered each question brilliantly, so amazing the learned scholar.

Rav Ashi apologized for his sarcastic remark, and humbly asked the ancient king of Judah, "If you were so learned, how did you come to worship idols?"

Manasseh replied, "Had you been there with me, you would have gathered up the hem of your garment and run after me to worship idols!"

[B. Talmud *Sanhedrin* 102b]

8. Hillel's Wife

An important man came to dinner at Hillel's home. All that day, Hillel's wife had spared no effort to prepare a perfect meal for their guest. But before they sat down to eat, a poor man appeared at the door. Hillel's wife greeted him and said, "Hillel is busy with a guest. How may I help you?"

"Mine is both a glad and sad story," the man replied. "Today is the day of my wedding. And for that reason I am glad. But I have no food to feed my wedding guests, and I have no money for food. And for that reason I am sad. I have come to ask Hillel for a loan to buy food."

Then Hillel's wife said, "We have something better than money to give you." She took the meal she had prepared and gave it to the poor man. But as soon as the man had left with his wedding feast, she heard her husband calling, "My dear, is dinner almost ready?"

She called back to him: "It will be a few minutes, my dear."

She set about baking bread, cooking a pot of stew, and fixing a salad. An hour passed and then another. At last, she called her husband and his guest to the table, placing the meal before them.

"My dear," asked Hillel, "why did you not serve us sooner?"

At once, Hillel's wife told the whole story: how the poor man had come to the door and how she had given him the meal that had taken her all day to prepare so he could serve it at his wedding.

Then Hillel smiled. "My dear," he said, "I asked only because I knew you had a good reason for waiting." He turned to his guest, saying, "You see, everything my wife does, she does for the sake of heaven."

[B. Talmud, *Derech Eretz Rabbah* 6; also in *Sefer HaAggadah*]

9. The Dowdy Dress

A middle-aged woman in a dowdy dress and her husband in a threadbare suit came to Jerusalem and walked timidly, without an appointment, into the outer office of Hebrew University's President. The secretary instantly knew that such bumpkins were entirely out of place.

"We'd like to see the president," the man said in a soft voice.

"He has a very busy schedule," the secretary snapped. "We'll wait," the lady replied. For hours the secretary ignored them, hoping they would leave in discouragement. But as they persisted in haunting her office, the secretary grew frustrated and decided to disturb the president, though it was a chore she always dreaded. "Perhaps, if you see them briefly, they will leave," she suggested.

He gave an exasperated sigh and nodded. A person of his importance obviously did not have the time for walk-ins, but he steeled himself and told the secretary to proceed. A moment later, the president, stern-faced and with dignity, met the couple at his door, escorted them into his study, indicated a couch on which they could sit, and sat down in an armchair nearby.

The woman explained, "We had a son who attended your university for one year. He loved Hebrew University. He was happy here. But last year, he was accidentally killed. My husband and I would like to erect a memorial to him somewhere here on campus."

The president wasn't touched. "Madam," he said, gruffly, "we can't put up a statue for every student who attended the Hebrew University and died. If we did, this place would look like a cemetery."

"Oh, no," the woman quickly replied. "We don't want to erect a statue. We thought we would like to give a building."

The president rolled his eyes. He glanced at the dowdy dress and the threadbare suit, then exclaimed, "A building! Do you have any earthly idea how much a building costs?" He went on to tell them what each building on campus was worth, enumerating them all from memory. When he thought he had impressed on them the foolishness of their proposal, he sat back in his chair and folded his hands on his desk.

For a moment the woman was silent. The president was pleased. Perhaps he would be rid of them now.

Then the woman turned to her husband and said quietly, "Is that all it costs to start a university? Why don't we just start our own?" Her husband nodded. The president's face wilted in confusion and bewilderment.

The couple rose, thanked the president, and started out of the office. The president hesitated a moment and said, "Forgive me, I did not ask your name."

The man in the threadbare suit grasped the president's hand and said, "Forgive us. We are Simon and Zelda Rothschild." With that, they left.

You can easily judge the character of people by how they treat those who seem of little use to them.

[based on an Internet fable]

10. The Benefit of the Doubt

🐾 Daniel, a poor farmer from the Galilee, hired himself out to work for three years for a man in the south. At the end of the three years, as the High Holy Days approached, he said to his employer, "Pay me my wages. I will go home to my wife and family."

The man said, "I have no money."

Daniel said, "Give me vegetables and grain."

The man said, "I have none."

"Give me land."

"I have none."

"Give me cattle."

"I have none."

"Give me linens for my beds."

"I have none."

With that, Daniel gathered his clothing and his few belongings, put everything in a sack, put the sack across his shoulder, and went home.

The day after Yom Kippur, his employer from the south appeared at Daniel's house. He brought Daniel's wages, along with three donkeys laden with food, drink, and gifts. He paid Daniel, saying, "All these gifts are for you."

Daniel's wife prepared a meal for them. After they had eaten, the former employer quizzed Daniel. "When you asked me for your wages, and I said I had no money, what did you think?"

Daniel said, "I thought you had bought goods cheaply, so you had no cash on hand."

"And what about the cattle?"

"I thought you may have hired them out, so you could not give them to me."

"And what about the land?"

"I thought you had probably rented it out, so you could not give me any."

"And the vegetables and grain?"

"I thought you had not yet tithed them for the Temple, so you could not give them to me."

"And about the linens for the beds?"

"I thought perhaps you had consecrated your property to God before the High Holy Days, so you could not give any of it to me."

The man said, "All you have spoken was the truth, Daniel. You see, I have a son who adamantly refused to study the Torah. I was so angry with him that I vowed everything that belonged to me to the Temple. If he would be foolish, I would leave him nothing. But my son repented during the High Holy Days and promised to study, so I went to the priests and they released me from my vow. Now I am a man of property again; and so are you. As you judged me favorably, so may God judge you."

[B. Talmud *Shabbat* 127b]

11. For the Sake of the Cattle

Alexander of Macedon visited King Kazia in Africa beyond the dark mountains. The king made a great feast to welcome his visitor. He served bread to all the dignitaries, but they set before Alexander two loaves of golden bread on a golden tray.

"Do you think that I need your gold?" Alexander demanded.

King Kazia said, "If not, why did you come to the end of the earth? Is there a famine in your country so that you are seeking something to eat?"

Alexander replied, "I came only because I am curious to see how you dispense justice."

King Kazia approved. They removed the golden tray with its golden loaves and in its stead gave Alexander bread and water.

When the table was cleared, the king ascended to his throne to dispense justice. A second throne was provided for Alexander so that he could sit beside the king.

Presently, a man approached with a complaint against his neighbor. "I protest against this man," he stated, "for he sold me a piece of worthless land and I found a treasure in it." The seller argued, "I sold him the land, which means he bought all that was in it, including the treasure." But the purchaser said, "I bought only the land. The treasure belongs to him."

King Kazia asked the seller, "Is it true you have a daughter of marriageable age?" "I do," the seller replied.

King Kazia asked the buyer, "Is it also true that you have a son not yet married?" "I do," the buyer replied.

"Then this is my judgment," King Kazia said. "His daughter shall marry your son, and the treasure will be her dowry."

The two men bowed and left the king's presence.

Alexander shook his head in wonder. Kazia noticed and asked him, "Have I not judged well?"

"They appear to be satisfied, Your Majesty."

Kazia noted his tone and said, "Apparently, you would have judged differently. Tell me, what would have been your judgment?"

"I would have put both men to death and kept the treasure for myself," Alexander said.

Kazia thought about that for a moment. He asked, "Does it rain in your country?" Alexander replied, "Yes."

"Does the sun shine in your country?" Alexander replied, "Yes."

"Do you have sheep and goats in your country?" "Yes," Alexander replied.

"Then, by heaven!," exclaimed King Kazia, "it is not for your sake that the rain comes and the sun shines. It is only for the sake of the innocent cattle!'

[Midrash Genesis Rabbah 33:1; J. Talmud Baba Metzia 2:5, 8c]

12. What Kind of People?

An old man sat outside the walls of a great city. When travelers approached, they would ask the old man, "What kind of people live in this city?"

The old man would answer, "What kind of people live in the place where you came from?"

If the travelers answered, "Only bad people live in the place where we came from," the old man would reply, "Continue on. You will find only bad people here."

But if the travelers answered, "Good people live in the place where we came from," then the old man would say, "Enter. Here, too, you will find only good people."

[Yiddish folk tale]

13. Barbuchin

A group of rabbis went forth to collect charity. Near a large farm, they overheard a conversation between the farmer and his son. The son asked, "What shall we eat today?" And his father, a Jew named Barbuchin, answered, "Go to the town market and choose the cheapest vegetables. That is what we will eat."

Hearing this, the rabbis thought that Barbuchin must either be stingy or poor. They decided to seek charity from others first; later, if they had time, they would return to Barbuchin for what would probably be a small donation. All that day, the rabbis collected small amounts from one Jew and another. Near dinner-time, they returned to find the farmer Barbuchin still working. The rabbis greeted him and said, "Tomorrow is Shabbat and many are in need. Perhaps you have a coin or two to spare?"

Barbuchin told them, "Go to my wife and say I instruct her to give you a bushel of coins."

The rabbis were surprised, but they did as they were told. And when the wife heard that she was to give the rabbis a bushel of coins, she asked, "Did my husband say to give you a level bushel or one that is heaped up?"

The rabbis answered, "He simply said 'a bushel.'"

Barbuchin's wife said, "Very well, I shall give you a bushel heaped-up with coins and if my husband objects, I will pay him back from my own money."

When the coins from the bushel were poured into bags, the rabbis struggled under the heavy load. As they walked, they came upon Barbuchin returning home from the field. They stopped to thank him.

He asked them, "Did my wife give you a level bushel or one that was heaped-up?" They said, "We told her 'a bushel,' as you said, but she gave us one heaped-up and said that if you complained she would repay you."

Barbuchin waved his hand. "A heaped-up bushel is what I had in mind," he said. "But, tell me, you must have been collecting all day, why did you not come to me straightaway?"

"In truth, we were close by this morning," the rabbis answered, "but we heard your son ask you what to buy for supper; and you replied, 'the cheapest possible vegetables,' so we thought you were either poor or stingy."

Barbuchin smiled. "With myself I am stingy, but with the requirements of God and the needs of the community, I am never stingy."

[*Midrash Esther Rabbah* 2:3]

14. Madness or Dancing?

🕮 It happened once in a small Polish town that all the people were invited to a great dance and celebration in the town hall. Now on the evening of the dance, a young boy from another town came to visit friends, but could not find them at home. Indeed, he could find no one at home in the whole town.

While he was searching for the people, and thinking how strange it was that the town was empty, he chanced to walk by the town hall. Looking in, from far away, the boy could plainly see that the entire town had gone crazy. People were jumping up and down, hugging one another, pressing one another, pushing and pulling at one another, bowing and raising their hands to one another. But as he came a little closer to witness this phenomenon, one of the people inside the town hall opened a window to let in some fresh air. It was then that the boy heard music pouring out of the hall. Suddenly, he realized that the people inside were dancing.

[Buber, *Early Masters*, p. 53]

15. A Barrel of Justice

🕮 Once upon a time, everyone entering the synagogue in Chelm sat wherever he pleased, but these days the rich reserved the seats closest to the Holy Ark for themselves, and the poor were forced to sit behind them. Naturally, the poor people grew jealous of the rich; and, for their part, the rich people began to fear the poor.

Finally, the poor complained to the rabbi. "Why should the rich dress in fine clothes, while we dress in rags? Why should the rich eat meat, while we drink soup? Why should the rich have the best of everything, while we live on air? Why is there no justice in Chelm?"

The rabbi considered their words and said, "Since the Torah speaks of justice, there must be justice somewhere in the world. If it is not in Chelm, we will have to find it elsewhere. Let us send two

Chelmites to Warsaw to search for justice. If they find it, they can buy some for Chelm."

The two Chelmites came to Warsaw and asked everyone they met where they might find justice. Time and again they received the same answer, "If there is justice here in Warsaw, we would surely like to find it for ourselves."

Now it happened that a couple of clever rogues overheard the Chelmites and thought, "Here is easy money to be made." They hailed the two. "Friends," they said, "how would you like a bargain? We just happen to have a warehouse of justice, more justice than we need, and we would gladly sell you some."

The Chelmites followed the rogues to an old warehouse. They could hardly believe their eyes! Before them, they saw barrel upon barrel stacked from wall to wall and from floor to ceiling.

"How much justice can you afford?" the rogues asked.

The Chelmites went to a corner to confer. When they returned, they said, "We would like a whole barrelful."

"Well," said one of the rogues, "Justice is not cheap. A barrelful will cost you a hundred gulden."

The Chelmites smiled, marveling at the wisdom of their rabbi. He had provided them with one hundred and fifty gulden. Now they could return fifty gulden and still bring a barrel of justice to Chelm. They paid the rogues, and the four men loaded the barrel on the Chelmites' wagon. A few farewells and they were bound for Chelm.

In Chelm, the word spread. Justice had arrived! Everyone—rich and poor—hurried to the synagogue. In front of the synagogue door, the barrel was taken from the wagon. Mottel the Mayor was given the honor of opening it. And the people crowded around as Mottel pried off the top.

Suddenly, the foul smell of rotten fish was in every nostril. Jumping away from the barrel, Mottel exclaimed, "This justice is spoiled."

The people of Chelm turned to one another in horror. "Alas, the justice is spoiled!"

But Gimpel, the richest man in Chelm, explained, "Now you know the truth. Spoiled justice is the only kind you will ever find outside of Chelm."

The rabbi had been sitting quietly, thinking deeply. Now, he rose to speak: "People of Chelm, now we know that justice is rotten in the world, so we must make our own. Here is what I propose: From now on, whenever an ox is slaughtered, let the entire animal consist only of the finest cuts. That way, no matter what part a person eats, it will be the finest part. From now on, there will be no difference between satin and cotton. Whatever garment you buy will be the finest material. From now on, all the synagogue will be equally close to the Holy Ark. Wherever a person sits will be the choicest seat.

"Now, if the rich are foolish enough to wish to pay a greater price for the seats that were formerly closer to the Holy Ark, let them. If they wish to pay more for what used to be the finest garments, let them. If they wish to pay more for the parts of the meat that were formerly choicer, let them. After all, foolishness is as foolishness does."

That is how justice came to Chelm. For the rich, things had not changed. But for the poor, everything was now different. They might still be poor, but they would always be equal to the rich. They would eat the finest meat, wear the finest clothes, and sit in the finest seats in the synagogue—no matter what they ate, no matter what they wore, no matter where they sat.

[adapted from Simon, *The Wise Men of Helm*]

16. A Leak at the Top

🐝 The richest merchant of Chelm bought a barrel of fine wine and stored it in his cellar. He sent his wife down to draw two glasses of wine for the Sabbath and, after the *Kiddush* prayer over the wine was made, both husband and wife agreed they enjoyed their fine wine very much. The next Sabbath, the merchant himself went down to the cellar to draw two more glasses of wine and, with a shock, he saw that the spigot had been leaking for a week. He took the top off the barrel and discovered, to his dismay, that the barrel was half empty.

He called his wife to the basement. "All that good wine lost and it is all your fault! You carelessly left the spigot open a small bit and half the wine leaked out the bottom of the barrel."

The wife was indignant. "It cannot be," she said. "Look, the leak was obviously not my fault. Only the top half of the barrel is empty. It is obvious, dear husband, that the wine leaked out the top!"

[adapted from Simon, *The Wise Men of Helm*]

17. The Young Judge

There were two storekeepers, one sold olive oil and the other sold spices. Their stores shared a thin wall. One evening the spice merchant discovered a little hole in the wall. Looking through it, he saw the oil merchant counting his money. The spice merchant carefully counted each coin to himself, even as the oil merchant moved the coins from one pile to another. When the oil merchant finished counting he placed all the coins in a sack and hid the sack on his shelf. In this way, the seller of spices knew that the oil merchant had exactly one hundred gold coins.

Now, this spice merchant was very greedy. He wondered, "How can I get those hundred gold coins?" And he hatched a plot. He ran into the street, shouting, "Thief! Thief! Someone has stolen my money!"

A crowd gathered and people asked, "Who has stolen your money?"

"Do I know?" he replied. "No one has even been to my store since noon. The only one even nearby is that oil merchant next door."

A policeman overheard this and asked, "How much was stolen?" to which the spice merchant said, "Exactly one hundred gold pieces."

Then, the policeman barged into the shop of the oil merchant, searched it carefully, and discovered a bag containing exactly one hundred gold pieces.

"Thief!" shouted the spice merchant. "You have taken *my* money!"

"You know me many years," the oil merchant said. "Do you think I would steal your money? Those coins belong to me."

But the policeman could not decide who was telling the truth, so he brought them both to the judge.

The two merchants testified before the judge. Each of them claimed that the money was his.

But the judge could not decide who was telling the truth, so he said: "Go to your homes, both of you. I will hold the money. In one week, I will make my decision and you will know who is the thief. Then the money will be returned to its rightful owner."

All week long, the town buzzed with gossip about the case of the two merchants. And all week long, the judge pondered his dilemma, but he was no closer to a wise decision at the end of the week than he had been at its beginning. He was walking toward the courtroom when he overheard some children at play.

One of the children said: "I will pretend to be the judge, and you two will pretend to be the shopkeepers." The other children agreed and the game began.

The "judge" sat on a large stone. The "spice merchant" stepped up and said: "The money is mine." The "oil merchant" said: "No, it is my money." The "judge" said: "We will soon know the truth. Let's put the coins in a pitcher of warm water. If drops of oil appear on the water, we will know that the coins belong to the oil merchant, because an oil merchant's fingers will leave oil on the coins. But if no drops of oil appear, then the coins belong to the spice merchant, since the dry spices will not leave oil on the coins."

The town judge ran over and hugged the boy who had played "judge." "You are very clever, my child. Thank you for showing me how to decide this case!"

The smiling judge hurried on to the courthouse. Soon, the two merchants appeared and the townspeople crowded in. Everyone was anxious to hear the judge's verdict. The judge ordered: "Bring a pitcher of warm water, and place the gold coins inside."

They brought the pitcher of water and placed the coins in it and, at once, the drops of oil floated to the surface. Everyone could see the truth for themselves. The judge pronounced his verdict and gave the bag of coins back to the oil merchant. And the crowd began to sing the praises of the judge, calling him "wise" and "clever."

The Judge called for silence. "Do not praise me," he said. "I learned how to judge this case from a clever child." And he pointed to the boy who acted the part of the "judge." And everyone, except perhaps the spice merchant, applauded for the boy.

[based on a story in Certner, *101 Jewish Stories*]

18a. The Bell of Justice

In the days of King John of Acre a bell was hung. Anyone who had suffered a great wrong could come and pull the rope to ring it. This was the signal for the king to assemble the judges of the realm in order that justice might be done.

In the beginning, the bell was rung but once or twice a year. As time passed, though, people had all but forgotten it. With no one to tend the bell, the rope attached to the bell's clapper slowly untwisted itself and frayed at the end. A clinging vine attached itself to the rope and grew tendrils all around it. At last, what was left of the rope could barely be seen.

Now, a certain great knight of Acre loved luxury so much that he sold his suit of armor, his pike, his helm, and three of his fine horses for a great deal of money. He kept only his favorite charger, a great white beast with a golden muzzle. He bought a fine villa and hired servants to tend to his every wish. He invested in the journeys of merchants, by camel and by sea so that his wealth grew each year. He spent his days drinking fine wine and eating fine foods and, for entertainment, he would count his money. From time to time, he would saddle his fine white charger and ride to the inn to join other old knights in drinking and remembering the good old days.

There came a day when the noble white horse was too old to ride. The knight lamented and thought to himself, "It is no longer of use to me and it will not fetch a good price in the market. All that is left for it is to eat at my expense." And the thought of the horse eating away some of the gold he had amassed gave the old knight a sore stomach. One night, he led the horse out of its stable and into the countryside near the town. When he came to a small grove of trees, he released the horse, saying, "You have eaten your last at my expense. Go now, and fend for yourself."

But the horse could not easily fend for itself. In the countryside, it was chased by wild beasts; and in the town, dogs nipped at its heels. It was soon so hungry that it would eat nearly anything, but hardly found anything to eat. Famished and exhausted, the horse chanced upon the vine growing beneath the old bell. It began to nibble at the vine. Now, the vine was stuck tight to the old rope of the bell and as the horse tugged at the vine to get it loose, the bell rang again and again.

The king heard the bell and remembered it. The judges heard the bell and remembered it. Despite the length of days that had passed since they heard it, they came running to the place where the bell was hung. The king said, "Here now is a sight to see. A horse has summoned us to do justice." The judges made inquiries and soon learned of the miserly old knight, his beautiful villa, his servants, and his habits. There was not a single person in the whole town who had not seen the knight riding upon his white charger. And, before them was that very horse, broken down and famished, its bones showing through its shriveled skin. Every heart in town was moved to pity.

The king summoned the old knight. "The Bell of Justice has tolled. You must stand trial for what you have done," the king said. Then the judges commanded that the knight should forfeit a thousand gold coins. A field was purchased for the horse, a groom was hired to care for it, and a stable was built to house it.

As for the bell, it was polished and provided with a new rope. The king commanded, "Neither man nor beast shall suffer wrongdoing so long as this bell can ring. In my kingdom, justice shall reign."

[adapted from *The Hundred Old Tales (Le ciento novelle antike)*]

The Hundred Old Tales (Le ciento novelle antike) was compiled toward the end of the thirteenth century possibly by a court minstrel. Scholars conjecture that this tale originated among the Crusader Knights of Acre. Henry Wadsworth Longfellow used it for his poem, "The Bell of Atri" and also as "The Sicilian's Tale" in the second volume of his *Tales of a Wayside Inn*.

In 1915, the National Woman Suffrage Association (later the League of Woman Voters) commissioned a 2,000 pound replica of the Liberty Bell with the words "Establish Justice" added to "Proclaim liberty throughout all the land unto all the inhabitants thereof" (Leviticus 25:10), The "Justice Bell" was created to promote the campaign for women's suffrage. The movement stated that "a woman's right to vote is a matter of justice." To dramatize their struggle, the clapper of the bell was chained to its side, ensuring that the bell would remain silent until the struggle succeeded. In 1920, after the passage of the 19th Amendment to the Constitution of the United States, the bell was rung for the first time. The Justice Bell now resides at the Washington Memorial Chapel in Valley Forge.

18b. The Bell of Justice (Version 2)

In the twenty-seventh year of King Jeroboam's reign over Israel, Azariah became the King of Judah. He was sixteen years old when he began to reign, and he reigned for fifty-two years in Jerusalem. Azariah tried to be a good king, as his father had been. But Azariah was afraid of the people, so he never lifted a hand against the high places where the Judahites worshiped foreign gods, where they sacrificed and burnt incense to idols. Then, God afflicted the king with an illness in his skin so terrible that he could no longer appear in public. The king gave command of the palace and the people to his son Jotham, while he prepared a separate place for himself, outside the palace—nor did he leave his quarters until the day of his death.

Jotham told his father, "You are the king and I will serve you. But you must not remove your wisdom from the people of Judah." So Jotham commanded that a bronze bell with an iron clapper be placed outside Azariah's quarters. To the clapper they attached a rope. Jotham said to his father, "I have made it a law that anyone with a wrong to be righted can pull this rope and ring the bell. Then you will listen to the complaint and call out your commands so that justice may be served."

The bell was seldom used. In time, a serpent made its home under the end of the bell-rope. It brought forth its young, and one day, when the little serpents were ready, it led them out of their nest for the first time. While they were away, a toad came and occupied their nest. The toad was so well settled, that it refused to budge when the serpent returned.

The serpent hissed and threatened, but it was all to no avail. Finally, in desperation it decided to lower itself into its nest. So it chanced that the serpent coiled itself around the rope of the bell and the bell rang.

From inside his quarters, Azariah called out, "State your case." He waited, but there was no answer. So Azariah returned to his bed.

But the bell rang again. This time, King Azariah said to his servant, "Go out and see who is ringing the bell." The servant went and saw the situation at once. All around the serpent's nest were the young serpents. Clinging to the bell-rope was the serpent. But in the serpent's nest was the toad.

All this the servant reported to the king. The king said, "Justice must answer the bell of justice, though it is merely justice for a serpent. It is clear that the toad is in the wrong. Therefore, drive the toad from the nest, and restore the serpent and its young to their place."

All was done as the king commanded.

Only a few days had passed, and the king lay in his bed, when the serpent came through the window and into the king's quarters. As it made its way to the king's bed, the servant took up a walking stick and came toward the serpent to kill it. The king commanded, "Put down the stick. This serpent will do me no harm. I have given it justice. Let us see what it will do."

At that, the serpent slithered up the side of the bed, opened its mouth, and laid a stone at the king's feet. Then it slid down the side of the bed and slipped away, never to be seen again. But no sooner had the stone touched the feet of the king than his pain vanished. His skin disease worsened each year, but, to the day of his death, so long as the stone touched him, the pain never returned. Such was the reward of King Azariah for answering the bell of justice.

[Rossel, based on 18a]

King Azariah is more popularly known as King Uzziah (ruled c. 785–734 BCE). Josephus recounts a tradition in which, on a festival day, Uzziah put on priestly robes, entered the Temple, and—over the protestations of the Temple priests—attempted to bring the incense offering to the golden altar. The earth quaked so hard that cracks appeared in the walls of the Temple, the sun shone through one of the cracks and fell directly on Uzziah's face. The king was immediately struck with "leprosy." He removed himself from the palace, placed Jotham over the kingdom, and slowly died of his disease (Josephus, *Antiquities*, 9:223ff.).

19. Hole in the Wall

In Yemen, women wore necklaces with their necklaces and bracelets with their bracelets. They wore nose rings and anklets. They adorned themselves with silver and beads from head to toe. And brides were bedecked and bejeweled beyond belief. The jeweler Shalom crafted silver and beads. He shaped and cut, filed and filigreed. He fashioned the most outstanding bracelets and the most exceptional necklaces in all of Yemen. Other Jewish jewelers bought Shalom's creations for their wives. Muslims came to his shop to purchase jewelry for their women. Shalom had a good trade and he loved it.

Now Shalom had one son and three daughters. His wife was busy day and night. She and the girls began baking bread before Shalom and his son rose in the morning; and breakfast was ready when the men came to eat. Shalom was not a rich man, but he and his son sold enough to keep the family in food and clothing. And in jewelry, of course.

One day, Shalom changed. He decided to make an amulet, a charm. Many jewelers made them. The Muslims called such an amulet "the Hand of Fatimah"—Fatimah was the daughter of the prophet Mohammed. Muslims thought that wearing a charm in the shape of Fatimah's hand would protect them against the evil eye. The Jews called the same amulet a *chamsah*, from the Hebrew word for five, as in the fingers of the hand. "Hand of Fatimah" or *chamsah*, the amulet usually had an eye in its palm, to show that the charm could turn away the evil eye.

Shalom's son, Mashiach, asked, "Father, why do you wish to make this *chamsah*? People love your necklaces and adore your bracelets. Would it not be best to keep making what the people buy?"

Shalom said, "My son, since before you were born, I have made bracelets and necklaces. My hands made bracelets while I slept; my heart designed necklaces while I was awake. But last night, in my dream, I saw a *chamsah*. It was silver, fashioned with fingers of filigree, an eye so delicate it seemed to see me when I saw it, and small blue beads like stars of night along its edge. Now, I can envision nothing else. I must create the hand I dreamed."

Mashiach shrugged. There were still many necklaces and bracelets ready to be sold. Before they were gone, he hoped, his father would return to his senses.

But Shalom worked many days, fashioning and discarding what he fashioned, cutting and throwing away what he had cut. Nothing he crafted seemed right. And, day after day, there were fewer bracelets and fewer necklaces left to sell.

Mashiach said, "Father, soon we will have no jewelry for people to buy. Why not stop working on this hand for just a little while to make a few more pieces for us to sell?"

Shalom said, "You have watched me many years. You can make necklaces and bracelets to sell."

"I am not your equal," said Mashiach. "I am good at selling what you make, but I am not the craftsmen you are."

Shalom nodded. His son was right. He looked at the silver shape he was holding. It was still not the *chamsah* of his dreams. Every night he dreamed of the hand and knew just how it was made; and every day he tried making it and found it was not what he had dreamed.

He turned to Mashiach and said, "I cannot stop now. I know I am getting close. You can make the necklaces and the bracelets and, if they are not as fine as the ones I craft, then sell them for less."

It came to pass that Shalom did finish his *chamsah*. In all of Yemen, he knew, there was no other like it. It was the very hand of his dream. He showed it to a few of his jeweler friends and their eyes widened. Once they had seen it, they spoke of it. They hardly spoke of anything else. More jewelers came to see it. All said the same thing, "Shalom, this is your greatest work. It will bring you hundreds of pieces of gold. The word has spread. Everyone in town has heard about your *chamsah*. Soon, very soon, someone rich will come to buy it."

And all were astounded—especially Mashiach—when Shalom answered, "I did not make it for money. I do not think I will sell it."

That night, Shalom's wife said to him, "My dear husband, shall we starve? Mashiach makes nice jewelry, but it does not fetch enough money for our family. Would it not be best to sell the *chamsah*?" But Shalom was silent.

The next day, a wealthy Muslim merchant came. He had heard of the amulet. He asked to see it. And Shalom showed it to him. "Allah be praised!" the merchant said, "I have never seen the like of this in all my travels. This is not just a Hand of Fatimah, it is the very likeness of Fatimah's hand for delicacy and the very likeness of the eye of the Prophet himself for craft. I must have this for my wife. Behold, I will give you two hundred gold coins, and without bargaining!"

Shalom thought of his wife and his family. Sadly, he took the bag of gold and handed his beloved charm to the wealthy merchant.

That night, Shalom dreamed that a thief came and stole his gold coins. He woke in a sweat. He could not get back to sleep. He tossed and turned and worried all night. The next morning, he went out behind his workshop to bury the bag where it would be safe. But that night again, he could not sleep. He worried. What if the bag of money was gone? What if someone had already stolen his gold?

The next morning, he went to where he had buried the coins. He dug in the ground and found the bag just as he had left it. He buried it again in the same place. But all day long, as he tried to make necklaces, his hands faltered. He was too tired to work. Days passed this way and everyone knew that Shalom's work was not as wonderful as once it had been. His customers began to go to other jewelers for their bracelets and their necklaces.

Every morning, he went to check on his bag of gold and, lo, one morning it was gone! His heart jumped into his throat. His worst fears were realized. He paced back and forth across the ground. Who had stolen the bag? Suddenly, he saw it: A little hole in the wall of his neighbor, Yakub. It was clear that Yakub was guilty. After all, Yakub was the laziest man in Yemen; and the greediest man that Shalom knew.

That night, Shalom went to visit Yakub. "I need your help," he said.

Yakub smiled and said, "My dear neighbor, what an honor you pay by asking my help. How can I help you?"

Shalom said, "A man paid me in gold coins. A few days ago, he gave me two hundred coins in a bag and I buried the bag to keep it safe. Today, he gave me four hundred coins in a bag and I do not know what to do. Should I bury the bag of four hundred with the bag of two hundred? Or should I bury the bag of four hundred somewhere else?"

Yakub did not hesitate. He replied, "Why should you have to look for your gold in two different places? If two hundred is safe in one place, then six hundred will be safe in the same place."

Shalom said, "Thank you for your wisdom. It is as you say. Tomorrow morning I will bury the bag of four hundred with the bag of two hundred."

That night, the crafty Yakub buried the bag of two hundred gold coins where he had found them. The next morning, he watched through the small hole as Shalom went to bury the bag of four hundred gold coins. Yakub rubbed his hands together, thinking of how soon he would have six hundred gold coins. What a simpleton that Shalom was!

As for Shalom, he took the bag of gold coins from their hiding place and buried two bags of rocks. Then he went to the home of the wealthy Muslim merchant. He knocked and the merchant came to the door.

"I am returning the two hundred gold coins," he said, handing the bag to the merchant. "I did not make the Hand of Fatimah for money. I made it because it was in me to make it. I do not need or want the gold. I only hope the amulet brings good fortune to your wife."

The merchant was surprised. "But you deserve the money for making it," he said.

"It is too much money," said Shalom. "It causes me worry and sleeplessness. I never had so much and we do not need so much."

"I will give you fifty gold coins," said the merchant.

"Too much," Shalom said.

"Twenty-five gold coins."

"Too much."

The merchant laughed. "If you bargain like this, by Allah, you will always be a poor man!"

"No," said Shalom. "I will never be poor. I have my hands and my art."

The merchant pressed ten gold coins in his hands and Shalom put them in his pocket. "Thank you," he said.

The merchant said, "Make another Hand of Fatimah. I will buy it."

Shalom replied, "You are speaking to Shalom, the jeweler. Shalom makes the finest necklaces and bracelets in all of Yemen. Come to my workshop if you need a necklace or a bracelet."

And, with that, the two shook hands and Shalom went home to his family.

[adapted from a Turkish folk tale]

20. Too Clever

🐌 Beggars often find themselves closer to the ground than other folk. And that is how it came to pass that the town beggar found a little bag half-buried in the mud of the road on the day after a huge downpour. He opened the bag and, much to his astonishment, it contained one hundred gold coins. Just as he was celebrating his good fortune, he heard the voice of the town crier announcing over and again, "Isaac the merchant has lost a purse containing a large sum of money. He offers a goodly reward for its return."

Just because a Jew is a beggar does not mean that he is not honest. Even a beggar knows God's laws. When you find something, you must seek its owner. You can only keep what you find if no owner can be found. So, with a heavy heart, but with high hopes for the reward money, the beggar soon presented himself at the home of Isaac the merchant.

Isaac brought the beggar inside and took the purse. Opening it, he spilled the coins on the table and proceeded to count them, one by one. Halfway through the counting, he realized that the beggar had indeed returned every one of the hundred coins. Isaac thought to himself, "What a fool this beggar is! Why should I give him any reward whatever?"

As he was thinking this, the beggar stepped closer and bowed a little. "Kind sir," he said, in his most beggarly fashion, "if I could just have my reward, I will be on my way."

"What kind of reward should I give to a thief?" Isaac cried. "Why, here before your eyes I have counted out one hundred gold coins, but there were two hundred in my purse when I lost it. Did you really think that you could get away with your theft?"

The beggar was stunned. "I found one hundred coins and returned one hundred coins," he said.

"No. You found two hundred and kept one hundred. Well, so be it. Just leave my house and keep the other hundred as your reward. You will get no more from me." And Isaac rose to drive the beggar out.

But the beggar did not like to be bullied. He did not like Isaac the merchant. And he did not like being turned away empty-handed. "Let's take the case before the rabbi," he said.

Isaac laughed to himself. His plan was so good that the rabbi would surely be fooled. Soon, he thought, people will praise me for allowing the beggar to keep the "other hundred coins." So he agreed to go to the rabbi. He grabbed his walking stick and the purse filled with the coins and the two of them walked the short distance to the home of the rabbi.

The rabbi listened to them both. They were not strangers to him. He knew the beggar was honest and he knew that Isaac was greedy. Still, he was acting as a judge, so he could not be prejudiced.

The rabbi said, "It is the law that when two people stand seeking justice, they must stand as equals. So before I give my verdict, Isaac, you must place the purse here on the table."

Hesitating just a bit, Isaac realized he had no choice. As much as he hated to part with the purse again, if he did not place the purse on the rabbi's table, it would be the same as saying he was a liar. So he did.

The rabbi asked Isaac, "Did you say the purse you lost had two hundred gold coins?" Isaac said yes.

The rabbi asked the beggar, "And you say the purse you found had one hundred gold coins?" The beggar said yes.

"If so," the rabbi concluded, "This is my judgment. The purse that was found does not belong to Isaac. Hopefully, my dear Isaac, someone will find your purse, soon. In the meanwhile, since no one has come forward to claim this purse…" And, as he spoke, the rabbi took the purse full of coins and placed it in the hands of the beggar. "The purse belongs to the one who found it."

[adapted from Ausubel, *Treasury*, p. 85]

21. The Secret of the Seedling

🐚 A kingdom needs many skilled workers: gardeners, builders, shoemakers, tailors, launderers, farmers, bakers, and so on. Some professions may seem less essential but are filled nonetheless— acrobats, jesters, beggars, dog-trainers, and the occasional thief.

His mother named him after the prophet Ezekiel, but this Zeke was no prophet. Zeke was a thief. He preferred gold but he would take whatever he could steal. If you stood close by him in a crowd, you might come away without a bracelet, a purse, or a belt. But Zeke was a thief with honor. Whatever he took, he sold to Yosef the Second-Hand Man in his shop at the edge of the marketplace—a few doors, a wall, and a moat away from the king's palace. If you "lost" something or if something "went missing" during the day, that very night you knew you could buy it back cheaply at the shop of Yosef the Second-Hand Man. In this way, Zeke the Thief made a living—not taking too much and not taking too little, either.

But one day Zeke stole one thing too many. It did not even seem a serious theft. He was walking near the king's fig orchard when he had a curious thought: "Why does the king place guards at these fig trees day and night?" Just then, he noticed a sleeping guard, so he sneaked into the orchard and took just one fig.

The moment he bit into it, Zeke knew he was in trouble. Five guards circled him; and a moment later, the captain of the guards appeared. "You have eaten the king's fruit," the captain said. "The king himself will pronounce the punishment." The guards clapped Zeke in leg chains and took him to the prison, deep in the basement of the palace.

Hours passed, then a whole day, but at last the king appeared. "Did you not know the law?" he asked Zeke. "It is forbidden for anyone but the king to eat the fruit of these fig trees. You sinned with your mouth, but your head shall pay." The king motioned for the captain of the guards and Zeke saw that the captain was carrying a huge axe. The king said: "Now, my dear thief, do you have any last words to say before we make you a whole head shorter?"

Zeke shrugged his shoulders. "It is a shame to die, of course," he said. "But it is a still greater shame that my grandfather's secret will die with me."

The king hesitated. Here was something more interesting than a mere thief. "What kind of secret could you have from your grandfather that would make any difference to me?"

Zeke replied, "Your Majesty, my grandfather taught me how to plant a fig tree seedling so that it grows branches, leaves, and fruit all in a single night."

"I do not believe you," said the king. "It takes seasons and patience and care for a fig tree to grow and even more patience before its fruit is worth eating."

Zeke shrugged again. "If everyone knew the secret, Your Majesty, it would not be a secret."

The king thought about that. "I will make you a bargain," he said. "If you can show me how to plant a seedling tonight and tomorrow have figs from that tree, I will let you go. Otherwise...." and the king pointed to the captain with the axe. Zeke nodded.

The king commanded the captain, "Alert the court and all my ministers. Have them assemble at my orchard at dusk. The thief will plant tonight and we will have fresh figs in the morning, or else...."

Toward dusk, guards came to his cell and led Zeke to the king's orchard. Behold, the orchard was dressed up like a ball-room. Lanterns were hung from every tree, the king and queen sat on thrones upon a platform, and all the lords and ladies paraded in finery—the men in ruffled sleeves and the women in pointed feathered hats.

The royal gardener brought a red silk pillow to Zeke. On the pillow was a single seedling, a little bit of a fig tree, ready for planting. Then the king rose and spoke: "Now, my little thief, you will plant this seedling using your grandfather's secret."

Zeke bowed low and said, "Your Majesty, forgive me, but I cannot plant this seedling."

"Your life depends on it," the king returned.

"I know, but the problem is my grandfather's secret. The seedling can only grow into a tree overnight if it is planted by someone who has never stolen anything. So, you see, Your Majesty, I cannot plant it because I am a thief."

Zeke went on, "Nevertheless, the magic will work if we call upon your Lord Treasurer, the one who guards your money. Surely, he has never stolen, so he can plant the seedling for us."

The Lord Treasurer blushed. He cleared his throat. "Your Majesty," he said, "I have been your loyal treasurer these many years. But—who can say?—a coin may have slipped one day from the table and landed in the cuff of my sleeve—or even, perchance, in my purse. I cannot guarantee that I have never stolen anything."

In the same way, Zeke presented the pillow to one minister of state after another, offering each one the chance to plant the seedling. This one said, "As a child, I may have taken a few coins from my mother's purse when her back was turned." Another said, "A piece of extra land may somehow, accidentally, have been attached to some of my land." Another said, "Collecting the king's taxes can sometimes be confusing, some coins could easily have fallen into the bottom of my saddle bags." Even the Queen refused to plant the seedling. She raised her royal head and even refused to say why she refused!

At last, Zeke brought the pillow with the seedling before the throne of the king. He bowed and said, "Your Majesty, it is up to you. Surely, if *you* plant the seedling it will grow overnight. Surely, *you* have never stolen anything."

The king laughed. "You are a very clever thief," he said. "You have proved that even honest people sometimes make mistakes; and that many who seem honest on the outside may be less than honest on the inside. It is true that no one is perfect."

The king said, "I will let you go, this time. But take my advice: It is one thing to make an honest mistake; it is quite another to be a professional cheat, liar, trickster, and thief. You should find a new profession, my friend. A clever person like yourself should not need to steal."

[Rossel, adapted from a story in Ausubel, *Treasury*, p. 365]

4
Avodah
Labor and Service

1. Tending the Fields

🐚 Once upon a time, a king had a field. He wanted to hire a farmer to care for it. The first farmer he asked, replied, "Your Majesty, caring for your field would be too hard for me. I barely have enough strength to care for my own field." The king asked a second farmer, a third, a fourth, and a fifth—and all answered the same way: "Caring for two fields is just too much effort."

Finally, the king came upon a strong young farmer and asked, "Will you accept the care of my field?" The young man answered, "I will, Your Majesty." The king asked, "Will you till my field, sow the seed, and reap the crop?" The young man answered, "I will, Your Majesty."

A year went by and the king came to visit his field. He was shocked to discover that the ground had never been tilled, the seed had never been sown, and the crop had never been grown. Instead, he found the young man sleeping beneath an oak tree.

Now, the question is: With whom should the king be angry? Should he be angry at the five farmers who said they had no strength to care for his field? Or should he be angry at the young farmer who said, "I will care for it!"?

So, with people; and so, with nations. When God decided to give the Torah, God offered it to many nations. But each nation said, "We have enough laws. We have no strength for more commandments." Finally, God offered the Torah to a strong young nation, the Israelites, and they said, "We will accept the Torah and its commandments." But, if the Israelites fall asleep under an oak tree—if they forget God and the Torah—why should God be angry at the other nations?—God has every right to be angry with Israel!

[*Midrash Exodus Rabbah* 27:9]

183

2. Hidden Treasure

A farmer in the Galilee knew he was dying, so he gave away all his money to the poor. His two sons came to him and said, "Father, do you mean to leave us nothing at all?" But the farmer said to them, "I decided not to leave you money. But there is a great treasure on our farm and I am leaving you the farm and hoping that you will find it."

When the farmer died, his sons went out to the field and started digging to find the treasure. Every day, they came out with shovels and worked from dawn to dusk, seeking the treasure. One day, they looked up, and one brother said to the other, "Look, we have dug holes in nearly the whole field and we still have not found the treasure. We could dig more holes and we would still be poor."

The other said, "We can search for the treasure next year. In the meanwhile, we have turned over all the rich soil in the field, so why not plant it?"

They planted barley in the middle of the field and filled the holes around the outside of the field with olive trees. That year, the barley grew tall and they sold it for much money. Meanwhile, the olive trees bloomed for the first time and they tended them.

The next year, they came back and dug again, looking for the treasure. Again, they ended up with no treasure, but they sowed more barley and tended the olive trees again. And so it went, for several years. After a while, they not only made money from their barley, but also from the wonderful oil they pressed from their olives.

One year, the two brothers came to the fields at the time for digging and one said to the other, "Brother, why should we look any more for the treasure? Look, we are already rich men. We do not need to find the treasure."

The other brother said, "My dear brother, in truth, I think we have found the treasure that our father meant us to find."

"Why, dear brother," the first one said, "I think you are right. Our father left this field to the two of us and, because we shared the work together, it has become our treasure."

The rabbi who told this story explained: When God sent Adam and Eve out of the Garden of Eden, God told Adam, "I have hidden a treasure in the earth. If you work, you will find it."

[based on an Iraqi Jewish folktale; also in Certner, *101 Jewish Stories*]

3. God's Slaves

Why is the Exodus from Egypt mentioned in connection with the commandments? We can compare this to a king who had a son. Once, the son was taken prisoner and held for ransom. The king ransomed the boy, but not as a son, rather as a slave. In that way, if the boy should ever disobey the king, the king could say, "You are my slave."

When the son returned to his father, the king said, "Bring me my sandals. Put them on my feet for me." Then the son protested. So the king took out the bill of sale, showed it to the son, and said, "Never forget, you are my slave."

When God redeemed the Children of Israel, God redeemed them not as children, but as slaves, so that if God imposed decrees on them, and they refused to obey, God could say, "You are My slaves." God commanded, "You shall not make idols." But they began to protest. "You are My slaves," God reminded them. "On this condition, I redeemed You from Egypt: that I should decree and you should fulfill My commandments."

But consider God's kindness: A person acquires slaves to look after him and sustain him. But God acquired the Israelites as slaves so that God could look after and sustain them.

[*Sifre Numbers* 35a; *Sifre Deuteronomy* 77a]

4. God and Beauty

It is written: "This is my God and I will praise God" (Exodus 15:2). But the Rabbis of the Talmud read these words differently, to say, "This is my God and I will beautify God."

Rabbi Ishmael asked, "Is it really possible for a person to make God more beautiful? It must mean that we can bring beauty to serve God. We are created in God's image, therefore, I will make myself beautiful to God through the commandments. How? I will make a beautiful *lulav*, a beautiful *sukkah*, beautiful fringes, beautiful *tefillin*....

"I will have the scrolls of the Torah written with beautiful ink and a beautiful pen by the hand of skillful scribes; and I will wrap the scrolls in beautiful silk.

"It is a *mitzvah* to serve God with the best and most beautiful of things."

[Mechilta *Beshalach*; B. Talmud *Shabbat* 133b]

5. It Could Be You

Our rabbis taught: When Rabbi Akiva died, Rabbi Judah the Prince was born. When Rabbi Judah the Prince died, Rabbi Yudan was born. When Rabbi Yudan died, Rava was born. When Rava died, Rabbi Ashi was born.

So we learn that a righteous person does not leave this world until another righteous person is brought into being.

One of the students asked, "When a righteous person dies, how do we know who the next righteous person will be?"

Our rabbis taught: "It could be you. We never know until your life too comes to an end. For everything depends on the way you live your life."

[B. Talmud *Kiddushin* 72b; also in *Sefer HaAggadah*]

6. Cooperation

The Baal Shem Tov told this story:

Once in a northern country, a gloriously colored bird alighted atop the tallest tree and nested in its branches. The king of the country was told of the unusual bird and asked that feathers be brought to him so that he might use them. The people decided to make a living ladder to reach the bird. One stood upon the shoulders of another until they had almost succeeded.

But it took a long time to build the human ladder and those nearest the ground lost patience, shook themselves free, and the whole enterprise collapsed.

[Buber, *Early Masters*, pp. 54-55]

7. The Goat that Made the Stars Sing

No one remembers now, but there was a time when the stars would sing all night. They sang because of the sacred goat. Now, the sacred goat was not extraordinary in any way, except that he had horns so long that they reached into the heavens. At night, when the stars came out, the goat would raise his head to the skies and brush the stars gently with his horns, so that the stars vibrated as they twinkled, making a heavenly music that soothed the world.

One night, the goat heard a wailing. An old Jew was bemoaning the loss of his favorite snuffbox. "First, it was the destruction of the Temple," the old Jew was crying, "then another Temple, and then the Jews were forced to leave the Promised Land, and now I have lost my snuffbox. Will troubles never end?" The sacred goat could not bear to hear suffering, so he bent down and said to the old Jew, "Cut a piece from my horns, as much as you need to make a new snuffbox."

The old Jew cut off just the tip of one horn. He carved his new snuffbox and filled it with tobacco. But everywhere he went, people who saw the snuffbox remarked, "This is not just a snuffbox, it is a bit of heaven itself. See how it gleams and twinkles like the stars at night." And they asked the old Jew, "Where did you get this magical snuffbox?"

When he told them, they ran to find the sacred goat. Time after time, the sacred goat lowered its head. Bit by bit, the Jews took pieces of the horns. One snuffbox was made after another. Every snuffbox added to the fame of the horns of the sacred goat. And, one night, the stars stopped singing.

They still sparkle at night, of course, but now they are silent. The sacred goat still paces the earth, but his horns that used to reach the heavens are gone.

[Buber, *Later Masters*, pp. 288-289]

8. How Should We Serve God?

Night had fallen and the Havdalah had been recited. The Sabbath was over and the new week had begun. The rabbi sat beneath a tree, lighting his pipe and sending puffs of grey smoke into the clear, dark heavens.

Two students, seeing that the rabbi was in such a peaceful mood, placed themselves by his side. For a while the three sat in silence. Finally, one student spoke, "Tell us, dear rabbi, how should we serve God?"

"Can I know?" the rabbi replied. Then the three fell silent once more, except for the small sound that the rabbi made as he drew upon his pipe in smoking. At last the rabbi told this story:

Two friends once climbed a mountain and found themselves faced with a deep chasm to cross. Together they managed to throw a rope with a rock attached to its end across the chasm. When the rock snagged in the crook of a strong tree, they repeated their trick. Using these two anchors, they were able to create a narrow rope bridge from one side to the other. The first friend then walked across the chasm on one rope while holding on to the other. He risked his life at every step; but ultimately he reached the far side in safety.

The other friend, still standing in the same spot, cried out across the chasm: "Tell me, dear friend, how did you manage?"

"I do not know for sure," the first friend yelled back, "but whenever I felt myself toppling over to one side, I leaned toward the other."

[Rossel, *When a Jew Seeks Wisdom*; Buber, *Later Masters*, pp. 59-60]

ᨒᨒ 5 ᨒᨒ
Merit

1. A Good Name

ᨒᨒ Well has King Solomon said, "A good name is better than good oil" (Ecclesiastes 7:1).

Good oil is poured downwards; a good name tends upwards. Oil, however good, gets exhausted; not so a good name.

Good oil can only be possessed by the rich; the poor as well as the rich can rejoice in a good name.

Good oil we can only put from one vessel into another; whilst a good name circulates everywhere.

The best oil if put on a dead body becomes offensive; the memory of a good name brings glory to the dead. Oil put on the fire will burn; a good name stands proof against fire.

[*Midrash Samuel* 23]

"Rabbi Simeon said: There are three crowns: the crown of learning, the crown of priesthood, and the crown of royalty; but the crown of a good name excels them all" (Mishnah *Avot* 4:17). Scriptures concurs: "A good name is rather to be chosen than great riches" (Proverbs 23:1) and, "A good name is better than precious oil" (Ecclesiastes 7:1).

2. Testing the Righteous

ᨒᨒ Rabbi Jonathan taught: "God tests the righteous" (Psalms 11:5). Think of a potter. If he has a cracked pot, there is no reason to test it. A single tap would break it. But if a pot looks whole, it can be tested a hundred times, for no matter how many times the potter tests it, a good pot does not break.

In the same way, God does not bother testing the wicked. They are already broken. But God does test the righteous.

[*Midrash Genesis Rabbah* 32:3]

3. Rothschild's Fortune

A businessman asked one of the heads of the House of Rothschild how much his great fortune totaled. Rothschild reached into a drawer and took out a ledger that contained entries of all of his charitable contributions. Patiently, he added the figures, and then reported the sum total of his wealth.

Believing his boss had taken out the wrong ledger by mistake, his secretary handed him the general ledger. To this, Rothschild answered gently. "I made no mistake! Everyone knows that I own mines and properties, business ventures and securities. But mines can be flooded and properties confiscated. War can disrupt my enterprises and render my securities worthless. Only the figures in my charity ledger record what is truly mine. This I am worth; this no one can take away from me."

[adapted from Bunim, *Ethics from Sinai*, v.3, p. 159]

4. Giving Wisdom to Fools

A Roman lady asked Rabbi Yose bar Chalafta, "Is it true, as it is written in the Book of Daniel, that God is always 'giving wisdom to the wise' (11:21)?" Rabbi Yose answered, "It is true."

The lady inquired, "Wouldn't it be better if your God gave wisdom to fools?"

Rabbi Yose asked, "Do you have any precious jewels?"

She answered, "Of course."

Rabbi Yose said, "If a beggar came and asked to borrow them would you give your jewels to the beggar?"

She laughed and said, "Surely, not!"

"If a wealthy merchant came and asked to borrow them, would you give your jewels to the merchant?"

"I would give the jewels, if the merchant were a responsible fellow."

"In other words," Rabbi Yose said, "you will lend your jewels to one you trust, but not to one of whom you are unsure. If so, you have answered your own question. God gives wisdom to the wise— to those who already have proved that they know how to use wisdom. Fools must take the first steps toward wisdom on their own."

[*Tanchuma Buber* 97a-97b]

5. Honor Your Father

🐚 When Rabbi Ulla was asked, "How far should honoring one's father and mother extend?" he replied, "Go and see what a certain pagan named Dama ben Netinah did for his father in Ashkelon.

Our sages sought to buy a jasper gem from Dama for the breastplate of the robe of the High Priest. They offered him sixty myriads of gold dinars—a princely sum. Dama said, "Allow me to go in the back and consult my father."

When he returned to the shop, he said, "I cannot sell the gem."

The sages were disappointed. They said, "We shall offer you eighty myriads of gold dinars," for they thought he wanted a better price. "Go and consult your father again."

Dama went in the back a second time, but when he returned he said, "I cannot sell it."

The sages grew angry. They needed this jasper for the High Priest, but there was a limit to how much they could afford. They whispered to one another, then said, "We can offer you ninety myriads, but tell your father we can offer no more!"

Dama left the shop the third time. When he returned he said, "I can sell you the gem now."

The sages began counting out dinars and when they reach sixty myriads, Dama handed them the jasper and said, "That was the bargain, sixty myriads."

The sages were mystified. "We thought you wanted a higher price," they said. "But if it was not the price that bothered you, then why did you not sell us the gem for sixty myriads in the first place?"

Dama replied, "The key to the drawer in which the jasper was kept was under my father's pillow. The first time I entered his chamber, my father was asleep. I could not disturb him. Nor could I disturb him the second time, for he was still sleeping. But the third time, he was awake and he was glad to hear that we could sell the jasper and proud to hear that the jasper would be placed in the breastplate of your High Priest."

For honoring his father in this way, the Holy One rewarded Dama, as we are told: The following year a rare red heifer was born in his herd. When the sages of Israel heard of it, they came to buy it for the Temple, Dama said to them, "I know you fellows. Even if I were to ask all the money in the world, you would pay me. But all I ask of you is the amount I lost the last time, when I honored my father."

Rabbi Chanina said: If a non-Jew like Dama—one who is not commanded to honor his father and mother—nevertheless honors them, and if Heaven rewards him in this way, how much more so will Heaven reward a Jew—one who is commanded—and does honor to parents!

[B. Talmud *Kiddushin* 31a]

6. Like Zusya

The students of Reb Zusya, hearing that their teacher was about to die, came to pay him one last visit. But entering the room, they were surprised to see him trembling with fear.

"Are you afraid of death?" they asked him. "What have you to fear? In your life, you have been as righteous as Moses himself!"

"When I stand before the throne of judgment," Zusya replied, "I will not be asked, 'Reb Zusya, why were you not like Moses?' I will be asked, 'Reb Zusya, why were you not like Zusya?'"

[Buber, *Early Masters*, p. 251]

7. Heaven Knocking

Our *rebbe*, Moshe Leib, was a great hulk of a man, but toward the end of his life, he suffered constant pain. Nevertheless, it was said that he rose every night at midnight to recite lamentations over the destruction of Jerusalem. When Rabbi Zvi Hirsh was a guest in our rabbi's house, he was awakened at midnight by noise from the rabbi's room and he quickly dressed and went to see what was the problem.

He saw Rabbi Leib go out into the night. Grabbing his coat and hat, Rabbi Hirsh followed at a respectful distance to see what would transpire. Our *rebbe* entered the shed and emerged carrying a load of firewood in his massive arms. He walked to a hut at the edge of town. Could any hut be more miserable? The porch had not been cleared of snow and Rabbi Hirsh could see by the chimney that no fire was lit. The hut must be very chilly, he thought. As our *rebbe* entered the hut, Rabbi Hirsh crept to a back window and peeked inside. On the bed, huddled beneath a blanket, lay a woman and her newborn child.

Our *rebbe* spoke to the woman in the local tongue, saying, "I have wood for sale and the load is heavy. I do not wish to carry it any more. I will sell it to you for a bargain price."

The woman groaned. "There is not a pfennig in the house," she said.

But our *rebbe* insisted. "I will return for the money later, when the weather changes."

The woman said, "The wood is of no use to me. I have no axe to chop the wood, and I do not think I could chop it myself, in any case."

"Think nothing of it," our *rebbe* said. He went back outside, picked up the axe he had carried under the pile of logs, and chopped the wood into small pieces. And while he was chopping, Rabbi Hirsh heard our *rebbe* singing the midnight lamentations under his breath. Then our *rebbe* took the wood inside and built a fire in the stove. As he added the wood, piece by piece, he still sang the soft prayers. The baby stopped crying; and mother and baby fell asleep, as the room warmed and the glow of the fire suffused the little hut in a golden haze.

Only then did our *rebbe* leave the hut, walking quickly to make his way home. Afterward, Rabbi Hirsh would say that only one thing could awaken our *rebbe* that way, night after night, precisely at midnight. It had to be heaven, knocking on his heart.

[Buber, *Later Masters*, pp. 86-87]

8. Choni the Circle Maker

No rain fell in the Land of Israel. The sun came by day and the moon by night, but no cloud darkened the skies. In the towns, people worried. Without rain, there would be no water in the valleys. Without water, there would be no grain. Without grain, there would be no bread. If rain did not come soon, there would be hunger by the end of the year. Farmers would lose their farms. Famine would spread. The whole month of Adar, when rain should fall, people watched the skies for a sign of a cloud, but not even a wisp of white was seen.

Everyone went to the synagogue to pray for rain, but their prayers went answered. The month of Adar passed and the rain never came.

The town elders met. "It may be that we have done something wrong," one of the elders said. "Perhaps God is angry with us."

"Could God have forgotten us?" asked another.

"In truth, we are not wise enough to know why God does not send the rain," said a third. "And our prayers cannot force God to send it."

To this, all agreed. One of the elders moaned, "For most things we need, we can work or study. When it comes to rain, only God can help."

Now the wisest stood and spoke: "Many of us are good people, but we seldom go to the synagogue. When we pray to God, we are like a dog or cat asking for food from its owner. God loves us, but it is as difficult for God to understand us as it is for us to understand our pets. Yet there is one among us who studies God's ways night and day. He is a master of the Torah, a great teacher and sage. He is not like God's pet; he is more like a member of God's own family. Let us call on Choni to pray for us."

So the elders came to Choni, saying, "Pray for rain to fall. We must have rain or we shall all suffer and die."

Choni prayed for rain. But no rain came.

"The Bible must reveal a way to force God to bring the rain," Choni thought. He studied. When he came to the books of the Prophets, he found the story of Habakkuk. "Here is the way," he told the elders. "When Habakkuk wanted God to answer his questions, he stood inside a circle and waited. That is what I must do."

With the elders of the town following him, Choni climbed to the top of a hill. Using his walking stick, Choni drew a circle in the earth and stood inside the circle.

"Holy One, Ruler of the universe," Choni called out, "Your children have asked me to pray for rain. I swear that I shall not leave this circle until You have mercy on Your children and send them rain."

Choni stood in his circle and waited. From out of the east, a breeze came forth and a single small gray cloud appeared like a dot. As it grew, Choni felt drops of rain fall on him. For a few minutes there was a gentle drizzle and then it stopped. The cloud passed over, and the rain ceased.

The elders of the town said, "Truly, we have seen a miracle: God has answered your prayer. But this was not enough rain to make a difference to us, only enough to answer your prayer."

Then Choni raised his voice to the heavens again. "Ruler of the universe, it is not for a drizzle that I prayed. I shall not leave this circle until You send a rain that will soak the land, fill the wells, and make the rivers rush."

This time there was no waiting. The skies darkened, the windows of the heavens opened, and rain gushed forth. Each and every drop could fill a bucket. The land was soaked in an instant. And still the rain beat against the earth.

Choni called out: "Holy One, I did not pray for such a rain. I only asked for a peaceful rain, a loving rain, a rain to save Your people."

At once, the rain turned gentle. It fell quietly from billowing white clouds, even as the sun shone through. The rain watered the land and filled the wells. It flowed down the hillsides into the valley and filled the rivers. The elders called to Choni, "Look there!"

Choni looked where the elders pointed and saw that the rivers were now flooding and the wells were overflowing. People were running for the tops of the hills to escape the rushing waters below. "If this continues," the elders said, "we shall all drown. As you prayed for rain to save our lives, now you must pray for it to end."

Choni turned his head to the heavens again. "Holy One, we thank You for the miracle You have done for us. Now hear the cries of Your people: When You ignore them, they seek Your voice. When You are angry with them, they cannot stand Your anger. When You give them too much of a good thing, they cannot bear Your goodness. Be gentle with them. Let the rain end so You may hear their words of thanks."

The breeze came again from the east. The clouds blew away; the skies cleared; and the rain ceased from falling. Choni left his circle and returned home. The people went to gather the mushrooms that sprout after the rain.

The next day, Simeon ben Shetach sent word to Choni: "You acted like a spoiled brat. You are like a child who says to his parents, 'I want a hot bath.' So they heat water and bathe him. Then the child says, 'I want a cold bath.' So they bring cold water and bathe him. Then the child says, 'I want grapes and dates, walnuts and almonds, peaches and pomegranates to eat.' So they bring him fruits and nuts. This time God has listened to you as parents listen to a spoiled child. But, beware, parents soon run out of patience. If you try to force God to work a miracle for you again, you may not be so lucky."

Choni never again tried to force God to answer a prayer. Yet the people remembered what Choni had done for them, and from that time forth, they called him Choni the Circle Maker.

[B. Talmud *Taanit* 23a; also in *Sefer HaAggadah*]

9. Pipe Dreams

🐚 A holy man, one of the great masters, died. To provide sustenance for his widow, and to keep his memory fresh, his followers came to buy his clothing and other mementos by which to remember him. When nearly all of the small collection of worldly goods that had belonged to the master were gone, the widow noticed that the master's chief disciple had bought nothing. "Surely," she said, "there is something that you want. And, if you cannot afford to buy something, perhaps there is something that I can give you."

"You are kind," the disciple replied. "And, as you know, I come from an affluent family. Money is not the issue. But I had fixed my heart to bid on only one object, and I have not noticed it at all."

"Speak then," she said. "What is it that you wanted?"

"I remember," said the disciple, "that the master spoke of having visions as he smoked his pipe. I had hoped to purchase that pipe for my own."

The widow said, "His pipe. I intended to keep that memento for myself. It was precious to my late husband."

"Nevertheless," the disciple said, "it might sustain you in your old age. Name a high price, and allow me the privilege of purchasing it."

After a moment's thought, she answered in a tentative voice, "Perhaps, a hundred rubles would cause me to part with it."

The disciple smiled, "The price is high. I should be allowed to try the pipe to be certain that it is sound. Let me smoke it once, then, just to test it."

The widow opened a drawer and handed him the pipe. The disciple sat down, filled the pipe from his own pouch of tobacco, and lit it.

As he drew upon the stem the first time, the widow, the room, and the cottage disappeared. He found himself in the foyer of a great palace with marble columns stretching into the distance as far as the eye could see.

As he drew upon the stem yet again, the marble columns melted away like ice. A light brighter than any he had known heretofore forced him to shut his eyes tightly. Grasping the pipe tighter in his hand, he drew upon the stem a third time.

With the third puff of smoke, the light faded. He found himself in a wasteland beneath a night sky populated with a myriad of stars. Looking up, he saw the seven gates of Heaven and felt himself being wafted gently upward like the smoke itself.

The vision was so overpowering that his mouth fell open in astonishment. With that, the pipe dropped from his lips, landing in his lap. Its scattering ashes threatened to set him afire. Jarred back to mundane reality, he jumped to his feet, seized the pipe in one hand, and brushed the ashes from his clothes with the other. Then he smiled at the astonished widow and counted out the hundred rubles she had asked.

Arriving home, the disciple immediately filled the pipe and lit it again. He puffed once, but nothing happened. He puffed again, but still remained in his room, smoking the pipe before his hearth. Time and again he drew upon the pipe, but no vision appeared. "I have been tricked," he thought darkly.

Deeply perturbed, he sought out another learned disciple of the master and told his story.

"It is a simple matter," his friend said. "The first time you smoked the pipe, it still belonged to our departed master. You saw what the master saw when he smoked. But then you purchased the pipe and it became your pipe. You saw what you always see! In this life, the dreams and visions we are granted are those we are ready to receive. Make yourself worthy and the pipe will serve for you as it served for our master."

[Rossel, *Bible Dreams*]

Once, a sorcerer's apprentice, after watching his master for many months, decided to commandeer the sorcerer's wand and do some magic on his own. But, no matter how much he waved, no matter what combination of words he uttered, the wand did not seem to work for him. He concluded that the wand had only one master at a time. Later, he offered this opinion to the sorcerer, who laughed and said, "Do you imagine that the wand is the secret? Have you given no thought to its passage through the air, to the hand and the way the wand is grasped, to the motion of the wave, or to the direction the wand must point? Have you forgotten to consider the spirits of the other world? Have you neglected to wear my robe, my cap, my shoes, and my purse? My dear young apprentice, none of these is of any use to you. The only way to become a sorcerer is to give yourself to the wand. Only then will you begin to understand that it is not the sorcerer making the magic, it is the magic making the sorcerer its path." As Rabban Gamaliel taught: "Make God's will your will, so that God may do your will as God's will. Set your will aside in the face of God's will, so that God may set aside the will of others before your will" (Mishnah *Avot* 2:4).

6

Rich and Poor

1. Only One Room

🖎 Wherever Jews spoke Yiddish—in Russia, Poland, Bulgaria, Rumania, Lithuania, Hungary, Germany, Czechoslovakia, and lands too numerous to mention—they told this story:

A man—a tailor—really, a mender of clothes—came to see his rabbi. "Rabbi," he said, "I am in pain and suffering. My head throbs from early morning to late in the evening. I am in misery and grief. Even my dreams are no relief. You must help me."

The rabbi asked, "Tell me, what is causing you so much trouble?"

"I live in a one-room house," the tailor replied. "One room used to seem like enough space for me and my excellent wife. But, rabbi, my excellent wife presented me with five excellent children—three excellent daughters and the excellent twins, both boys. Naturally, what one child touches another demands. So there is crying and screaming from dawn to dusk. One day, my wife's mother came to visit and stayed to live with us. My own mother, may she be blessed, heard of this, so she came to live with us, too. The table is too small, so we take turns eating. Everyone is talking and yelling all at once, all the time. In all the commotion, I can hardly thread a needle. When customers come to bring me work… Well, they flee before they ever find me. Who wouldn't? Our little room is mad with people scrambling and running, talking and jabbering, jostling and kicking."

"What would you like?" the rabbi asked.

The tailor sighed a huge sigh. He said, "If only I were as wealthy Reb Shmuel the merchant, or as well-off as Reb Yoni the forester. If only I could afford to add another room to my house." Then he stood silent before the rabbi.

The rabbi pointed a finger at the tailor and spoke to him like a father. "I will tell you what to do," he said, "and you must do ex-

199

actly as I say. You must bring your chickens into your house and return to me in one week's time."

The poor man gave the rabbi a quizzical stare. Finally, he said, "Very well, rabbi, if that is your wisdom, I shall try it."

A week later, the tailor appeared again. The rabbi asked, "How is your room now?"

"Rabbi, things are worse than before. We used to trip over one another, but now we trip over one another and trip over chickens, too. Chairs fall and plates break. The twins pull at the chickens' wings. And the squawking... How can I tell you about the squawking? Tell me, Rabbi, what can I do to make things better?"

Like a loving parent talking to a child, the rabbi said, "I will tell you what to do and you must do exactly as I say. Bring your goat into your house and return to me in one week's time."

The tailor just stared. Finally, he shrugged and said, "If that is your wisdom, rabbi, I shall try it."

In exactly one week, the tailor appeared again. He did not wait for the rabbi to ask him how things were. He just started talking. "Rabbi, the goat eats my thread; the chickens eat my bread; the children kick the goat; the goat kicks the chickens; my wife screams from day up to sun down; my mother threatens my mother-in-law; my mother-in-law tells my wife to leave me. There is no room to move. Everything is worse than before. Tell me, Rabbi, what can I do to make things better?"

The rabbi said, "I will tell you what to do and you must do exactly as I say. You must bring your cow into your house and return to me in one week's time."

One week passed. When the tailor appeared his coat was in shreds and his trousers had holes in them. There were big black rings beneath his eyes as if he had not slept in days. "Tell me," the rabbi said, "how is your one room now?"

The tailor spoke slowly, with tears in his eyes. "The noise is dreadful. The smell is awful. We sleep standing up because there are animals on every bed. We eat from pots because the table cannot be reached. Even if we could reach the table, there would be no space to set the chairs beside it. Rabbi, I will tell you in truth, if before I was a poor man, today I am destitute."

The rabbi pointed his finger at the tailor. He spoke like a commanding father. "Do exactly what I say: Take the chickens out of your house, remove the goat, and put the cow back in the yard. Return to me in one week's time."

A week passed and the tailor returned. His coat was mended and so were his trousers. His eyes were clear and sparkling. There was a smile on his lips. "Rabbi, O Rabbi," he said, "you have turned my house into a castle. I never before imagined how big a single room could be! What can I say, Rabbi? You are a worker of miracles!"

[Yiddish folktale]

2. Six Days

Rabbi Yochanan was walking with Rabbi Chiya from Tiberius to Sephoris. They came to a farm. "You see this farm," he said to Rabbi Chiya. "I used to own this farm. I sold it so I could spend my time studying the Torah."

Walking a little farther, they came to a grove of olive trees. "You see these olive trees," Yochanan said. "I used to own them. I sold them so I could spend my time studying Torah."

Reaching the hills, they saw a vineyard with grapes hanging from every vine. "You see this vineyard," said Yochanan. "I used to own it. I sold it so I could spend my time studying Torah."

Suddenly, Rabbi Chiya became very sad.

"Chiya, my friend, what makes you sad?" asked Yochanan.

"Looking at all you owned and all you sold makes me sad," replied Chiya. "If you had kept these things, you would have been rich in your old age."

Rabbi Yochanan smiled. "Do you think I was foolish? I sold things that were worth only six days, and I gained something worth forty days and forty nights. It took God only six days to create the entire world, but God spent forty days and forty nights revealing the Torah to Moses at Sinai."

[*Midrash Leviticus Rabbah* 30:1; also in *Sefer HaAggadah*]

3. *Matzah* Is a Reminder

A poor man found a treasure and suddenly became rich. Even so, he ate *matzah* at every meal to remind him of the hard bread he ate when he was poor. In time, the same man lost his fortune and became poor again. Even so, he went on eating *matzah* at every meal. His friends asked, "Why do you always eat *matzah*?" He answered, "One day, I will be rich again. The *matzah* is just a reminder."

The Maggid of Dubno explained: "When we were slaves in Egypt, we ate hard bread. When we went free, we felt rich. Even so, we ate *matzah* to remind us of the many years we were slaves. Today, some of us are free and some are not. One day, all Israelites everywhere will be free. The *matzah* is just a reminder."

[Rossel, *Storybook Haggadah;* adapted from *Parables of the Preacher of Dubno* (Yiddish)]

4. Reb Yechiel's Candlesticks

In a tavern, two Jews were gossiping about a certain Reb Yechiel, a wealthy merchant, famous for never giving charity. If a needy Jew came to Reb Yechiel, the merchant would give the Jew what he thought was necessary, saying, "This is a loan. In God's good time, you will pay me back—you can pay me in a lump sum or in installments, whatever you think best. And, if I am no longer here, you will take care to give the money back to someone else." So, you see, the gossipers agreed, Reb Yechiel never gave charity.

That evening, Reb Yechiel came home from the synagogue. When he entered his doorway, he was shocked to find a stranger in his home. As Yechiel approached, the stranger's face turned white; and Yechiel immediately saw that the stranger was hiding something beneath his coat. It seemed obvious that this was not a professional thief, but a poor Jew who had given in to temptation. He had stolen something.

But Reb Yechiel faced the stranger with a friendly smile. "I see that you have come to borrow some money," he said, "and that you have brought something of value with you to secure your pledge. Would you be kind enough to show me what you brought?"

Slowly, the thief took two gold Sabbath candlesticks from under his coat and put them on the table. Reb Yechiel sat down and studied them carefully, as if he had never seen them before. "These are worthy items," he said. "How much do you think I should lend you against these?"

But the stranger was speechless. His mind said "Flee!" but his feet seemed nailed to the floor.

"I will tell you what," Reb Yechiel went on. "I will speak. All you need do is nod or shake your head. So, let's see, Passover is coming and you probably need money for *matzah*. Am I correct?"

The stranger nodded.

"That was easy," Reb Yechiel said, "The next is more of a wild guess. Do you have a daughter at home, one who wants to be married but has no dowry?"

The stranger nodded and started to weep.

Reb Yechiel said, "Come, now. I am here to give you a loan, not to put up with tears. Kindly compose yourself, and let's do business as equals."

"I think you might sell these candlesticks for thirty-five or forty rubles. I'll lend you thirty—all right, I'll make it forty rubles. Fifteen rubles will be enough for Passover, another fifteen will be enough for a dowry for your daughter, and you can use the extra ten rubles for a wedding dress. I am sure that whatever else you need, God will provide. In God's good time, you will pay me back— you can pay me in a lump sum or in installments, whatever you think best. And, if I am no longer here, you will take care to give the money back to someone else."

And so the would-be thief left Reb Yechiel's house with forty rubles in his hand, a loan of forty rubles he had secured with Reb Yechiel's own candlesticks!

[I.L. Peretz, possibly from the same source employed by Victor Hugo in *Les Miserables*, often anthologized as "The Bishop's Candlesticks"]

5. Making *Aliyah*

"Going up!" That is how Jews throughout history have always announced that they are returning to the Holy Land. "Going up" in Hebrew is *aliyah*, and so Jewish pilgrims say, "I am 'making *aliyah*.'" Many years ago, in the city of Chelm, a beggar named Ammi suddenly felt ready to go to the homeland of his ancestors. "I am making *aliyah*," he told people on the street. "I am making *aliyah*," he told people in the synagogue.

To his surprise, that week, people gave Ammi an extra coin here and there. Ammi thought, "This is good. People like the idea that I am making *aliyah*."

Taking some of the extra coins to the tavern, he bought a drink. He asked the men, "How far is it to Jerusalem?" Most shrugged their shoulders, but one rogue said, "Seven hundred hours, but if you go by way of the city of Luvov, taking the foot-path, you will save a quarter of an hour."

So Ammi, in order to save the quarter of an hour, went by way of Luvov. And that was not a bad thing. If you don't take advantage of life's little helps, you will never get any large ones. It's always easier to save or to earn a *grosz* than a *zloty*, but thirty *grosz* make a *zloty*. And if a pilgrim making a journey of seven hundred hours could save a quarter of an hour every thirty hours, how much would he save during the whole trip? Who wants to figure it out?

Of course, Ammi was going toward the Holy Land, but his deeper concerns were an easy life and good food, so Luvov was as good as Chelm to him. As the old proverb says, "A beggar can never take a wrong turn." Ammi could beg in Luvov just as he had in Chelm.

So Ammi bethought himself to travel the high road, to pass by wealthy houses, places known for good cooking. He worked out a plan for eating well all the way to the Holy Land. Whenever he came to a good inn, run by nice Jewish folk, he would enter and say, "I am making *aliyah*, can you spare some water soup with pebbles for a poor pilgrim?" When the sympathetic Jews said, "Pilgrim, pebbles will sink to the bottom of your stomach and lay there like dead weight," Ammi would reply, "Right! That's why I choose them. Pebbles last longer than bread and it is a long way to Jerusalem. But if you could spare a little wine with them, to help a pilgrim to the Holy Land, then of course I could digest them more easily."

Always the innkeepers would say, "But, pious pilgrim, such a soup can surely give you no strength, Here, won't you take some bread, some chicken soup, and maybe a few forkfuls of vegetables, or a little piece of meat?" With that, Ammi would sit at the table like a king, attacking the meal with gusto, until he had consumed the last crumb, strand, and drop of the bread, wine, meat, vegetables, and broth.

Finally, Ammi would say, "Bless you, my dear innkeeper. All I wanted was some pebble soup, but now I am too full to eat it. But do me this favor: save the pebbles for the pilgrims who follow me. It's a long way to Jerusalem, and pebbles last longer than bread."

Lo, these many years later, Jerusalem is still waiting to catch sight of Ammi. But, no matter. As Ammi himself will tell you, "A Jew can make a profitable business out of making *aliyah!*"

[Rossel based on *"Die Jesuiten in Wien," Schweizerbote*, v. 1, no. 38 (September 21, 1804), pp. 302 ff.]

6. How It Feels to Be Poor

One cold winter evening, the shoemaker's wife gave birth. The shoemaker suddenly discovered that he had run out of wood to light the stove for heat and had no money for wood or food. Not knowing what else to do, he went to see the rabbi. The shoemaker explained the reason for his visit. But the rabbi said, "I have dispensed every bit of charity given to me this week, so I cannot help you. Perhaps, one of our richer folk would be willing to help."

The two of them walked to the house of the town's richest man and knocked at his door. "Who is there?" the rich man called. His voice sounded annoyed. And, in truth, he had been lying in bed, trying hard to fall asleep.

"It is your rabbi," came back the voice beyond the door.

The rich man grumbled, but he arose, dressed quickly, and opened the door. "Come in, rabbi, come in," he said, trying to sound friendly.

"No," said the rabbi, "let us talk right here."

"Why here?" asked the rich man. "It is awfully cold outside and all three of us are shivering."

"What we need to discuss is urgent," said the rabbi, "I do not have even the time to come inside."

"Then, let us close the door," the rich man offered. "The cold is more than I can bear."

But the rabbi stood firmly in the doorway and the door remained open.

Now, the rabbi was well-known as a teller of tales and he began to tell one story after another. He spoke of Abraham and of Moses; of Micah and of Jeremiah; of Rabbi Yochanan and of Akiva. He talked. He quoted. He taught. Time slipped on.

"Yes, yes, rabbi," cried the rich man. "I know these were all worthy Jews, but I am dying of the cold and you have still not reached your point."

The rabbi said, "That is precisely my point! You stand in the open door for only a few minutes and already you are chilled to the bone. Now, look at our poor shoemaker! His wife just gave birth, he has no wood to heat his house, and his wife and baby are cold and hungry. You are cold for only a minute, yet you do not suffer what he suffers day and night."

"Dear rabbi," the rich man said, "well have you made your point. If you and the shoemaker will be kind enough to come inside and close the door, I will give him money enough to help him buy wood and feed his family." The rabbi then suffered the door to close behind them and the three proceeded to the rich man's study, where he gave the shoemaker a generous gift. Then the rabbi and the shoemaker left. And the rich man found, when he reached his bed and his warm covers again, that he fell immediately into a very restful sleep.

> [variously attributed to Rabbi Levi Yitzchak of Berditchev, Rabbi Shmelke of Nikolsburg, the Maggid of Dubno, and other Chasidic masters]

The rabbis opined: "More than the householder does for the beggar, the beggar does for the householder" (*Midrash Leviticus Rabbah* 34:8).

7. Ready to Receive

🙶 Once on the Great Sabbath, the Sabbath which comes just before Passover, Rabbi Naftali of Ropchitz came home exhausted from the synagogue. "Why are you so tired?" his wife asked.

"It was the sermon," he replied. "Passover is coming and the cost of *matzah* and wine and everything else is terribly high this year. So I spoke about the poor and their many needs."

"Was your sermon successful?" his wife inquired.

"Halfway," he said. "You see, the poor are now ready to receive. As for the other half—whether the rich are ready to give—it's still too early to say."

> [Buber, *Later Masters*, p. 197]

8. Torah Is the Best Merchandise

🙶 A well-known scholar of Torah was journeying by ship with some wealthy merchants. As the passengers quizzed one another, each telling what merchandise they had stored in the ship's hold, they finally turned to the scholar and asked, "What kind of merchandise did you bring?"

"My merchandise," the scholar replied, "is beyond value."

"I watched every bit of cargo being loaded," one said, "but I did not see you watching after the safety of any."

"My merchandise," the scholar answered, "is not in the hold of the ship."

"In that case," said another, "there must not be much of it."

They had not sailed far, when the ship was attacked by pirates. The pirates transferred all the goods in the hold to their ship, took everything valuable from the travelers, and left. Both passengers and crew were grateful to have escaped with their lives.

When the ship made port, the merchants, dressed in the rags that had been left them by the pirates, were forced to beg. The scholar, however, had worn no finery to begin with, so the pirates had found nothing to take from him. Soon, he was invited to teach at the House of Learning. His talks were so edifying that he attracted great crowds. People invited him to house after house to dine; and finally they offered him a great sum to settle there and stay among them as their teacher.

The merchants he had sailed with did not fare so well. Not only had they lost all their merchandise, but they had no trade or profession to practice. In near desperation, they turned to the scholar for help. The scholar used his influence to find them all employment.

It was clear to them now that, indeed, it had been the scholar who had brought the most valuable goods aboard the ship. "Torah," they all agreed, "is the best merchandise."

[Tanchuma *Terumah*]

7
The World and Its Ways

1. Suffering

While Rabbi Shmelke was visiting his teacher Rabbi Dov Baer, the Maggid of Mezeritch, he asked the Maggid, "Why do the sages of the Talmud demand that we praise God for suffering in the same way that we praise God for health and well-being? It is easy to be joyful when God sends good our way, but, tell me, do the sages truly believe we can receive suffering with joy?"

The Maggid said, "Go to the House of Study. Zusya is there, smoking his pipe. Zusya can give you the answer."

Rabbi Shmelke went to ask Zusya his question. Now, it was well-known that Zusya was what people call "ill-fated." Since the day of his birth, Zusya had been visited by all manner of hardship. Rabbi Shmelke did not want his question to seem personal; and he certainly did not wish to embarrass Zusya in any way. So, when he saw Zusya, puffing on his pipe, he whispered a quiet hello, then pulled a chair nearby and sat in silence.

Zusya took the pipe from his mouth for a moment to welcome Rabbi Shmelke. He asked, "Were you sent to me by the Maggid?"

"He sent me because I asked a question. The Maggid said you could answer it."

Puffs of white smoke rose like little curls in the air above Zusya's head. "Ask me your question," he said.

Rabbi Shmelke spoke his piece, ending with, "Do the sages truly believe that we can receive suffering with joy?"

At that, Zusya laughed.

Rabbi Shmelke was taken aback. "Do you think mine is a foolish question?" he asked.

"Oh, no," Zusya replied. "It is only that I cannot imagine why the Maggid would send you to me for the answer. I know about being joyful. I feel the need to praise God at all times. But, in truth, I cannot ever recall experiencing suffering."

With that, Rabbi Shmelke had his answer. Others knew Zusya as a man of suffering, but Zusya met suffering by turning his heart to God in joy. In that way, Zusya felt only the love of God. Zusya did not know suffering at all.

[Buber, *Early Masters*, pp. 237-238]

2. The Princess and Rabbi Joshua

A beautiful princess saw Rabbi Joshua in the marketplace. "What a pity you are so ugly," she said. "You have so much wisdom, but Your God put it into such an ugly body."

"Does your father have much wine?" Rabbi Joshua asked the princess. She nodded, answering, "Very much."

"In what does he keep his wine?" the rabbi asked.

She answered, "In clay jugs."

"Clay jugs are all very well for the common people," said Rabbi Joshua, "but you are royal folk."

The princess asked, "In what should we keep our wine?"

"You are so important," Rabbi Joshua replied, "that you should keep your wine in jugs of silver and gold."

The princess went off and told her father what the rabbi had said. Then the emperor placed all his wine in jugs of silver and gold. But when the wine touched the metal, it began to sour. Before long, all the emperor's wine had turned to vinegar.

The emperor asked his daughter, "Who gave you this advice?"

"The wise Rabbi Joshua."

So the emperor called for Rabbi Joshua and asked him, "Why did you tell my daughter to place wine in silver and gold?"

"She thought all things of beauty should come in beautiful containers," answered Rabbi Joshua. "I was just letting her learn: We should not look at the outside to tell if something is ugly or beautiful—all depends on what is inside."

[B. Talmud *Taanit* 7a-b; B. Talmud *Nedarim* 50b; also in *Sefer HaAggadah*]

3. Who Is the Ugly One?

Our Sages taught, "Have no regard for outward appearance, all depends on what is contained within" (Mishnah *Avot* 4:20). And what is the proof? Consider what happened to Rabbi Eleazar:

Leaving the House of Study, Rabbi Eleazar turned his donkey toward the river for a stroll. Torah was so much on his mind that only half of him was grounded while the other half soared upward toward Heaven.

A man offered greetings, saying, "Shalom, sir," and, when Rabbi Eleazar took his eyes off the trees and looked down at the man, what he saw was an exceedingly ugly man. Feeling peeved because his mood was interrupted, Rabbi Eleazar replied, "Empty one! How ugly you are. Are all the people around here as ugly as you?"

The man frowned and answered, "I cannot say. Why not ask the One who crafted us all? Say to God, 'How ugly is this thing You made.'"

All at once, Rabbi Eleazar felt guilty for having spoken to the man in such an unkind fashion. He got off his donkey and fell to one knee before the man, saying, "Forgive me, I beg of you. There is no excuse for what I have said."

"I shall not forgive you," the man said. "You cannot unsay words; or call back hurt feelings." An the man turned to walk away.

Rabbi Eleazar followed him on foot, leading his donkey, stopping once and again to beg forgiveness. As the two proceeded in this way, they came to a small town. When people in the town saw Rabbi Eleazar coming, they came out to greet him, calling, "Shalom, O Teacher, O Master!"

The man whose feelings had been hurt asked the others, "Whom are you welcoming in this way?"

The people said, "Do you not recognize him? The one walking behind you is none other than the great Rabbi Eleazar."

"Humph!" the man grunted, "If this fellow is a teacher, may there be no other teachers like him in all Israel!"

Then Rabbi Eleazar explained to the townspeople what he had done and how sorry he was for it. The townspeople begged the injured man to forgive Eleazar, "for he is greatly learned in the Torah."

The fellow finally relented. "For your sake," he said, "I will forgive him, but only if he promises never to act in this way again."

[B. Talmud *Taanit* 20a-b]

4. The Praying Hands

🐚 In the fifteenth century, a family with eighteen children lived in a small village near Nuremberg. To keep food on the table, Albrecht Durer the goldsmith not only worked at his own profession, but took on any paying chore.

Among his children were two who showed early promise as artists and both wished to study art. Their father sadly informed them that the school in Nuremberg was too expensive for the family to afford—too expensive even for one child, and most certainly too expensive for two.

But the two boys, Albert and Albrecht, entered into a pact. One would become a laborer in the mining tunnels nearby, and help support the other at the academy in Nuremberg. One Sunday, after church, they tossed a coin, and Albrecht Durer the Younger, won.

Albert took to the mines, dangerous and dirty work that it was. For the next four years, he struggled to finance his brother. At the academy, young Albrecht Durer's work earned high honors. Everyone agreed that his etchings, woodcuts, and oils were outstanding. By the time he graduated, he was earning commissions that began to pay considerable fees.

When Albrecht returned home, the Durer family held a festive dinner to celebrate his triumph. After the meal, the young Albrecht offered a toast to his brother for his years of sacrifice. With great joy, he said, "Albert, my beloved brother, your turn has come. You can go to the academy at Nuremberg to study art, and I will take care of you."

But Albert's eyes were filled with tears. He rose to his feet and spoke quietly. "No, dear brother. I cannot go to the academy. It is too late for me. Look for yourself." Albert put his hands out for all to see. "This is what four years in the mines have done to my hands! Nearly every bone in my fingers has been smashed at least once and now the arthritis in my right hand is so bad that I cannot even hold a glass to return your toast, much less trace delicate lines on canvas with a brush. For me, it is too late."

Hundreds of years have passed and hundreds of masterful portraits, sketches, watercolors, charcoals, woodcuts, and copper engravings by Albrecht Durer hang in the world's museums. But his most famous work is a portrait of two abused hands, palms together, and fingers pointing to the heavens. These are the hands of Albert, drawn by his brother Albrecht. He called the picture, "Hands," but the world knows it best as "The Praying Hands."

[Internet anecdote]

5. Silence and Interruption

A *gabbai* is an "assistant." Many rabbis had assistants who took care of small details so that the rabbis could be free to concentrate on more important things. Rabbi Naftali of Ropchitz had a *gabbai* named Leizar who was more than a little quirky. Leizar had a head for thinking, but he was not always willing to consult it.

Two stories about silence will illustrate what I mean: Among traditional Jews—especially among the followers of Rabbi Naftali—silence was considered a great virtue. Some moments, especially, should never be interrupted by talk. No chatter should interrupt a person at prayer. And there is a time before meals—from the moment the hands are washed to just after the blessing over the food is said to just after the first bite is taken—when a Jew should silently think only of gratitude to God. There is also—though the modest seldom mention it—a time for silence when we visit that necessary place, the place we call the "rest room," and the place Rabbi Naftali even more politely called "where there is neither day nor night."

The holy Reb Naftali washed his hands for the afternoon meal. He glanced at the table and saw that his *gabbai*, Leizar, had provided bread and hot coffee, but had forgotten to provide a spoon. Reb Naftali always used a spoon to cool his coffee as he brought it to his lips. Just then, though, the rabbi could not "interrupt" his silence. What did he do? He tried to get Leizar's attention by coughing.

Leizar, though, did not take the hint. He sat like a statue, waiting for the rabbi to begin the meal.

What did the rabbi do? He took a little bread, then he gulped down a small mouthful of the burning coffee. His tongue was still stinging when he turned to Leizar and said, "Why didn't you place a teaspoon here? Did you not hear me cough?"

"Aha," Leizar said, "Is that why you coughed? I did not know that coughing meant, 'Bring me a teaspoon.'"

By the time Leizar fetched a teaspoon from the kitchen the coffee was cold. But Reb Naftali always found it difficult to be angry with anyone. So he took the rest of his meal in silence.

Leizar, though, thought the silence was directed at him, so he apologized by saying, "Next time I will know what your coughing means."

One day, Reb Naftali was in that place "where there is neither day nor night." Leizar, too, needed to go there, but when Leizar tried the door, he found it was locked. He sat down on a bench to wait for the door to open. But, as he waited, it seemed to him like a thousand years passed, so he stood up and banged on the door. He did not even knock politely, because Leizar was growing desperate.

At that moment, though, the rabbi could not "interrupt" his silence. What did the rabbi do? He coughed.

So Leizar went and fetched a teaspoon.

[Langer, *Nine Gates*, pp. 79-80]

6. Pegfuls of Troubles

A man came to Rabbi Nachum and said, "My burdens are too great. I cannot endure them any more. My shoulders are bowed and my legs threaten to give up under me."

"Yes. Yes," the rabbi said. "I am certain that it is so. But do you imagine that you are the only one with troubles?" And Rabbi Nachum told this story:

Once God tired of hearing so many complaints. God made a large room and angels gathered the souls of all the human beings on earth and brought them into this room, lining them up around the four walls. God spoke gently, soothingly, to all humanity. "I make no excuses. Suffering is necessary. Everyone must have a share. But I am tired of all the complaining that you do, so I am giving you a choice. On the wall, behind each of you is a peg. Hang your troubles on this peg and go around the room. Seek out any peg of troubles that you like best."

"When all was said and done," Rabbi Nachum said, "each soul returned to its own peg and chose its own troubles—the troubles it knew best—for everyone else's troubles seemed even more difficult to bear."

[Buber, *Later Masters*, p. 73]

7. *Neshamah*

One Jewish tradition has it that the human soul is composed of three parts. The basest part is *nefesh* (literally "animation"), which humans share with all forms of life, plant and animal. The second part is *ruach* ("spirit," in the sense of personality) which humans share with animals. The highest part is *neshamah* ("breath"). *Neshamah* derives from the moment of human creation when God breathed the *nishmat chayim*, "the breath of life" (Genesis 2:7) into Adam. It is the *neshamah*, bequeathed directly by God, that separates human beings from the rest of living creation.

Reb Zusya of Anipoli, a leading Hasidic teacher, was stricken with blindness toward the end of his life. As we would expect, whenever tragedy strikes, people doubt and question. "Would a merciful God allow this to happen?" "Why does God not put an end to the suffering of the righteous?" Such questions tend to be on the levels of *nefesh* and *ruach*. Overcoming tragedy without jeopardizing faith requires a deeper strength. In this spirit, Reb Zusya assigned himself the difficult task of finding a blessing where there seemed only a curse. Using his *neshamah* to overcome the lesser forces of his soul, he offered up the prayer, "Thank You, O God, for making me blind so that I might perceive the inner light."

There is no law commanding one to thank God for personal tragedy. Any such law would be both cruel and bitter. And there is no commandment requiring us to accept whatever happens without anger, disappointment, or discouragement. Reb Zusya realized through his *neshamah* that no blindness is as destructive as the blindness of the heart.

Because *neshamah* is that segment of the soul directly attuned to the Divine, we read in Proverbs (20:27), "The *neshamah* of a person is the lamp of God, searching all the inward parts."

[Rossel]

8
Hospitality

1. Solomon the Poor

King Solomon ruled for many years. For most of those years, he brought peace and well-being to his people. And his people, the Twelve Tribes of Israel, loved their king. Yet, there came a time of several years when taxes were too heavy, too many young men were taken off to the military, and too many people were conscripted as corvee labor for the king's projects. What had gone wrong?

In those evil days, the rumor grew that the real King Solomon was no longer on the throne. People said that Solomon had been tricked by Asmodeus, king of the demons, who had stolen Solomon's magic signet ring. Asmodeus exhaled a foul wind that lifted the king and sent him far away. Now Asmodeus looked like Solomon, lived in Solomon's palace, and sat on Solomon's throne in Jerusalem. All the evil things happening were the fault of the king of demons, not of the real king of Israel—or so the people said.

Meanwhile, the real Solomon wandered in some distant land. The evil breath of Asmodeus had shred his royal robes to rags and tatters. Like an ordinary beggar, he passed from house to house asking for a meal and a place to stay the night. And, like an ordinary beggar, most folk ignored him, shooing him away. When he would say, "I am Solomon, King of Israel," they would laugh and mock him, replying in sarcasm with: "If so, we are all Queens of Sheba!"

Lonely, weary, and hungry, Solomon once happened on the house of a merchant who had visited Jerusalem many times. "I know you," the merchant said. "You are the King of Israel. I have seen your face as you passed through the streets of Jerusalem." So the merchant invited Solomon to come in and dine with him.

"My, my, but it is a terrible shame," the merchant said to the king as the appetizer was served. "Look, how you have become

215

nothing more than a commoner. What has become of your riches and your gold? Where is your palace and where are all your servants?" So it was with the soup. "My, my." And with the salad. "It's a terrible shame." With the main course, it was, "What a pity." With every word and every course, Solomon felt more and more sorry for himself. Tears came to his eyes, rolled down his cheeks, and fell to his plate. Soon, he pushed the food away, unable to take another bite.

The next night Solomon came to the door of a poor wood cutter, one who had certainly never been to Jerusalem. "I have not much to offer," the wood cutter apologized, "but come and share it with me. There is bread enough for us and a pot of lentils freshly made." Slowly, as they ate, Solomon told his story, and the wood cutter responded, "I am sure that things will turn out all right," or, "Tomorrow is yet another day; things may seem brighter then." Gradually, Solomon's mood changed. The wood cutter's words gave him a glimmer of hope that one day he might regain his throne. He felt reassured that he was indeed Solomon, the King of Israel.

One day, the people of Jerusalem noticed a change. A spate of good was overtaking the kingdom. Tax collectors asked for less. The army required less men. The work crews required less workers. The rumor passed among them, "The demon has been defeated. King Solomon has returned to his throne." As this was true for them, it was true for Solomon, too. Solomon had overcome the demon and banished him. He was now a changed Solomon and all that had happened—even the meal with the merchant who was kind in a cruel way and the meal with the wood cutter who was kind and considerate—seemed as if a dream.

[Yalkut *Proverbs*, #953]

2. Friends

Rabbi Shmelke of Nikolsburg once told the story of a king who was overthrown and exiled from his own kingdom. For years, the king wandered through the world like an outlaw, a stranger with no place to rest. Luckily, the king remembered one friend from the days of his youth—a friend who was also outside the old kingdom, so the king sought refuge with his friend.

The friend was poor, but ready to share everything. He offered the king hospitality in his small cottage and did what he could to make the king's stay sweet. Inside, his friend's soul grieved for the king's troubles; but outwardly his friend would rejoice and remind the king of the days of the king's glory. In this way, he lightened the king's heart through laughter and song, and even entertained the king by dancing to his tunes.

"And who is this king?" Rabbi Shmelke would ask. "It is none other than the Holy One, God, the Blessed!" In our hearts, we may be sad that God is in exile with us, that we have become poor and separate from our Holy Land, that God's Temple is gone, and that God is forced to witness Jerusalem in ruins. But, outwardly, what better friend could God have than the Jewish people? We have known God since our youth and we tell God's stories day and night, we entertain God with dance, praise God with song, and lighten God's heart with laughter. The day will come when God will return to the Holy Land. Then, we will be invited home, too, to enjoy the hospitality of our Friend.

[Langer, *Nine Gates*, pp. 162-163]

3. An Honored Garment

🐝 The town hired a new *melamed*, a teacher for the *cheder*, the one-room schoolhouse. The position of *melamed* carried honor and respect in the Jewish community. But, let's face it, the position did not command much of a salary. So it was usually occupied either by an unmarried young man or an older man who was a widower. To compensate for the small recompense, the position came with frequent invitations to dinner.

Our hero, whose name was Baruch, came from a poor family. He dressed in peasant clothing. He could not afford a special set of robes for the Sabbath. And yet, one day, he received an invitation to a Sabbath dinner at the home of the richest man in town, the wealthy money-lender Reb Moishe.

All week long he looked forward to this event and on the appointed evening he went to the house on the hill. The servants took just one look at Baruch, saw his ragged clothes, and drove him away with a broom—the way you might sweep some unwanted dirt beneath a carpet.

On Sunday, when the Sabbath was over, another invitation like the first arrived at the *cheder*. On it was a handwritten note saying, "We hope you are not ill or suffering, and that you did not think our first invitation was insincere. We look forward to seeing you for Shabbat dinner this week."

But the same thing happened this time as before. He was swept out with the crumbs. In fact, the crumbs were inside, but Baruch was never allowed to enter. He left with a grumbling stomach and with the fragrant odors of a Sabbath meal in his nostrils.

When the third invitation arrived, Baruch determined to do something about this unacceptable situation. Taking a day off, he traveled to his home village some miles away and conferred with his mother. She rummaged through an old trunk and found a white robe that his grandfather used to wear for the Sabbath. It was dated and out-of-style, but it was definitely a Sabbath robe.

When he appeared at the door of Reb Moishe for the third time, the servants behaved as if they had never before seen him. They bowed and curtsied and welcomed him into the warmth of the merchant's home. He was led to the table and seated among the other honored guests.

But when the soup arrived, Baruch dipped the sleeve of his robe into it, saying, "Eat, my garment, eat."

And when the roast was placed before him, he dipped the buttons of the robe into the gravy and touched the meat with a corner of the robe, saying, "Enjoy, my honored garment, enjoy!"

Reb Moishe dropped his fork and knife. "What is the meaning of this?" he demanded.

"My honored host," the young man began, "twice before I came to your house looking forward to a Sabbath meal with you. But both times, I was dressed like a peasant and your servants drove me away. This time I came dressed in my grandfather's Sabbath robe, and your servants ushered me in. Obviously, at the home of Reb Moishe, it is not the guest that is honored, but the garment. Well and good, then, it is the garment that should take pleasure in eating!"

Reb Moishe laughed. "You are quite right to be angry, young man. And you are welcome to continue feeding your garment if that brings you pleasure. But know this: I myself was not always a wealthy man. In fact, I was the first *melamed* of the *cheder* in which you now work. And I did not always have fancy clothing to wear, so I, too, dressed in peasant style. The fault here is mine and I apologize heartily. From now on, I will make sure that you are welcome no matter what you wear. And just to set things right between us, I will have my tailor make you a Sabbath coat beyond compare. Let this be my way of thanking you for teaching me a lesson. In my house, it is not the garment that is honored, but the learning. Now, eat and enjoy. Today is the Sabbath."

[Sufi folktale; adapted from Ramsay and McCullagh, *Tales from Turkey*]

4. Treachery

In the days when the Christians of Spain lived side by side with the Moorish Muslims, no love was lost between the two peoples. Fights were common, and some ended tragically. It was this way when, once, a Christian arguing with a Moor drew out a dagger and struck the Moor in the heart, killing him instantly. As the victim slumped in a pool of blood, the murderer fled for his life.

No matter how fast he ran, he could barely outpace his pursuers. Finally, out of breath and out of choices, he clambered over a wall and into an orchard, hiding himself behind one of the trees. Suddenly the orchard's owner appeared, a Moor of stately appearance. The young Christian's heart sank.

"I have done a terrible thing," he said to the Moor, and he told the story of his quarrel and the way it ended. The Moor was not shocked, for he was well aware of the violence and bloodshed that had become common in the village. Life and death were in his hands, he knew, and yet the requirements of hospitality took precedence over both.

"This could have happened to anyone," the Moor said. "When you are young, you are hot-blooded. I know this well, for I have a son about your age. Come, then, have no fear. I shall not give you over to the mob. You shall stay with me this night and, in the morning, you may seek freedom through flight."

Now the Moor took an apple from his tree, cut it, and offered half to the young Christian. He said, "It is our custom that a person who has eaten our food becomes a protected guest, so eat, be my guest, and I will swear to protect you." He led the frightened young man to his house, fed him, and prepared a place for him to sleep.

As night fell, a messenger came to the Moor. The messenger told the man how his son had become involved in a fight with a Christian who drew a dagger and stabbed him. "Your son is dead," the messenger concluded.

At once, the bereaved Moor realized that he was protecting the very man who had killed his own son! As soon as the messenger departed, the Moor saddled one of his best horses and woke up his guest. "My only son meant more to me than anything in the world. And the man you killed today was my son!"

He bade the man dress and led him to the horse. "I have saddled this horse for you, so please take it and leave my house as fast as possible. For my part, I will keep my promise to protect you. But if one of my relatives finds you, you are lost! Say nothing more to me, just mount and be gone!"

As the Moor let the killer escape, his heart was heavy and his hands shook. "Hurry!" he said, as the Christian mounted the horse. "Hurry and flee! And thank God for the customs of my people."

As the young man galloped out of sight, the Moor sank to his knees, put his head in his hands, and wept.

[adapted from Certner, *101 Jewish Stories*]

5. Abraham and the Old Man

🕮 Abraham would greet all travelers, whether friends or strangers, with open arms, welcoming them into his tent. We are even told that Abraham set his tent in the center of a crossroads with openings on every side, so that a passerby coming from any direction would be encounter his hospitality.

It was Abraham's custom to wash the feet of the traveler (as all nomads do), and to feed the traveler. Then, when the traveler would thank Abraham for his hospitality and for the meal, Abraham would say, "Nay, do not thank me, but thank *Adonai*." The traveler would ask, "Who is this *Adonai*?" And so Abraham could enlighten each traveler with knowledge of the One God, the Creator of heaven and earth and all that is therein.

Once an old man appeared at the door of Abraham's tent and Abraham welcomed him as always, washing his feet and preparing him a meal. But after the meal, when Abraham asked the old man to thank *Adonai* for the blessing of food, the old man replied that he worshiped only fire, and would thank no other god but the god of flame and ash. "Moreover," the old man said, "when I am forced to build my own fire, the only god I thank is the god of my own fingers!"

This aggrieved Abraham and he drove the old man out of his tent into the chill of the desert night. At once, God's voice came to Abraham saying, "Wherefore have you done this shameful thing? For seventy years I have suffered this old man. Can you not suffer him even for one night?"

Then Abraham made haste to chase after the old man. He brought him back to the warmth of his tent and kept him there for the night.

[based on *Midrash Genesis Rabbah* 43:8 and 42:4;]

In Paris, Benjamin Franklin once grew impatient at a dinner party when gratuitous prejudicial remarks were aimed at the Jewish people. Franklin called for a copy of the Bible. Opening it, he read the story of "Abraham and the Old Man," stating that it was found in Genesis, chapter 67. In this way, the American sage had delivered a rebuff regarding prejudice in general and "the People of the Book" in particular. On closer scrutiny, though, Genesis ends with chapter 50 and the story of "Abraham and the Old Man" is nowhere to be found in the Bible. Franklin had carried off a masterful hoax.

Franklin's version was published in 1790 in sixteen "verses" of English styled on the King James translation. Verse 11 reads: "And God said, Have I borne with him these hundred, ninety and eight years, and nourished and clothed him, notwithstanding his rebellion against me; and couldst not thou, that art thyself a sinner, bear with him one night?" Versions found in *Midrash Genesis Rabbah* (43:8 and 42:4) fall short of transmitting the full story. The earliest known complete version is found in the dedication of George Gentius' Latin translation of *Shevet Yehudah* ("The Scepter of Judah") by Solomon ibn Varga published some time before 1667. The well-known clergyman, Jeremy Taylor, produced an English version around the same time. It is likely that Franklin's telling was based on Taylor's.

There remains a strange twist of fate: In 1844, some years after Franklin's account was published, a version in classical Hebrew in sixteen verses was composed and published by Nachman Krochmal who evidently had Franklin's English version before him as he worked! A folktale about Abraham had at long last found hospitality among Abraham's people.

9
Friendship

1. The Magic Ring (Version 2)

Throughout his life, the merchant named Itzik was successful. Those who traded with him and those who knew him felt drawn to his warmth and even a few moments in his presence served to cement relationships that lasted a lifetime. He was called "Itzik, Friend of All." When people sometimes asked him why this was so, he would point to a gold ring he wore day and night, saying that this was "the Friendship Ring" which had been passed from father to son through the generations of his family. Anyone who possessed this magic ring, he would say, held the power of friendship in his hand.

Now Itzik had three sons, all of them loyal and deserving children. At one time or another, thinking little of it, he promised each of them the magic ring. As his age increased and his life force abated, he realized that he had created a problem with no easy solution. He expended much time and energy thinking of what to do.

On his death bed he called his eldest son to speak with him privately. He handed the magic ring to his eldest son with the admonition to use its power only to do good in the world. When his eldest son had left his bedside, he called in his middle son, presenting him too with the magic ring and admonishing him to use its power only to do good in the world. As his middle son left the room, he called his youngest son, handing him too the magic ring and advising him to use it only for good. As his youngest son departed his side, he was satisfied; and Itzik, Friend of All, breathed his last.

While mourning their father, all three sons claimed that they had been their father's favorite and, as proof, each one produced the magic ring. How shocked they were to learn that all three had rings and all three rings were identical. At the funeral, they accosted their father's jeweler and demanded that he examine the three rings and tell them which was the authentic "Friendship Ring."

It was the jeweler who explained how, shortly before his death, Itzik had given him the golden ring, charging him to create two copies of it so artfully crafted that no one—not even the jeweler himself—could tell them apart. He confessed, as he looked at the three rings, that he had been successful. He could no longer identify the original. "Of course," he added, "in the end, the one of you who makes the most friends, who is known by the whole world as 'Friend of All,' he is the one with the true magic ring."

[Rossel, based on Giovanni Boccaccio, *The Decameron*, day 1, tale 3]

2. The Dragon of Jerusalem

For seven hundred years, the people of Jerusalem came to the Temple on Sukkot to pray for rain. Jerusalem is on top of the hills of Judea, in a place where water was always hard to find. So, when the rains came, it was always a blessing; and the people believed that God was granting them a special gift. And everyone knew that, without the prayers for rain on Sukkot, there was little hope for God's special gift.

The prayer for rain, like the one for lighting Sabbath candles or the one over wine, included a ritual. Every year, the people went down to the Siloam pool, a pool of water at the end of the tunnel dug long ago by the workers of King Hezekiah. From the Temple they took a giant golden pitcher. When they came to the water gate at the pool's opening, they sounded the *shofar*: *Tekiah, Teruah, Tekiah.* They filled the giant pitcher with water and carried it back up the hill to the Temple, where they gave it to the priest.

Then the priest went up the ramp to the altar. There were two silver bowls on the altar, a very large one and a smaller one. Each one had a spout. The larger was for the water and the smaller was for wine. As one priest poured the water of Siloam from the giant golden pitcher into the large silver bowl, the water came out of the spout and spilled across the altar. At the same time, another priest poured wine into the smaller bowl and the wine spilled out on the altar, joining with the water. It was a beautiful sight.

When the priest poured the water from the giant golden pitcher into the silver bowl, all the people called out, "Raise your hand high!" because one time a priest had accidentally missed the silver bowl and poured the water on his feet, and the people were so sure that no rain would come that year that they grew angry and threw their *etrogim* ("citrons") at the priest. You can be certain that priest never made the same mistake again!

Such was the ritual for beseeching rain at the Temple in Jerusalem—spilling water on God's altar, in the hope that God would bring rain from the heavens spilling down in its season.

This particular year, when the people took the giant golden pitcher from the Temple, when they blew the *shofar* and went into the gate that led down the steps to where the water would be drawn from the pool, something strange happened. I'll tell you what happened in just a minute, but first you have to know a little more about the wonderful waters of the pool of Siloam.

Siloam was one of two pools of water that the people of Jerusalem relied on. Every day, water-carriers went to these pools, bringing pitchers and jars, filling them, and bringing water to the people. Without these pools, there would be no water in Jerusalem. One pool is fed by a little stream that everyone can see. And, through the years, the people of Jerusalem dug large pits to hold any rain that fell and to feed the rain into that pool. But the other pool, the Siloam pool, is much more mysterious.

Everyone knows that if you linger on the steps you can witness a little miracle. Sometimes it occurs two or three times a day; sometimes it happens just once a day; and sometimes it happens four times a day. All of a sudden, the still, clear water starts to bubble and churn and the stream rises up over the bottom step and inches higher and higher until it nearly reaches the top step. If you are standing on the bottom step when that happens, you will soon be up to your waist in bubbling, churning water. But, if you wait just a little while longer, the water stops bubbling and it stops churning. It settles down to the bottom step, as if nothing ever happened. And there it stays, a gentle, still stream only a few inches deep.

Of course, the best time to draw water from the Siloam pool is when it begins to bubble and churn, when it rises up close to the top step, because then the pool is high enough that you can put any size pitcher or jar into it, even the giant golden pitcher from the Temple.

Now, let us return to what happened that particular day, the first day of Sukkot, when the people came with the giant golden pitcher to draw water from the pool. They stood and waited, knowing that if they waited long enough, the stream would begin to bubble and churn. But it did not. It did not budge. It just stayed still and calm. Time passed, but the stream never rose—and there was no way to put the giant golden pitcher into the little bit of water at the bottom of the pool.

This was an emergency. The people grew anxious. No one could remember a time when the water did not bubble, churn, and rise. If they could not get enough water from the Siloam pool, then it was certain that the prayers in the Temple would be ineffectual. There would be no rain that year!

They sent a message to the High Priest, but he had no idea of what to do. The waters of the Siloam pool had never failed in his lifetime. So the High Priest sent a message to the Great Assembly, the council of Israel's wise sages. This was the Great Assembly that had decided what prayers would be spoken and when they would be said. This was the Great Assembly that began the work of assembling the Spoken Torah. If anyone would know what was wrong, it would be the elders of the Great Assembly.

But when the message reached the Great Assembly, it caused a stir. The sages were disturbed and conferred with one another all at once so that it seemed as if they were bubbling and churning and rising, even when the waters of the Siloam pool would not. Finally, one sage shouted out his question, "Where do the waters of the Siloam pool come from?"

No one knew. The stream always flowed through the tunnel that King Hezekiah's workmen dug hundreds of years before. No one remembered where the tunnel started. Now, they thought, "Perhaps a rock has fallen somewhere in the tunnel and blocked the stream. Maybe dirt has gathered near the opening of the stream and must be cleared away."

But the oldest and wisest sage did not agree. He held up his hand until there was silence. "I will tell you what my grandfather told me," he said, "if you promise not to laugh." The other sages nodded. "My grandfather once brought me down to get water from the Siloam pool, and I fell off the bottom step. He grabbed me quickly and raised me up. Lucky for me that he was quick, for a moment later the water churned and rose upward, so that, if my father had not taken hold of me, I would surely have drowned.

"Then my father said, 'You must be vigilant at the pool of Siloam because an enormous dragon lives at the end of the tunnel. And every time the dragon moves, his tail stirs the water so that it rises to the top of the steps. So, at Siloam, you must watch your step—and beware of the dragon's tail.'"

A dragon? In the tunnel? Could it really be that there was a dragon living under Jerusalem, causing the waters of Siloam to churn and rise? The sages were of mixed opinions. Some believed it was possible. Some said it could not be. But one said, "My grandmother once told me that Solomon could speak the language of the animals and the birds. She said he once commanded a dragon to come to Jerusalem to help the people. I thought she was telling me a tall tale." He scratched his head. "I wonder," he said, "could Solomon's dragon truly be living beneath Jerusalem?"

Again, the sages spoke all at once. If it was a dragon, then it was a dragon who worked very hard. It was a dragon who moved every day, turning and twisting and stirring the waters. But, if it was a dragon, then what had happened? Why was the dragon not moving today when the people of Jerusalem needed to draw water for the Sukkot prayer for rain?

So it went, until a small voice rose higher than any other. It was Benjamin, the youngest member of the Great Assembly, a youth not yet twenty years old. "I will go into the tunnel to its very end," he said. "If there is a dragon, I will find it and discover why it has stopped moving."

The oldest sage replied, "This may be dangerous. What if the waters start to bubble and churn while you are in the tunnel? You will be drowned and no one will be with you to save you."

But Benjamin said, "If someone does not go to the dragon, there will be no rain this year, and our people will die of thirst. Surely, Solomon forced the dragon to promise to serve the people of Jerusalem. Maybe the dragon has forgotten his promise. Let me go. I will remind the dragon of his promise."

So they sent Benjamin down to the pool of Siloam. He stepped into the water, which only came up to the soles of his sandals. He walked alone into the darkness of the tunnel, carrying nothing but a torch to light his way. In this way, he soon arrived at the tunnel's end, a huge dark cave. But he saw no dragon. And there was no rock blocking the stream and there was no dirt to be cleared away. And Benjamin wondered what to do. Finally, he called out a single word: "Dragon."

Back at the pool of Siloam, the people saw the stream suddenly bubbling and churning. The water rose higher that day than ever before—higher even than it has risen since. From above the steps, the Temple's giant golden pitcher was filled. The water carriers rushed to the Temple, racing to reach it before the sun could set.

But most of the people remained at the pool, wondering, "Where is Benjamin?"

Slowly, the waters settled down. Slowly, the bubbling and the churning stopped and the stream was once more below the lowest step. And, when it had been that way for a while, out of the tunnel came Benjamin.

The people hugged and kissed him. They blessed him and called him a hero. They asked, "Did you see the dragon? Is there really a dragon beneath Jerusalem?"

But Benjamin was wise. He just smiled and said, "You can count on the pool of Siloam, just as you always have. Every day, a few times each day, it is sure to rise to the top step and give water for all the people of Jerusalem."

And he returned to the Great Assembly where the sages hugged and kissed him. They blessed him and called him a hero. And they asked, "Did you meet the dragon? Did you see the dragon?"

But Benjamin was wise. He just smiled and said, "Of course, the dragon is a legend. And some legends are just tall tales and some legends tell the truth in ways that help us. Maybe there is a dragon living under Jerusalem and maybe there is not. If there is, it may be a dragon that gets lonely living alone and needs a visit every seven hundred years or so. And, if there is no dragon, then maybe someone should just walk to the end of the tunnel every seven hundred years or so. It worked this time, and it may work again."

To this very day, the waters still do their daily dance. Scientists say that, somewhere along the tunnel, there is probably a narrow place that acts like a siphon and makes the waters rise and fall. But the old-timers of Jerusalem swear that it is the dragon that stirs and makes the waters rise and fall. And who knows the truth? Some legends are just tall tales and some legends tell facts in ways that help us.

[Rossel based on a factual account in Millgram, *Jerusalem Curiosities*]

3. The Third Friend

&ₑ. There was a king who loved the presence of money more than the company of people. His favorite sound was coins jingling, his favorite thrill was touching silver and gold, and his favorite place was the vault in his treasury.

One day, as he was stacking and counting coins, he heard an odd noise coming from behind a chest of gold. He called his guards to investigate and, to their surprise, they found a tunnel hidden behind the chest. And, there, at the tunnel's entrance, they spied two feet. The commander of the guards grabbed the feet and pulled. In a moment, he had pulled a man from the tunnel. And the man was still dragging a bar of gold in his hands—a thief! The guards set the man on his feet and brought him before the King.

"Why steal from me?' asked the king.

"Your Majesty, you have so much and I have so little," the man replied.

"You will have even less on Sunday," the king said. "On Sunday. the chief executioner will remove your head and you will forfeit your sorry life."

The thief said, "Your Majesty, my head is not all that important, I know. But there is something very important to me. If you will only let me go now, I promise that I will return on Sunday."

"Let you go? Now? Why would I agree to that?"

"Your Majesty, my daughter is to be married this Saturday. I was taking the gold to pay for her wedding dress. She is my only child. I promise: If you will let me see her wed, I will return to face my death."

"I am sorry for your daughter," said the king. "But what guarantee do I have that you will return?"

The thief considered, then spoke again: "I have a friend and I believe he will take my place until I return. Will you let me go?"

"If you have a friend like that—someone who trusts you with his life—I will let you go until Sunday. But I swear, if you do not return, on Sunday your friend will lose *his* head!"

When the friend was brought before the king, he agreed to stay in prison while his friend, the thief, went to his daughter's wedding. The king was amazed, but since he had agreed, he gave the thief freedom and placed his friend in the dungeon.

Saturday came and the thief's daughter was wed. He danced and drank at the wedding and toasted her all the night through. At dawn he woke, knowing he must ride hard to save his friend. But he had not gone far when he was attacked by highwaymen in the woods. They took his purse and left him for dead. When they were gone, the thief managed to catch his horse. He traveled on, riding hard.

But at the river he was dismayed to see that a flood had washed out the bridge. Desperate, he plunged into the waters on his horse and horse and rider braved the swift river current to get to the other side. Time was passing too quickly.

When he reached the town, he had to fight his way to the castle; and when he reached the castle he had to fight his way through the crowd. He was horrified to see the court gathered round watching his friend kneeling on the ground as the chief executioner raised his axe.

"No! No!" he screamed. "I am back! I am the one you want!"

The king heard him and saw him pressing through the crowd. He stopped the execution and commanded that both the thief and his friend be brought before him.

The king said, "I have decided to give you both your freedom, but first I must ask you three questions."

He turned to the thief's friend. "Why did you take his place?"

"Your Majesty, I have known this man my whole life. He would never steal if he could find another way. But he loves his daughter so much that he wanted only the best for her. We are friends and I trust him. So I knew he would return just as he had promised."

The King nodded. He asked the thief, "Why did you return when you could have been free?"

"Your Majesty, you were holding my friend. He trusted me and I gave my word. I would never let him take my place in death."

The King nodded again. "I have one more question," he said. He came close to the two men and almost whispered in their ears. "May I be your third friend?"

[European folktale]

4. The Visit

🕮 They were study-partners in the *yeshivah*, but when they grew older they were sent to opposite ends of the country and became rabbis in towns far distant from one another. At first, they corresponded frequently but, with all the troubles of the Jews in those days, who could find time to write? So, many years, but few words passed between them. Still, the warmth of the friendship of their youth bound them close.

Imagine the delight Reb Menachem felt one Chanukah when a letter came by messenger from his distant friend. He fairly tore open the envelope to drink in the words of the companion of his youth, Reb Nachum. But as he read, his expression changed and furrows knit his brow.

"My brother," the letter said, "I have had a dream and I know that it will come to pass. I see dark days coming for our people—especially for you and the people of your village. Soldiers on horseback will invade—burning and looting, destroying and despoiling. I sense that my prayers alone are not enough to stem this evil tide for you. Yet, I have not lost faith. Perhaps what I cannot accomplish alone, you and I can still accomplish together. When the Holiday comes, I will come to you." And it was signed, "Your brother, Nachum."

Reb Menachem sat and penned a short reply. "My brother," he said. "I too have heard the trembling of the earth and the beat of hooves that will soon come against our people. And, I confess, I had no idea what I alone could do. But your letter brings me new hope. Perhaps with both our voices raised to heaven, the Holy One, the Blessed, will accept our plea. " And he signed the letter, "Your faithful servant, your brother, Menachem."

He entrusted his note to the messenger and bade him make all speed in delivering it to his distant friend. But no sooner was the messenger on the road than the rabbi realized he had made an error. He had forgotten to ask the simplest of all questions: On what holiday would his friend be coming?

Certainly, it would not be Purim, for the mood of Purim was inappropriate for their serious task. On the other hand, it *was* Purim when the Jews were delivered from the hands of Haman and all their enemies. So perhaps it would be Purim, after all.

As Purim approached, he prepared to receive his friend and prayed that Nachum's long journey would be safe. But Purim came and went and there was no letter and his friend did not arrive. The rabbi thought to write a second letter just to ask "What holiday?" but the more he thought about it, the more it seemed to him that he should wait. Passover was coming soon and surely his friend would come for the Seder. For wasn't Passover the perfect holiday for their prayers? After all, the cries of the Jews suffering in slavery had reached heaven and discomfited the Eternal, so that God sent Moses to free them on Passover. Surely, Passover was the holiday that his friend had intended all along.

But Passover came and went. And again there was neither letter nor word from the companion of his youth. Moreover, hints of danger were growing day by day. The time was growing short and the mission was becoming urgent. Reb Menachem numbered the days of the Counting of the Omer each morning and soon came to believe that his friend had meant the holiday of Shavuot, the Festival of Weeks. Yes, it would be Shavuot, the season of the making of the covenant, a time when all Jews—the Jews of every generation past, present, and future—had stood at Mount Sinai together, as close to God as Jews had ever been. This would be the right moment for the two rabbis to join their vital prayer.

He made all preparations to greet his friend on Shavuot, as he had on Purim and on Passover. Instead of his friend, though, a messenger appeared with a new letter. "To the esteemed Rabbi Menachem," he read, "It is my terrible fortune to inform you of the death of your good friend, Reb Nachum. Fever took him on the seventh day of the Counting of the Omer and God now cares for him. To you, his friend, he gave his final greetings—directing me to send this message to you and telling me to say that he knew you would understand." It was signed by his friend's good wife.

Learning in this way that he would never see his friend again was almost too much for Reb Menachem's poor heart to bear. He had been in such a high state of expectation that the letter dealt him a devastating blow.

All summer long, he was disconsolate. His followers watched him sink deeper and deeper into despair. It was so unlike him that they were truly afraid for his life. Even as the High Holy Days approached there was little change. Even the lilting chants of the cantor on Rosh Hashanah could not awaken him from his stupor.

Only when Reb Menachem heard the voice of the *shofar* on Yom Kippur did he seem to stir from his long torpor. Suddenly his eyes grew bright and his mood lightened, as if a great weight had lifted from his soul. That night, Reb Menachem himself took the hammer to drive the first stake into the ground, beginning the yearly labor of building a *sukkah*.

He seemed entirely renewed. He delighted in building and decorating the *sukkah* with his family. He took pleasure in cutting and placing the tree branches that loosely formed the *sukkah*'s "roof." And he prepared to celebrate the holiday of Sukkot in joy, as he had in better times.

Surely, Reb Menachem thought, Sukkot had all along been the holiday that his friend had intended in his letter so long ago. Sukkot is the only holiday that Jews call *HeChag*, "The Holiday." It is the time when—following the mystic practice called *Ushpizin*—Jews invite Abraham, Isaac, Jacob. Moses, Aaron, Joseph, and David to join them in their *sukkot*, to come and visit. In the *sukkah*, Jews share a meal with these celebrated heroes of their people.

Tonight, Reb Menachem reasoned, there will be visitors. If not his old friend, then at least the old friends and mighty heroes of the Jewish people. So he and his family ate in the *sukkah*, looking up from time to time at the stars winking through the leaves above their heads. Afterward, the dishes were cleared and his wife left to put the children to bed. Reb Menachem sat alone in his *sukkah*, thinking.

And a man sat with him.

"I have come as I promised," the man said. Looking up, the rabbi recognized his old friend Nachum beside him. He was speechless. Could it be his feverish imagination? But no, Nachum seemed real, touching his arm and looking deep into his eyes.

"Come," his friend said, "the time is short and the storm has begun. The wicked Cossack, Chmielnicki, leading all his forces, are drawing close, just as I dreamed. Now we must raise our voices together to Heaven."

The two fell to prayer, reciting psalms, repeating words of comfort. First, one led and then the other. The night passed in this way, devotion after devotion, adoration after adoration, plea after plea; and when the first light of dawn broke, Reb Menachem found himself alone in his *sukkah*, still sitting at the table.

In the morning, the Jews came to the synagogue carrying *lulav* and *etrog* to celebrate the holiday. And, when they returned for the afternoon prayers, they heard the good news: Inexplicably, the Cossack armies had wheeled and turned away the night before, sparing their village and all the small Jewish towns around them.

That afternoon, Rabbi Menachem wrote a letter telling his friend Nachum the good news. Of course, he did not send it by messenger. Instead, he slipped it in his pocket.

Ever after, the Jews of his little town were mystified by the rabbi's new behavior. Deep in prayer, Reb Menachem would sometimes reach into his pocket and bring out a folded piece of paper, holding it up on high, as if he were handing it to heaven. Then, as the cadence of the prayer wore down, he would return that hand to his pocket and bring it out open and spread, as if he were offering himself and all he had to God.

[Rossel]

5. The Wind and I

Once upon a time, the wind ruled the hills and valleys of Talpiyot, close by Jerusalem. The wind swept down the mountain, through the valley, and across the plains, as if Talpiyot belonged to him alone.

When I first came upon Talpiyot, somehow I knew it was a special place for me. As I walked alone, I saw my future there. But then, the wind saw me.

He blew a gust in my face. "Why are you here?" he wheezed.

I said, "I'm out for a walk."

He puffed and my hat went sailing; and when I bent down to pick it up, he whooshed my coat inside out so it flopped over my head. When I straightened up to adjust my coat, he huffed so hard, I lost my balance and fell plop down on my bottom. He roared with laughter. "You are leaving now," he said.

When I got to my feet, he pressed at my back, pushing me all the way to Jerusalem. I thought, "It's hard to argue with the wind."

Though I tried to adjust to the city, my heart sent me back to Talpiyot and my feet followed. Thinking about the wind, I brought a tent to Talpiyot and set it up. I settled in the tent, with just a cot, a table, and a candle.

Then, one night, a breeze came in and blew out my candle. I went outside my tent and there was the wind, spiraling around like a little grey tornado. "Hello, neighbor," I said. "Would you like to come in?"

He spun around faster, throwing dirt in my eyes and choking me with dust. I fled into my tent and pulled down the flap. But the noise outside grew moment by moment, until suddenly the tent pegs were flying out of the ground and the tent took off like a giant canvas wing, flying away across the plains. Then the cot took off in another direction and the table flew into a thousand pieces.

I went back to Jerusalem, but always I dreamed of fresh air. And there is no air so fresh as the air of Talpiyot, so I made my way to Talpiyot again. This time I brought wood and built a cabin. I liked my cabin. It was not big, but it was roomy enough for a person like me, a person who does not need much.

Then, one day, the wind blew by and saw my cabin. The wind asked, "What is it?"

"It is a cabin," I replied.

The wind huffed. "I have never seen anything so flimsy as this thing you call a cabin."

I huffed back, saying,. "So, here is something that you never saw before."

The wind puffed himself up. "Let me inspect it," he howled. When he inspected the door, the door splintered and fell. When he inspected the windows, the windows cracked and shattered. When he inspected the roof, the roof creaked and groaned and crashed to the ground. "I am through inspecting," he wailed. "Now, where is this cabin of yours?" And the wind laughed a breezy laugh,

I did not laugh. I just thought, "Yes, where is my cabin?"

When I returned to Jerusalem, my heart was set more than ever on beautiful Talpiyot. So I decided to build a house that would withstand the wind. I bought the huge white stones that are the best building blocks used in Jerusalem. I bought lots of mortar. And I bought strong timbers for the frame of my house. Then I hired workers to lay a strong foundation and build a house no wind could collapse.

As soon as the house was finished, the wind came to visit me. He tested my walls with squalls and blasts. He tortured my roof with howls and blows. But he could not move the stones and he found no way in. I sat inside, cozy and warm, and I heard him banging at the window.

"Who is at my window?" I asked. The wind huffed, "It is your neighbor."

"Why does a neighbor come calling on such a windy night?"

The wind laughed. "I am here to give you a housewarming."

"Can this be true?" I asked. "For I have never heard of a neighbor coming through a window like a thief.

Now the wind knocked on my door. "Who is knocking?" I asked. The wind blew his answer: "It is I, the wind, your neighbor. Why do you lock your door against me? Open up!"

"I am not fond of the storm," I said. "Come back when the sun is out and I will open the door for you."

In a while the weather changed and the sun came out. I opened my door, but the wind was nowhere to be found. I smiled. Standing in the door, I could breathe the fresh air and see the marvelous vista of Talpiyot. And it was then I thought, "There is nothing outside my house but dirt and rock. Where are the trees and plants? Where are the flowers and grass?" So I decided to plant.

It was hard work turning the earth to make it ready. But, in the end, I planted some young trees. Rain came to water them, dew to refresh them, and sunlight to teach them to grow toward heaven. Before long, my trees were strong in trunk and branch. I put a bench beneath the trees and sat in their shade. I waited to see if the wind would come again.

When the wind came, it was at night, and the wind came howling and shrieking like a hurricane. I ran inside my house and waited, The wind struck the trees and they bent almost to the ground, but when the wind paused for even a moment, the trees struck back. The wind gathered up his strength and struck a second time. And a second time, the trees struck back. In the end, the trees stood where they had been before the squall, but the wind was out of breath. Finally, the wind blew himself away.

Ever since, the wind has been more humble. He breezes in like a real gentleman, so I treat him like a gentleman, too. When he visits, I invite him to rest beside me on the bench in the garden, in the shade of the trees. He sits with me, bringing me the fresh mountain air. We do not speak about the way we met or how he acted in those days. And when he draws in his breath to blow away, like a good neighbor, I invite him to come again. In truth, I like him very much. And, who knows? It may be that the wind likes me, too.

[adapted from a tale by S.Y. Agnon]

✥ 10 ✥
Tzedakah
Charity and
Righteousness

1. Two Brothers

✥ The building of the Temple ranks as Solomon's greatest achievement. He himself attached such great importance to it that he watched over every detail of its construction. But the most monumental decision that he faced and the one which vexed him for the longest time, was where exactly the Temple should be placed.

Solomon was awakened by a dream. He could still hear the voice in his dreaming directing him to go to Mount Zion. He dressed hurriedly and walked by the light of the moon until he reached the top of the mount. He looked about, and behold, he witnessed a strange sight, indeed.

It was harvest time. Solomon saw a beautiful field in the moonlight. Its grain had all been harvested and, at the east boundary and at the west, bundles of grain stood beside a threshing floor, awaiting the morning's work.

As he watched, a man crossed the field carrying a bundle of grain from the east threshing floor. When he reached the west threshing floor, he added the grain he was carrying to the pile already there. A while passed, and another man carried a bundle of grain from the west threshing floor to the east, leaving it there. This happened several times: the two men crossing the field, each carrying a bundle of grain, each leaving it across the field from where it had been. But the two piles of grain stayed at the same levels as before. Solomon was mystified.

Once, as the two men practically ran into one another with their bundles of grain, Solomon called to them and they stopped to look at him. A moment later, they saw one another, dropped their bundles, and embraced.

Now Solomon called them near. When they saw him in his royal robes, they bowed. "Who are you?" Solomon demanded.

"We are brothers," one said to him. "This is the field that we own and work together."

Solomon turned to the one who had spoken. "Why are you carrying bundles from one threshing floor to the other?"

"Your majesty," the man said, "I am a bachelor and I have few needs. But my older brother is married with four children. When we finished harvesting, we divided the bundles equally. But, to feed his family, he needs more grain than I. So I was carrying a few more bundles from my threshing floor to place it with his. It is only right that he should have more grain to sell."

Solomon now turned to the other. "Why were you carrying grain to your brother's end of the field?" he asked.

"Your majesty," the man said, "I am happily married. My family and I have enough to satisfy us. But my poor younger brother is a bachelor. He does not have the money to find himself a wife and begin a family of his own. So I was carrying a few bundles to his threshing floor, so that he would have more grain to sell."

"Your hearts are large," said the king. "Now, I shall make you both rich. For the two of you have made this field holy through your devotion to one another and through your acts of _tzedakah_. Now, let me purchase this field from you and give you both what you deserve—more than enough for a man with a family and more than enough for a bachelor to start a family of his own. Heaven led me to this place to discover a worthy site for God's Holy Temple."

So it was that Solomon built the Holy Temple on a field that called forth _tzedakah_ from two brothers; and ever after called forth _tzedakah_ from all Israel.

> [Uriel Costa, _Mikveh Israel_, No. 59, based perhaps on Berthold Auerbach, who refers to this legend in his _Village Stories_]

2. The Temple in Ruins

🐝 Once, as Rabban Yochanan ben Zakkai was leaving Jerusalem, Rabbi Joshua accompanied him and they saw the temple in ruins.

"Woe unto us," Rabbi Joshua cried, "that this place where Israel atoned for its sins through sacrifices is now laid waste!"

"My son," Yochanan replied, "Be not grieved; Israel has another atonement as effective as this. And what is it? It is *gemilut chasadim*, 'works of lovingkindness,' as it is said, 'For I desire mercy and not sacrifice'" (Hosea 6:6).

[*Avot deRabbi Natan* 4]

Gemilut chasadim, "works of lovingkindness," is a sub-class of *tzedakah*. It is made up of works for which no reward should be expected in this life: clothing the naked, providing a dowry for the bride, offering hospitality to the stranger, visiting the sick, comforting the mourner, and accompanying the corpse to the grave (B. Talmud *Sotah* 14a, *Eruvin* 18a, *Shabbat* 127a-b).

3. Buy Me a Town

Although Rabbi Tarfon was very rich, he did not often give money to the poor. One time, he was walking through the marketplace with Rabbi Akiva when Akiva asked, "Tarfon, how would you like me to buy one or two towns for you?"

Rabbi Tarfon said, "Yes, towns would be good to own." He gave four thousand gold dinars to Rabbi Akiva.

What did Rabbi Akiva do? He took the money and divided it among the poor students in the house of study.

A while later, Rabbi Tarfon met Rabbi Akiva in the market. "Where are the towns that you bought for me?" he inquired.

"Come, I will show you," answered Akiva. He took Rabbi Tarfon by the hand and led him to the house of study. There he found one of the poor students reading from the Book of Psalms. He pointed to a verse and told the child to read it aloud. The child read, "He has divided it among the people; he has given to those in need; he will always be called righteous" (Psalms 112:9).

Then Rabbi Akiva pointed to the room full of young men studying. He spoke to Rabbi Tarfon, saying, "This is the town I bought for you."

Rabbi Tarfon hugged Rabbi Akiva and kissed him on the forehead. "You are my teacher and my friend," he said. "With your wisdom, you teach me. By what you do, you prove that you are my friend."

Rabbi Tarfon took more gold dinars from his purse and pressed them into Akiva's hands. He smiled and said, "Now, go and buy me another town."

[B. Talmud *Kallah* 2a; *Midrash Leviticus Rabbah* 34:16; also in *Sefer HaAggadah*]

4. Shipwrecked

🐟 Rabbi Eleazar ben Shammua was walking on the rocks by the sea, when he saw a distant ship suddenly sink with all on board. As he watched, a single survivor sitting on a wooden plank was carried from wave to wave until he simply stepped ashore. The man was nearly naked and at once he hid himself among the rocks.

Other Israelites also witnessed the sight, and the man behind the rocks called to them, saying, "I am an Edomite, a child of Esau the brother of Jacob. Please give me clothing to cover my nakedness. The sea has left me with nothing." The Israelites answered, "We wish all the children of Esau were stripped bare!" And they passed him by.

But Rabbi Eleazar was dismayed to see the Israelites act this way. He removed his outer coat and offered it to the man. He also led the Edomite to his house, provided him with food and drink, gave him two hundred dinars, drove him fourteen Persian miles, and treated him with great honor, bringing him all the way to his own door.

Some time later, the king died, only to be replaced by a new king who hated Jews. He sent a decree to the entire province: In five days time, all Jewish men will be killed and all Jewish women taken as spoil. The Jews came to Rabbi Eleazar, saying, "Do not let this happen. Please, go and plead on our behalf."

The rabbi replied, "Pleading will not be enough. We must pay a ransom."

So the Jewish community entrusted him with four thousand dinars, saying, "Offer this as our ransom."

Rabbi Eleazar took the money to the gate of the royal palace and called to the guards, "Go, tell the king that a Jew stands at the gate and wishes to greet him." The guards brought him to the throne room.

But when he entered, the king got to his feet, stepped down from his throne, and bowed low to the rabbi. The king asked,

"Have you forgotten me? Or, perhaps, you have forgotten your kindness: giving me your coat, feeding me, and bringing me home?" Then Rabbi Eleazar saw that this king was the very Edomite who had been shipwrecked.

The king asked, "What is your business here?"

Rabbi Eleazar said, "I come to beg mercy for the Jews of the province."

The king said, "You have faith in your Torah, I know. And it is written there: 'You shall not hate an Edomite, for he is your brother' (Deuteronomy 23:8), yet these Jews treated me as an enemy. They are deserving of death."

Rabbi Eleazar said, "Though they are guilty, forgive them. Take the ransom instead of their lives. Here is their gift of four thousand dinars. Take the money, but show mercy to the people."

The king said, "These four thousand dinars belong to you in exchange for the two hundred you gave me. The Jews will be spared in exchange for the food and drink you shared. And for your one robe, take seventy robes of mine. And let us be brothers, as Jacob and Esau were."

[*Midrash Ecclesiastes Rabbah* 11:1]

5. The Glass and the Mirror

🐟 A rich man who never gave to charity came to visit the rabbi. "My daughter is engaged to be married and we would like you to perform the ceremony."

The rabbi replied, "I know another man's daughter who wishes to be married, but she has no money for dress or dowry, and the family cannot afford the wedding."

The rich man said, "Rabbi, let's stick to my business. I did not become rich by giving away my money."

The rabbi rose from his desk and walked to the window. "Come over here," he said.

"All right," the rich man said, joining the rabbi. "Now I am looking out your window."

"Tell me, what do you see?" the rabbi asked.

"I see people," came the reply.

The rabbi crossed the room. Between two bookshelves, there was a small mirror. He pointed to the mirror and said, "Now, come close and look here. Tell me, what do you see?"

"It is a mirror, Rabbi. I see what I always see in a mirror. Myself."

"Aha!" the rabbi said, raising both hands in the air. "That's the whole story."

Feeling perplexed, and a little impatient, the rich man asked, "What am I missing?"

"Think with me," said the rabbi. "What is a window made of?" And they both answered, "Glass." The rabbi continued, "And what is a mirror made of?" And they both answered, "Glass."

"And what is the difference between the window and the mirror?" the rabbi asked. And he waited. Finally, the rich man said, "The glass of the mirror is coated on one side."

"Yes," the rabbi said. "It is coated on one side with silver. And the silver keeps you from seeing past yourself. But if you could stop seeing the silver, you would see other people."

The rich man smiled. "Aha," he said. "You will perform the wedding for my daughter. I will pay all the expenses for the daughter of the other fellow to get married."

"Yes," said the rabbi. "Provided…"

"There's more?" asked the rich man.

"Provided that you promise, from now on, to look out your window as much as you look in your mirror."

"I will try, Rabbi. I promise you, I will try."

[adapted from Ausubel, *Treasury*, p. 60]

6. Get a Fair Price

🕮 Rabbi Shmelke of Nikolsburg was so generous that he and money barely coexisted. Any beggar could knock at his door and carry away something. As for Rabbi Shmelke and his family, they could hardly afford lentil soup. If the rabbi received money during the day, he managed to give it away before the evening. And, if a beggar knocked when there was no money, Rabbi Shmelke would find something else to give. One time, he gave a precious ring to a beggar.

His wife berated him, "Look what you have done! Do you realize that the ring you gave that man was worth four hundred ducats?" She was surely a woman of *tzedakah* herself, always ready to give food and clothing to beggars. She was not complaining because the good rabbi had given *tzedakah*. Heaven forbid! But four hundred ducats was four hundred ducats! It was not just a ring, it was a fortune!

"Was the ring really worth that much?" Rabbi Shmelke asked, shaking his head.

"That much and more!" his wife replied. And she smiled when she heard Rabbi Shmelke send his *gabbai* to call the beggar back. But she threw her hands in the air when she heard what the rabbi told the beggar.

"Listen," he said to the man, "I have just learned that the ring I gave you is worth four hundred ducats. Be careful! When you go to sell it, be sure you get a fair price."

[adapted from Langer, *Nine Gates*, pp. 146-147]

7. Giving Charity

🐟 On his way to Danzig, Rabbi Simcha Bunam stopped in a small town to spend the Sabbath. He heard about a pious and learned man who was living in extreme poverty. Rabbi Bunam invited himself to the man's house for the Sabbath. But first, he had a table and chairs, couches, beds, sheets, and pillows delivered to the man's house. Next came deliveries of dishes, pots and pans, forks and knives. Then came deliveries of food and wine in great quantities. The rabbi even sent the town tailor with special robes for each member of the poor man's family—"Fine clothing for the Sabbath," the town tailor said.

The result was a Sabbath fit for a Chasid, for the Chasidim love to splurge on all the best that God has offered us in this world—especially on Shabbat.

When Shabbat was over, Rabbi Bunam bid farewell to the poor man and handed him a bag of silver coins. But the poor man refused to accept the gift. "Look at all the charity you have already given me and my family," he said to the rabbi. "Surely, it is enough."

"Up to now," Rabbi Bunam said, "I have given you no charity. All that was given, benefitted me and did honor to God's Sabbath. I did not want to see you and your family in poverty, otherwise I might have pitied you. Now that I know you, I do not pity you. Like all of us, in some ways you are rich and in others poor. What I am giving you now is *tzedakah*, not charity. Charity is given out of pity; but *tzedakah* is 'righteousness,' given to fulfill God's commandment. It is my *mitzvah* to give *tzedakah*; it is your *mitzvah* to accept it."

[Buber, *Later Masters*, p. 242]

8. Hit Him Again

At one of our congregations—or so the story goes—an emergency meeting of the Board of Trustees was held to discuss how to raise the funds necessary for making repairs to the building. The old building was literally falling apart. Everyone knew it, but no one wanted to face the fact. The rabbi stood and made an impassioned plea and the board applauded.

You can imagine how surprised everyone was when one board member—the one who had always given the least; the one who had always been the most miserly—stood, and offered to donate the first five hundred dollars toward the building repair fund. Before he could take his seat, a bit of plaster fell from the ceiling and hit him square on the forehead. Surprised and bemused, the board member rubbed his head and said, "I suppose I had better make that the first *one thousand* dollars."

One of the other board members looked at the ceiling, shook his head, and spoke out in a deliberately loud voice, saying, "Go ahead, God. Hit him again."

[Rossel, based on urban folklore]

11
Humility

1. The Tower of Babel

In those days, all human beings spoke one language. People said: "We are a mighty breed; united, nothing can withstand us. Let us build a tower to heaven, so that we can make war on God. Our arrows will rain on heaven and heaven will fall before us!"

They set out to erect their tower. Brick by brick the tower rose. People carried bricks to the top, one by one, and the tower's top rose. The higher the tower, the longer it took to get a brick to the top. When the tower reached seven stories, it took a full day to carry a single brick to the top.

When a person fell from the tower, the workers paid no attention. But when a brick fell, work stopped for a time of mourning. All sat down and wept for the loss of the brick. "Much depends on getting the bricks to the top," they reminded one another. And all agreed: "Every brick is precious."

Finally, God pitied their foolishness and disdained their misplaced sorrow. God thought, "They care more about bricks made of mud than they do about one another. Very well, then, let them speak to one another like bricks speaking." And God confounded their one language into all the seventy languages of the earth.

Unable to communicate, their unity was shattered. They fell to gesticulating wildly, pointing and jabbing one another, grabbing and jostling to be understood. Workers more frequently dropped bricks; and those bricks that made it to the top were taken where they were not needed. People quarreled over trifles, wrestled, bloodied one another, and cast opponents against the tower walls. From bottom to top, bricks were loosened, chipped, shattered, and broken. Even mud sun-dried hard as stone could not withstand human strife. Brick by brick, as they had built it up, so they themselves brought the massive tower down. The once-

245

mighty human breed could not even grieve over their loss. They could only babble; that is why the place is called Babel.

When the tower was a ruin, people gathered in groups according to their tongues—those who could speak the same language and understand one another. One by one, the groups abandoned Babel to found their own cities. And so it went, until human beings were scattered over the face of the whole earth.

[*Midrash Genesis Rabbah* 38:6; also in *Sefer HaAggadah*]

2. The Little Sheep and the Lowly Bush

Moses was a wonderful shepherd. He never lost a single sheep.

Once, a lamb ran away from the herd and Moses ran after it. He caught up just as the little beast started to drink from a stream. "Poor lamb," Moses said, "I did not know you were thirsty. Slake your thirst; drink as much as you need." When the lamb finished drinking, Moses lifted it on his shoulders and carried it back to the flock. God saw this and said, "Moses truly understands compassion. He shall be the shepherd for My flock. Through Moses I will rescue the Children of Israel."

Moses' sheep ate the long grass until there was no more. When the grass of the field was gone, they climbed the mountain higher and higher to find more grass to eat. One day on the mountain, Moses looked up and saw a little bush burning. He thought, "I will turn aside to get a closer look." As he approached, behold, he saw a marvelous thing. The bush was truly aflame, yet its branches and leaves were not consumed by the fire.

Suddenly, the voice of God spoke to Moses from behind the burning bush. God said, "I have heard the painful cries of My people, the Children of Israel. You must return to Egypt and bring them out so that they may be free to worship Me."

The Rabbis taught: The burning bush was always there; the flame set in it by God in the days of Creation. From that time forth, many climbed the mountain and passed it without stopping. To ordinary people, it seemed a little thing. But Moses noticed that little thing, just as Moses had noticed the little lamb that strayed. Sometimes, the Rabbis said, the greatest miracles are hidden in little things, if only we turn aside to notice them.

[*Midrash Exodus Rabbah* 2:2; Rossel, *Storybook Haggadah*]

3. The Thorn Bush

🐾 Someone asked Rabbi Joshua ben Karchah, "Why did God speak to Moses from a thorn bush?" Rabbi Joshua told this story: When it was time to tell Moses to go down to Egypt to set the Israelites free from slavery, God decided to speak from a tree. Then, the trees vied to be chosen by God for this purpose.

The fig tree said, "God should choose me. When Moses wandered through the wilderness, he went for days without water. He grew hungry, tired, hot, and thirsty. He did not know the way. But he saw the green leaves of my crown from a distance, and he knew that where I grow there is always water. He came to where I stood. And how I welcomed him! He drank from the water at my roots. He ate my figs until his hunger was gone. He cooled himself in the shade of my branches. And when night came, he slept on the soft earth beside me. I have been Moses' friend, and that is why God should choose me."

But the carob tree said, "God should choose me. When Moses came out of the wilderness, he married Zipporah, one of Jethro's daughters. She picked beans from my branches and ground the pods into flour. Then she baked the flour to make bread. At that holy moment of Moses' life, at his marriage feast, Moses blessed God over a loaf of carob bread. Moses used my fruit to give thanks to God, and that is why God should choose me."

In this way, each tree came forward to tell why it should be chosen as the tree of destiny. Some had provided wood for the fires Moses needed for warmth. Some had given Moses shelter from the sun while he tended the flocks. Every tree had some reason for being chosen. All but one, the lowly thorn bush, which did not speak at all.

God asked, "Thorn bush, why are you silent?"

The thorn bush replied, "I am a small and insignificant tree. Animals hate me because they become entangled in my branches. Human beings hate me because they prick themselves on my thorns. My branches are too thin and frail for building fires or making houses. I am too short for people to use for shade. There is no reason You should choose me."

But God said, "Nevertheless, I have chosen you. I will speak to Moses from your branches."

Then all the trees asked, "Why should the Holy One choose this basest and most despised of all trees?"

God replied, "To show that I am in all things on the earth, even in the lowly thorn bush."

[*Midrash Exodus Rabbah* 2:5; *Midrash Song of Songs Rabbah* 3:10; also in *Sefer HaAggadah*]

4. King David and the Frog

King David held his harp on his knee. He strummed and sang softly as he looked out the window. Before him was Jerusalem, his city, the City of David. He loved it by day as the sun reflected from its rosy stones. He loved it by night as the light of oil lamps glimmered in the windows of its homes. As he played the harp, he sang a poem of thanks to God, a psalm.

He smiled to himself. He loved being king. He was proud of his city. He was proud of his harp. He was proud of his psalm. And he was proud of his singing. How well he knew that everyone agreed his was the finest voice in all the land.

When he finished his song, he yawned and looked across the room. Was the couch he used for sleeping calling him? He was tired; surely, it beckoned him to rest. He hung his harp on the hook by the window and gazed out on the city one more time. The moon over Jerusalem was a golden ball hung in a cloudless velvet sky. Satisfied, he stretched out on the cushion of his couch, closed his eyes and fell fast asleep, a smile playing on his lips.

Toward midnight, a breeze came up and blew into Jerusalem from the south. It swirled into the open window of David's bedroom and caused the harp to sway back and forth on its hook. Like a million tickling fingers, the breeze crossed over and around the strings until the harp gave forth sweet music. The sounds of a Jerusalem night joined in—insects chirping, frogs croaking, and the mournful whoop of the hoopoe bird.

David sat upright on his couch. He was wide awake, yet it seemed to him that he was still dreaming. What a beautiful melody! he thought, as he listened to God's creatures sing. And still the breeze played on, moving the harp to and fro, a lullaby rising from its strings. David could not go back to sleep. He had to listen.

He lit the small oil lamp on the table and sat in his chair. He opened the Torah scroll that he kept on the table and set himself to study. The scroll had opened to words of song: "I will sing to God, for God has gained a glorious victory.... God is my strength, and God is my song!" So David studied and listened, listened and studied, until nearly the whole night had passed away. Slowly, the breeze softened, and the harp rested and played no more.

Then David spoke to God, saying, "O Blessed One, look how mighty I am! I am a great student of Your Torah, studying all night. And I am a great singer, singing to You all the time. Have You ever had any one who sings You finer songs than I?"

No sooner were these words out of his mouth than David heard a croaking louder than any noise he had ever heard before. David looked and saw a bull frog sitting on his window's ledge. He thought, "Surely, I must be dreaming. How could a frog jump so high as to land on my window ledge?" As if in answer, the frog croaked out its speech.

"Is that a proper prayer for a king?" the frog inquired. "You sound like a rooster crowing, 'Look at me, how wonderful I am!' Surely, those words are fine for a show-off. But are they words fit for a king?"

David replied, "But it is all true. I am a good student of Torah. And I do sing songs to God all the time."

When the frog heard this, he leaped from the ledge of the window to the table. Sitting before the king, the frog said, "I like your songs, Your majesty, but I am tired of your bragging. I am an old frog, and you can take a lesson from me. Long before God created human beings, we frogs were already croaking, birds were already singing, and insects were already chirping. Every song we creatures sing is a psalm for God. God created our songs for all the world to hear. You, on the other hand, sing a little bit each night; and yet you brag that you are the greatest singer in all the world! But we frogs sing all night every night. We let our song speak for us."

David said, "Old frog, you are right. Sometimes when we are happy, we human beings brag too much about how great we are. It would be better if we were more like you. From now on, I will try to let the songs I sing and the things I do speak for me."

The bull frog said no more. It puffed up its throat and croaked a little song to God. David took his harp from its hook and plucked the strings. Then David and the frog sang together, sending up a psalm to God, even as the sun rose over Jerusalem.

[*Midrash Lamentations Rabbah* 2:22; also in two versions in *Sefer HaAggadah*]

A king dressed himself in old garments, lived in a small hut, and refused to allow anyone to bow to him. One day, the king glanced in a mirror and thought, "What good has all this humility done for me? In truth, I am as proud now as ever I was." He called for a philosopher and asked him to explain how it was that his regimen of modesty was having no effect. The philosopher said, "My dear king, you have it backward. Dress like a king; live like a king; allow your subjects to show you deference; but be humble in your heart."

5. Two Wise Children

The disciples of Rabbi Joshua asked him, "Why do you always pay such close attention to everything we say?"

Rabbi Joshua answered, "I am your teacher, but that does not mean I always know more than you. I listen carefully to your words because I have been taught many good lessons even by little children."

"What have children taught you?" they asked.

Rabbi Joshua gave them two stories:

Once, as I was walking between two towns, I saw a road that cut through a field. I thought, "My way will be shorter if I take that road." So I started walking through the field. I had gone but a short way, when a little girl called to me.

"Master," she said, "are you so cruel that you would trample the grain in this field?"

"No," I replied, "but this is surely a path that many feet have traveled before mine. The grain here is already trampled."

"That is true," said the little girl. "It was trampled by others as cruel as you. They, too, set their feet to go through the field instead of around it. Would you follow in their footsteps to do evil?"

"You are absolutely correct," I told the girl. Then I turned back and walked around the field.

Another time, I was walking between two towns when I saw a little boy sitting at a crossroads. I asked him, "My son, by which of these roads should I go to the town?"

First, the boy pointed to one road, saying, "This is the shorter road but longer." Then he pointed at the other road, saying, "This is the longer road but shorter."

Being very tired, I decided to take the shorter road, but after I walked some distance, I found that the road came to an end. Bushes and weeds blocked the way on every side. So I turned back and returned to the crossroads. The little boy was still there.

"My son," I inquired, "did you not tell me that the road I took was shorter?"

"You listened, but you did not hear," said the little boy. "I said that the road you took was shorter but longer. It is longer because you would have to struggle through the weeds and thorns to get to town. But the other road, O Master, is longer but shorter. It ends in the center of the town."

So I kissed the boy on the head and said to him, "We are truly blessed, for even the youngest of the Children of Israel are wise."

[B. Talmud *Eruvin* 53b; also in *Sefer HaAggadah*]

Rabbi Joshua said: "If all seas were ink, and all the reeds were pens; if heaven and earth were scrolls; and all human beings were scribes, still they would not suffice to write down the teachings I have learned, even though I abstracted from my masters no more than a person would take when dipping the point of a painting stick in a pool of paint" (*Midrash Song of Songs Rabbah* 1:3, #1).

6. The Toothpick

🐟 Rabbi Zeira was so old and weak that he needed help when he walked. So Rabbi Haggai became his constant companion, walking with him, and allowing Rabbi Zeira to lean upon his shoulder. As they were walking one day, a man carrying a bundle of wood chips passed by them. Rabbi Zeira said, "Good Rabbi Haggai, kindly stop that man and ask him for a single chip of wood that I may use as a toothpick."

Rabbi Haggai started after the man, but then he heard Rabbi Zeira call him back. "Hold. Do not take even a single chip," Zeira said. "I have thought it over, and it was wrong of me to make such a request."

"Surely, it cannot hurt to take a single chip from a whole bundle of wood chips," said Rabbi Haggai.

"Oh, it can hurt very much," Rabbi Zeira responded. "If everyone would ask for but one chip, soon the man would have no bundle at all. God forbid that I should do such harm to this man."

[J. Talmud *Demai* 3:2, 23b; also in *Sefer HaAggadah*]

7. The Farmer's Boast

A farmer often bragged: "I am the most important person around. If I do not plow the field, sow the seed, and harvest the crop, what will you eat?" Pretty soon, people grew weary of his bragging.

Once, a wheel of his wagon struck a rock and broke. The farmer went to the blacksmith. "I need to work," he said. "Please mend my wheel."

"I will not fix it," said the blacksmith.

"Why not?" the farmer asked. "Without a wagon I cannot gather my wheat."

The blacksmith laughed and said, "You are always bragging that you are the most important person of all. I will only fix your wheel, if you will fix your bragging."

The farmer promised. From then on, he bragged: "Everybody depends on the farmer except the blacksmith."

To harvest the wheat, the farmer needed new shoes. But when he asked the shoemaker to make them, the shoemaker said, "I will not!"

"Why not?" asked the farmer. "Should I go barefoot in the fields?"

The shoemaker laughed and said, "You are always bragging that you are the most important person of all. I will make you shoes, if you will fix your bragging."

Again, the farmer promised. From then on, he bragged: "Everybody depends on the farmer except the blacksmith and the shoemaker."

When the harvest was in, the farmer needed the miller to grind the wheat into flour. The miller refused unless the farmer would promise to fix his bragging. From then on, the farmer bragged: "Everyone depends on the farmer, except the blacksmith, the shoemaker, and the miller."

In the same way, the farmer needed the carpenter, the tailor, the baker, the butcher, and all the other folk who lived in town.

And all of them refused to help him, unless he added them to the list of people he needed. Finally, one day, the bragging stopped. From then on, the farmer would say: "Everybody depends on the farmer—and the farmer depends on everybody."

[adapted from Certner, *101 Jewish Stories*]

8. Forgetting Torah

🐟 The people of Simona sent word to Rabbi Judah the Prince, "Send us one of your rabbis who is a Torah scholar, a judge, a scribe, and a teacher for our children." Rabbi Judah sent Levi ben Sisi.

Levi went north to the town of Simona. When he arrived, the people made a great party for him. They gave him a beautiful house in which to live. They took him to the bath house and gave him new clothing. They brought him to the house of study and said, "We have made a throne for you to sit upon."

He stepped up on the platform they had built and sat on the throne of wood and silver. He placed his hands on the arms of the throne and looked down on the people of the town. "I am ready to help," he said.

They asked him a question concerning a commandment of the Written Torah. He could not answer. They asked him to expound a ruling of the Spoken Torah. Again he could not answer. They asked him question after question, but he knew no answers whatever. At last, they told him, "You are not the kind of man we need." Levi left Simona and returned to Jerusalem.

Soon, the elders of Simona appeared before Rabbi Judah. "Is this the kind of man you send to us?" they asked. "He knows nothing of Jewish law and nothing of Jewish lore."

Judah sent for Levi and said to the elders of Simona, "Ask your questions again."

They asked the same questions. This time Levi gave an answer to each question. And in every answer there was wisdom.

Rabbi Judah asked Levi, "Why are you able to answer these questions now, when you could not answer them in Simona?"

"When I came to Simona," replied Levi, "they set me on a throne and worshiped me like a god. My heart was full of pride, and all I could think was, 'How wonderful I must be to sit on a throne.' For the life of me, I could not remember any of the Torah that I had studied."

Rabbi Judah said, "They paid you honor because you studied Torah. But you forgot what Torah teaches: We must seek wisdom, not honor."

[J. Talmud *Yevamot* 12:6, 13a; *Midrash Genesis Rabbah* 81:2; also in *Sefer HaAggadah*]

9. Do Not Think of I

Once Rabbi Melech of Lizensk visited a small town. When he went away, the whole community followed him, walking behind his carriage and singing.

He asked the coachman, "Where do all these people go?"

The coachman said, "But, Rabbi, they are following you! They want to gain merit in Heaven by honoring your wisdom."

"You don't say," Rabbi Melech replied. He immediately forgot his "I" and thought only of what the people were doing. So he jumped down and joined the crowd, singing and walking along behind the carriage. "If they wish to gain merit in Heaven," he thought, "why should I not join them?"

Therefore, the Chasidim say, to be a spiritual Jew you must forget your "I,"—your soul must think of God and not of self.

[adapted from Langer, *Nine Gates*, p. 129]

10. What to Wear

Albert Einstein's wife tried mightily to have her brilliant husband dress more professionally when he headed off to work. "Why should I?" he would invariably argue. "Everyone there knows me."

When the time came for Einstein to lecture before his first major conference, she begged him to dress up a bit. "Why should I?" said Einstein. "No one there knows me!"

[Internet anecdote]

Einstein observed: "My religion consists of a humble admiration of the illimitable superior spirit who reveals himself in the slight details we are able to perceive with our frail and feeble mind" (*Einstein Quotes*, collected by Kevin Harris, 1995).

11. Sound the *Shofar*

🕮 A former chief rabbi of Israel, Rabbi Abraham Isaac Kook of Jerusalem lay in the hospital recovering from a heart attack. It was the month of Elul and, in accord with the tradition of preparing for the coming High Holy Days, he asked that the *shofar* be blown each morning so that he could fulfill the commandment to hear the blowing of the ram's horn. The rabbi's doctor feared that the violent blasts of the *shofar* might have an adverse effect on his critically-ill patient. He argued in vain against Rav Kook's request.

Then, one of Rav Kook's disciples said to the doctor, "You are trying in the wrong way. Only suggest to Rav Kook that the other patients might be disturbed by the blasts."

As soon as the doctor proffered this suggestion, Rav Kook immediately replied, "If that is the case, do not permit the *shofar* to be blown!"

[adapted from Goodman, *Rosh HaShanah Anthology*, p. 139]

12
Shelom Bayit
Domestic Tranquility

1. Choose One Thing

The wedding was the finest ever held in Sidon. Everyone who was anyone was invited. The bride was dressed in fine wool. Perfumed oil was poured on her head and her hair was decorated with a crown of gold. For the groom, a branch of an olive tree was twisted and bent into a crown. Flowers were set around the bridal canopy. Food was served on large shells brought from the seashore and there was more wine and fish than the guests could consume. The groom—a wealthy fisherman—was treated like a king and his bride like a queen. And the Jews of Sidon praised the bride's beauty and danced to celebrate the marriage.

Ten years passed, but the fisherman and his wife were not blessed with a single child. One day, the wife said to her husband, "It seems that we shall never have a child together. You must leave me and marry another."

"I do not wish to leave you," answered the fisherman. "I love you very much."

"And I love you, too," said the woman, taking hold of his hand, "but to have a family you must have children; and we have no children."

The fisherman was sad. He hardly slept that night. In the morning, he told his wife, "I have heard that of a great rabbi named Simeon ben Yochai. Perhaps he will bless us so that we may have children."

The next day, they set out on the road to the south to find Rabbi Simeon ben Yochai. The fisherman and his wife held hands and, from time to time, they glanced at each other with love. So it was for the three days of the journey. They hardly spoke a word along the way. At last, they came to the home of Rabbi Simeon.

256

"Great master of Torah," the fisherman said, "either you must bless us so that we can have children or else we must part one from the other."

Rabbi Simeon shook his head. "This thing you ask is beyond my skill. The Torah explains that it takes three to make a child—a father, a mother, and God. It is clear that you wish to be a father. It is clear that your wife wishes to be a mother. But God alone decides when the time is right."

"Does this mean we must be divorced?" asked the fisherman's wife.

"Yes," said Rabbi Simeon, wincing as he saw their bodies bend in pain and their faces grow long. "But I declare you must separate in joy and not in sadness. You have told me how wonderful was the feast at your wedding. Now, you must make a feast just as wonderful for your divorce. You shall be separated with food, with wine, and with love."

They left the rabbi and returned to Sidon. Along the way, when the wife would begin to cry, her husband would say, "Why should you cry? Think of the beautiful feast we shall soon have." And when the husband would start to weep, his wife would say, "This is no time for weeping. We must think about who should be invited to our feast."

So they made a great feast, setting out the seashell plates, cooking fish and roasting lamb, making bread and baking cakes, and bringing wine in great jugs to the tables. It seemed that all the Jews of Sidon were invited, and the dancing, singing, and drinking went on from evening to the early hours of the next morning. Even as the last cup of wine was passed, and the last dance danced, the fisherman and his wife were filled with the joy of celebration.

Then the fisherman said to his wife, "My love, I have decided that you may choose any precious thing you desire from our home and take it with you when you return to your father's house."

What did she do? She waited for the fisherman to fall asleep. Then she called her servants and told them, "Lift the couch with my husband on it, and carry the couch and my husband to my father's house."

In the morning, the fisherman rose from his sleep, rubbed his eyes, and looked around. "My love, where am I?" he asked.

"Do you not know?" she asked. "You are in the house of my father."

"But what am I doing in the house of your father?"

"Do you not know? You said to me last night: 'Choose anything precious from my home and take it with you when you return to your father's house.' There is nothing in the world more precious to me than you."

The fisherman took his wife in his arms. "I shall never leave you," he said. "We shall return to Rabbi Simeon, and this time he will pray with us."

And when they again stood before Rabbi Simeon, he said, "I am pleased that you have returned. The last time, you asked me to pray for you. That is fine, but it would not be enough. This time, you ask me to pray with you. So let us pray together, for it is when we pray together that God hears us best."

A season passed before the fisherman's wife took her husband's hand, saying, "My love, place your hand just here and feel the life that is growing. Together—God and you and I—we shall soon have a child."

[*Midrash Song of Songs Rabbah* 1:4, #2; also *Sefer HaAggadah*]

2. Close the Door!

One cold winter night, Asher and his wife Basha were awakened by a loud noise and a gust of icy air.

"The wind has blown the door open," Asher said. "Kindly get up, and close it."

"No. You get up and close it," Basha said.

"I shall not," Asher said. "I asked you to do it."

"I have no wish to do it," Basha said.

"We shall see," said Asher. "Let us make a bargain: The first to utter a word must get up and shut the door."

To this bargain, both agreed, both certain that the other would speak first. So the long silence began, and with it the creaking of the door, the gusting of the icy breeze, the shivering, the waiting, and the growing stubbornness of them both.

Came the robbers. First, there were footsteps. Then, voices saying, "An open door! Here's a job that is easier than most! These people deserve a good robbery." Next, the clatter of silverware and pots and pans thrown into sacks. From there, the sound of furniture creaking as pieces were lifted onto the crooks' shoulders and whisked out the open door: books, table, loom, couch.

Soon the thieves reached the bedroom and began taking it apart. They saw Asher and Basha in bed, both sitting absolutely silent. One thief said to another, "They must be blind, deaf, and dumb." The other one answered, "Take it all, just leave them and their bed." And still the stubborn couple refused to speak.

The thieves departed and, what was worse, they had not even closed the door behind them. It was silent in the house, quiet as the grave. At dawn, the couple rose and inspected their home. All that was left was lonesome walls, empty cabinets, and the bed.

Basha looked at Asher in anger. He looked back at her in anger. But neither spoke. He pointed to his belly. She pointed to hers. They were hungry. Basha pointed to the door and made a little walking motion with her fingers. She was going to get some groceries. She left through the door, but she did not close it.

A little later, the barber arrived. "I am here as I promised," he said cheerily. Looking around, the barber said, "Are you moving out of town?" But there was no reply from Asher. Asher just went into the bedroom and sat on the bed.

The barber took out his scissors and set to work. "Tell me when to stop," he said to Asher. Of course, Asher said nothing, so the barber cut and sheared, sheared and cut, pausing at times to wait for Asher to say "Enough!" But Asher never spoke. It was the barber who ran out of what to cut, for Asher was now bald as an egg—no hair above and no beard below.

The barber said, "Pay me and I will be on my way," But Asher was too stubborn about remaining silent even to say that his wallet had been taken by the thieves.

The barber soon passed from frustrated to infuriated. "I'll teach you!" he said. He grabbed soot from the stove and dumped it on Asher. "There," he said. "That's what you deserve!" Asher said nothing. The barber gathered his tools and walked out. Nor did he close the door.

That's when Basha returned. Taking one look at Asher, covered in soot, missing his beard, shaved to his bald head, she forgot herself and screamed, "Asher! Asher!"

Very, very slowly, Asher's lips formed a big, broad grin and he hugged himself with his hands. "Aha!" he exclaimed, "You spoke first! Now, dear wife, get up and close the door!"

[folktale adapted from Swynnerton, *Indian Nights' Entertainment*, no. 11, pp. 14-15]

3. The Wooden Bowl

An old and feeble man came to live with his son's family. His legs were weak, his eyes were dim, and his hands shook. Seeing this, the son worried that his father might accidentally break the fine china. One day, the son took some wood and carved a wooden bowl for his father to use.

Not long after, the son came home and discovered his own son carving a hollow in a piece of wood. "What are you making?" he asked.

The boy looked up at his father said, "I am making a wooden bowl for you. When you are as old as grandfather, you will have a wooden bowl, too."

After that, whenever the family sat down to eat, the grandfather was served like everyone else, on a fine china dish.

[B. Talmud *Kiddushin* 31a-b]

4. The Puddings

A wife and husband came to visit Rabbi Israel, the Maggid of Koznitz. They sat at the table across from him. The Maggid noticed that the wife's hand was in her husband's, so he was surprised when the husband stated that he wished to divorce his wife.

"What is the problem that cannot be solved?" the Maggid asked.

"It's the Sabbath pudding," the husband said. "All week, as I work, I dream of the Sabbath pudding." He looked at his wife. "The taste of her pudding is like the sound of the angels singing. No other taste on earth can compare."

"If so, what is the problem?" the Maggid asked.

The husband continued: "Every Sabbath it is the same. As soon as I finish reciting the *Kiddush* prayer and drinking the wine, my wife serves the first course." He looked at his wife. "The first course is fish prepared with such love that every bite is pure pleasure. It is impossible to eat my wife's fish without finishing every morsel on the plate. When the fish course is complete, she brings out the onions and the chicken." He glanced again at his wife. "What can be said to describe the worlds of flavors in the onions and the chicken? It is impossible to set aside the plate without finishing the onions and cleaning every speck of meat from the bones of the chicken. My wife, as all will freely attest, is the finest cook in all of Koznitz."

"So," the Maggid said. "What is the problem?"

"Dear Rabbi, you can only empathize with my suffering if you can imagine how full a person's stomach can be after the fish, the onions, and the chicken. When at last the Sabbath pudding arrives on the table, I have no strength left to eat it. I know how delicious it is. I know what paroxysms of pleasure await. But I am simply too full to eat it. Week after week, I beg her to serve the pudding first, to let me have this gratification when I can appreciate it. But she refuses." He glanced at his wife again. "There is no choice. We must have a divorce!"

The Maggid shook his head. The couple was still holding hands; and every gaze and glance they shared was filled with love. He turned to the wife, asking, "Why not serve the pudding first?"

She immediately lowered her eyes so as not to offend the holy man. In a small voice, she answered, "My mother taught me to cook. If I am a good cook, she was an excellent cook. If my pudding is wonderful, hers was miraculous. And she taught me our family traditions. Shabbat is celebrated first with fish, then with onions and chicken, and last with the crowning achievement, the Sabbath pudding. O Holy Rabbi, is it not written that I must honor my mother and my father? Is it not true that I must be faithful to my family tradition, especially now that my mother watches me from Heaven? Not to serve the pudding last would be an insult to all the generations of women in my family!"

The Maggid nodded. "I understand," he said. "But we have been taught that, when it comes to family, there is always a middle way—a path that brings *shelom bayit,* 'peace-at-home.' And I think I know a middle way here." And the Maggid was pleased to see the couple look hopefully at one another. "From now on, I pronounce, you must make two Sabbath puddings. You will serve the first right after the *Kiddush* in honor of your husband. And you will serve the other, as before—the crowning achievement—at the very end of the meal, in honor of your mother and the tradition of your family."

As if a great light dawned, the couple smiled. They rose together, bowed to the Maggid, bid him farewell, and left—still holding hands.

The Maggid's wife overheard the whole conversation from the next room. She came and kissed her husband on the head, saying, "My husband, you are truly wise."

"Wiser than you think," said the Maggid. "From now on, my dear wife, it is my wish that you, too, shall prepare two Sabbath puddings—one to serve after the *Kiddush* and one as dessert." Thus was born a new tradition in the house of the Maggid of Koznitz; a tradition carried forward in the homes of his children and of his children's children. And, ever after, the pudding served immediately after the *Kiddush* was known as the "*Shelom Bayit* Pudding."

[Buber, *Early Masters*, pp. 293-294]

13

Leshon HaRa and *Yetzer HaRa*
The Evil Tongue and
The Evil Impulse

1. Removing an Evil Tongue

In the days before printing, when every book was copied by hand, young Ismail (Samuel) ibn Nagrela came to the attention of the court through the beauty of his handwriting. Starting as a scribe, he became the vizier's private secretary, then rose to the office of vizier at the court of the Berber King Habus, the Muslim ruler of Granada. The Jews called him *Shmuel HaNagid*, "Samuel the Prince."

The king was Muslim and Samuel was Jewish, a difference that did not keep them from being friends. Samuel was a poet and the king was an ardent lover of poetry. But their friendship and mutual admiration gave rise to much jealousy among the Muslim poets at court.

It happened once that a Muslim poet came before the king to demand justice. "What wrong has been done to you?" the king asked.

"The Jew, Ibn Nagrela, plagiarized a poem I wrote, calling it his own," the poet claimed. "He even dared to read it before you, Your Majesty. I beg you, O King, have this liar's tongue cut out for this crime."

"We shall see," the king replied. He sent a messenger to bring Samuel to the throne room immediately.

"What have you to say to this charge?" the king asked his Jewish friend.

"I am innocent, Your Majesty," Samuel said.

263

"Can you prove your innocence?" the king asked.

"In this way," Samuel replied. And from beneath his robe he pulled out the original manuscript of his poem. "Here is my first draft," he said, "and upon it are all the markings and changes which I made to better the poem. All of my work is here to be seen, from its first rough form to the final work which I read before the king."

The king turned to the poet who had accused Samuel. "And you," he said, "can you show me your original work?"

With that, the jealous poet withered. "There is none," he admitted, almost in a whisper.

"Then let your punishment be in the hands of Samuel Ibn Nagrela," the king said. And, turning to his friend, he added, "I command you to cut out the evil tongue of this man, just as he would have had yours cut out."

Later that day, the king passed Samuel's room and heard the sound of laughter within. Opening the door, he was astounded to see the two men, Samuel and the Muslim poet who had been his accuser, laughing and playing a game of chess together.

"Samuel," the king said, "this man is your enemy. Why have you not removed his evil tongue as I commanded you?"

"But, I have done just as you advised, Your Majesty," Samuel replied. "You see, I have turned him from an enemy into a friend. I have cut out his evil tongue and put a kind one in its place."

[adapted from Abrahams, *Chapters on Jewish Literature*; see also, Heinrich Graetz, *History of the Jews*, vol. 3, p. 254]

Leshon hara (literally, "the evil tongue") is "slander" which the Torah condemns in the Holiness Code, stating, "You shall not go about spreading slander among your people; nor shall you stand idly by when your neighbor's life is at stake" (Leviticus 19:16). The sages observed that the two parts of this verse were purposely connected. Destroying a reputation is tantamount to imperiling a person's life. In Jewish law, both are capital crimes.

2. Daniel Prays

🕮 The enemies of Daniel slandered him before the king. When the king sent for Daniel to answer the charges made against him, the time for the afternoon prayers had come. So Daniel ignored the summons, remained in his rooms, and prayed.

Even the king was surprised by this behavior. Daniel's enemies could hardly have been more pleased. "What shall be done with one who is guilty and will not answer his king?" demanded the enemies.

In this way, Daniel fell into the hands of his enemies. They took him to a den full of lions and threw him to the voracious, growling beasts.

It came to pass in the morning, when the enemies returned, that Daniel was still alive. All night long he had prayed, and the lions, instead of eating him, had settled down on every side of him.

Sensing a miracle, the king had Daniel removed from the lion's den.

But Daniel's enemies protested, saying, "The lions were not hungry."

Then the king said, "Let us test and see if they were hungry or not." With that, the king commanded that all Daniel's enemies be thrown in with the lions. So it was that Daniel's enemies were destroyed by ravenous beasts, while Daniel was saved through prayer.

[Rossel, *When a Jew Prays*; based on Daniel, Chapter 6]

3. A Tongue for Good and Evil

🔖 How flexible is the tongue and how great is its power! It is related of a Persian king that his physicians ordered him to drink the milk of a *livayah*, a lioness, and one of his servants offered to procure this rare medicine. Taking some sheep to lure the beast— and risking his life at every moment—he actually succeeded in milking a lioness.

On his journey home, the servant was so tired that he fell into a deep slumber. While he slept, the members of his body began to argue which of them had contributed most towards the man's success in obtaining so rare a commodity as the milk of a *livayah*.

Said the feet: "Without a doubt, we were the most critical factors in this successful undertaking. Without us, the man could not set out, nor journey, nor slip up in stealth, nor return without mishap."

"Not so," said the hands, "setting out would have been of no avail had we not proven so handy. By us, the rig was built to hold the lioness, the lambs were led to the slaughter, and the milk was extracted."

"Feet and hands had a small share, of course," exclaimed the eyes, "but without us the man would have walked and groped in vain."

"And yet," interrupted the heart, "had I not inspired the idea, none of the things you all think you accomplished would have been possible."

At last the tongue put in her claim, but she was utterly ridiculed by the unanimous opinions of all the contending members of the body.

"You?" they said scornfully, "You have no free power to act—whereas, each and every one of us does. You are imprisoned in the narrow space of the human mouth—whereas, every one of us rules over all the other parts at one time or another. How can you dare claim to have contributed to this success?"

The parts of his body were still arguing when the servant awoke, stretched, and set himself back on the road. He traveled on, until he appeared before the king, carrying the much-desired *livayah* milk. The man prepared to say, "Here, I have brought your Majesty the milk of a *livayah*," but, by a slip of the tongue, he said, "Here I have brought your Majesty the milk of a *kalbah*."

The savage king was insulted and embarrassed by these words. He ordered the servant to be seized and immediately hung on the gallows.

On the way to be executed, all the members of the man's body—heart, eyes, feet, and hands—trembled with fear. But not the tongue! "I told you so," said the tongue to the other parts, "Is my power not greater than all yours put together? Are you ready now to acknowledge me as the master of all?"

What choice did the other members of the body have? They all admitted what the tongue claimed. Whereupon, the tongue requested a short reprieve from the hangman, so that it could make a last minute appeal for clemency to the king. When the servant was brought before the king, the tongue spoke eloquently:

"O great and just king," the tongue began, "Is hanging a fit reward for a servant who gladly offered his life to fulfill the king's desire? Has any man before been known to risk death itself in order to bring the king the medicine he required?—And to take it from a terrifying beast of the jungle, who at any moment might have ended the life of this loyal servant of the king?"

"But," the king answered, "By your own admission you brought me dog's milk instead of lioness' milk."

"Not so, My Liege," replied the tongue, "I brought the milk your majesty required; but, in my excitement, and because they sound alike, I confused the words *kalbah*, 'dog' and *livayah*, 'lioness.' Drink the milk of the *livayah* that I brought and you will know that I have spoken the truth."

The milk was submitted to the test, and was found to be the milk of a *livayah*, and no mistake. That is how the tongue triumphantly demonstrated its great power for good or for evil.

[*Midrash Psalms* 39]

4. Lies Like Feathers

A woman came to her rabbi to confess that she was addicted to gossiping and spreading rumors about her neighbors. She pleaded for his help. How could she change her ways?

"Pluck a chicken," the rabbi said, "and scatter its feathers along the road from your home to the town square. Then return the way you came, gather the feathers in a basket, and bring them to me. When you have done this, I will give you my answer."

She readily agreed to do as the rabbi asked. The next day she returned, but, lo!, her basket was nearly empty. "Rabbi," she said, "I followed your instructions. I plucked the chicken and scattered its feathers, but when I returned the way I had come, I found that the wind had scattered the feathers in all directions." She pointed to the basket. "These are all I could collect."

"Now you see, my dear child," the rabbi sadly said, "gossip is like feathers; once it is scattered, it cannot be retrieved. It flies off in all directions, doing damage wherever it reaches. As our rabbis taught us, 'What is spoken in Rome may kill in Syria' (*Midrash Genesis Rabbah* 98:23)." The rabbi raised a finger to his lips. "When you hear gossip, practice silence."

[Yiddish folktale; see also the version in Certner, *101 Jewish Stories*]

5. Freedom of Choice

Rabbi Akiva said, "Everything is foreseen, yet freedom of choice is given." (Mishnah *Avot* 3:19) Yet, if God knows all things in advance, how can it be said that human beings have free will?

Imagine a lighthouse along a rocky shoreline. God is the keeper of the lighthouse. In the midst of a storm, with the searchlight ablaze in the darkness, God looks out and sees the many ships approaching the shore. From above, God can tell which ships will avoid the jagged rocks and reach land safely. God can also tell which ships will strike the rocks and be destroyed.

Even so, aboard each ship, each captain is free to choose how to steer and what course to pursue. Some will heed the warning light of the lighthouse; and others will not. Naturally the chances are better if the captain sees the warning light and steers accordingly. Still, each captain makes his own choices. God's knowledge does not affect the captain's free will.

[Rossel based on a comment by J. H. Hertz, in *Sayings of the Fathers*]

6. Before This World

🐚 Before creating this world, God created many others without the Torah. Because God created them, each of these worlds was perfect, each beautiful—yet they were static and did not grow or change. In these previous worlds there was no lust, but there was no love, either. There was no cruelty, but there was no compassion, either. There was perfect satisfaction, but there was no ambition. There was no strife, but no peace. There was no sorrow, but no joy, either. Everything was without flaw, but there was no hope of anything becoming better.

The real spark of life—freedom, free will, the opportunity and ability to choose good from evil, to sin with a chance to repent, the ability to create and the right to fail—these were missing.

This world, which God created using the Torah as a plan, is a dynamic world in which every choice we make, makes a difference.

[Zohar 1:24b]

7. The Laws of Sodom

🐚 Can a whole community deserve punishment?

The people of Sodom served the *yetzer hara*, "the evil urge." For example, they forbade sharing. When a stranger came to town, they took gold, silver, and jewelry from the town treasury and gave it to the stranger. But when the stranger complained of hunger and tried to buy food, the Sodomites refused to sell him any. When the stranger begged, they ignored him. After the stranger died of hunger, the jewels and money were returned to the city treasury and used to snare other strangers.

One time, the people of Sodom put a little girl to death for sharing. It happened this way: Two girls came to a well to draw water. One asked the other, "Why are you so pale?"

The other girl answered, "My family has no more food. We are starving to death."

What did the first girl do? She went home and filled her pitcher with flour instead of water. Then, the girls exchanged pitchers, each taking the other's. But when the Sodomites discovered this act of sharing, they burnt the first girl to death, for the law of Sodom strictly forbade anyone to give charity.

It was because they worshiped the *sitra achra*, "the evil side," and the *yetzer hara*, "the evil urge," that the whole community of Sodom deserved to be punished.

[B. Talmud *Sanhedrin* 109b; *Pirke deRabbi Eliezer* 25; *Midrash Genesis Rabbah* 49:6]

8. The *Yetzer HaRa*

The *yetzer hara* ("the evil urge") is crafty. At first, it gains a foothold by asking us to do a small thing. "It has been long since you borrowed this book, but its owner seems not to miss it—why bother to return it?" Soon it requires us to do something more serious. "Why bother asking? Just take the book you need, for yours is a good cause and the book should be yours."

The *yetzer hara* may say to us, "Just do this thing one time— it cannot hurt anyone if you only do it one time." Then soon it requires us to do evil all the time. "Come and hurt this one," then "Look how weak that one is: that one cannot hurt you in return."

At first, the *yetzer hara* is like a spider's web, but in the end it is like heavy ropes.

At first, the *yetzer hara* is like a passerby, later it is like a guest, and finally it becomes the master of the house.

At first, the *yetzer hara* is sweet; in the end it is bitter.

[B. Talmud *Sukkot* 52a and 52b; J. Talmud *Shabbat* 14c; *Midrash Genesis Rabbah* 22:6]

A young man asked the rabbi of Rizhin how he could secure God's help in breaking his evil impulse. The rabbi smiled knowingly. "You want to break the *yetzer hara*?" he asked. "You will break your hip and break your back, but you will never break the *yetzer hara*! Yet, if you pray and study, if you expend your energy in doing good, the *yetzer hara* will vanish of itself."

9. My *Yetzer HaRa* Made Me Do It

A poor Jew had a wife and children, but no way to earn a living. Up stepped his *yetzer hara*, his "evil impulse," and whispered in his ear a single word, "Steal." He waited to see if he would hear from his *yetzer tov*, that is, his "impulse to do good," but no word came from that quarter. "That's it," he decided, "I have heard all my life about highwaymen. Now, I shall be a highwayman." And suddenly it seemed possible to him that he could make a great deal of money by choosing the right kind of people to rob.

The very next morning, he prepared for his new profession. He put a sack over his clothing as a disguise, stuck a hatchet in his belt, took along his prayer book, and made for a section of road deep in the forest. The morning passed, but no one came along the road. By late afternoon, he shrugged his shoulders and prepared to say the afternoon prayers.

But when he was midway through reciting the Eighteen Blessings, the very heart of the afternoon service, a Jew came down the road. Naturally, the prayers could not be interrupted, so the highwayman motioned for the Jew to wait. The Jew, seeing that another Jew was praying, waited politely.

The highwayman finished his prayers with a loud, "Amen!" Then he drew the hatchet from his belt and turned on the Jewish traveler. "Your money or your life," he yelled. And, then, thinking of stories of highwaymen, he added, "Stand and deliver!"

"Are you mad?" the startled traveler demanded. "Do you really mean to kill a fellow Jew in cold blood? Besides, I have a wife and children to support. Surely, you don't intend to make my wife a widow and my children orphans! Moreover, you can see for yourself that I am not a wealthy man."

"My luck," thought the highwayman. "A husband and a father; and a poor man, to boot!" But this was no time to give up. "Okay," he said aloud, "I will not kill you, but give me a ruble."

The traveler threw up his hands. "Do you think I am Rothschild?" he asked. "Where would I get a ruble to give you."

"Then, give me ten kopeks," said the highwayman.

"No one gives ten kopeks to a beggar," the traveler observed, "not ten kopeks at one time!"

"You must give me something," said the highwayman.

The traveler took out his snuffbox. "Have a pinch of tobacco," he said.

The highwayman took a pinch, stuck it in his nose, and sneezed.

The traveler said, "*Gesundheit!* God bless you!" Then the traveler took a pinch and he also sneezed. The highwayman said, "*Gesundheit!* God bless you!"

They stood looking at each other as the sound of their sneezes echoed in the forest. Finally, they shook hands and said goodbye.

In one ear, the highwayman heard his *yetzer hara* saying, "*Oy!* Some highwayman!" In the other ear, he heard his *yetzer tov* laughing.

[adapted from Ausubel, *Treasury*, p. 348]

10. Catching the *Yetzer HaRa*

🐟 Our sages once caught the *yetzer hara* and bound it up with golden chains. At first, they were very pleased with themselves. Thievery stopped; murder ceased. People were suddenly friendly and loving toward one another. There was no jealousy; and in all of Israel no arguments occurred between two Israelites. Moreover, no one died.

Then, slowly, our sages came to a strange realization. People were so satisfied and contented that they did not bother to toil. There was no competition, so people quit striving. No new houses were built. People no longer married or wanted to have children. No babies were born. Even the sages themselves became lazy and put off their study of Torah.

In this way, our sages learned how important the evil urge is to the world. They broke the golden chains and set free the *yetzer hara*.

[*Midrash Genesis Rabbah* 9:7]

14

Kindness to Animals

1. Beating a Donkey

🐾 A sage was walking down the road one day and came upon a man beating a donkey.

"Why are you beating that poor animal?" asked the sage. "Have you no mercy?"

"I am beating this donkey to get its attention," the man replied.

"Why don't you just talk to the donkey?" asked the sage.

"I will," said the man, "just as soon as I get its attention."

[anecdote related by an Israeli Arab guide]

2. All God's Creatures

🐾 In the beautiful city of Sephoris, in the Galilee, Jewish scholars who had been raised in Babylonia had their own synagogue. One morning, Our Teacher, the great Rabbi Judah HaNasi, was sitting on a bench beside that synagogue, studying the Torah. A butcher passed by, leading some cattle toward his shop, when one calf broke away and dashed under Rabbi Judah's bench. It looked up at him and cried out in agonizing bleats, as if it were pleading to be saved.

Rabbi Judah spoke to it sternly, saying, "'What can I do for you? In truth, you were fashioned for slaughter." And he helped the butcher reclaim the little calf.

For this heartless act, Rabbi Judah was punished. For thirteen years, from the moment the calf was slaughtered, he suffered a toothache that jumped from place to place in his mouth, so that it mystified all who tried to cure it.

Then, one day, just outside his house, a scorpion hurried past him. His daughter saw it, too, and she ran to help her father. She raised her foot to kill the scorpion, but Rabbi Judah stopped her,

272

saying, "My daughter, let it be. Since we see the scorpion, we can step out of its way and it will not bother us. For we were taught, 'God's tender mercies are over all God's works'" (Psalms 145:9).

Suddenly, his own words echoed in his ears and in his mind there flashed an image of the little calf he had not saved. "If only I had been kinder to that calf," he thought. And, with that, his toothache disappeared, never more to cause him suffering.

[*Midrash Genesis Rabbah* 33:3; B. Talmud *Baba Metzia* 85a]

3. The Ox that Kept the Sabbath

🐂 It is commanded: "You shall rest on the Sabbath—you and your male servants and your female servants and your beasts" (Exodus 20:10).

A Jewish farmer owned an ox. He used it to make his living. He rented himself out, along with his plow and his ox, to farmers throughout the region. Six days he worked and, in accordance with the law, on the seventh day, the Sabbath day, he rested, and his ox rested, too.

There came a long drought and farmers did not plant so they had no need to till or turn the soil. The Jewish farmer grew poorer and poorer until, at last, he was forced to sell his ox. He got a good price for it and found a good home for it with a non-Jewish farmer who lived some miles away.

A few weeks passed, no more than a month, when the non-Jewish farmer appeared at his cabin, leading the ox behind him. "You sold me an ox and I expected an ox that would work," the non-Jewish farmer said angrily. "This one will not work! He lies down in the field. Even if I beat him, he just remains where he is, stubbornly refusing to plow."

"It cannot be!" the Jewish farmer said.

"Nevertheless, it is true," said the non-Jew, adding, "and I want my money back."

"The money has been spent—all but a very small part," the Jew said. "But, tell me, is the ox refusing to work all the time or only some of the time?"

"Most of the time, the ox works," said the non-Jew.

"And, is there a particular day on which he refuses to work?" the Jew asked.

"Now that you mention it, he lays around only on Saturdays."

"Aha," the Jewish farmer said. "Allow me to explain." He explained the Jewish week to the non-Jew and told him of the commandment to rest on the Sabbath and to allow beasts to rest on the Sabbath, too. "Come," he said, "let me help you. Tomorrow is Saturday, so I will walk to your farm and speak with the ox."

The non-Jew shrugged his shoulders.

The next morning, as promised, the Jewish farmer appeared to speak with the ox. "My dear friend," he said to the beast, "when you worked with me, you were working for a Jew, so we rested on the seventh day. But I was forced to sell you to a non-Jew who does not keep the commandment to rest. If you will just work for him for a little while, I will try to raise the money to buy you back."

Lo and behold, as if the ox understood all that was said, he immediately rose from where he was lying and allowed himself to be yoked to the plow. The non-Jewish farmer was amazed by this new behavior. He started to lead the ox to the fields, but then he thought better of it. He removed the yoke and spoke to the ox, saying, "If God in Heaven believes that you should rest one day a week, perhaps you should. From now on, you and I shall both rest on Saturday."

He turned to the Jewish farmer and asked, "What else is commanded by God?"

They spent the whole day conversing about the Torah; and long after Havdalah—which separates the Sabbath from the ordinary days of the week—and well into the night, the two continued to talk.

Not many months later, the non-Jewish farmer and his family converted to Judaism. The talks with the Jewish farmer became studies in a *yeshivah*, and before another year passed, the non-Jewish farmer became a rabbi. He assumed the name Rabbi Chanina, because he loved the teachings of that sage of the Talmud, and soon enough, he himself was the rabbi of a town.

And what became of the ox? No longer a farmer, the rabbi had no further need of it, so he returned it to the Jewish farmer with his blessings.

[*Pesikta Rabbati* 56b-57a; see also Gaster, *Sefer Ha-Maasiyot*]

15
Tikkun Olam
Repairing the World

1. The Strength to Try

🕮 A group of Chasidim came to study with their *rebbe* and found him sitting and weeping. They tried to console him.

"Why are you crying?" they asked.

"When I was a young man," he said, "I thought I could change the world, so I set out to try. That's how I learned that the world is a very difficult thing to change.

"When I turned thirty, I decided that it was just as important for me to perfect my small corner of the world, so I placed all my energies in trying to improve my community and my students. That's how I learned that communities and classes cannot be made perfect.

"At the age of forty, I set about to change just my family. I spent hours and hours with my wife and my children, trying to make my family perfect. But I learned that even families cannot be perfected.

"When I reached my maturity, I realized that there was only one who would listen to the lessons I had been placed in the world to teach, so I set out to perfect myself. But now I know that even that is beyond my powers."

The students were afraid. If even the *rebbe* could not perfect himself what chance had they? They turned to consoling him even more. "*Rebbe*, you have become a *tzaddik*, a holy man—what you do is right and just. You should not mourn because you are not perfect. After all, only God can be perfect."

"No," said the *rebbe*, "You misunderstand. I am not weeping because I am sad. I am weeping because of the great blessing God granted me."

"What blessing?" the students demanded.

"All through my life," the *rebbe* answered, "God has given me the strength to try."

[adapted from a tale of Rabbi Chaim of Zans in Buber, *Later Masters*, p. 214]

2. Beruriah's Advice

In Rabbi Meir's neighborhood a band of hooligans annoyed him so often that he lost patience and prayed for them to die. His wife Beruriah asked, "What makes you think that your prayer should be answered? Are you thinking of the verse, 'Let the sinners be consumed' (Psalms 104:35)? But in fact, the verse does not say 'sinners,' but 'sins.' And consider the whole verse: 'Let the sins be consumed and let the wicked be no more.' This can only mean that once sins cease, the wicked will be no more. You must pray for mercy for these hooligans, that God will allow them to repent of their sins, then they will be wicked no more." Rabbi Meir then prayed for mercy for them, and, in the end, they repented.

[B. Talmud *Berachot* 10a]

3. Eighty Witches

Rabbi Shlomo Yitzchaki, famously known as Rashi, tells a story in his commentary on the Talmud, about a rabbi and an innkeeper, who died on the same day and in the same village.

Now the rabbi was a righteous man and the innkeeper was a sinner. But, both being Jews, their relatives brought the two bodies to the same cemetery. As the innkeeper's mourners were carrying his body to its final resting place, the mourners carrying the rabbi's body crossed their path.

Suddenly, a mounted troop of nomadic raiders came galloping through the cemetery, trampling graves as they took their brazen shortcut. Just the sight of the charging horsemen caused both funeral groups to scatter. The coffins were left in the field as the people fled.

When the raiders had passed, the two groups once more took up their burdens. But those who were carrying the rabbi's body accidentally picked up the coffin of the innkeeper and those carrying the innkeeper's body were left with the rabbi's coffin. Since both were plain pine boxes, the mourners did not realize that the mistake had even occurred.

So it came about that the rabbi was buried ignominiously, while all honor and pomp was accorded to the undeserving inn-keeper. That night—and for many nights thereafter—the rab-bis' chief disciple found no rest in sleep. He grew certain that a mistake had been made and that the rabbi's grave was occupied by a sinner.

When he finally fell asleep, he dreamed that the rabbi came to him, saying, "Be comforted, my child. Though the innkeeper may be occupying my grave, I hold a place of honor in Paradise and the innkeeper's punishment is just. And there was a reason for the switching of the coffins. My burial was marred because my soul was marred. Once I overheard people speaking ill of the sages and I did not raise my voice to oppose them. But once the innkeeper was to hold a feast for the governor and the governor cancelled at the last minute, so the innkeeper diverted all the food and drink to the poor—for this, he was deserving of a righteous burial. And, when the time of his punishment in Gehenna is ended, this one righteous act will also guarantee him a reward in Paradise."

The rabbi's disciple asked, "How long will it be before the inn-keeper receives his reward in Paradise?" The rabbi answered, "He awaits the death of Rabbi Simeon ben Shetach, who will take his place in Gehenna." The rabbi's disciple was shocked. "What did the righteous Simeon do to deserve a punishment in Gehenna?"

The rabbi answered, "His punishment awaits him because of what he did not do. This very moment, he knows that there are eighty Jewish witches in Ashkelon, yet he idly suffers them to ply their evil trade."

The next morning, the rabbi's disciple went in search of Rabbi Simeon ben Shetach. He found the great sage studying beneath the shade of a weeping willow. With a heavy heart, the disciple poured out his whole story—the confused burials, his own misgiv-ings, the dream, and the suffering that Rabbi Simeon was to suffer on account of the witches.

Rabbi Simeon listened carefully, then spoke words of comfort to him, saying, "Do not worry overmuch for me. Your rabbi has given me a warning. No one's fate is sealed until it is actually sealed; so, while I live, I can still avert the evil decree."

The next day, Rabbi Simeon set out to take action against the eighty witches of Ashkelon. He recruited eighty Jewish men—all of them young, strong, and unmarried. He promised each of them a worthy wife, if they would only follow his directions precisely. They were to gather on the edge of the city of Ashkelon at the first sign of a rainy day.

It was not long before the rains came. On the first rainy day, the eighty men, mounted on eighty horses stood ready to do the bidding of Rabbi Simeon. For his part, Rabbi Simeon gave each of them a robe neatly folded and tucked inside an earthen vessel. He instructed them to wait for his signal, then to break the pots, put on the robes, and each lift up one of the eighty witches and carry her off on horseback.

"Do not worry overmuch," Rabbi Simeon told them, "for witches only possess their power while they are in direct contact with the earth—bare feet on bare ground. Lift them off the ground and their powers are broken. Keep them apart from each other and they are fine Jewish women. Take care," he concluded. "you must wait for my signal."

Leaving the men in ambush, Rabbi Simeon took a robe from his own earthen vessel, unfolded it, and put it on in place of his own. Then he summoned all his courage and entered the enormous cave wherein dwelled the eighty Jewish witches of Ashkelon.

"Who are you?" the witches demanded, forming themselves into a circle for protection.

"I am a wizard," he said, "come to experiment in magic."

"What proof do you have?"

"Do you see that the day is rainy? And do you see that I am dry? Surely, that is proof enough!"

"How is it that you are dry, though you come in out of the rain?" they asked.

"I walked between the raindrops," said he. "And I can give you more proof, too. Even though it is raining, with a snap of my fingers and a wave of my hand, I can produce eighty strong men, all of them in dry clothing, too."

They mocked him with smiles, and said, "Let us see!"

Rabbi Simeon went to the mouth of the giant cave and snapped his fingers. Inside, the eighty witches heard the snap of his fingers and the noise of an echo so loud it seemed the sky itself had cracked. For, in that instant, all eighty men had shattered their pots and were putting on the dry robes inside. Now, Rabbi

Simeon waved his hand and, starting from ambush, the riders came on in small groups of twos and threes, riding into the caves in their dry robes. The moment all eighty were arrayed before the witches, Rabbi Simeon snapped his fingers again and each young man snatched up one of the eighty witches, lifting her off the ground, throwing her upon his steed, and riding away with her to his home. In this way, the rabbi arranged eighty marriages, defeated eighty witches, made happy eighty young men, and averted the evil decree against him in heaven.

Later, when the rain stopped, Rabbi Simeon brought workers and they filled the cave with boulders, from its deepest point even to the sealing of its enormous opening. To this day, travelers point to the bulge of rocks marking the place where once the witches' cave was a gaping sore on the landscape of the Holy Land.

[Rossel, adapted from Rashi's commentary on B. Talmud *Sanhedrin* 44b]

4. Repaired Souls

Once, Rabbi Isaac Luria, the Holy Lion, was strolling through the fields of Safed, transmitting kabbalistic lore to one of his disciples. Looking up, he glanced a number of souls perched in a tree. He interrupted his instruction to remark to the disciple, "The trees here are full of souls beyond number. Many more stand farther on, in the fields."

The disciple asked, "Why should there be a gathering of souls here?"

The Holy Lion explained, "God cast these souls out for failing to repent. But these souls have heard that I have the power to repair exiled souls. When I pray, they don the robes of my prayer and accompany it to God's very throne. Yet, I fear that soon I shall be gone and people will neglect to help souls in exile."

The disciple inquired, "Can you tell me the secret of this power?"

The Holy Lion said, "There is no secret! Souls can aid one another. If only a righteous soul reaches out and joins itself to one that is exiled, together they can batter a way through to God."

[from Isaac Luria, *Tales of the Ari* (Hebrew)]

5. The Blemish on the Diamond

A king owned a large and flawless diamond. It was so valuable and he loved it so much that he kept it in a locked box. But, now and again, he would take it out of its box and turn it over in his hands to admire its fire and to see the way the light played upon its every surface.

One time, as he was lost in contemplating the stone, it fell from his hands and struck the marble floor. With stunned silence, he picked it up and turned it over, examining it. His heart dropped when he saw that the diamond had suffered a crack. The flawless diamond was no longer flawless.

The king called in jewelers and diamond cutters, and every expert in gemology he could find. He consulted with them all. But all agreed that no amount of polishing could restore the stone and no cutting could safely insure that the stone would again be flawless.

The king suffered nights of sleeplessness, thinking, "If only I had not been so careless. I myself destroyed the stone's perfection." Finally, he gave the diamond to the Minister of the Treasury, saying, "Take it away from me and put it on public display. Let all admire what a wonderful diamond it once was, but let me not see it again, for it pains me too greatly to be in its presence."

Many came to admire the diamond and, despite the king's disappointment with it, it seemed wondrous enough to those who had not known it when it was flawless. Now, among those who came was a jeweler from a distant land who remarked aloud, "So beautiful a gem! If only it were carved, it would be perfect."

The guards reported this remark to the Minister of the Treasury who reported it to the king. The king said, "Bring me this jeweler."

When the jeweler stood before the throne, the king asked him, "Can you remove the blemish from my diamond?"

"No one can do so, Your Majesty," the jeweler said, "nevertheless, the diamond can become something at least as beautiful as it was before it was cracked."

"How will you accomplish this?" the king asked.

"Trust me," the jeweler said, "I have a vision of what the diamond can become."

The king pondered his options. He hated being reminded of the diamond's blemish. He wished the diamond could be perfect again. On the one hand, the jeweler was unknown to him. What distant place had he come from? Could he be trusted? On the other hand, the jeweler had a plan.... At last, the king tired of turning his mind up-side-and-down. "So be it," he said. "My own jeweler will prepare a workshop for you. Do whatever you can do."

The jeweler had cut many stones, but from the moment the great gem was placed in his care, he knew he had been born to repair this diamond. He placed his chisel alongside the blemish, lifted the hammer, and tapped gently, creating the first cut. One cut followed another until an etching appeared along the flaw. The jeweler worked without a pattern, trusting the instinct of his soul. A touch of the chisel here and a stem emerged. Another tap, and a leaf appeared; then, another leaf. And above the stem and the leaves, he tapped and carved a perfect image of many tiny cuts. The jeweler was pleased. The flaw had been transformed into a delicate many-petaled rose.

If the jeweler was pleased, the king was ecstatic. "It was always meant to be this way!" he exclaimed, embracing the jeweler and promising a fine reward.

Of course, the king's first thought was to lock the diamond away, to keep it to himself alone, as he had at first. But then he realized that sharing its beauty, knowing that his people admired what he himself admired, had brought its own special pleasure.

So the king commanded that the gem be placed where all the people of his kingdom could see what the jeweler had achieved. Those who had seen it before, were awed by its new perfection. And, whenever the king visited, he marveled anew at how a flaw could become a virtue.

> [adapted from Ausubel, *Treasury*, p. 66; also in *Parables of the Preacher of Dubno* (Yiddish)]

6. Hidden Blessings

People say, "Inside every problem there is an opportunity." Jews add, "Inside every trouble, there is a hidden blessing."

Jacob was a handyman, busy from dawn to dusk repairing things. He had no time to spend among the learned in the House of Study. He had to make a living: another child was on the way.

Nevertheless, on days when there was nothing to repair, he could spend a few minutes resting beneath a tree. He could study what he wanted in his free moments. Magical books, mystical books—those were the ones he kept under his arm. *The Book of Creation*, *The Book of the Angel Raziel*, the *Zohar*—books that kept demons away, books that could be slipped under his wife's pillow when she was giving birth; they were charms that could protect him and protect her.

He would open a book on his lap and turn the pages. A man like him could not actually understand what was written in such books, but the words were surely sacred. Just gazing at the pages, even if you were a sinner, the books revealed awesome images: so many stars, so many chariots, so many powers, so many angels, so many worlds.

Jacob remembered what he heard about the book called *The Tree of Life*. There it was written that evil was like the emptiness that came into being when God made space for the earth. It was as if a holy pot were broken to make enough space inside for a lump of clay. Little pieces of holiness fell to earth from the shattered pot. Holy people searched for these little pieces of holiness. Their righteous deeds helped God raise the pieces, helped God put the holy pot back together. That kind of thing made a handyman think.

Jacob might not comprehend it all, but he understood the meaning of "repairing." If the world was in need of repair, who should be called but a handyman? Maybe God needed Jacob the way Jacob needed God.

A handyman understood: Repenting and turning away from evil could change sins to holy pottery. Doing the right thing could lift a little broken piece and fit it back into its place in heaven. Bad things could be made good again. A handyman knew the kind of help God needed.

[adapted from Singer, *The Slave*]

7. The Boulder

🐌 Imagine yourself walking down the path of your life. Many other people are walking on what seems to be the same road. The more you watch, the more you discover that the road may be the same, but each person walks differently. Some sing and swing their hands as they hike. Some carry heavy packs and troubled faces. Some hike alone; others hike with a partner. Some organize many hikers together. And some pause to sit by the roadside; while others rush along.

You come to a place where a boulder blocks the roadway. Being a student of human nature, you watch as different people approach the boulder. Many come finely dressed as merchants, doctors, lawyers, and government officials. Encountering the boulder, they choose to squeeze past it, leaving it there blocking the roadway. Others, in blue jeans and tie-dyed shirts, in khaki and scrubs, study the boulder and pause to curse the king for not keeping the roadway clear. But they, too, do not lift a hand to move the boulder.

Along comes a farmer. He is carrying a heavy load of vegetables to market. He sees the boulder, sets down his load, and with great effort, he pushes and slides the boulder off the road.

As he picks up his load of vegetables, the farmer notices something on the roadway where the boulder had been. It is a purse. He opens it and, wonder of wonder, it is full of gold coins and there is a paper in the purse with writing on it. Now the farmer looks up at you, approaches you, and hands you the note. By the way he shrugs his shoulder, you know he cannot read. So you read the note to him:

The gold in this purse belongs to you. It is a gift from your king. I placed the boulder to block this road as a test. Many will pass the boulder and ignore it, but someone will say, "If this boulder is an obstacle to me, then it is an obstacle for others, too." Someone will be kind enough to move the boulder aside. And the person who reaches out to help others, that is the person who will be rewarded. The gold in this purse is your reward.

You smile and return the note to the farmer. As he leaves with the note, the purse of gold coins, and his load of vegetables, his burden is a little heavier, but a whole lot lighter. As you watch him walk away, you are no richer in dollars, but you are wealthier in wisdom.

From now on, every time you face an obstruction on the road of life, you will face it knowing that choosing to cope with it has its rewards. From now on, when you solve a problem in your life, you will look to see what kind of message the king gave you for placing that problem on your road. From now on, you will face every trial with the knowledge that there may be plentiful days ahead, days of pleasure and laughter, days of love and family, days of beauty and sunshine, if only you choose to overcome life's obstacles.

[Rossel, based on a European folktale]

8. Spanning

When the first suspension bridge was built over the gorge near Niagara Falls, New York, no boat could carry the necessary suspension wires across the turbulent Niagara river. The solution? A prize of five dollars was offered to the first boy who could fly a kite from the American to the Canadian side. A kite string soon made the crossing, whereupon a succession of heavier cords and ropes was pulled over until cables finally spanned the river.

[Internet anecdote; but compare to *Sifre Numbers* 33a]

9. The Soap Maker and the Rabbi

A man who manufactured soap came to his rabbi and expressed his doubts about life and its meaning. The rabbi invited him along on a stroll.

As they were walking, the soap maker posed his problem. "What good is being Jewish?" he asked. "The world is misery and woe despite thousands of years of teaching about kindness, justice, mercy, and peace. The prophets are still lonely voices crying out in the wilderness. All the study of Torah, Talmud, and Midrash is like a lantern throwing light in one direction or another, but failing to illumine the darkness of our souls. If being Jewish is essential, why does the world remain so unenlightened?"

The rabbi was silent until they passed near a small group of children playing in the dirt. Every child's face and hands were filthy with soot and grime. The rabbi pointed to the children.

"See those children? Your soap should make them clean. But after all your manufacturing, those youngsters are still covered with filth. What good is soap? Why bother making it?"

The soap maker replied, "Rabbi, surely you know the difference between the existence of soap and the use of it. Soap cannot clean these children, unless they use it!"

"Aha!" the rabbi said, smiling. "Should being Jewish make a difference if it is not applied?"

[adapted from Certner, *101 Jewish Stories*]

10. The Shadow of God's Image

Our Holy Scriptures often mentions the hand of God, the right hand of God, God's ears, the eyes of God, God's mouth, and the feet of God. Yet God cannot be revealed through human description. God is beyond measure, beyond time, and without form. Why, then, do we speak of the "eye" of God, the "feet" of God, God's "heart," God's "mind," and so on? Ohev Yisrael of Apta explained:

Whenever we cast a shadow, our body forms a likeness of itself. The shadow is not our body. It may or may not have the precise shape of our body. Yet it is cast from our body. As we move, the shadow changes. In the same way, as we follow God's commandments, we cast a shadow of God's likeness.

If we do good, we form God's right hand. If we resist evil, we form God's left hand. By turning away from evil, we form God's eye. By denying falsehood, we form God's ears. If we walk in the way of the Torah, we form the feet of God. We are not only created in the image of God, we also cast God's image with our actions, with our thoughts, with our very breath. One who loves God casts a giant shadow that embraces all worlds.

[Langer, *Nine Gates*, pp. 170-171]

🌀 16 🌀
Women in Israel

1. Zelophehad's Daughters

🌺 The Israelite camp was abuzz with the news. God had commanded Moses to divide the Promised Land. Now, every man would receive a share for his family, a portion that would belong to his family forever. Everyone agreed this was good news. All, that is, except one family.

In the tribe of Manasseh, there were five sisters whose names were Machlah, Noach, Hoglah, Milcah, and Tirtzach. Their father, Zelophehad, had died and none of them had yet married. For them, the news was bad. There was no man in their family so they would not receive a portion of the Promised Land.

Machlah, the oldest, said to her sisters: "It's not fair! God created us equal to the men of Israel, but the men of Israel do not behave as if we were equals."

Milcah said, "You are right, my sister. It is not fair. Moses says that God is good to all and God cares for all of Creation—not just for men, but for women, too."

Hoglah said, "We must speak out."

Noach said, "Moses appointed judges. We can go to the judges and demand justice."

Tirzach said, "Absolutely. Our family deserves a share of the Promised Land, even if there is no man among us."

The five sisters went to the local judge—who was allowed to judge for ten families—and said, "Justice must be done. Our family must receive an equal portion, even though we have no man among us." The local judge replied, "This is a hard case. I do not know how to decide it. We must go to a judge who rules over me, a judge of fifty families."

The local judge took the five sisters to the court of the judge of fifty families and said, "The daughters Zelophehad demand their fair portion." But the judge of fifties said, "This case is too difficult for me. We must take it to a judge of a hundred families." So the sisters, with the judge of ten and the judge of fifty, came to the judge of a hundred and asked him, "How will you decide?"

When the people of Israel heard what was happening, they came to the tent of the judge of a hundred to see what he would decide. But the judge of a hundred was also puzzled. "Above me," he said, "is the judge of a thousand families. Let us take the case to him, for surely he will be wise enough to decide." So the women and the judges and all the people came to the judge of a thousand. And he said, "I, too, have a superior. Let us take this matter to the elders of Israel."

Standing before the elders, the judge of ten, the judge of fifty, the judge of a hundred, the judge of a thousand, and all the people of Israel listened. The sisters said, "We have no man among us, but women are equal to men. Therefore, we demand that you give us a portion of the Promised Land." The elders replied, "It is not up to us to decide. We must take your case to Eleazar the Priest. He will know what to do." Everyone who had gathered went to Eleazar, but Eleazar said, "I cannot judge this case, there is only one who can decide. Let us submit your case to Moses himself."

Moses was surprised when the judges, the elders, Eleazar the Priest, and all the people of Israel came to stand before him. The five sisters spoke again, saying, "Our father died and none of us is married. Yet, we are members of the tribe of Manasseh. Our family should have a portion of the Promised Land equal to the portion of every other family." Moses heard how the judges had decided to ask the elders for wisdom, and how the elders had asked Eleazar for wisdom, and how Eleazar had decided that he must judge. He thought, "If all these good people have asked for wisdom, I, too, should ask for wisdom."

"Wait here," Moses said to the sisters, "for there is One even wiser than I. I shall take your case before God."

Then Moses entered the Tent of Meeting to pray. The people waited outside. Although there were many of them, they were silent. Some of them may have been praying, too—praying that God would give Moses wisdom.

After a while, Moses returned. "It is good that you brought this case to me," he said to the judges, the elders, and Eleazar the

Priest. "It is good that we are all together to hear this judgment," he said to all the people of Israel.

"Pay close attention," Moses said. "God created all of us equal. Male and female, God created us in God's own image. The daughters of Zelophehad deserve the portion of the land that would have gone to their father. Equal justice: This is the law of God, and this is the law of Israel."

[*Sifre Numbers* 49a-b; also *Sefer HaAggadah*]

2. Hannah's Prayer

✥ Hannah was distraught because she and her husband had no child. Once, at a festival season, Hannah followed the crowds of Jews to Shiloh. She stood beside the tabernacle there and prayed, "O God of hosts, look at all the people who gather to honor You. You have created multitudes of people in Your world. Is it too difficult for You to give me just one child?"

Rabbi Eleazar told a parable to explain what Hannah had done:

Once there was a king who gave a great feast for his servants. A poor man came and stood outside the door, begging, "Give me just a little piece of bread." But no one paid him any attention. So he forced his way into the hall and went up to the king. "Your Majesty," the poor man said, "you have made a great feast. Can you not find just a morsel of bread for me?" Then the king's heart was moved. He left his throne, found the finest loaf of bread, and personally gave it to the poor man.

In the same way, Eleazar concluded, God's heart was moved by Hannah's prayer. God spoke directly to Hannah, saying, "Go home to your husband, Elkanah. In one year, you shall have a child. Call the child Samuel, which means 'God has heard,' for I have heard your prayer." And Samuel became a great prophet in Israel.

[B. Talmud *Berachot* 31b; also *Sefer HaAggadah*]

3. Can a Woman Be a Judge?

✥ Day after day, Deborah studied Torah while her husband, Lappidot, worked in the fields. At night, Lappidot returned from his work to eat his dinner. Then Deborah would say, "Listen to what I learned today," and she would read to him the words of the Torah. But Lappidot was tired; his back ached and his shoulders were sore. Whenever he heard Deborah say "Listen to what I learned today," he would prop his head in his hands and promptly fall asleep.

Deborah said to herself, "God wants us to study Torah and do good deeds. I know that my husband is a good man, even if he does not study. I must help him to do good deeds." So she meditated until she had conceived a plan. She twisted threads until they were thick as cords. Then she collected wax from the hives of bees and melted it, forming little towers around the threads.

One day, when Lappidot came home from the fields, Deborah said, "Look, I have made candles. Take the candles to the holy place at Shiloh where the men sit and study the Torah day and night. In this way, scholars will study by your light, and you will have a place among the wise." And Lappidot did as Deborah asked.

God saw the wisdom of Deborah and said to her: "Because you have taken care to make the wicks thick so that the candles will give good light, I will call you 'woman of light.' Because you have cared for others and helped them, I will make your light shine for all Israel to see." Then God told Deborah to sit beneath a palm tree. "Many will come to you," God said. "You shall be a judge in Israel."

Far away, in the school of the prophet Elijah, a student heard this story and asked, "Can a woman be a judge?" Elijah taught: "I call heaven and earth to witness that whether it be a Jew or a non-Jew, a man or a woman, a boy or a girl, the holy spirit will shine forth from any one of them who does good deeds."

[*Tanna devei Eliyahu*, p. 48; *Yalkut Judges* #42; also *Sefer HaAggadah*]

4. Rachel and Akiva

Rachel was the daughter of a rich man named Kalba Savua. She lived in a beautiful home. The floors were mosaics of birds and lions fashioned from Roman tiles. The windows looked out on gardens of roses. Her father and mother loved her. All the same, Rachel was lonely. She was old enough to marry but she knew none of the young men in town. "When it is time for you to marry," Kalba Savua often told her, "I will find the right man for you."

One morning, Kalba Savua called for Rachel. "I need some help, my dear. Please take water from our barrel and carry it to the shepherds who watch my flocks."

Kalba Savua had many flocks and Rachel carried the water pitcher from one flock to another. At each stop, the shepherd boys gazed at her and smiled. She studied each of them closely, thinking, "This one seems too old for me," "This one seems too silly for me," or "This one seems too tall for me. " The afternoon was slipping away by the time she reached the last flock.

The last shepherd boy was not very handsome. He was too shy to look at her. But she studied him closely. He was dressed in an old robe, a sure sign that he came from a poor family. His hair was neither brushed nor oiled. Still, there was something about him that attracted her.

She began her conversation tentatively, inquiring, "Do you think you will always be a shepherd?"

He shook his head. Rachel was surprised. Could it be that he was even too shy to speak? "What else can you do?" she pressed. "Can you forge iron or make sandals?"

He shook his head. "I would like to read," he said, softly.

"You cannot read?" she asked.

He shook his head again.

It was getting late. Rachel returned home. But her thoughts kept turning to that shy shepherd. He was poor, which did not bother her. There was a special feeling she felt being near him, a feeling that tantalized her. Of course, she knew her father would never permit her to marry a common shepherd.

In a few days time, Rachel returned to visit her shepherd. As she drew near, her heart beat more quickly. Could this be love? she wondered. "Be brave," she thought to herself, "for he is too shy to tell me what is in his heart. I will have to talk for us both."

They sat awhile, watching the sheep. Then Rachel asked, "Pray tell me your name."

"I am Akiva ben Joseph," the young man answered.

"Akiva," she repeated, liking the way his name sounded. Then, she surprised herself by asking, "If I promise to marry you, Akiva, will you promise to go to a house of study?"

He looked into her eyes for the first time. "Yes," he answered, and she heard excitement in his voice. In that moment, she knew she had chosen the right man for her. And they pledged to keep their plan a secret.

That night, Rachel's father came to her room. "One of the shepherds saw you sitting with Akiva. I forbid you to see him again."

"Father," she answered, "I love you very much. But I love Akiva, too. In truth, I want to marry him."

Her father was angry. "That can not be," he said fiercely. "I will find a rich man for you to marry."

"My heart is set on Akiva," Rachel answered.

Kalba Savua's eyes flashed. He was not used to having his intentions questioned. He fairly yelled at his daughter: "Marry him, and you will be forced to leave my house! Marry him, and you shall not have even a single coin from me as long as you live!"

Another girl might have grown afraid. Another girl might have acceded to her father's wishes. But not Rachel. She simply left her father's home and married Akiva.

Of course, life was not easy for them. By winter, they were so poor they had to sleep in a bin of straw where donkeys fed. Akiva picked bits of straw from her hair and said, "If I were rich, I would give you a golden tiara such as the ladies of Jerusalem wear."

"I do not wish that you were rich," she replied. "I wish what you wish: that you could read and write. Now, go to study Torah, as you promised me you would."

The next morning, Akiva kissed his wife and left home to find a house of study. Rachel worked in town. After some days had passed, she received a letter from Akiva. "How wonderful!" she thought. "Akiva has learned to write." In time, his letters were filled with beautiful words. "How wonderful!" she thought. "He has learned so much." In this way, letter after letter, twelve years passed.

One day, she heard a commotion outside her door. She went out to see what was happening. A great teacher was entering the town, and hundreds of his students were following him. The people of the town turned out to welcome the sage and Rachel joined them. All at once, she recognized him: it was her own Akiva at the head of all the students! But when she ran toward him, the students tried to protect their master by pushing her aside.

"Let her be," said Akiva to the students. "Everything that you and I know is only because of her." Then he held her in his arms, kissing her with the whole town looking on.

Not a moment later, Kalba Savua pressed to the front of the crowd. When he saw Rachel and Akiva, he began to cry.

"Why are you crying?" asked Akiva gently.

"I made a vow that Rachel would never have even a single coin from me as long as she lived."

"Would you have made that vow if you had known that her husband would become a teacher of many?" asked Akiva.

"If her husband had been able to read even a single word, I would never have made such a vow," answered Kalba Savua.

"I am her husband. I am the same Akiva who worked for you as a shepherd."

Kalba Savua stared at Rachel and Akiva. At last, he said, "Forgive me, my children." And turning to Rachel, he added, "You and your husband shall have half of everything that is mine."

Ever after that, Rabbi Akiva would say, "Rachel made me happy, wealthy, and wise: happy through her love for me; wealthy because she trusted me; and wise because she sent me to study Torah."

[B. Talmud *Ketubot* 62b-63a; also *Sefer HaAggadah*]

🎨 17 🎨
Reward

1. Treasures for the World to Come

🎨 A lengthy drought descended on the land of Adiabene in the days of King Monobazus. Without rainfall, the rivers sank low in their beds, irrigation ditches dried up, and crops failed. People died of starvation. The king ordered that all his wealth—whatever was in the treasury—should be used to buy food for the poor.

The king's relatives called him foolish and complained about his behavior. "The drought will end," they said, "but by then you will have nothing. The treasures of your ancestors will be spent, wasted on the poor."

King Monobazus had been expecting these relatives and anticipated what they would say. He was ready, too, with his answer: "My ancestors stored up treasures for below. I have stored my treasures for above. They stored treasures in a place where force could rob them; I stored treasures in a place where no force can harm them. They stored treasures that can yield no fruit; my treasures will be productive. They stored treasures of gold; I stored mine of souls. They stored treasures for others, I for my own good. They stored up treasures for this world; but I have stored my treasures for the World to Come."

[Tosefta *Peah* 4:18; B. Talmud *Baba Batra* 11a]

Adiabene was a kingdom in northeastern Mesopotamia. In the first century, CE, its rulers converted to Judaism. The most famous of these was the righteous Queen Helena who built palaces for herself and for her son in Jerusalem, made contributions to the Temple, brought food from Egypt and Cyprus to help feed Jerusalemites during a famine, and herself took the vows of a Nazirite. She returned to Adiabene, but when she died ©. 64 CE), her sarcophagus was sent back to Jerusalem for burial. Josephus relates these details in the *Antiquities* (20:17-96) and the *War* (45:253), adding that it was the influence of Jewish merchants which convinced the rulers of Adiabene, and perhaps many of its leading citizens, to convert.

2. One Golden Leg

🐌 Rabbi Chanina was a kind man who loved his wife very much. If only he were a rich man, he could afford to get a servant to carry water for her, another servant to knead and bake the bread for her, and still another to cook the meals for her. He sighed. If only he were a rich man!

Chanina's wife once said to him, "You work hard and I work hard. Yet we have very little. How long shall we suffer?"

"What shall we do?" he asked.

Chanina's wife said: "I have heard that the reward for studying Torah in this life is riches in the world-to-come. Why not ask God to send you some of the riches that you have already stored up in the world-to-come?"

Chanina fasted for three days. He sat on the ground, putting his head between his knees, and prayed in deep devotion. His head was reeling when he looked up and saw a hand reaching down from heaven to offer him a long stick of gold. "Heaven has heard my prayer," he said to himself, "and God has given me gold from the world-to-come."

Before he could tell his wife the good news, Chanina fell asleep and dreamed. In his dream, he and his wife were in the world-to-come. All the sages were sitting with their families at tables of gold. And each table had three golden legs. But he and his wife were sitting at a table that had only two legs so they had to prop the table up with their hands.

"Are you happy with this table of two legs?" Chanina asked.

"What happened to the other leg?" she inquired.

"I prayed for heaven to send us riches from the world-to-come, and I was given one of the three golden legs from our table."

Chanina's wife shook her head. "When you wake up from this dream," she said, "you must pray for heaven to take back the leg of gold."

Chanina awoke and prayed that the leg of gold be taken back. He opened his eyes and looked at his hand. His hand was open and, lo, the leg of gold was gone. Then he looked at his wife. "My dear, I have prayed twice to heaven: once for heaven to give us riches and once for heaven to take the riches back. In truth, we are already rich; we have what we need in this world."

It was said of Rabbi Chanina that his prayers for heaven to take back the leg of gold produced an even greater miracle than the giving of the golden leg itself. For we have been taught: "Heaven gives a thing; but once a thing is given from heaven, it is never again removed."

[B. Talmud *Taanit* 24b-25a; also in *Sefer HaAggadah*]

3. The Gem from Heaven

On the day before the Sabbath, Rabbi Simeon ben Chalafta discovered that he had no food and could not afford to buy any. Thinking how this would disappoint his wife and how they would be unable to serve God by beautifying the Sabbath day, Rabbi Simeon went a distance outside the city gates and wept and prayed to God for help. A precious jewel dropped down from heaven.

Wiping his eyes in disbelief, he picked up the jewel and ran to his wife. He told her, "God has provided us with the money we need for the proper observance of the Sabbath." He handed her the jewel and said, "Now, go and buy all that is required."

His wife said, "I will not buy even the smallest morsel of fish until you tell me where you got this jewel."

Rabbi Simeon explained, "I prayed to God and the jewel was sent down to me from heaven."

"We will find food enough to manage for this Sabbath," she said, "but you must promise me that you will return this precious jewel as soon as the Sabbath is over. Do you think it will be right when we reach the world to come that, because you have taken your reward in advance, your table shall be poorer than the tables of all the other sages?"

Rabbi Simeon went and told the story to Rabbi Judah the Prince. Rabbi Judah said, "Return to your wife and tell her this: When we are all safely arrived in the next world, if anything is lacking at the table of Rabbi Simeon, I shall personally make it up from whatever is on my table."

When Rabbi Simeon told this to his wife, she answered, "Take me to your teacher, Rabbi Judah."

She said to Rabbi Judah: "Master, it is kind of you to offer assistance to us in the world to come. But we can learn from the Bible that one righteous person may not see another in the World to Come. It is written, 'Because man goes to his world when the mourners go about the streets' (Ecclesiastes 12:5). It says 'his world' and not 'the world-to-come!' So it teaches that, after death, each righteous person rules a world of his own."

When Rabbi Simeon heard his wife's teaching, he went out of the city gate to the place he had prayed. There, he wept and prayed and begged again. When he at last stretched out his hand to restore the jewel to heaven, an angel descended and took it from him. And, it was said, this miracle of returning the jewel was more difficult for Rabbi Simeon to perform than the miracle of bringing it down.

[*Midrash Exodus Rabbah* 52:3]

4. A Good Investment

🐟 It is well-known that the emperor Hadrian, may his bones rot, was no lover of the Jews. But his sister's son, his nephew Onkeles, loved the spirit of Jewish thought and wished to embrace Judaism. Not wishing to offend Hadrian, Onkeles went to the emperor and asked for leave to "undertake a certain enterprise," though he did not state what that enterprise might be.

His uncle was entirely supportive, offering him money which Onkeles did not accept, saying he had enough. Instead, Onkeles asked his uncle for good advice, since in that regard he said, he was "inexperienced in the ways of the world." This request pleased the emperor and Hadrian gave Onkeles the following advice: "Purchase goods which are not too expensive at the moment, but which you have reason to believe will eventually command a higher price. This is the path to true success."

Onkeles left the emperor and went to Judea where he immersed himself in study. After a time Rabbi Eliezer and Rabbi Joshua came to admire this young student. They offered him instruction, helped him solve difficult problems, and befriended him.

In time, Onkeles returned home. He went to pay his respects to his uncle Hadrian. The emperor said, "You look pale, my child. Did you meet with monetary reverses in your new enterprise?"

Onkeles said, "No, uncle, I have been studying intensely and so I have been indoors and out of the sun." He quietly added, "Also, I was recently circumcised."

"Who advised you to undergo circumcision and for what purpose?" Hadrian inquired.

"I acted on your advice," said Onkeles. "I purchased a thing which stands at a low price right now but which will, I am certain, soon rise in value."

When Hadrian asked him to explain further, Onkeles said, "The prophet Isaiah wrote: 'Thus said *Adonai*, the Redeemer and Holy One of Israel ... Kings shall see [Israel] and rise up; nobles, and they shall prostrate themselves...' (Isaiah 49:7). You see, Uncle, I found a nation that momentarily stands in low esteem, but no other nation is as sure to rise in value as the people of Israel."

[Tanchuma 41a *Mishpatim* 3]

5. As Kind as Rebecca

&&& One hot summer day, Rabbi Joshua found himself traveling to do a *mitzvah* in a distant place. He had gone a long way under the glaring sun without finding even a drop of water to quench his thirst. Late in the afternoon, he came to a small village and saw a girl filling her pitcher at the village well.

"Please grant a thirsty traveler a drink from your pitcher," he said to her. "If not, I may well perish of thirst."

The maiden answered with words like those of the kind Rebecca of the Torah, "Drink your fill, O sage; and I will also draw water for the donkey which carried you here." So saying, she handed her pitcher to Rabbi Joshua.

The rabbi drank deeply, then returned the pitcher, as he complimented the maiden: "How good it is and how pleasant to hear your words and see you act in the merciful ways of our mother, Rebecca."

The maiden was quick to rejoinder: "Therefore," she said, "I hope you will equally remember how to imitate the generous ways of Abraham's faithful servant, Eliezer!"

Rabbi Joshua smiled at the *chutzpah*, "the arch self-confidence," "the nerve," "the gall," of the girl. "I well remember the generosity of Abraham's servant," the rabbi answered, "and, by right, you deserve rings and bracelets and other golden trinkets for your kindness." He waited until the maiden smiled, then continued: "You deserve them, but you do not need them. Why, anyone can tell that there is already the jewel of mercy in your kindly soul; and that is the best and the brightest ornament one can possess. All that I can add to your luster is my prayer that God may allow you to cling to your merciful nature throughout the days of your life."

With this, Rabbi Joshua departed.

[*Midrash Lamentations* 1]

6. The Harlot Who Went to Heaven

One of Rabbi Akiva's disciples—the one who sat at the head of Akiva's twenty-four thousand pupils, was once passing through the street of the harlots. He saw a woman there and, from the moment his eyes lighted upon her, he fell desperately in love. He sent a go-between to her to make an appointment for that evening.

Towards evening the woman went to the roof of her house. From there, she could see Akiva's disciple sitting at the head of the rest as a prince would be enthroned over a host. It even seemed to her that the angel Gabriel was at his right hand.

She said to herself, "Misfortune is my lot. All the punishments of hell await me. Such a great man, like a king! Shall I bring him to ruin, so that when I die and leave this world, I will inherit Gehenna? But, if I can make him listen to me, I will rescue both him and me from hell."

That evening, when he came to her, she said to him, "My son, what you desire is the thing least worthy of all." She begged him and chided him, she used her guile, her charm, and her wit. At last he was persuaded. From that moment he was chaste, and a heavenly voice went forth saying, "That man and that woman are appointed for the life to come."

[adapted from *Tanna devei Eliyahu*]

7. Murals

When the king built a new ballroom in his beautiful palace, he wished to decorate its two long walls with murals. He called for the two finest painters in his realm. Then, he thought, "I want each mural to be entirely unique." So he had a long curtain stretched the length of the ballroom. Each artist would work only on his side of the curtain, unable to see the work of the other. He gave them six months to paint their masterpieces.

One of the artists set to work at once, beginning with pencil drawings in his sketch book. As he sketched, he settled on the notion of portraying the first six days of Creation. He outlined his work on the long wall—the darkness and light of the first day; the heavens and oceans of the second day; the third day of earth and sea, flower, and fruit, and tree; the fourth day of moon and sun; the fifth day of birds and fish; and the sixth day of animals and Garden of Eden and Adam and Eve. Next came color, light, and texture as oil paint spread through the story, enlivening the wall. The more he worked, the more his work brought him pleasure. The more pleasure he had from his work, the more certain he was that the work was good. Weeks passed quickly, but he remained on schedule. He would finish by the end of the sixth month.

From time to time, he wondered how the other painter was doing. He could hear nothing from the other side of the curtain, but he imagined his colleague was also busy.

Nothing could be farther from the truth. The second artist was among the laziest of men. For months, he sat on his side of the curtain, daydreaming about how he would spend the money that the king had promised to pay for the mural. And, while he could imagine the money, he imagined little else. Time passed, and he remained uninspired. Suddenly there was but one week left and he had done no painting at all, not so much as a sketch. He searched his mind for a clever idea—and that is what he found. In the last week, he worked furiously to finish his wall.

When the day of the great unveiling arrived, the king and queen and all the courtiers gathered to view the murals in the new grand ballroom. The hard-working artist was excited and ready to show his work first. When the group stepped into his side of the ballroom, they let go their breaths in a long "Ah..." The scenes of Creation were so lively, so bright, so vivid that everyone immediately remarked on the genius of the artist! Could any other mural compare with this? A long time passed as the king and queen and all assembled stood and admired the mural.

At last, the king ordered that the curtain be removed so that they could view the work of the second great artist. But when the curtain was removed, the sight was breathtaking! Amazingly, the king and queen and all the courtiers beheld an exact image of the scenes of the story of Creation painted by the first artist. What a work of magic! How had the second artist known what the first artist was painting? How did he make his work entirely identical to the mural on the other wall? How?

Only when the king moved closer to the second artist's wall, did he see how the painter had achieved this magic. The painter had not lived up to his reputation in any way. Up close, it was obvious that there was no mural on the wall, nothing but a coat of paint. The king understood at once. The second artist had painted the wall orange, polishing it so that it reflected light like a mirror. Everything drawn by the first artist was reflected in the polished surface.

The king himself then had a clever idea. He whispered to the captain of the guard. In a short while, the captain returned with two soldiers, each carrying a heavy bag of gold and silver coins. Both soldiers approached the mural painted by the first artist and right where the Garden of Eden started, they poured out all the coins from both bags in two big heaps. The king turned to the artist who had done such fabulous work and said, "This is your well-deserved payment for your masterpiece."

Then the king turned to the lazy artist. He pointed to the orange wall—to where the two heaps of gold and silver coins were reflected in the orange wall. The king said, "And this is the payment you deserve."

[adapted from Certner, *101 Jewish Stories*]

8. As Many as You Want

A merchant was traveling through a small village on his way home to Odessa. He stopped for the night and the innkeeper told him that his visit was a great coincidence. At that very moment, a teacher who had come from Odessa two years before lay dying in a nearby house. The merchant wondered if he knew the dying man so visited him. "I do not know you," the merchant said to the teacher, "but because we are both from Odessa, I am sorry that you are suffering."

The teacher thanked him. "It is true. I am suffering and I am dying. But if you are headed home to Odessa, there is a favor you can do for me."

The merchant hesitated. He had not bargained on doing a favor for a dying man. After all, everyone dies. All he said was, "Perhaps."

The teacher said, "Once I had a good job in Odessa. When I lost it, I had to leave my family just to earn a living as a teacher. Now I have earned a hundred gold coins but I cannot trust them to a common messenger. They are in a bag under my pillow right now. Take the bag of coins to my wife and give her as many as you want."

The merchant saw a chance to earn a lot of money for little work. He took the name of the teacher's wife and he took the purse of gold coins from under the head of the dying teacher. The next morning the innkeeper told him that the teacher had died in the night.

When the merchant arrived in Odessa, he went to the house of the teacher's wife. "I have brought you sad news," he said, and he told her that her husband was dead and she was a widow. "But he sent you two gold coins," the merchant added, handing her two coins from the purse of one hundred.

The teacher's wife was no fool! She told the merchant, "My husband wrote that he was sending me one hundred gold coins. Have you stolen the rest?"

"Heaven forbid!" sad the merchant. "But your husband and I made a bargain. I was to give you as many of the coins as I wanted." With that, the merchant tied up the purse and left.

The next morning, the merchant was summoned to the Beit Din, the Jewish court of justice, and brought before a rabbi who was serving as the judge. The rabbi listened to the woman, who told him that her husband sent one hundred pieces of gold. Then he listened to the merchant who told him, in all honesty, that the husband meant for him to give the widow only as many of the coins as he wanted.

The rabbi asked the merchant, "How many coins did you want?"

The merchant said, "I wanted ninety-eight coins."

The rabbi said, "What a shame that you were so greedy. If you wanted less, you could have kept more. And what a smart teacher this widow had for a husband. As you yourself testified, you agreed to his terms. So now you must give the widow 'as many coins as *you* wanted.' She gets ninety-eight coins, which is as many as you wanted. And you may keep the other two coins."

[Yiddish/European folktale; also in Certner, *101 Jewish Stories*]

9. The Marvelous Clock

A new town hall, with a fine tower and belfry, was erected. The elders of the city sent out calls to clockmakers everywhere, inviting them to submit designs for a unique clock. Many clockmakers sent designs, but the elders rejected them for all seemed too ordinary. The town remained without a clock.

One day, an old craftsman came to the city. He went directly to the office of the city elders, saying, "I can build you the most unusual clock in the world—such a clock as no other town, city or nation has ever possessed. It will be my masterpiece."

"That is precisely what we want!" said the elders. Eagerly they escorted the old clockmaker to the tower and told him to order whatever materials he needed.

For seven years the craftsman worked day and night. Food was sent to him, along with springs and gears and all the bits and pieces of a giant clock. Finally, he had finished. The scaffolding which had hidden the belfry tower for seven years was removed, revealing the new clock.

Behold! It was marvelous, musical, and magical. It rang and sounded each hour on the hour, on the half, and on the quarter. A finely-crafted image showed the phases of the moon, while images above the clock showed the cycle of the night skies. At dawn and dusk, the clock played engaging melodies that caused the people to stop whatever they were doing and look heavenward in wonder.

The town elders realized that people would soon come from far and near to visit this magnificent clock. But the elders began to worry. What if some other city should order a similar clock from the old clockmaker? Might he not create a second masterpiece to rival this one?

In the end, they did not wait for him to ask for his reward. Instead, they had him seized and bound and brought before them. "You are accused of sorcery," they told him. "Only by a bargain with the devil could you have created a clock like this!"

They had him thrown into prison where he was tortured night and day until he finally admitted that he had made a bargain with the devil. Beaten and broken, they had him brought to the town square beneath his clock, where they announced his punishment to the whole town. "For dealing in sorcery, the clockmaker's eyes will be put out."

When the clockmaker heard the horrible decree—his only reward for all his genius and labor—he pleaded with the elders: "You know I am innocent of all guilt, but you are bound to do what you will with me. Grant me only one favor before you blind me. Let me gaze once more on the workings of my clock, so that I will have this sight to remember when all other sight is taken from me."

The elders conferred. Finally, they agreed to honor his last wish. They had him taken up into the clock tower and granted him a few minutes alone with his clock. When this was done, they brought him back to the town square. Before the whole assembled populace, they had his eyes pierced with white hot nails. They released the poor blind man and he left town that very night, the bandages still wound around his head.

The next day, they noticed that their clock was running slow. Its chimes ceased to function and soon after that the clock itself came to a halt with a painful grinding noise. They sent clockmaker after clockmaker into the tower to repair the clock, but none could find the problem. So it dawned on the elders that the old clockmaker had taken his revenge. They were ashamed and full of remorse, but there was nothing they could do. They could not bring back the clockmaker's eyes and they could not bring back to life the glorious clock he had created.

[Yiddish/European folktale; adapted from Alois Jirasek in his book *Stare Povesti Ceske* ("Old Czech Legends"), based on an Internet translation]

The story of "The Marvelous Clock" was originally told of the famous Horologium, located in a tower of the Municipal Building on Prague's Old Town Square. Hourly, the clock displays a procession of apostles marching to the tune of a bell tolled by a skeleton opening and closing its jaws. In the Middle Ages, the Horologium was judged so unique that it gave rise to the legend that the city fathers blinded the person who constructed it, fearing he might build another elsewhere. Actually, town records show that the Horologium was constructed by clockmaker Mikuláš of Kadaòman in 1410 with the help of a professor of mathematics named Jan Šindel. The impressive moving figures were added later, some as late as the nineteenth century.

10. The Rich Man and His Son

A rich man was disgusted by his lazy son. "Do you ever work at anything?" he berated the boy. The boy shrugged and said, "I am comfortable, my father. You provide my every need. Why should I think of working?"

The father said, "To get the money to make you comfortable, I had to work hard most of my life. What if you have a son and I am gone?"

So the lazy son agreed to try working. The father got him a job with a farmer, but he insisted that the boy should be paid only one hundred silver coins for a whole year's labor.

Seeing how lazy the boy had been, and knowing that he came from a wealthy family, the farmer was careful to give his new hired hand only simple tasks to perform. At the end of a year, the lazy boy's hands were hardly more callused than they had been before the year began. Nevertheless, as agreed, the farmer gave him a bag of one hundred silver coins and sent him home.

The son gave his bag full of coins to his father. The father said, "Let us take a walk by the river." Arriving at the river, the father casually tossed the bag full of coins into the water. The boy made no protest, nor was he perturbed at the loss of the money.

The next year, the father apprenticed his son to another farmer. Once again, it was agreed that the boy would be paid one hundred silver coins for his work. This farmer also treated the boy kindly because of his rich father. He gave the boy good things to eat and fine clothes to wear and he assigned hm only the lightest of chores. Again, when the year was up, the boy returned to his father and gave the bag of silver coins to him. The father did as before, throwing the money into the river. The boy made no protest.

The third year, the father brought his son to a third farmer. This time no wage was set in advance. The rich man did not even tell the farmer that the boy was his son. He just asked the farmer to teach the boy how to run a farm.

From the first, things were different. The boy was forced to work from early morning to late at night. He received only coarse food to eat and he was forced to dress in ragged clothing. When the boy paused to rest, the farmer insulted him for being lazy. "Do you think you can earn your bread without working?" the farmer would yell.

At first, the boy was too exhausted even to complain. At night, he fell asleep on his bed as soon as he reached it. But soon, he grew accustomed to the work and even began to like the lifting and the digging, the feeding and the milking. Once in a while, the farmer even praised the boy for doing a good job.

The year passed. The boy had grown strong. His hands were rough and callused. The farmer gave him a small sack of silver coins for all the hard work he had done for the year. "You earned more," the farmer told him, "but I kept some to pay for your food and shelter."

The boy returned to his father, placing his small bag of coins in his father's hand. The father once more took the boy down to the riverside. But the son said, "Father, do not throw the money away. I would like to keep this bag of coins."

The father asked, "What difference does a small bag of coins make? One day, you will inherit all my wealth!"

"Yes, Father," said the son, "but I earned this money with my labor. It means a great deal to me."

[adapted from Certner, *101 Jewish Stories*]

The Chinese tell this story: A fifty-year-old man had a lazy son of thirty years. Even at age thirty, the son depended entirely on his father for food and clothing. The father was concerned about this, so he took his son to the fortune teller to have his fortune told. The fortune teller predicted that the father would live to eighty and the son to sixty-two. Both of them were convinced that the fortune teller's words would come true.

The son was sad. His father comforted him, saying, "Don't be sad! You are only thirty now. You still have thirty-two years of good days ahead of you."

"I am not worrying about my age, dear father. It is your age which causes me such anxiety."

Hearing this, the father was deeply moved. In tears, he said, "Do not worry about me so much. I have thirty years ahead of me, too."

"I'm not much worried about that," said the son, "but I have figured out that you will die two years earlier than I. Upon whom shall I depend in the two years after your death?"

11. The Widow and the Wind

A frail and weary woman, her frame bent with sorrow, threw herself to the ground before King Solomon as he sat judging in Jerusalem. "My king," she cried, "I have come to avenge myself. Hear my plea and grant me justice."

Solomon looked about, but saw no other person standing near her. "Against whom do you plead your case?" he asked.

"Against the wind, O mighty king. The wind has cast me down and battered me. The wind has taken every thing I held dear. A king of justice will hear my case and judge against the wind!"

"Pray, tell me what happened," said Solomon in kindly tones, "Speak and I shall listen."

Now the woman spoke: "I am a widow and alone in the world. I lived by the sea, weaving the nets fisherman need. But then came many days of furious storms at sea. Near six months passed with no fisherman even putting out to fish. Not a net was sold. I was near starving when the time for harvest came.

"Having no flour I had no choice. I went to work among the poorest of the land. I gleaned in the fields, picking up what the workmen dropped as they harvested and sharing in the grain the farmers leave for the poor in the corners of the field. Back-breaking work it was, but I was more ashamed to be in need of it than harmed by the honest labor. At the end of two days, I harvested enough grain that when it was ground into flour I had enough to tide me over for a week or so. I wrapped it in my kerchief and tied it all tightly.

"I started home with the wind still thrusting and buffeting me now from one direction and now from another. Then, the wind drove a skeleton to the road beside me. He caught my arm and cried out, 'Woman, help me! Fire devoured my home and family. I am all that escaped and three days I have had nothing to eat.' So I opened my bundle and gave him a third of the flour. I thanked God I could help save a starving man, just as the farmer helped me.

"I went on and was still some distance from my hut when the wind nearly caused me to trip over a man lying on the path. This poor wretch had been kidnaped and held for ransom. Once they had the ransom money, his kidnappers took him a long distance, far from everyone he knew, far from everyone who knew him. Thank God, they did not murder him, but they tied him up and left him there on the path to live or die. I untied him. What was I to do? Obviously God had provided me with the flour for this purpose. So I untied my bundle and gave him half of what was left."

King Solomon was so moved by her story that he interrupted her to say, "O noble widow, saving a life is like saving a whole world. And you saved two lives! But why do you accuse the wind of doing you wrong? Could it be that the wind only blew in order to place these two lives in your path so that you could save them?"

"If that were all, your majesty, I would have no case against the wind, But there I was with only a single portion of flour left in my bundle when I looked for my hut. Lo, it was gone! The storm had blown so fiercely that the roof flew away and the boards of the walls had scattered in every direction. Bed and table were blown away, too, though somehow a single bench survived. The wind brought this evil upon me! Exhausted from all that had happened, I still made no protest. I set the bench upright, sat down on it, placed my precious bundle on my lap, and fell fast asleep.

"The wind would not let me rest. It screamed in its fury and a single icy blast came across my lap and lifted the bundle of flour. I jumped up, but all I could do was watch as the bundle flew on the wind's wings out into the sky above the storm-tossed sea.

"Now, I beseech you, O wise king, place the wind on trial for what it has done to me. If I cannot have home and bread, at least let me have justice!"

The king spoke gently. "Poor widow, my servants will give you food, a place to sleep, and time to rest. When you are refreshed, we shall see what justice a King of Israel can bring you."

While the widow was eating, three strangers appeared in the courtyard of the palace, each with a donkey, and on each donkey a large bundle. The strangers called out that they wished to see the king. When they were brought before him, King Solomon asked their business.

One replied, "We are three merchants who were strangers to one another. We met aboard a boat bound for Egypt. One of us sells silver and gold. One of us trades in precious stones and ornaments and crowns. And the third trades in spices. The first day at sea, we shared stories and became friends. Then came the storm that tossed the boat up and down and side to side like a sliver of wood in a river rapids. Day after day, the storm pounded. At last, a small hole was opened in the side of the boat. It could not have been more than a hand could cover, yet the force of the wind drove the water into the boat so that we knew our lives would soon end."

Another of the merchants took up the tale. "Each of us prayed to our own god or goddess. When that did not work, we prayed to every god and goddess that we had ever heard of. Still the hole let the water in and the danger grew moment by moment. Suddenly, I remembered the stories of the God of Israel saving the Israelites by opening up the sea so that they might cross on dry land. We pledged all our goods to the God of Israel if only our lives would be spared."

The third merchant then spoke, saying, "It was the wind that tried to wreck us, but now the wind blew a bundle aboard our ship and the God of Israel worked a great miracle for us. The bundle flew directly to the hole, where it lodged and plugged the leak. The wind ceased to blow and the clouds broke overhead, so the sun came through like a welcome visitor. And the boat gently landed upon the shore of your kingdom. We did not forget our pledge, O glorious king. In thankfulness for our lives, we bring all our wares here to you for your God."

King Solomon asked, "What became of the mysterious bundle?"

The first merchant spoke, saying, "Your majesty, we would not leave behind that which saved our lives. Here is the kerchief that wrapped the bundle."

Solomon sent for the widow. "Do you know this cloth?" he asked. Her eyes grew wide. "That is the kerchief I used to hold my precious bundle of flour," she said.

"In that case," Solomon said, "the wind has answered your charges and bestowed on you these three large bundles of silver and gold, precious stones, and fine spices." Solomon told the merchants about the bundle and how it came to be sent on the wind. And Solomon told the widow about the merchants, about their prayer to God, and how their lives were saved by her bundle.

"Your majesty, the merchants pledged these sacks to God. Far be it from me to take what belongs to God. All I want is to work with spindle, needle, and hook as before to earn my bread."

Then Solomon gave his verdict. "Your words are precious to God. The three sacks will be sent to the Temple in your name, as your freewill offering. As for you, you shall have a place among the pious and goodly women who weave curtains and fabric for the Temple. You shall live there so long as you live."

That is how the widow came to live in the Chamber of Hewn Stones in Jerusalem. The curtains woven by her hand and embroidered by her fingers became famous throughout the land, so that even the priests praised the splendor of her skill and admired the wisdom of her heart in every piece she wove. And whenever they passed a curtain that was her work, they would call out in wonder, "Behold, the curtains of Zipporah, the net-weaver."

[adapted from Bialik, *And It Came to Pass*, pp. 148-155]

12. Prince of Onions, Prince of Garlic

The king called his oldest son and said, "It is not enough to be a prince, you must also learn to earn your way. See, I have outfitted a ship with sailors and merchandise, sails and provisions. Go forth into the world and find your fortune."

The prince sailed to and fro, from port to port, trading merchandise and making friends in many places, but he found no fortune. Slowly, he was forced to trade merchandise for provisions, until at last he had little, if anything, left to trade. With his tail between his legs, he steered the ship homeward, stopping only at a small island to purchase a little more food for his sailors.

The king of the island invited the prince to a banquet. After they had eaten, the king inquired, "Do you approve of the work of our excellent chef?" The prince said, "In all honesty, your majesty, I have hardly ever had such a regal repast. The puddings were beyond compare, the bread was sweeter than cake, and the pies were extraordinary." The king inquired, "What about the roast?" The prince answered, "In all honesty, your majesty, the roast would have benefitted from onions."

"Onions," the king said, "What are onions?"

So the next night, the prince invited the king to dine aboard the ship. The prince instructed his cook to prepare a roast with onions. When the king had eaten his fill, he said, "These onions are a wonder! Bring me as many onions as you can and I shall trade you. For every bag of onions, I will give you a bag of greater value."

Now, although he had no more merchandise, the hold of the prince's ship was loaded with onions. The next morning, the sailors unloaded bag after bag of onions on the dock. And, true to his word, for every bag of onions, the king gave the prince a bag of greater value: bag after bag of shining, glittering gold.

Happy to have earned his fortune, the prince returned to his father. And, whenever the prince explained how he became rich, people laughed and clapped.

In a little while, the king addressed his younger son, saying, "I have outfitted a ship for you. Go out into the world like your brother and find your fortune."

But the younger brother saw no reason for struggling. He removed the merchandise his father had placed in the hold of his ship and replaced it all with bags of garlic. He set sail straight for the small island his elder brother had visited last.

The king of the island invited the young prince to a banquet. After they had eaten, the king inquired, "Was everything to your liking?" The prince answered, "It was a meal beyond compare, your majesty, quite nearly perfect." "Nearly perfect?" the king asked. "Oh yes," replied the prince, "it would have been perfect indeed, if only the chef had made the roast with garlic!"

"Garlic," the king said, "What is garlic?"

The next night, the king dined aboard the prince's ship. The prince instructed his cook to prepare a roast with garlic. When the king had eaten his fill, he said, "Do you have more of this wonderful garlic? For every bag of garlic, I will give you a bag of greater value."

The young prince smiled. The next morning, the sailors heaped bag after bag of garlic on the dock. And, true to his word, for every bag of garlic, the king gave the young prince a bag of greater value: bag after bag of golden-skinned onions!

[adapted from a story by Chaim Nachman Bialik, *Kol Kitvei Bialik* (Hebrew)]

✣ 18 ✣
Death and Life

1. Beruriah and Rabbi Meir

🐟 On the Sabbath, Rabbi Meir lingered in the House of Study, praying and studying. His beloved wife Beruriah often lingered with him, praying and studying by his side. But not this Sabbath. A plague was ravishing the town and both sons of Meir and Beruriah had contracted it. Beruriah put one cool cloth after another on their foreheads but it was all to no avail. All through the afternoon, their bodies grew more feverish. Toward sunset, one after another, both boys died in her arms. Beruriah lovingly placed their bodies side by side on a single couch and spread a sheet over them.

The Sabbath ended and Rabbi Meir returned home. He asked, "Where are our two sons?" Beruriah replied, "They went to the House of Study." Meir said, "That is odd. I hoped that they would feel well enough to come. I looked, but did not see them."

Beruriah was silent. With enormous effort, she held back her grief. She handed Meir the cup of wine, the candle, and the spicebox so that he could recite the Havdalah prayers marking the division between the Sabbath and the new week of work.

After the Havdalah prayers, Meir again asked, "Where are our two sons?" Beruriah said, "They went walking together. They should be home soon." She brought food for him. After he had eaten, Beruriah said, "My husband, my teacher, I have a question." Rabbi Meir said, "Ask."

"My teacher, a while ago a man came and deposited something in my keeping. Now he has returned to claim what he left. Shall I return it to him or not?"

"Beruriah, you know the law as well as I. If you hold something on deposit, you are required to return it to its owner, whenever the owner requests!"

Beruriah said, "Even so, I would not have returned it without asking your opinion first."

She took Meir by his hand, led him up to the chamber, and brought him near the couch. When she removed the sheet that covered them, he saw the ashen bodies of his children. Meir began to weep, crying, "My children, my children, my teachers, my teachers. My children in the way of the world. My teachers when they brightened my eyes with their love of Torah."

Now Beruriah comforted her husband. "My love, you just taught me that we are required to restore to the owner what is left with us in trust. God gave us our sons for just a little while. It was God who required their return."

[Midrash Proverbs 31:10; Yalkut Proverbs #964]

2. Comforting the Mourner

When the son of Rabban Yochanan ben Zakkai died, the rabbi's students came to comfort him. One student offered, "Be comforted by the example of Adam and Eve. When their son Abel died, they were comforted by having another son." Rabban Yochanan countered, "In the midst of my grief over my own son, should I be reminded of the grief of Adam and Eve?"

A second student offered, "My master, be comforted by the example of Job. When Job lost all his sons and daughters, God granted him a new family." Rabban Yochanan countered, "I am shattered by the loss of my one son. Should I be reminded of the many losses Job had to suffer?"

A third student said, "Think of the example of King David who lost a son and was comforted when God sent him Solomon, whose name means 'peace.'" Rabban Yochanan countered, "The loss of my son gives me no peace. Must I also suffer because David lost a son?"

At last, Rabbi Eleazar ben Arach spoke: "A king once gave a gem to a man, saying, 'Guard this jewel for me.' Every day, seeing the gem, the man worried: 'When will the king return to claim his gem so that it will be safe?' You had a son. He loved the Torah and studied the legends and laws of our people. In the end, God asked for the return of your precious jewel, and you returned him safely. You have done all that you could for the sake of heaven."

Rabban Yochanan said, "Eleazar, yours are words of wisdom. You have eased my burden. This is the proper way to comfort mourners."

[Mechilta *Yitro, Bachodesh*; also in *Sefer HaAggadah*]

3. Birth and Death

There were two ships: one was leaving the harbor and the other returning home. Onlookers expressed their joy over the ship that was leaving but hardly noticed the incoming one. Among the people on the dock was a person of sound sense who pointed out to the crowd that their joy was misplaced. There should be more joy for a ship safely returned from its voyage than for the ship whose fate no one could foretell.

No doubt, this is what King Solomon meant when he wrote: "The day of death is better than the day of one's birth" (Ecclesiastes 7:1). No one can foretell the destiny of the newly-born child though everyone knows when a person goes hence with a good record behind him. Such a death is better than a new birth. As Solomon said: "A good name is more precious than fine oil" (*ibid.*). Moreover, when a person is born, we begin counting the days to death; but a person who dies is accounted for the world to come.

[*Midrash Exodus Rabbah* 48:1]

4. Twins in the Womb

Imagine twins in the womb. What do they need? They are fed though their mouths are closed. Their lives are serene. The womb is their whole world. In time, though, they begin to wonder, "Why are we shifting lower and lower? If this continues, we will slip out one day. What will happen when we slip out?"

Now one twin is a believer. He says, "There will be another life after this womb." He cannot prove what he says, but he feels it is true, so he says it. The second twin is a skeptic. Legends do not deceive him. There is no evidence of any other life. Why imagine one? Why believe in one? Anyone who "slips" is obviously dead; and that's that.

The first twin says, "You should have faith, brother. After our 'death' here, there will be a new world. Who knows? We may eat through our mouths. We may see wonders, and we may use our ears to hear things. Our feet may grow strong. And our heads may be up and our bodies down."

The second says, "Forget it, brother. It is all in your imagination. There is only this world. There is no world to come! All that lies ahead is death."

"Well," asks the first, "what will death be like?"

The second twin thinks before answering. "Bang!" he says. "We will go with a bang. The world will collapse under us and we will sink into blackness. We will forget and we will be forgotten."

Suddenly, there is a sound like rushing water. The womb convulses with turmoil and writhing as everything lets loose. The twins begin slipping faster and faster, lower and lower.

The first twin exits, falling out. The second twin silently shrieks, startled by this "accident," mourning the loss of his brother. Why? Why wasn't he more careful? Why did he have to fall?

While he is lamenting, he hears an awful crying coming from the abyss and he trembles, "Terrible! Horrible! Just as I predicted!"

Meanwhile, the first twin has "died" into the "new" world. The awful cry is a sign of health and vigor. And, even though the second twin did not believe it possible, he, too, is about to be pulled into that new world.

[adapted from a story by Rabbi Maurice Lamm]

5. Appointment with Death

🐦 One morning, as King Solomon awoke, he heard chirping outside his window. Sitting up in bed, he paid close attention, for he understood the language of the birds. As he listened, he overheard the birds say that the Angel of Death had been sent to take the lives of two of the king's closest advisers.

King Solomon was startled by this unexpected information. He summoned the two doomed men and revealed to them what he had learned of their fate.

At once, the two were terrified. They begged the wise King Solomon for advice. Solomon observed that their only hope was to reach the charmed city of Luz, for it was well known that the Angel of Death was forbidden to enter that city. Indeed, the citizens of Luz were known to live forever—as long as they remained within the city walls. Among mortals, few knew the secret of reaching Luz, but Solomon was one.

King Solomon imparted the secret path to his two frightened friends and they set forth at once. They whipped their camels across the hot desert all day; and at nightfall they finally glimpsed the walls of that fabled city. Immortality was almost at hand and they rode as fast as they could to reach the city gates.

But as they approached they saw, to their horror, the Angel of Death waiting for them before the gates.

"How did you know to look for us here?" they asked. The angel replied: "This is where I was instructed to meet you."

[B. Talmud *Sukkot* 53a]

🏵 19 🏵
Choosing Life

1. Hillel on the Roof

🏵 Pupils came from near and far to study at the great academy of Jewish learning in Jerusalem where the famous masters, Shemayah and Avtalyon, taught Torah and law. Even in faraway Babylonia, young Hillel had heard of them and determined to be their student. He made the long and arduous journey to Jerusalem on foot. Arriving at the gate of the academy, he said to the watchman: "I have come from Babylonia to study with the sages."

The watchman answered: "To study, you must pay. To enter the house of study, you must give me half a *tropaic* each day."

Each day, Hillel found some kind of labor. He worked each morning until he had earned one *tropaic*. Half of this he used for lodging and for meager meals. The other half he gave to the watchman at the academy so that he could spend each afternoon in study. He found no hardship in this, for in truth Hillel was always hungrier for wisdom than for food.

But it happened one Friday that Hillel could find no work at all. He ended his morning with not even half a *tropaic* to pay the watchman. Sad and soul-stricken, he felt as gray as the overcast sky. Indeed, without the words of his teachers to warm him, he was nearly as cold as that winter day in Jerusalem.

"I have no money today," he told the watchman, but the watchman was stern: "No money, no lesson."

Then Hillel had an idea. He climbed to the roof of the house of study and stretched himself out on it. And he put his head over the skylight, covering half the glass panel in the roof. In this way, he could listen to the daily lecture. Intent on the words, Hillel did not notice the snow beginning to fall.

Morning came. It was the Sabbath. Shemayah and Avtalyon rose, wrapped themselves in warm clothing, ate breakfast together, and entered the main room of the academy to study.

316

"It is a cold day, Brother Shemayah," said Avtalyon, crossing his arms and shivering. "And since it is the Sabbath, we are not even permitted to make a fire to warm us."

"Yes, a cold day, Brother Avtalyon," Shemayah agreed. "But, tell me, do you not notice a strange thing?"

"What is that?"

"Every day, this house of study is bright with light, but today it seems almost dark. Tell me, is the day so cloudy?"

"It was clear from the window of my bedroom," said Avtalyon. "I could easily see the beauty of Jerusalem covered in the white blanket of yesterday's snow."

At that, both looked up at the skylight where they saw the shape of a young man like a dark shadow.

"Unbelievable," Avtalyon said, "I see a shape like a frozen person on the skylight."

"I see it, too, Brother Avtalyon," Shemayah answered.

They ran out of the house of study and climbed to the roof. There was Hillel covered over by the snow.

"Quickly," Avtalyon said, "let us save the young man if we can."

They called the watchman to help them, and all three struggled to carry the frozen Hillel from the roof into the house of study. They took the snow from his body and bathed him with warm water.

While they were doing so, the anxious watchman said: "It is my fault, Masters. The boy is Hillel the Babylonian. He had no money and I told him he could not enter unless he paid. He must have climbed to the roof to listen through the skylight."

"No, it is not your fault," said Shemayah, "it is our fault. For we instructed you, 'Do not let students enter without paying,' and you were only doing as we commanded."

"That is true," said Avtalyon, "but from now on you are to let this student enter even if he has no money at all."

They rubbed him with warm towels, but Hillel was still shivering wildly.

"We must build a fire to warm him, Brother Shemayah," said Avtalyon. And Shemayah fetched logs for the fire.

"Masters," the watchman said. "It is the Sabbath and we are forbidden to build a fire on the Sabbath."

"I am the teacher," Avtalyon said in a kindly way. "So learn this, my friend: To save a life, we are permitted to break the law, even the Sabbath law."

"Truly," said Shemayah as he lit the fire, "this young man deserves to have the Sabbath law broken on his behalf."

"Yes," said Avtalyon, as he sat the boy by the open fire. "His love of learning is great. It is certain that one day this Hillel will become a great sage in Israel."

[B. Talmud *Yoma* 35b; also in *Sefer HaAggadah*]

It is written: "You shall therefore keep my statutes and my ordinances; for the one who does shall live by them" (Leviticus 18:5), The sages of the Talmud interpreted this to mean that a person must be enabled to "live" by God's commandments and not die as a result of obeying them (B. Talmud *Sanhedrin* 74a; B. Talmud *Yoma* 85b).

2. Medicine

Once, Rabbi Ishmael and Rabbi Akiva were walking through the streets of Jerusalem when a sick man approached them complaining about his ailment and soliciting their advice. When they instructed him regarding a remedy, an onlooker was incensed. "If it is God's will that this man should have contracted this disease," the man argued, "who are you to counteract God's decision by removing the disease which has been decreed for him?"

"What is your occupation?" demanded the rabbis.

The onlooker answered, "You have only to look at the tools I am carrying to see that I am a gardener."

"But why do you interfere with the earth which God has created?" the sages inquired.

The man retorted, "If I did not manure, prune, and water the trees, how could I expect them to produce their fruit?"

"Even so," the rabbis replied, "this man is like a tree of the field. He requires tender treatment and attention to his body to make it flourish and keep it in good health."

[*Midrash Samuel* 4]

3. The Donkey

A farmer's donkey once fell into a well. The poor donkey cried piteously for hours as the farmer considered what to do. In the

end, the farmer decided that the donkey was too old to be useful
and the well was dry and should be sealed up anyway. It was probably best not to retrieve the donkey. The farmer invited his neighbors to come and help him. Everyone grabbed a shovel and began
to throw dirt into the well. When the donkey realized what was
happening, it cried horribly. Then, to everyone's surprise, the donkey quieted down. A few shovel loads later, the farmer leaned over
the well to see what was happening and was astonished at what he
saw.

As each shovel of dirt hit its back, the donkey would shake it
off and take a step up. As the farmer's neighbors continued to
shovel dirt on top of the animal, the donkey shook off the dirt to
take another step up. Not long after, the people were amazed as
the donkey stepped up over the edge of the well and trotted off.

Dirt falls on every life—all kinds of dirt. The trick to getting
out of the well is to shake it off and take another step up. Each
spot of trouble is a stepping stone and we can trot out of the deepest well if we never stop and never give up.

[attributed to Edwin Friedman]

4. Whose Life Should Be Saved?

🕮 Ben Petura posed the following problem:

Two men are traveling through a desert. Ploni ("Man A") has
a flask of water. Almoni ("Man B") does not. Both of them are dying of thirst.

If Ploni were to drink the water in his flask, he might be able
to reach the town at the desert's edge. On the other hand, if Ploni
and Almoni share the water, neither of them will reach the town
and both will die.

Should Ploni drink the water? Or should he share it with
Almoni? Whose life comes first, when only one may be saved?

Ben Petura himself offered the first answer. He said, Ploni and
Almoni should share the water. The central issue, Ben Petura argued, is not really "Who shall live?" but "What is the right thing to
do normally? And normally," he said, "any of us would share the
water with another person."

Rabbi Akiva disagreed. Akiva argued that it is better to have
one person die than two. Therefore, since the water belongs to
Ploni, he must drink it all.

None of the sages argued that Ploni has an obligation to give the water to Almoni. Why? Because Jewish law requires equal treatment for all. Therefore, if Ploni were required to give the water to Almoni, Almoni would equally be required to give the water to Ploni. Both would die in the desert, passing the flask of water back and forth, with no one ever drinking it.

[*Sifra Leviticus* 25:36; B. Talmud *Baba Metzia* 62a]

5. Is It Alive or Is It Dead?

In a small town there lived a rabbi well known for his wisdom. Jews from miles around came to study with him. They challenged him with difficult questions for the pure joy of hearing his brilliant answers. And the people of the town took great pride in bragging of their resident sage.

One youngster grew very jealous of the rabbi. "I am as smart as that old man," he thought to himself. "I can surely pose some question that he cannot answer. Of course," he added, "I will have to think of it first. But, when I do, people will not think that old rabbi is so wise."

So the youngster set himself the task of devising questions that the rabbi could not answer. Every day the student went to the House of Study. Every day he asked the rabbi a question that he imagined was too difficult for the rabbi to answer. Yet, every day, to the bitter disappointment of the young man, the rabbi would answer his question; and all the people gathered around would marvel at the rabbi's wisdom.

Finally, the youngster conceived a clever plan. He caught a small bird and brought it to the rabbi. He cupped the little bird in the space between his two hands in such a way that the bird could not be seen.

"Rabbi," the young man said, "I have a question that, with all your wisdom, even you cannot answer. In my hands I am holding a tiny bird. Tell me, is the bird alive or is it dead?"

What a strange question! The people gathered closer together the better to hear the rabbi's answer. But how would the rabbi know?

And the youngster smirked. He was certain that the rabbi could not answer this question—for he really did have a clever plan. If the rabbi replied, "The bird is dead," then the boy would open his hands and the bird would fly away, very much alive. And, if the rabbi replied, "The bird is alive," the student would quickly crush the tiny bird with his palms, then open his hands and reveal a dead bird.

For a while the rabbi sat deep in thought. His eyes were closed and one hand played with his beard. At last, he opened his eyes and looked at the young man.

"My child," he said, "in your hand you are holding a life. Choose very carefully what you will do with it."

[Yiddish/European folktale; Rossel, *When a Jew Seeks Wisdom*]

⚜ 20 ⚜
The Sabbath

1. Sabbath Angels

🔖 Rabbi Yose ben Judah taught: Two angels, one good and one bad, visit our homes before Shabbat. If the Sabbath lights are lit, the wine is blessed, the table is arranged, and all is ready for the Sabbath feast, the good angel says, "May it be God's will that the next Sabbath will be as beautiful as this one." To this, the bad angel is forced, against its will, to say, "Amen."

But if the table is not ready, the lights are not lit, and the wine is not blessed, then the bad angel intones, "May it be God's will that the next Sabbath will be like this one." To this, the good angel is forced, against its will, to say, "Amen."

[B. Talmud *Shabbat* 119b]

God calls the Sabbath "a sign between Me and the children of Israel forever" (Exodus 31:17). Rabbi Israel Meir Ha-Kohen, the *Chafetz Chayim* ("Lover of Life"), compared the "sign" of the Sabbath to the sign above a shop. As long as the sign remains, it signals that the business thrives. If the sign is removed, its loss indicates the demise of the enterprise. So, too, with the Sabbath, the *Chafetz Chayim* concluded, as long as we observe it, it is a sign that the belief in God lives in our hearts (*Machnei Yisrael*).

2. The First Sabbath

🔖 As the sixth day of Creation ended, something new and strange happened: The sun dropped lower and lower in the western sky. Slowly, slowly, the light of day faded away. Slowly, slowly, the air grew colder. Adam and Eve were dismayed to see the light dying. They huddled close together, warming one another. Even so, they soon began to shiver. And shivering frightened them even more.

All at once, the sun disappeared, swallowed by the horizon, and the world was darker than the inside of the darkest cave. "This must be our end," Adam thought. "Soon we will sink into the earth like the sun." Adam and Eve were so tired and so terrified that they began to cry. "This must be the death of which God spoke," said Eve, weeping.

Then Adam noticed little fires appearing in the darkness. He called the tiny fires, "stars." Soon, a very large one rose up in the sky. "It is like a little sun," said Eve. "Let's call it 'moon.'"

All night, they huddled close, watching. "This cannot be death," said Eve. "See how the moon and the stars make the leaves glitter and their light glows on the fur of the rabbits as they feed. And see how the yellow eyes of the owls pierce the night."

In this way the hours of darkness passed. The light of dawn glowed red in the eastern sky until the sun rose to shed its golden rays. And God said, "This is My Sabbath. On this day, all shall rest." And Adam and Eve saw that it was good. "Darkness and light, night and day, are the way of nature," they said. And they rested by the light of the day.

When the Sabbath day passed, the sun began to fall again in the sky. God said, "You shall not go into this new week in cold and fear. Behold, I am giving you a great gift. It is the gift of fire itself. If you are careful, you can control it. It will warm you by night and help you work by day."

Adam and Eve praised God for the fire. And, even now, every week begins with blessing the fire of the *Havdalah* candle and every week ends and every Sabbath begins with blessing the fire of the Sabbath lights.

> [B. Talmud *Avodah Zarah* 8a; B. Talmud *Pesachim* 54a; *Midrash Genesis Rabbah* 11:2]

3. Remember the Sabbath Day

In a small village in the Holy Land, there were three friends: a Muslim, a Christian, and a Jew. Each kept the Sabbath—the Moslem on Friday, the Jew on Saturday, and the Christian on Sunday.

One Friday, the Jew and the Christian set out for their fields. The Jew saw the Muslim's field and noticed that only half of it was plowed. He thought, my friend cannot plow on his Sabbath. But what if it rains tomorrow? As long as I am plowing my field, I will plow his a little, too.

The Christian also sensed the rain coming and, thinking much the way the Jew thought, he also plowed some of the Muslim's field. But since they each plowed from opposite sides and at different times, neither the Jew nor the Christian was aware of what the other had done.

The next day, the Muslim came and found his field completely plowed. Amazed, he thought, "Allah sent angels to help me with my work." And he gave special thanks to Allah in his prayers that day.

Some months later, it was time for reaping. One Sunday, the Jew and the Muslim went to their fields, while the Christian kept his Sabbath. The Muslim saw the Christian's field. The grain was ripe and tall and ready to be cut. He thought, my friend cannot reap on his Sabbath. Yet, it could rain tomorrow. As long as I am reaping, I will cut a little of his crop for him."

The Jew thought the same way and did the same thing. But since they each reaped from opposite sides of the Christian's field and at different times, neither the Muslim nor the Jew was aware of what the other had done.

The next day, the Christian went out to reap and found his work already done. Amazed by this, he thought, "Jesus sent angels to reap for me." He dropped to his knees and pressed his hands together in a prayerful way, thanking Jesus for sending him help.

After the reaping, it was time for threshing. On Saturday, the Jew observed his Sabbath. The Christian and the Muslim went to work. The Muslim said to himself, "The wind is perfect today for threshing. It is not too still and it is not too windy." He thought of his Jewish friend resting and said, "Perhaps tomorrow there will be no wind or the wind will be too strong. I will thresh a little of his grain when I finish threshing mine."

The Christian thought the same way. So, toward the middle of the afternoon, the Christian and the Muslim found one another at the threshing floor of their Jewish friend. Suddenly, the Muslim understood how his field had been magically plowed and the Christian understood how his field had been magically reaped. They embraced, and together they threshed the grain of their Jewish friend.

On Sunday, the Jew went to his threshing floor and saw the grain freshly threshed and ready for the mill. He was amazed, as his friends had been when work had been done for them. Lifting his eyes to heaven, he blessed God for sending him angels to help.

The next day, all three met on the way to the mill. The Christian and the Muslim told their Jewish friend how they met at the threshing floor. The Muslim said, "When the two of you plowed my field, I gave thanks to Allah for sending angels. But you two were my angels." The Christian said, "When the two of you reaped my field, I gave thanks to Jesus for angels. But the two of you were my angels." The Jew said, "When the two of you threshed my grain for me, I gave thanks to God for sending me angels. But the two of you were my angels." Then all three prayed together, each thanking his God for the blessing of friendship.

[Rossel, from a story in Hanauer, *Folk Lore of the Holy Land*; also in Certner, *101 Jewish Stories*]

4. Joseph-Who-Honors-the-Sabbath

🕮 Have you heard the story of Joseph who loved the Sabbath so much that everyone called him "Joseph-Who-Honors-the-Sabbath"? If you have not heard it, I will tell it. And, if you have heard it, I will tell it, anyway, for stories are like the Sabbath—they are most enjoyable when they come around often.

Joseph's neighbor, a non-Jew, owned much property. One day, this neighbor visited a soothsayer who told him, "One day Joseph-Who-Honors-the-Sabbath will enjoy all your property." The non-Jew immediately consulted another soothsayer who told him the same thing. Now, when he had heard the same thing from a third soothsayer, he knew it must be true.

What did he do? To protect his wealth, the non-Jew went and sold all his property. He took the proceeds and bought a pearl. And he secured the pearl in his headdress so that he would be able to keep track of his wealth wherever he might go.

This did not have the desired effect, however, because as the non-Jew was crossing a bridge, the wind blew off the headdress and carried it out to sea where a fish swallowed it. The fish was caught and arrived at the marketplace at twilight on the eve of a Sabbath. The fish-monger was dismayed. He asked, "Who will buy such a large fish at this late hour?" Finally, someone told him, "Go, take it to Joseph-Who-Honors-the-Sabbath. He is always eager to buy fine things in honor of the Sabbath."

When Joseph saw the fish, how sleek and grand it looked, he thought how it would do great honor to the Sabbath if he could serve it at his table. So he reached deep into his pocket to find enough money to purchase it. He thought, "So what if I starve the rest of the week? The honor of Shabbat is worth the price."

Lo and behold! When he cut the fish open to bake it, he found the pearl in it! After the Sabbath was over, he sold the pearl for so many golden *denars* that he became as wealthy as his former non-Jewish neighbor had been.

One day, not long after, a certain venerable elder—and some say it was Elijah himself—met Joseph and leaned over to whisper to him: "The one who lends to the Sabbath, the Sabbath will repay."

[B. Talmud *Shabbat* 119a]

Why do Jews speak of "the Sabbath Queen"? When God completed Creation, the Sabbath came before the Holy One and complained: "Each day of the week has a mate—the first day has the second; the third has the fourth; the fifth has the sixth—and only I have no mate." But God consoled the seventh day, saying, "You, too, have a mate. Your mate is the people of Israel. Each week they will welcome you to a wedding feast, even as a king greets his intended on the occasion of their marriage" (*Midrash Genesis Rabbah* 11).

5. Light a Candle

🕮 Up in the north, where many houses have basements, a student came to the rabbi and said, "I wanted to go down into the basement of the study house to fetch wine for the Sabbath, but the darkness prevented me. Tell me, Rabbi, is there a way to chase darkness out of the world?"

The rabbi went to the closet and took out a broom. He handed it to the student and said, "Go sweep the darkness out of the basement."

It was not long before the student returned. "Rabbi, I swept and swept, but the darkness did not budge an inch. I still cannot see anything down there."

The rabbi nodded. "Darkness in the world can be a stubborn thing." He reached in a drawer and took out a ruler. "Take this stick," he said. "See if you can drive the darkness out by beating it."

It was not long before the student returned. "Rabbi, my arms are sore from beating with the stick, but the darkness is still too stubborn to budge."

"I see," said the rabbi. "But here's the next possibility: Go down to the basement and protest the darkness. Raise your voice and scream at it. Yell out that you want it to disappear."

Of course, the student soon returned. "Rabbi, I am hoarse from screaming and yelling, but the darkness must be deaf."

The rabbi led the student to the cupboard, opened a box, and took one of the candles used to welcome Shabbat. He put the candle in a candlestick and struck a match to light it. He handed the candlestick to the student, saying: "Darkness is like evil. It sometimes seems that it is too prevalent for any single person to drive away. But let's take this little light to the basement."

Then the two went down the steps to the basement and wherever the light's glow met the darkness, the darkness evaporated like fog dissipating in the warm sun.

The rabbi said, "This little light is like the Sabbath. If we only stop long enough to bring this little bit of brightness into our world, suddenly the darkness and evil disappear and the light dawns on us all."

[Yiddish/European folktale]

6. The Sabbath Miracle

🐚 Once two Chasidim were bragging about their respective *rebbe*s. "See here," one said, "it happened once that my *rebbe* was driving along in his wagon when a terrible storm appeared. What did he do? He stretched out his hands in prayer. Behold! On the left there was darkness and rain and on the right there was darkness and rain. But, in the middle where the wagon drove, the sky was clear and the sun was shining."

"*That* you call a miracle?" demanded the other Chasid. "It happened once that my *rebbe* was driving in his wagon on a Friday afternoon and he saw that the sun was going down. He knew that the Sabbath would begin before he could reach the *shtetl*. He knew that he would be desecrating the Sabbath if he was still riding on his wagon when it began. So he stretched out his hands in prayer. And behold! A miracle! On the right there was Shabbat and on the left there was Shabbat. But, in the middle where the *rebbe*'s wagon drove, it was still Friday!"

[adapted from Ausubel, *Treasury*, p. 131]

7. Sabbath Spice

Rabbi Judah the Prince invited the emperor Antoninus to dine at his home on Shabbat. Because it was Shabbat, there was no fire for cooking, and the rabbi served the emperor cold dishes: salads, cheeses, and cakes. The emperor ate and thanked Rabbi Judah for a wonderful feast.

Another time, on a weekday, Rabbi Judah invited Antoninus to come to dinner. This time, he served the emperor hot dishes.

The emperor again thanked Rabbi Judah. Then he said, "It is strange, my friend. I enjoyed the hot meal you served me tonight but, in truth, I prefer the cold meal you served me on my last visit even more."

Rabbi Judah agreed. "These hot dishes are just fine," he said, "but they lack a secret spice."

Antoninus asked, "What spice would make a meal as delicious as the cold one you served? Send me some of that spice and I will have my cooks use it."

"I do not think your cooks can use this particular spice," replied Rabbi Judah, laughing. "The secret spice is Shabbat. For those who observe Shabbat the spice works; for those who do not observe Shabbat, it does not work."

[B. Talmud *Shabbat* 119a; also *Sefer HaAggadah*]

21
Shalom
Peace

1. Yochanan and Vespasian

🖎 Rabbi Yochanan was in Jerusalem when the Roman armies laid siege to the city. For three days, Rabbi Yochanan begged the Zealot leaders of Jerusalem to surrender and make peace with the Romans, but they were too proud. They refused.

It happened that Vespasian had spies in the city. The spies wrote messages on the heads of arrows and threw the arrowheads over the walls to the Roman soldiers below. In this way, they sent a message to Vespasian, saying, "In all Jerusalem, there is only one sensible man and his name is Yochanan."

Devising a plan, Rabbi Yochanan called his students and told them, "Prepare a coffin for me and I will lay in it. Carry me out of the city."

At sunset, the students came to the gates of Jerusalem, carrying the coffin. The gatekeepers asked, "What is this?" The students answered, "There is a corpse in the coffin. Jewish law states that a corpse cannot be left in the city overnight." The gatekeepers nodded, and said, "If so, take it out."

Solemnly, the students carried the coffin out and took it to the Roman general Vespasian. Before Vespasian's bodyguards could stop them, they lifted the lid of the coffin and the rabbi stepped out. The bodyguards surrounded the rabbi, but Vespasian ordered them to stand down. He recalled the message of his spies and guessed the truth. He asked, "Are you Rabbi Yochanan?"

Rabbi Yochanan said, "I am he. I come in peace. If it were possible, I would open the gates of Jerusalem for you, just so that you would spare the city and the Temple."

Vespasian said, "But if you cannot deliver the city to me, what do you want?"

329

"I ask for a small favor," Rabbi Yochanan said. "Let me go in peace to the little town of Yavneh."

"What will you do there?" Vespasian asked.

"We will pray to our God. I will teach my students. And we will live there peacefully according to God's commandments."

Vespasian considered the rabbi's words. At last, he answered, "My enemies are armies; my foe is in the city. Go in peace. Do whatever it pleases you to do in Yavneh."

In that moment, two fates were sealed: The Temple would be destroyed; but, thanks to Rabbi Yochanan, Judaism would be saved.

[*Avot deRabbi Natan* 4:11b-12a]

2. Golda and the Arab Nations

Following the Six Day War, no peace treaty was signed between Israel and her Arab neighbors. In 1969, Golda Meir became Prime Minister of Israel. She hoped that her new administration could conclude a treaty, but she insisted that this was only possible if she could meet the Arab leaders face to face.

In one interview, a reporter commented that face to face negotiations were probably unnecessary. "Even divorces are arranged without personal confrontation," he offered. Golda Meir riposted: "But I am not interested in a divorce. I am interested in a marriage."

Another reporter asked her if she truly believed that peace with the Arab nations could be achieved.

"We will have peace with the Arabs," Meir confidently replied, "when they love their children more than they hate us."

[adapted from two anecdotes: "not interested in a divorce...," original source unknown; "We will have peace...," statement to the National Press Club, Washington, DC, 1957]

3. Loving Peace and Pursuing Peace

Our rabbis taught: Moses' brother, Aaron, was loved by all the people of Israel. When Aaron died, the people mourned for thirty days. "Aaron was a man of peace," they said. "He knew how to pursue peace, and he knew how to love peace."

When two friends had an argument, Aaron would go to one of them and say, "Look how your friend walks with his eyes down, wringing his hands in sorrow! Your friend truly misses you." Then Aaron would go to the other and say, "Your friend is sorry for arguing with you. Look for your friend among the people!" The next time the two met, they would hug and kiss each other. In this way, Aaron brought peace to the house of Israel.

It is likewise told that when Aaron was walking and chanced upon a man who was reputed to be evil, he would greet the man saying, "*Shalom*, peace be with you."

The next day, if that man thought to do something evil, he would say to himself, "If I were to do this thing, how could I then lift up my eyes and face Aaron? I would be ashamed before him, for he gave me a greeting of peace." So the man would refrain from doing evil.

[*Avot deRabbi Natan* 12; also in *Sefer HaAggadah*]

4. Proverbs of Peace

The sages observed: Beloved is peace, for God has granted peace to those that are near God, and also to those that are far off (who have removed themselves from God's presence), as it is written, "Peace, peace, to the one that is far off and to the one that is near" (Isaiah 57:19).

Rabbi Levi said: Beloved is peace, for all our prayers end with "peace."

Rabbi Simeon bar Chalafta said; See how beloved is peace: In seeking to bless Israel, God found no other vessel which could contain all Israel's blessings, save peace. How do we know this? For it is written: "God will give strength to God's people; God will bless God's people with peace" (Psalms 29:11).

[*Midrash Deuteronomy Rabbah* 5:15]

Moreover, it is taught: "Great is peace, for *Peace* is God's name" (*Midrash Numbers Rabbah* 11:7) And the sages recorded the following prayer: "You who are majestic on high, who abide in might, You are peace and Your name is *Peace*. May it be Your will to bestow peace on us" (B. Talmud *Berachot* 55b).

IV
FAITH

1

Prayer

1. You And I

O God, my God,
You are the Master and I am the servant.
Who cares for the servant, except the Master?
You are God and I am the mortal.
Who cares for the mortal, except God?
You are the Living and I am the dying.
Who cares for the dying, except the Living?
You are the Potter, and I am the clay.
Who cares for the clay, except the Potter?
You are the Shepherd and I am the sheep.
Who cares for the sheep, except the Shepherd?
You are the Listener and I am the speaker.
Who cares for the speaker, except the Listener?
You are the Beginning and I am the end.
Who cares for the end, except the Beginning?

[Yemenite Hebrew prayer, *Ani V'atah*, published by Herbert Weiner in Oesterreicher, ed., *The Bridge*, Vol. III, pp. 25f.; new translation by Rossel]

2. Who to Thank

A boy who had just eaten lunch said to his mother, "Thank you very much." But his mother said, "You should not thank me alone, for I only prepared the food."

The boy wondered, "Whom should I thank?" He went to the grocery store and saw the grocer. "Thank you, Mr. Grocer, for the very fine food I ate for lunch."

"You are welcome," said the grocer, "but you should not thank me alone. I only sell food. I do not produce it. Take the bread, for example, it comes from the bakery."

So the boy went to the bakery and found the baker. "Mr. Baker," the boy said, "thank you for the wonderful bread that you bake."

The baker laughed and said, "I bake the bread, but it is good because it is made from fine flour. And the flour comes from the miller who grinds it."

"Then I will thank the miller," said the boy and he turned to leave.

"But the miller only grinds the wheat," the baker said. "It is the farmer who grows the grain which makes the flour so fine."

So the boy went off in search of the farmer. He walked to the edge of the village and there he saw the farmer at work in the fields. "Thank you for the bread I eat every day."

But the farmer said, "Do not thank me alone. I only plant the seed, tend the field, and harvest the grain. It is sunshine and good rain and the rich earth that make the wheat grow."

"But who is left to thank?" asked the boy, and he was confused, tired, and hungry again, for he had walked a long way in one day.

The farmer said, "Come inside and have dinner with my family and then you will feel better."

So the boy went into the farmhouse and sat down to eat with the farmer's family. Each person took a piece of bread and then, all together, they said, "We thank You, O Eternal, our God, Ruler of the universe: You cause bread to spring forth from the earth."

Suddenly, the boy realized that it was God whom he had forgotten to thank.

[Rossel, *When a Jew Prays*]

3. Heaven Knows Her Children

Rabbi Levi Yitzchak of Berditchev loved all Jews, those who studied Torah and also those who did not. On Rosh Hashanah, before the blowing of the *shofar*, he assured his congregation that God would receive their prayers and penitence, and God would inscribe them for a good year in the Book of Life. He told this story:

He was at an inn where merchants stopped. It was far from Berditchev and no one recognized him. Several young Jewish merchants rose early, anxious to complete their morning prayers so that they could get to the marketplace. But there was only one pair of *tefillin* ("phylacteries"), so they passed them from one to another, putting them on and taking them off. When everyone had prayed, Levi Yitzchak called them together and said, "I need to ask you, *Ma... meh... ma...; va... veh... va...?*"

"What do you mean?" the merchants asked. But the rabbi only repeated, "*Ma... meh... ma...; va... veh... va...?*"

The young men grew restive, thinking the person before them a fool. They were about to take their leave, when the rabbi fixed them with his eyes and said, "Do you not understand the very language in which—in your rush to complete your prayers—you just addressed God?"

The merchants were startled. Finally, one recovered enough to challenge the rabbi, "Think of a baby in the cradle. It makes sounds like the ones you made, the ones you say we made: '*Ma... meh... ma...; va... veh... va....*' Sages and wise men shrug their shoulders and turn away, but a mother hears these sounds and knows exactly what the baby means."

Levi Yitzchak said to his congregation, "In that moment, my heart danced with joy. I realized that, no matter what language we use to disguise our prayers, our parent in Heaven understands us. Dance and sway, tremble and shake, sing and sign, God hears. Shout and whisper, mumble and gibber, hem and haw, God knows what you mean. Who can deny it? Heaven knows her children."

[Buber, *Early Masters*, p. 214]

4. Horses Can Pray?

🐎 Before modern times, a Polish nobleman was called a *pan* ("Sir" or "Knight"). It happened once that two Polish pans were drinking and bragging. Each believed his estate the more beautiful and desirable. They contended over all their possessions, each claiming the best, the most, the greatest. One pan bragged, "I have just purchased, for a great sum of gold, a fabulous white stallion, the most elegant horse in all the world."

"Of what use is a stallion to you?" asked the second pan.

"Why, I can ride him as the clouds ride the wind," said the first.

"That may be," said the other, "but can your stallion give you wisdom?"

"No," the first answered, "Why do you ask?"

338 - *The Essential Jewish Stories* - FAITH

"I have a servant in my court," said the second, "who is the world's greatest teacher. He can teach anything to anyone."

"But can you ride him?" asked the first pan, laughing loudly.

"How much better it is to have a wise adviser and great teacher than a white horse!" said the other.

But the first pan said, "I would bet that your teacher is not so great as you say."

"What do you mean?" asked the second pan.

"I bet your teacher cannot teach my horse to pray."

The second pan should have shrugged this off but the wine had taken effect. He could not resist any bet! "Of course," he replied.

"If your wise man can teach my horse to pray in three weeks," said the first, "then the horse is yours. But if he cannot, you must pay me in gold what I paid for the stallion." And so the matter rested.

The next morning, though, when the second pan awoke, the white stallion had been delivered to his stable. Through his hangover, he remembered the bet and he was dismayed. Horses can trot, they can gallop and canter; but can horses pray? Still, he had made the bet. So he called for Yussef to be brought to him.

"Can you teach a horse to pray?" he asked Yussef. Then, he told him of the wager.

When Yussef heard the story from beginning to end, he shook his head. "I do not know," he said. "It seems an impossible task. But I will do my best."

All morning, Yussef kept the white stallion away from food. When afternoon came, the beast was ravenous.

Late in the afternoon, Yussef brought out a wooden stand and placed a prayer book on it. Now he opened the prayer book to the very first page and spread oats upon the page.

When the horse smelled the oats, he came over to the prayer book and ate them from the page where Yussef had placed them.

The next day, Yussef again spread oats on the first page of the prayer book, but this time he also put oats between the next two pages. When the horse had eaten the oats on the first page, he still smelled more oats. The horse sniffed and sniffed, and finally he put his tongue out and licked the top page. And the page turned! So the beast ate the oats Yussef had placed on the second page.

The next day, Yussef put oats on the first page, the second, the third, and the fourth. And whenever the horse finished eating the oats on one page, he put out his tongue and flipped to the next page full of oats.

Soon the time of the wager was up and the two Polish pans met again to see who had won the bet. Yussef led the white stallion into the room and set up the stand, placing the prayer book on it. Now, of course, there were no oats on the prayer book pages, but the smell of oats remained on every page.

The horse came up to the prayer book and sniffed up and down the first page. Finding no oats to eat, he flipped the page with his tongue and ran his nose up and down the second page. Soon he had leafed through the entire prayer book, sniffing up and down each page; snorting, grunting, and turning pages with his tongue. No one could deny it, the horse seemed to be praying.

"You see," said the second pan to his unfortunate friend, "I have won the bet. My teacher has taught your horse to pray."

The rabbi who told this tale added, "Too many of us, my friends, pray like horses looking for oats: flipping pages and reciting words, but offering God little from our hearts."

[Yiddish folktale; Rossel, *When a Jew Prays*]

5. Consecration

🐾 Imagine this setting: The sanctuary of the synagogue has a huge vaulted ceiling. The *Aron Kodesh* ("Holy Ark") is set two steps higher than the *bimah* ("pulpit"). The Holy Ark is behind two burnished brass doors which rise nearly all the way to the ceiling. The brass doors, too heavy to be opened by hand, are cleverly attached to two motors installed beneath the *bimah*. A foot switch, strategically located beneath the carpet atop the steps, operates the doors. At the appropriate moment, the rabbi steps on the foot switch and the enormous doors slowly and majestically open. Stepping on the foot switch again produces the opposite result and the doors slowly and majestically close.

Once, a rabbi of this congregation was rehearsing the children of the nursery and kindergarten classes in preparation for Consecration (the modern Jewish ritual in which children new to the religious school are called to the *bimah* to recite the *Shema* prayer). When the rabbi brought the children to the sanctuary, took them up on the *bimah*, and had them climb the steps to the level of the ark.

Now, imagine yourself a small child looking up at those brass doors intended to impress adults seated in the congregation. Imagine how lofty they seem as you look up at them from below. The children were visually awed by the experience.

The rabbi said, "This is where we will stand when we say the prayer," and he asked them to recite it now. After they repeated the words of the *Shema* prayer, the rabbi stepped on the concealed foot switch and the doors slowly ... and majestically ... opened.

The children were mesmerized by the sight! Closing the doors and seeing how excited the children were, the rabbi asked them if they would like to do it again. Of course, young children like nothing better than repetition. Their heads bobbed up and down in unison. They spoke the words again; and the rabbi again stepped on the switch. And the doors slowly and majestically opened and closed again. Afterward, the rabbi led the children back to their classroom.

A little while later, the rabbi was passing by the darkened sanctuary when he heard a sound coming from within. Opening the door to investigate, he saw a single young man, aged five, standing on the raised step before the ark, looking upward at the doors, stamping his foot, and crying out, "*Shema, Yisrael ... Shema, Yisrael ...*"

[Rossel]

6. Service of the Heart

🖎 Can we really give God anything in return? Can our prayer really mean anything to the Creator of all the World, to the King of kings? A Chasidic rabbi told this story to explain why God loves the prayer of man:

Once there was a king who loved music very much. In his palace he kept a whole orchestra to entertain him. All day long the musicians would practice and practice, studying new songs and new melodies to delight the king. Every evening, they would play for the king in his great throne room. The orchestra never failed to please the king.

Now one of the king's advisers brought the king a gift: a beautiful songbird, a nightingale. The nightingale sang night and day, flittering from place to place in its golden cage. Whatever the king was doing, he would pause to listen to the bird's song. Though the bird knew only one tune, the king loved its singing more than the playing of his whole orchestra, for the song of the nightingale came, not from rehearsal and skill, but from its heart and soul.

So, too, God, the King of kings, loves the singing of human beings in prayer more than all the perfect prayers of the angels, for authentic human prayer comes from the heart and soul.

[Rossel]

7. Praying Every Hour

The emperor Antoninus asked Rabbi Judah, "If the Jews are so close to God, why don't they pray to God every hour of the day?"

Rabbi Judah answered, "It is forbidden. If we prayed every hour of every day, God would soon grow tired of us."

"I think you are mistaken," said Antoninus.

What did Rabbi Judah do? Early the next morning, he entered the throne room of Antoninus and said, "Hail to you, Emperor!" An hour later, he returned and said, "Hail to you, mighty Antoninus!" Each hour, he returned and offered words of praise: "Peace be with you, great Caesar!" "Long life to you, King of Rome!"

After several hours of this, Antoninus grew angry. "Why do you treat me this way?" he asked Rabbi Judah.

Rabbi Judah replied, "I only wish to show you the truth of what I said. If you, a man of flesh and blood, feel angered when I come every hour just to give you greetings, imagine how disturbed God would be if every Jew everywhere on earth prayed every hour of every day."

[*Tanchuma Buber* 98a-98b; also in *Sefer HaAggadah*]

On the other hand, Rabbi Meir taught, "A person is commanded to find reasons to pronounce one hundred blessings every day" (B. Talmud *Menachot* 43b).

8. Why We Talk All Night

🐝 The Passover *Haggadah* tells of five rabbis who sat at the Seder table all night! They talked about how the Jewish people were slaves to Pharaoh. They talked about how God rescued us from Egypt. They talked about freedom. They talked so long that they did not notice the night had passed and the sun was coming up. Suddenly, there was a knock at the door! The rabbis looked up and saw their students standing in the doorway.

"Where have you been?" the students asked. "It's time for the morning prayers!"

"Where have *you* been?" the rabbis asked. "While you were sleeping, we were slaves in Egypt, we were rescued by God, we crossed the sea with Moses, and we received the Ten Commandments at Mount Sinai. We did all this— and we never left this table!"

If you can do all this while sitting at your table, you too will have a Passover filled with mystery and wonder. And that is why Jews sit so long at the Passover table.

[Rossel, *Storybook Haggadah*]

9. Dancing with the Bear

🐝 One time, in a kingdom very far away, a circus performed before the king and all the royal court. When the circus left town the next day, it was suddenly noticed that the little prince had disappeared. The king sent messengers everywhere looking for the prince, but the prince could not be found. Nor could the messengers find the circus to ask if the prince was with them.

In fact, the prince had left with the circus. The circus folk were accustomed to little boys running away to join them. They had no way of knowing that this particular boy was a prince. So they continued traveling from kingdom to kingdom. In time, the little prince grew to be a teenager. He learned to set up the tents when the circus reached a new town; and to take tents down when the circus was ready to move on. He learned to walk the tightrope. He learned to stand on the back of horses as they ran around the circus ring. But, above all else, he loved to dance with the dancing bear. No one was better at dancing with the bear than he, so that became his job. He tended to the needs of the bear day and night, and danced with the bear at each performance.

In time, the circus returned to the kingdom of the prince's father. The circus folk saw the notices posted on trees everywhere. The king had never given up hope. He was still offering a reward for the return of his son, the prince. The circus manager suddenly realized that the king's son and the circus' dancing boy must be one and the same! He said nothing to the boy, but led him to the kingdom's capital.

The prince thought it was the most wonderful city he had ever seen. As he and the circus manager passed through the marketplace filled with shops and stalls selling colorful cloth, food of every variety, golden cups, and silver ornaments, the boy thought it was the most wonderful market he had ever seen. As they entered the palace where the soldiers marched before them in rows, the boy thought the splendid uniforms were the most wonderful costumes he had ever seen. But when they came to the throne room—when the prince saw the king sitting on the throne—he thought this was the most marvelous person in the world. All these things he had long ago forgotten, nor could he know that before him was his very own father.

For his part, as soon as the king saw the prince, he knew it was his son. The king called to the boy and bade him come very close. Then he confided, "You are the prince, my son. You are the very one who has been missing for so many years. To welcome you home, we wish to give you a gift. You can have anything in the world you want. Tell me, What would you like?"

The prince thought for a moment. He still hardly believe how lucky he was. Finally, he looked up at the king and answered, "Well, I do need a new pair of dancing shoes."

Rabbi Simcha Bunam always ended this story by saying, "This is what it is like for us when we pray. We stand before the Ruler of the World, God Almighty. And God asks us, what would you like if you could have anything in the whole wide world? And we are as simple as that little boy standing before his father. We ask for the needs of the hour."

[Rossel, based on a tale of Simcha Bunam in Buber, *Later Masters*, pp. 252-253]

10. How Shall I Bless You?

A man went wandering through the desert. He traveled for many days without finding a village or a town. He traveled for many days without finding an oasis. He traveled for many days without finding water. He did not see animals along his way. And even birds did not fly where he went.

Twenty days passed, and at the end of them he finally saw a tree standing alone in the distance. "I must reach this tree," he thought. "There may be water beneath it." Truly, when he was beside the tree, he was happy to see a little pool of water in its shade. He was also very pleased since the tree was green and full of dates and beneath the shady tree was a perfect place to rest.

The man sat beneath the tree, looking at its reflection on the water. When he was cooled by the shade, he picked some dates and ate them. Then he drank the water and felt refreshed. When he rose to leave, he spoke to the tree.

"Tree, O tree," he said, "you have blessed me, and I would like to leave you with a blessing. But what blessing can I offer to you? Can I pray that your shade be pleasant? It is already pleasant. Can I pray that you grow straight and tall? You are already straight and tall. I cannot bless you by asking for water, for you already stand over water. And I cannot bless you by asking that your fruit be delicious, for it is already delicious."

Then he said, "How shall I bless you? I shall bless you by asking that all new trees that come from your seeds shall be just like you."

[*Midrash Numbers Rabbah* 2:12; B. Talmud *Taanit* 5b]

11. The Watchmaker

Once upon a time the watchmaker of a small village died. No one else in the village knew how to repair watches, so the townspeople were at a loss if a watch slowed down or if a clock stopped. As time passed, no one really knew the correct time.

Some of the people, when their watches stopped, just threw the watches in the bottom of a drawer and left them there, piling other things on top of them, entirely neglecting them. Other people, when their watches stopped, carefully wrapped and stored them, taking them out from time to time just to dust them off and wind them.

One day an itinerant watchmaker came to town. All the people brought their stopped watches to the watchmaker. Now, as for the watches that had been carefully stored and continually wound, the watchmaker had only to make a few minor adjustments, dust their inner works, set them to the correct time, and those watches were as good as new. But, as for the watches that had been neglected, every part had to be cleaned, and many parts had to be replaced before those watches would even tick again.

The rabbi who told this story, Abraham Joshua Heschel, went on to explain that it is this way with our prayer, too. If we stop praying when our prayers do not seem to work, and we do not pray again until we feel that we absolutely must, prayer will be difficult for us. We will be like the townspeople who neglected their watches. But if we emulate those who wrapped their watches carefully, who took them out and wound them even though they did not know the correct time, if we keep on praying though we do not know the effect of our prayer, then when we feel we must pray, we will be ready to pray with all our hearts.

In a way, prayer is like flying a kite. You prepare the kite, tie the tail just right, attach the string to it, and run with all your might to get the kite off the ground. At times, the wind is right and the kite lifts off to soar through the skies. At times, the wind is wrong and the kite refuses to fly, though everything you did was right. One thing, however, is certain: Unless you try, the kite will never fly. Unless you pray, your prayer will never soar to heaven.

["Watchmaker" section attributed to Abraham Joshua Heschel; kite section by Rossel]

2
Trust in God

1. This Too Is for Good

🐝 There was a certain man called Nachum of Gamzo. Why was he called *Gamzo*? Because whenever something went wrong for him, he would always say, *Gam zo letovah*, "This too is for good." And things were always going wrong for him.

He was blind in both eyes. He said, "*Gam zo letovah*, 'This too is for good.' Now I can learn to look into my heart to love God more."

He was crippled in both legs. He said, "*Gam zo letovah*, 'This too is for good.' Now I can spend more time in studying Torah and less time walking from place to place."

His body was covered with sores. "*Gam zo letovah*, 'This too is for good.' Now I can stop thinking about being handsome and pay closer attention to the beauty of God's creation."

His house fell down, leaving only ruins. He said, "*Gam zo letovah*, 'This too is for good.' Now I can spend less time making my home better and more time making God's world better."

No matter what happened to him, no matter how bad it seemed to others, Nachum of Gamzo would merely say, "*Gam zo letovah*, 'This too is for good.'"

One time, the Jews decided to send a gift to the emperor. They came to Nachum. "We wish you to take a chest full of diamonds and pearls to the emperor."

Nachum said, "Why should I be chosen for such a great honor?"

"Because, no matter what, you always find a way to make things good," they said.

So Nachum loaded the chest of jewels on one donkey, climbed on another donkey, and set out to see the emperor. On the way, he stopped for the night at an inn. "I am on my way to see the emperor," he said to the innkeeper, "and I need a room for the night." Then the innkeeper helped Nachum put the chest in his room.

"This chest is very heavy," said the innkeeper to Nachum. "It must be filled with books."

"Not books," said Nachum, "it is filled with precious gems for the emperor."

The innkeeper smiled. When Nachum was fast asleep, the innkeeper crept into his room and stole all the diamonds and pearls from the chest, filling the chest with dirt. The next morning, he helped Nachum load the chest back on the donkey. "You must be very careful with this treasure," he told Nachum. "You should not tell everyone what is in this chest. Someone might steal it."

Nachum thanked the innkeeper and went on his way. When he reached the emperor's palace, the guards brought Nachum and the chest before the emperor. "I have brought a gift from your loyal friends, the Jews of Israel," said Nachum.

But when the chest was opened, the emperor was wroth at what he saw. "Is this the gift the Jews send to me? A chest of dirt? Am I not the emperor of Rome? Do I not deserve gifts of gold and silver, gifts of precious spices, gifts of jewels and silks?" Then the emperor said, "I will show you what I think of your gift. I will have you tortured and killed."

Nachum said, "*Gam zo letovah*, 'This too is for good.'"

"How can this be ' for good'?" demanded the emperor. But, just at that moment, the king's wise man whispered in the king's ear, "Your majesty, this may be magical dirt. For I have heard how Abraham, the father of the Jews, once threw earth at his enemies, and the earth turned into swords and arrows and drove his enemies away."

"We shall see," said the emperor. He sent the chest of earth to where his soldiers were doing battle. In the heat of the struggle, the emperor's soldiers threw the dirt in their enemies' eyes. And when the dirt blinded their enemies, the soldiers defeated them. They sent word back to the emperor, saying, "Your secret weapon has helped us conquer a city!"

The emperor had Nachum Gamzo brought forth from the dungeon. "Your God has worked a miracle for me. In return, I will show you honor." He called his soldiers to bring a chest larger than the one the Jews had sent and to fill it with diamonds and pearls. The emperor announced, "I give these gems and pearls as a gift to the Jews." And he sent Nachum on his way.

As it happened, Nachum stopped at the same inn for the night and once again the innkeeper helped him with his chest. "This chest is bigger and heavier than the last one," said the innkeeper. "You must have bought even more books."

But Nachum replied, "No. I gave the emperor what was in the last chest, and the emperor gave me this chest of diamonds and pearls."

The cunning innkeeper did not steal from Nachum this time. Instead, the next morning, after Nachum left, the innkeeper filled a heavy chest with earth and took it to the emperor. "Great Caesar of Rome," the innkeeper said, "I have brought you a great gift, more of the same earth that was given to you by Nachum of Gamzo."

"We shall see," the emperor replied. He sent the chest of dirt to his soldiers. But this time, when the soldiers threw the dirt at their enemies, their enemies were wise to the trick. They covered their eyes with their hands. Then they drove back the emperor's soldiers, defeating them. When the emperor heard how his soldiers had lost the battle, he had the innkeeper put to death.

That same day, Nachum brought the emperor's chest to the Jews. "You have truly worked a miracle," they told him. "We sent you with a small treasure and you returned to us with an even greater treasure."

All Nachum said was, "*Gam zo letovah*, 'This too is for good.'"

[B. Talmud *Taanit* 21a; B. Talmud *Sanhedrin* 108b-109a; also *Sefer HaAggadah*]

In *A Treasury of Jewish Folklore*, Nathan Ausubel tells the story of the funeral of the richest man in town, when many of the townspeople came out to pay their respects to the deceased. One wept through the eulogy, cried even more pathetically as he followed the hearse, and fairly fainted as the rich man's casket was lowered and the people began to shovel spadefuls of earth into the grave. The rabbi turned aside to console the man. "Were you a close relative of the deceased?" he asked. "Relative?" the man said in a plaintive voice. "Why, I am no relation at all." "Then, why do you weep and suffer so?" the rabbi asked. "But, rabbi," he answered, "that *is* the reason!" (p. 398).

2. Zusya's Breakfast

In his old age, Rabbi Zusya of Anipoli would rise and go to *shul* for the morning prayer. When he returned home, he would say: "O Sovereign of the universe, Zusya is hungry; may Zusya be granted nourishment!" This was the signal for his *gabbai* ("attendant") to bring him his morning meal. In time, though, the *gabbai* grew weary of this little charade. He asked himself: "Why does Rabbi Zusya speak to God about breakfast? I am the one who brings him his breakfast. Why doesn't he just ask me?" So the *gabbai* determined not to listen to Zusya's prayer. He decided to wait until the rabbi spoke directly to him.

That morning, as Zusya was returning from *shul*, he approached a stranger, a traveling merchant who did not recognize him. The cobblestone path was narrow and Zusya was dressed in simple clothes. Little wonder, then, that the merchant thought the rabbi was a beggar. Typically, Zusya's mind was far away—thinking more of what matters to God than what matters to Zusya—so he did not step aside. *Nu*, the collision was no one's fault! But the merchant's temper flared. And the upstart was, the merchant shoved Zusya into the gutter!

Zusya was not bothered by this. He had suffered far worse. When he was young, he often received beatings from peasants who simply liked hurting Jews. In fact, many Chasidim believed that Zusya had turned suffering into a kind of prayer. Zusya was beaten? Okay. Zusya thanked God for choosing him to be beaten so that other Jews would not be hurt. This day, Zusya picked himself up out of the mud and thanked God that no other Jew had slipped into it.

Meanwhile, the merchant went to the inn where he told his story about the comical old beggar and how he shoved him aside. But when he described the "comical old beggar," the innkeeper was horrified. He wrung his hands, saying, "*Oy*, you do not know what you are saying! *Vey*, you do not know what you have done! That beggar you shoved is our holy Rabbi Zusya!"

Being at heart a good Jew, the merchant was mortified. He decided he must beg the rabbi's forgiveness right away. He asked the innkeeper for his best cakes and finest wine. Carrying this feast in his hands, he went to see the holy rabbi.

Meanwhile, Rabbi Zusya came home, sat at his table and said, "O Sovereign of the universe, Zusya is hungry; may Zusya be granted nourishment!" But his stubborn *gabbai* sat still, waiting. A while passed, and the rabbi repeated, "O Sovereign of the universe, Zusya is hungry; may Zusya be granted nourishment!" The *gabbai* thought, "Now I have got him! If he keeps asking God for help, there will be no breakfast for Zusya today. Let him ask me— and he will have his breakfast."

Imagine the *gabbai*'s surprise when a knock came at the door and breakfast arrived for Rabbi Zusya.

From then on, whenever Zusya said, "O Sovereign of the universe, Zusya is hungry; may Zusya be granted nourishment!" the *gabbai* ran to get breakfast for his rabbi, knowing that, in truth, it was God and not the *gabbai* who was feeding Zusya.

[Newman, *The Hasidic Anthology*, p. 151]

3. Three Gifts

It happened once that a simple Jew died and his soul went upward to the gates of heaven. Immediately the angels prepared the trial. First they set up a scale with two large pans on either side and a pointer in the middle. Then, they appeared with two enormous bags. One bag contained all the good deeds that the Jew had done in his days on earth. The other bag contained all the evil deeds that the Jew had done in his days on earth. The soul was amazed. Not only had he never imagined that all his good and evil deeds were being collected to be weighed after his death, he also never imagined that he had done so many evil things or, for that matter, so many good things.

Now the two attorney angels stepped forward. One was the advocate angel. He was given the bag full of good deeds. The other was the prosecuting angel; the bag full of evil deeds was given to him. As the prosecuting angel poured the contents of the bag of evil deeds on one side of the scale, the advocate angle poured the contents of the bag of good deeds on the other side. For a moment, the evil deeds outweighed the good ones and all the angels standing around sighed. But when the advocate poured out more good deeds, so that the scale was tipped toward the good, the angels rubbed their wings together, making a heavenly sound.

By this, the soul understood that his fate hung in the balance. If his good deeds outweighed his evil ones, then he would be admitted to heaven. If not, well, heaven forbid, because his fate would be with evil ones.

What happened next had never happened before. The good deeds were not all that good; and the evil ones were not all that evil and, when both bags were empty, the scales tipped one way and another and came to a stop with the pointer straight up—there was not a bit of difference, not one whit, between the weight of the good and the evil deeds of this simple Jew.

The prosecuting angel stepped forward and intoned, "This soul cannot be condemned."

The advocate angel stepped forward and intoned, "This soul cannot be admitted to heaven."

The angel who was the court clerk said, "We have no guidance for a situation like this. This soul will have to wander the earth until God notices him and chooses to send him one way or the other."

But the advocate angel whispered to the soul, "Take my advice. Where you wander, pay close attention to the human beings. If you see something especially wondrous or exceptionally beautiful, grab hold of it and bring it to the gatekeeper of heaven. Tell the gatekeeper that I sent you. If you collect three acceptable gifts, then the righteous will demand that the gates of heaven be opened for you. Do this, because otherwise you will wander forever."

Then the soul plummeted to earth, flying across fields and villages, pausing at every Jewish village. Whenever he saw a Jew, he would come close and wait to see if the Jew would do something to sanctify God's name or perform some special act of kindness. But, alas, most Jews were simple folk doing simple everyday things.

Seasons passed and one year followed another. Cities turned into cemeteries; cemeteries became plowed fields. Forests were cleared away; walls were built and fell, rivers shifted from one bed to another, comets blazed, and many souls passed on their way to heaven, but still the wandering soul found no wonderful deed of goodness.

The soul was nearly beyond hope when he saw a fabulous house with bright light burning in the topmost window. He flew to the window and saw a truly remarkable sight. A Jew was tied up in a chair and a robber was going through his possessions, gathering them up—a golden menorah here, a silver kiddush cup there, a gold ring, a bag full of silver coins. Each time the thief found something he brought it to the Jew and showed it to him. He held a dagger to the Jew's throat and asked, "Is there more?" Each time, the Jew would nod and the villain would go off in search of something else. The Jew did not seem to care at all. What if the robber took everything? What difference would it make? He had been born with nothing and, in the end, he could take nothing with him. Why struggle for the sake of some possession or other?

But then the robber reached under the mattress of the bed and pulled out a little brown bag, tied at its neck. He brought it over to the Jew and held the dagger to the Jew's throat, asking, "Is there more?' This time, the Jew strained for the bag, saying, "Take everything else, but leave me this!" Then the thief thought, "I have found the finest treasure." He whipped his hand and the dagger did its awful work, spilling the blood of the Jew. Elated, the robber put down his dagger and opened the little bag to see the Jew's greatest treasure.

What a bitter mistake the robber had made! There was nothing in the bag but some dirt. The thief dumped the dirt on the Jew's body, gathered up all his booty, and left. But the wandering soul at once knew the meaning of the dirt. It was a bag full of earth from the Holy Land and the Jew had been saving it to have it put under his head in the coffin when he died. He had given his life for the love of the Holy Land. The wandering soul picked up a pinch of the blood-stained earth and flew upward to heaven. He presented this first gift to the gatekeeper, who held the earth in his palm and nodded sadly.

The wandering soul needed two more gifts. Now, he was in high spirits as he flew back to earth, but as the seasons passed again, his high spirits faded. He searched in vain for a beautiful word, a valiant deed. Then, all at once, he saw a court in session in a town square. The judges were dressed in velvet and a Jewess was on trial. Beside her, ten men were holding the ropes attached to a wild horse. The head judge rose and said, "This Jewess is guilty of a terrible crime. On the occasion of our last festival, she stole out of the ghetto and polluted the streets of our fair city with her footsteps. She saw the sacred images that we carried in procession and defiled them with her eyes. She heard the hymns we sang and defiled them with her ears. Perhaps, this rabbi's daughter even touched one of our sacred artifacts! No doubt she is possessed by a demon, for one knight actually turned aside from the procession to stare at her beauty. But our soldiers captured her and she did not even struggle against them. So, I pronounce this sentence on this Jewess:

"Her long demon's hair shall be braided into the tail of this wild horse. Then the horse shall be released and drag her like a corpse through the holy streets that her footsteps defiled. Let her wash the streets clean with her blood."

The judgment pronounced, all the spectators shouted wildly. It was justice pure and sure. The judge held up his hands for silence and said to the Jewess, "Do you have any last request?"

"I do," she answered quietly. I would like a few pins."

The crowd laughed. The judge said, "If you want pins, you can have them."

While her hair was being braided into the tail of the wild horse, the young girl doubled up her body and drove the pins through the hem of her skirt and into her flesh. Her only thought was of modesty. Only the wandering soul realized her true intention. The crowd and the judges watched the hair being braided, and the ten men had all they could handle just to hold the wild horse still.

Suddenly, the judge cried out, "Release the horse!" The poor young girl was dragged through the streets with the townspeople whipping at the sides of the horse and urging it to complete its dreadful work. When all was done, the soul drew a single blood-stained pin from the body of the corpse and flew with it to the gatekeeper of heaven. The gatekeeper looked at the pin in his hand and nodded. "Only one more gift," he said.

A long time passed before the soul was attracted to another tragic scene, this time by the sound of military drums. A Jew was being forced to run the gauntlet between two lines of a regiment of men. And the men were betting on how far he could run before he died.

The Jew ran as quickly as he could, but the men beat him mercilessly. Then, suddenly, the Jew realized that he had lost his skullcap. He was running bareheaded! So, he turned and ran back, suffering blow after blow, until he found the skullcap where he had dropped it. Putting it back on his head, he turned to run forward again, but his strength had given out. He fell senseless to the ground a few feet from where the skullcap had fallen, and he breathed his last.

The wandering soul swooped down and carried the skullcap off to the gatekeeper of heaven. Now, the righteous in heaven were all alerted. Their cries rose to God's ears, and the gates were thrown wide for the wandering soul. A bit of earth, a pin, and a skullcap. Useless gifts they were, yet truly wondrous.

[Rossel, based on a folk tale related by I.L. Peretz]

4. The Commissar

❧ When World War II threatened, the famous Rabbi Israel Spira moved to Luvov, which was then under Soviet rule. Here, he was faced by a new dilemma, for the Soviets would exile to Siberia anyone not productively employed. Even a Chasidic rabbi had to find a job. In fact, the very title "rabbi" was outlawed. So it was that Rabbi Israel Spira of Bluzhov became an insurance agent, forced to demonstrate at the end of each month that he had earned at least one thousand rubles.

Actually, this was no problem for the rabbi, since he had many followers. Each month he was able to provide receipts for at least one thousand rubles and a list of those he had insured. Yet, in truth, he was still employed in serving his Chasidim. Nor was he the only rabbi that used this ploy. The Rabbi of Boyan had also become an insurance agent.

It happened once, though, that the Russian commissar announced a compulsory meeting of all the local insurance agents to be held on what happened to be the first night of Chanukah. Now, it pained Rabbi Spira to think that he would miss the festive celebration of the kindling of the Chanukah menorah, so he devised a scheme. That afternoon, he went to the commissar's office. And, all along the way, he kept dipping into his snuff box, inhaling, and sneezing, until he was certain that his nose was beet red.

He was still sneezing as he came into the commissar's presence. "It is a very bad cold," he told the commissar, "surely, I will be unable to attend the meeting this evening."

The man he faced wore a uniform decorated with a great many medals and sat behind a huge desk piled high with papers. "This is indeed a strange coincidence," he said, hardly looking up from his work. "A few minutes ago, another insurance agent with a beard and side-locks like yours came to see me. His nose too was as red as the Soviet flag and he too could not stop sneezing. Like you, he asked to be excused from tonight's meeting."

Rabbi Spira knew at once that the other agent must have been the Rabbi of Boyan. He sneezed and said, "It seems only logical that two people might catch a cold at the same time."

The commissar made no reply. Instead, he sifted through the papers on his desk until he found what he was seeking. He read for a moment, then looked up at the rabbi. "Aha," he said, "I have found the cause of your suffering. According to this Jewish calendar, tonight is the first night of Chanukah. Surely, a man of your learning should know better than to try to pull the wool over the eyes of a Soviet official. Here in Russia, when one concocts a story, it should be a good one. After all, you never know who is dressed in the uniform of a Soviet commissar. If I were some other commissar, you and your sneezing friend would be nursing colds in Siberia!" The commissar paused, then smiled, "Just your luck. I happen to be the son of a Jewish butcher. Go home and light your menorah."

[adapted from Eliach, *Hasidic Tales of the Holocaust*]

3

Kavanah
Intention

1. Flying with the Torah

🐝 A cantor named Chaim had a voice like the clear, round sound of a rosewood flute. When Chaim sang, the congregation felt uplifted by the prayers. And when he chanted, his *kavanah*, his heart's "intention," caused the words to rise to the heavens.

It happened once, on the morning of Shabbat, as Chaim held the Torah scroll in his arms, carrying it through the congregation and singing, that his voice rose steadily more sweetly and the words brought new meanings to the congregation, as if each person were hearing them for the first time.

Up in heaven, the story goes, God was listening to the singing of the Jewish people in congregations throughout the world. Yet, one voice topped the rest, a voice filled with such love and sincerity that every word echoed God's Name. "What voice is this that rings so true?" asked God of his angels.

"It is the voice of Chaim the Cantor, who sings with all his heart, with all his soul, and with all his might," came the reply.

Far below, Chaim was concentrating so hard on what he was singing that when he lifted the Torah scroll above his head, it felt like the heavy scroll had no weight at all. Suddenly, the Torah began to rise and Chaim with it. His feet left the floor and still the scroll would not let him loose. Instead it carried him ever upward.

The awestruck Chaim soon stood before the heavenly throne and heard the voice of the Holy One. "Chaim," the voice said, "tell now the secret of your wondrous prayer. How is it that your words have the power to reach My very throne?"

Chaim bowed low and replied, "When I sing, I see the words before my eyes, I feel the words in my throat, I hear the words in my ears, I taste the words in my mouth, and I try with all my heart to understand what I sing."

And the voice of God said, "That is true *kavanah*. It has lifted you and your prayers to the heavens."

Chaim looked and, lo, he was in his congregation, the scroll still in his arms. The people seemed to have noticed nothing, yet he had flown to heaven, Chaim knew. So he thanked God in the words of the Bible: "Eternal One, You are near to all who call upon You, to all who call upon You in truth" (Psalms 145:18). And the cantor's eyes shone with joy.

[Rossel, *When a Jew Prays*]

2. The Power of the Broken Heart

🐟 The Baal Shem Tov knew that every sound of the *shofar* on the High Holy Days has a deeper, inner meaning. These "meanings," taught by the mystics, are called *kavanot*, "intentions." The Baal Shem Tov asked his student Rabbi Wolf Kitzes to learn the *kavanot* for the blowing of the *shofar* so that he could lead this part of the liturgy during the High Holy Day season.

Now, because he had been asked by the Baal Shem Tov himself, Rabbi Wolf was very nervous. As he studied the *kavanot*, he made a note of each one; and he copied all these notes on a single slip of paper that he slipped into his pocket before the service began. Some say, "Rabbi Wolf only thought he slipped the note in his pocket." Others say, "The note must have slipped *out* of Rabbi Wolf's pocket." And still others say, "Somehow, the Baal Shem Tov himself caused the note to disappear from Rabbi Wolf's pocket."

The time came for calling out the notes of the *shofar*. Rabbi Wolf reached into his pocket and found ... nothing! He tried to remember each *kavanah*, but nothing would come to mind. Tears filled his eyes. He wept as he read the order of the sounds of the *shofar* from his prayer book. He made no errors, but he could only speak the names of the sounds as they were written. He could not remember the mystical meanings that he had studied.

Later, the Baal Shem Tov consoled him, saying, "The *kavanot* are only useful to help us achieve emotion, gather our feelings, reach into ourselves for true caring; while you achieved emotion, gathered your feelings, and reached into yourself all at once and without the *kavanot*. Rabbi Wolf, you stood at the door to heaven today—a door that has many keys. Even with the right keys, that door is difficult to open. It was better the way you did it. An axe is always more direct than a key. And an axe opens every door in the castle of heaven."

[Buber, *Early Masters*, p. 64]

3. Sanctified Before Birth

Before human beings made their first appearance on earth, the angels were instructed to sanctify God's Name in hymns to anticipate the human prayer that God desired. They sang, "Blessed be the Eternal God of Israel from everlasting to everlasting."

When Adam was created in the Garden of Eden, the angels asked, "Is this the human creature we awaited? Is this the very one whose prayer God so anticipates?" But they were told that this was not the one. For Adam was destined to prove himself dishonest.

At Noah's birth the angels exclaimed, "Lo, this time we behold the awaited man!" "Not this one," they were told. For Noah was destined to become a drunkard.

The angels guessed again when Abraham appeared on the earth. But they did not guess well. For Abraham was destined to disappoint God by attempting to kill his son Isaac.

Soon, the angels expressed their hope that Isaac was the sought-for human presence. But Isaac proved weak by preferring Esau over Jacob, so that God's people were saved only through the wisdom of Isaac's wife, Rebecca. Nor was Rebecca the one. She was also flawed, since she achieved her goal through deceit instead of honesty.

Then, the angels thought, Jacob should be the one they were told to anticipate with their hymns. And this time God said to them, "At last, you have fixed on the right one. This one shall be singled out as "Israel" and all his descendants shall be called by that name."

Many years later, God spoke to Moses, saying, "Tell the children of Israel that they were sanctified in heaven even before they were called into existence on earth. They must therefore be holy even as their God is holy."

Just so, a human king who brings his newly-married bride into his palace might say to her: "You are now united to me. I am king, therefore you shall henceforth be my queen. If you honor me, all shall honor me. If you dishonor me, all shall dishonor me."

[Tanchuma, *Kedoshim*]

4. Twelve Loaves

A Jewish couple, Jacobo and Esperanza, are expelled from Spain and go to live in Israel. Jacobo attends Shabbat services in the synagogue, but he doesn't know Hebrew all that well and he doesn't always understand everything in the service.

But one Shabbat he hears the words of the Book of Leviticus (24) in which the people of Israel are told to offer a sacrifice to God of twelve loaves of *challah* bread in the tent of meeting every Sabbath.

Jacobo is overjoyed. He rushes home to tell Esperanza: God likes *challah* for Shabbat! And you, Esperanza, make the best *challah* in the world! So the next week, before Shabbat, Esperanza baked twelve loaves of her best *challah*—kneading her good intentions and her desire to serve God into the bread. Friday before Shabbat, they put the twelve loaves into the Holy Ark, said *"buen apetito"* to God and went home.

It happened then that Itzik, the janitor, came into the synagogue, stood before the Ark, and prayed, "God, my children are starving. I need a miracle." He opened the Ark, saw the *challah*, thanked God, and took the twelve loaves gratefully home to feed his family—God provided, just as the janitor had trusted.

The next day at services, when the old rabbi opened the Ark, Jacobo and Esperanza could see that the loaves were gone. God had eaten every crumb! They smiled at each other in satisfaction.

This went on, week after week, for thirty years.

One Friday as Jacobo and Esperanza were leaving the *challah* in the Ark for God, Esperanza spoke to the Almighty, "God, I'm sorry about the lumps in the *challah*. I'm not as young as I used to be, and my fingers don't work as well as they used to. But I hope you enjoy the loaves anyway."

Just then the old rabbi opened the synagogue door, saw something strange happening and cried out, "What are you doing, you fools?"

"We're giving God his twelve loaves of *challah*!"

The rabbi sputtered, "Don't you know that God doesn't eat?"

"Well, you may be a rabbi, but there seem to be things you do not know. God most certainly does eat. For thirty years we've been leaving loaves of *challah* and God has never left so much as a crumb."

The rabbi thought for a moment, then decided. "Hide behind this curtain with me," he said, "and let us see what is really happening to your loaves of *challah*."

Before long, Itzik came in. He stood before the Ark and prayed: "God, I don't want to complain, but your loaves have been getting a little lumpy lately. Still, they are keeping my family alive and I am grateful."

The old rabbi leaped out from behind the curtain. "Stop, you fool! Don't you know anything? The great scholar Maimonides taught us that God has no body!" He turned to Jacobo and Esperanza, saying, "God does not bake." He turned to Itzik, saying, "And God does not eat. From this day forth you must stop all this nonsense. It is a sin to make fun of God."

By now, Jacobo, Esperanza, and Itzik—all were weeping. The good couple wept because all they had wanted to do was to serve God. Itzik wept because he suspected the rabbi's edict meant no more loaves of *challah* to feed his family.

Just then, the great mystic Rabbi Isaac Luria came into the synagogue. He shook his head at the old rabbi, "You have wisdom, my friend—but little understanding! Know this: Thirty years ago, it was your destiny to die. But God instructed the angel of death to wait, because God was having fun watching what was happening in your synagogue. Well, now that's all over, and soon you will be called to the court of heaven."

Luria turned and spoke to Itzik, Jacobo, and Esperanza. "Now you know who has been baking your *challah* and you know who's been eating your *challah*. Nevertheless, Esperanza, you must continue to bake the loaves as before. You, Jacobo must take them directly to the janitor. And you, Itzik, must eat them with your family as before. And you all must believe with perfect faith that it is God who bakes and God who eats and God is no less present among you than before."

[Rossel, based on a story of Isaac Luria, *Tales of the Ari* (Hebrew)]

5. A Jeweler's Dream

🕮 As he reached his teen years, Abe gave more and more thought to the kind of career he wanted for himself. He went from shop to shop in the marketplace, as if he were shopping for the occupation that interested him most. In the end, he made his decision and presented himself to the jeweler. "Please take me on as your apprentice," he said. "I want to become a jeweler."

The jeweler considered the young man for a while, then asked, "Pray tell me, what did you dream last night?"

Abe replied, "I dreamed that I made a lot of money."

The jeweler said, "I am not looking for an apprentice right now. Return some other day."

Abe was disappointed, but not discouraged. The jeweler needed to know that he was determined. So he returned to the jeweler's shop the very next day. "I am ready to be your apprentice," he told the jeweler.

Once again the jeweler asked, "What did you dream last night?"

Abe answered, "I dreamed that I was a king and all my subjects bowed low to me."

The jeweler said, "I am not really interested in taking on an apprentice today. Try me again some time."

Abe was discouraged. As he returned home, he looked again at all the various shops. Perhaps, he thought, he should choose another trade for his future. But that night in his dreams he saw himself sitting in the jeweler's chair, wearing a loupe, and crouching to repair the delicate mechanism of a watch. When he finished the repair, he felt himself sweating. Then he watched himself setting down the watch and smiling.

When morning came, he nearly ran to the jeweler's shop and, before the jeweler could ask, he blurted out everything he had dreamed.

"Now you are ready to be my apprentice," the watchmaker said. "Keep dreaming the dream of jewelers and one day you will be a great jeweler."

[adapted from Certner, *101 Jewish Stories*]

6. The Alphabet

🔖 One Yom Kippur, as evening fell and the time for saying the *Kol Nidre* prayer approached, a single Jewish man bemoaned his fate. He was lost in a dense forest with absolutely no sense of north, south, east, or west. He knew he could not possibly be more than six or seven miles from the *shul*, yet it was equally certain that the sun would set before he could reach it. Because it was forbidden to travel on the High Holy Day, he was doomed to spend this night and all of tomorrow right here in the woods.

Sitting all alone on a tree stump, our hero pondered an even more important fact. A Jew was in need of prayer on Yom Kippur. A Jew could not ignore the holiest day of the entire year. On Yom Kippur, God wrote the fate of every Jew into the Book of Life: who would live and who would die in the coming year. Our hero needed to pray, but he had no prayer book. What could he do?

He felt so sorry for himself that tears began to come to his eyes. He wiped his cheeks and blew his nose. This would never do. A Jew should not give up. There must be a way for him to pray.

He turned his face upward and spoke. "God of my ancestors Abraham, Isaac, and Jacob, hear my voice. My heart is filled with love for You and for the world You created. But I am not an educated man. I am a simple Jew who cannot even find his way through a forest. I have forgotten all I ever studied. I am lost for words before You. Yet You, Beloved God, You can do all things. So I offer You the letters of the alphabet and pray that You will combine them into all the words and thoughts in my heart." Then, all that evening and all the next day, our hero recited the alphabet over and over, "*Alef ... Bet ... Gimel ... Dalet ...*"

The rabbi who told this story added, "Of all the prayers spoken that Yom Kippur, God found this one the most precious."

[Rossel, *When a Jew Prays*, based on a story in Agnon, *Days of Awe*, p. 227]

7. The Need to Whistle

🔖 The boy was a shepherd who could neither read nor write. His older brothers studied day and night, bringing pride to their father. But when his shepherd boy would return at night from the sheep fold, his father only shook his head from side to side and sighed. All the same, on the day of Yom Kippur—and only this once each year—the father brought the boy to the synagogue along with his brothers. He kept the boy close to him. And, who knows, perhaps the father whispered a special prayer for his simple son.

Now, the boy's most treasured possession was a little whistle that he always carried in his pocket. He played it to lead the sheep. He played it to calm them. He played it to entertain himself. And he played it when his heart was bursting with joy.

For many hours, as the congregation prayed, the boy sat quietly listening. As the morning prayers ended and the additional service called *Musaf* began, the boy whispered to his father, "I feel like playing my whistle now."

His father was surprised. "Did you bring your whistle to the *shul*?" he asked.

The boy nodded. "It is here in my pocket."

Then his father placed a hand over the pocket and kept a close grip on the whistle through the whole *Musaf* prayer.

As the afternoon service called *Minchah* began, the boy shifted in his seat. "Father, I feel like I should whistle now."

But the father shook his head and held the pocket with the whistle in it even tighter. "Not now," he told his son. "Not here."

The time soon came when everyone in the congregation stood up for the closing service called *Neilah*. With a twist, the boy pulled away from his father and slipped the whistle out of his pocket. Then came the clear sweet notes of the shepherd, but in the synagogue they seemed only brash and unexpected.

Everyone stopped praying and turned to the boy. The father was embarrassed. His older brothers were mortified. Like all the rest, his family stood and stared, until the boy finished his melody and slipped the whistle back into his pocket. Though everyone else was distracted, the rabbi of the congregation, the great Baal Shem Tov, had been tapping a foot to the beat of the music, even as he continued praying without a stop.

Finally the congregation joined the rabbi's prayers, taking up where they had left off. The father grabbed his son and was about to escort him out of the shul when the Baal Shem stopped him with a friendly smile. "What a mighty whistle!" he said. "The gates of repentance were about to close, then suddenly the prayers of our entire congregation rode through the gates on the notes of that whistle. If only your son could teach us all how to whistle when we feel the need."

[Buber, *Early Masters*, pp. 69-70]

8. The Full Shul

For a long time the Baal Shem Tov served as an itinerant preacher, traveling from town to town, teaching, preaching, and leading congregations in prayer. As he traveled through the mountains of Moravia, his reputation grew, so that when he came to a new town, he was welcomed as a hero. The town elders took pride in ushering him into their synagogue.

In one town, the elders eagerly led him to the door of their synagogue, but the Baal Shem Tov stopped upon the threshold. They urged him to go inside, but he told them, "I can go no farther. There is no room for me inside."

The elders remonstrated, saying, "But no one is inside yet."

"Look closely," the Baal Shem Tov said. "Your *shul* is filled with prayers and teachings from floor to ceiling and from wall to wall. They never left this place, for they were not spoken with a full heart. True, they were spoken to fulfill God's commandments, but they were spoken without *kavanah*. So they remain and fill your *shul*, leaving not a speck of space for me to enter!"

[adapted from Buber, *Early Masters*, p. 73]

9. The Tightrope

The famous teacher Rabbi Chaim of Krosno was a follower of the Chasidic way, a disciple of its founder, the Baal Shem Tov. One time, Rabbi Chaim attended the circus along with his students. They watched in awe as a man walked a tightrope.

One student asked, "Why does he risk his life to walk a rope?"

Rabbi Chaim thought a moment and then spoke. "I do not know why he is risking his life in this way. But this I know: As long as he is walking that tightrope, he must focus all of his mind and soul on walking it. If, for one instant, he thought of the money he is earning or of how he looks as he is walking, he would forfeit his life and fall to his death. It is only by concentrating his entire being on the task at hand that he can hope to succeed."

[Buber, *Early Masters*, p. 174]

10. Baseless Love

Before the establishment of the State of Israel, the gregarious and generous soul, Rabbi Abraham Isaac Kook, would greet everyone—believer, agnostic, and atheist alike—with the words *Shalom aleichem*, "Peace be with you." Once he was asked how he managed to love all people equally. In reply, he explained, "Jews speak of a sin called *sinnat chinnam*, 'baseless hatred.' It arises when a person hates without real reasons for hating. But, in modern times, there is need of a new *mitzvah* we could call *ahavat chinnam*, 'baseless love,' that is, loving a person whether or not the person is deserving. In our day, to be a true seeker of peace, we must practice love for all, for those who agree with us and those who disagree with us, for those we like and those we dislike. We must practice *ahavat chinnam*."

[based on a teaching of Rav Kook related by Rabbi Ben Zion Bokser]

11. The Fragments of the Broken Tablets

God commanded Moses to build the Ark of the Covenant, saying to him, "In this Ark you shall place the stone tablets given to you on Mount Sinai." But what became of the first set of two tablets of commandments that Moses had shattered?

Rabbi Judah taught: There were two arks. When Moses first came down from Mount Sinai with the commandments, he saw the people of Israel worshiping a golden calf. Anger flared in him like a flame. He raised the tablets and threw them to the ground, breaking them.

When God forgave the Children of Israel, Moses climbed the mountain again, returning with a second set of two tablets. Now these tablets were placed in the Ark of the Covenant. But Moses carefully gathered all the broken pieces of the first set of tablets, placing them in another ark. In this way, Moses taught that everything God created is holy—not only those things that are whole, but even those things that to us seem shattered.

[J. Talmud *Shekalim* 1:1, 49c; Yalkut, *First Samuel* 101; also in *Sefer HaAggadah*; in relation to aging, see B. Talmud *Berachot* 8b; B. Talmud *Baba Batra* 14b]

4

Defiance

1. Defiance

🐚 Overwhelmed by the many sorrows of his people, Rabbi Levi Yitzchak of Berditchev offered this prayer:

Good morning to You, Lord of the world! I, Levi Yitzchak, son of Sarah of Berditchev, approach you with a legal matter concerning Your people of Israel.

What do you want of Israel? It is always: "Command the Children of Israel!" It is always: "Speak unto the Children of Israel!"

Merciful Father: There are so many other peoples in the world! Persians, Babylonians, Edomites! Russians, Germans, English… What do they say: "Our kingdom is the kingdom!" "Our emperor is the emperor!"

But I, Levi Yitzchak, son of Sarah of Berditchev, say: *Yiskadahl, Veyiskadash Shemay Rabo!* "Glorified and sanctified be God's great name!"

And I, Levi Yitzchak, son of Sarah of Berditchev, say: I shall not go hence, nor budge from my place until there be a finish, until there be an end, to our suffering…

"Gloried and sanctified be God's name!"

[Newman, *The Hasidic Anthology*, p. 398]

2. Berel Forgives God

🐚 One Yom Kippur, as the congregation filed out of *shul*, Rabbi Levi Yitzchak of Berditchev waited by the door. When he saw the tailor, he called him aside. "I know you argued with God," the rabbi said. "Tell me everything that happened." The tailor then told his story:

"May I be forgiven, Rabbi, I was angry at God … and with good reason. Before Rosh Hashanah, the Count called me to his castle, gave me some fine mink furs, and ordered me to make him a coat.

366

I measured carefully and cut the furs as precisely as I could. When the fitting was done and the coat complete, there were a few skins left over. Of course, I was paid for my work, but I have five children. And, since no one asked me to return the extra furs, I placed them in my cart under a blanket when I left the castle.

"I had not traveled far, when a horseman came thundering after me. This is bad, I thought. Who shall feed my wife and children if I am thrown in prison as a thief? What could I do? Quickly, I grabbed the blanket with the furs and hid the bundle behind a tree, praying that the horseman would not notice. I had barely left the tree, when the horseman came up and ordered me to return to the Count at once. I tell you, Rabbi, fear and trembling both sat beside me on my ox-cart all the way to the castle.

"The Count was proudly showing off the new fur coat to his family when I entered his chamber. He turned to me, stared into my eyes, and said, 'Is this the way a tailor finishes his work?' I was too terrified to utter a word. 'Is it not customary for you to make a loop in the coat so that it may be hung? And such a perfect coat! Surely, Berel, it deserves a loop!'

"My soul jumped a thousand parasangs. Was this what I was so worried about? A loop? So I made a leather loop for the coat and sewed it inside, beneath the collar. The Count sang my praises and sent me on my way.

"All the way back to the tree, I sang hymns of praise to God for sparing me. But when I reached the tree, the bundle—blanket and furs—was gone. Perhaps, it was the wrong tree, I thought. So I looked behind every tree that stood at the side of the road. It was no use.

"I sat and thought, 'Berel, God does not want you to be a thief.' But then I thought, 'Berel, God does not want your wife and children to eat so well. God does not want you to dress them so well. God does not want you to have a dowry for your oldest daughter.' What can I say, Rabbi, the more I thought the matter through, the more defiant I became. I thought about nothing else from Rosh Hashanah to Yom Kippur. Then, on Yom Kippur, the grief and anger poured out like water breaking through a dam.

"On *Kol Nidre* eve, I whispered in my heart, 'God of Abraham, You call me to repent my sins, but I have only little sins to repent. God of Isaac, is it so terrible that a tailor should keep a bit of left-over cloth? God of Jacob, should I be called to account just for wanting to feed my family?'

"By Yom Kippur afternoon, I was seething. I cried out in my heart, 'I, Berel the Tailor, call Heaven and Earth to witness against You this day, O God. I have committed small sins but You have committed grievous injustices. You have taken babies from their mothers, and mothers from their babies. You have given poverty and exile to Your children. Now, God, it is only fair. If You will forgive me, then I, Berel, will forgive You.'

"I swear, Rabbi, these were the last words I spoke as the Gates of Repentance closed and Yom Kippur ended."

Rabbi Levi Yitzchak nodded. He told the tailor, "There was great commotion in the heavenly court, Berel, but you prevailed. For your sake, the repentance of the whole community of Berditchev was accepted. But, tell me, why did you let God off so easily? Just then, you might have forced God to redeem the entire Jewish people!"

[Newman, *The Hasidic Anthology*, p. 57]

3. Denying God

🎕 Rabbi Moses Leib taught us that God created all things with a purpose. Even the freedom of people to deny God was created by God. But what purpose can denying God serve? Charity!

Rabbi Leib explained: Imagine a world in which every person was absolutely certain of the truth of God's power. In a world like that, if the poor sought help from the rich, the rich could reply, "Why turn to us for help? God is all powerful. Ask God for your reward." And whole communities might turn aside from the poor, saying, "You can trust in God to help you."

Not in the world that God created. While there is still a hint of doubt, a dollop of skepticism, and a morsel of uncertainty, the denial of God can be redeemed in order to serve God. When someone requires your help, you cannot delay helping. You must act as if God did not exist, as if only you in all the world could help. Only you.

[adapted from Buber, *Later Masters*, p. 89]

5
Atonement

1. Enjoying Life

🔖 Nazirites were commanded to bring sin offerings for their ascetic way of life. Rabbi Eleazar HaKappar Berebi asked, "Against what soul did the Nazirites sin? Obviously, they were required to atone because they had denied themselves the enjoyment of wine. It stands to reason that, if people who deny themselves only the enjoyment of wine are considered sinners, all the more so are the rest of us sinners if we deny ourselves all the enjoyments of life."

[B. Talmud *Taanit* 11a-b]

2. Praying Once a Year

🔖 The Maggid of Dubno noted that several Jews in his congregation had hardly attended the synagogue the rest of the year, but now on the High Holy Days, they stood wrapped in their prayer shawls, piously reciting the service. This is what the Maggid preached:

My dear Jews! There was once a shopkeeper who lost everything in a fire. Worse still, most of the goods he lost had been bought on credit, leaving him not only poor but deep in debt. The largest sum of all he owed to a particular manufacturer for whom he had a deep affection. The two of them had known one another and done business together for many years.

When the time to pay the debt came, this particular manufacturer sent his bill. The shopkeeper was dismayed and sought advice from his friends. Everyone made the same suggestion. "Go to the manufacturer and explain your misfortune. Tell him about the fire and perhaps he will delay his bill, or perhaps he will even cancel it entirely."

The shopkeeper decided to follow their advice. He went to the city where the manufacturer lived. But when he stood before the

369

door of the manufacturer's house, his heart deserted him. He did not have the courage to knock. He kept asking himself, "How can I come here empty-handed? He trusted me with all that money. How can I let him down?" Standing there and thinking this way, he burst into tears, sobbing and crying like an infant.

The manufacturer heard the commotion at his door and opened it. Surprised to see his old friend and disturbed to witness his distress, the manufacturer tried to console him. "What could possibly make you cry this way?" But the manufacturer's solace only caused the shopkeeper to sob and weep all the more. When he half regained his composure, he said, "I weep because I owe you so much money and I have no way of repaying you. All I owned went up in flames!"

The manufacturer behaved like a *mensch*, a "decent soul." He ushered the shopkeeper into his home, offered him food and drink, and spoke to him words of comfort. "My dear friend," he said, "We know one another for many years. I know you to be an honest merchant and a good man. Forget what you owe me from the past. I will provide you a new consignment of goods so that you can begin your business again." Then, to the shopkeeper's wonder, the manufacturer removed a sheaf of invoices from his file drawers and tore them to shreds.

The shopkeeper was overcome. That night, having dinner at the inn, he told all the lodgers how good the manufacturer was and how generous the manufacturer had been. Everyone marveled as he described how the manufacturer tore up the invoices.

One listener excused himself and hurried to the manufacturer's home. Standing outside the door, he wept and wailed loudly. The manufacturer opened the door to see a person he had never seen before. He asked, "Why are you crying?" and the stranger answered that he was destitute. "I have come to ask you for a large consignment of goods so that I can start a business."

The manufacturer was astounded. "Why should I trust you with goods to start a business?" he asked.

The stranger said, "I know that you trusted the shopkeeper I met at the inn. Am I any worse than he?"

"Can you compare yourself with him?" the manufacturer demanded. "I have known that shopkeeper for many years. I have been doing business with him for many years and I have always realized a profit! But you are a stranger to me. What right have you to ask anything of me?"

The Maggid of Dubno concluded his sermon by saying, "It is the same with God. When a Jew who attends services regularly and tries to do good, accidentally sins and then repents, the Holy One forgives him. But when a stranger—one who seldom speaks with God, who seldom attends the synagogue—suddenly appears and asks for forgiveness, God asks, 'What right have you to ask anything of me?'"

[adapted from *Parables of the Preacher of Dubno* (Yiddish)]

3. Little Stones and Big Stone

🐟 A young fellow appeared before his rabbi. "The time of repentance comes once a year," he said, "and usually this is no problem for me. I can think of something that I have done wrong in the past year and so I prepare myself to repent for my wrongdoing. But honestly, rabbi, this year I can remember nothing that I have done wrong. So I ask you: While others are repenting, what should I do?"

The rabbi said, "You must do exactly as I say. Go down to the riverbed and choose a large stone and bring it to me."

The young man walked down to the riverbed and stared at the stones around him. He chose a stone that was not too large for him to carry and he put it in a sack and threw the sack across his shoulder. A short while later, he appeared before the rabbi. He drew the stone out of his sack and placed it on the table.

The rabbi admired the stone for a moment. "You have done well," he said to the young man. "Now, please take this stone and return it to the exact place where you found it. And, this time, bring me ten pebbles."

The young fellow wondered what the rabbi had in mind, but he did as he was instructed. He returned the large stone to its place on the riverbed and looked around for ten nice pebbles to bring back to the rabbi. He made his selection carefully, trying to find ten smooth stones, placing each one in his sack one by one.

It was early evening before he again appeared at the rabbi's table, placing the ten pebbles in a neat row before the rabbi.

The rabbi admired the ten pebbles for a moment. "You have done well," he told the young man. "Now follow my instruction carefully: Take the ten pebbles back to the river bed and place them each exactly where you found them."

"But, rabbi," the young man objected, "that is impossible! I searched up and down the river for these ten pebbles. I shall never remember the exact location for each of them!"

The rabbi nodded. "Now, you have learned something about sin and repentance," he said. "When it comes to a large sin, none of us have any trouble remembering exactly what we have done, where we have done it, and how to set it right. But all year long we do small things that are wrong, every one of us sins in small ways. These small sins are like your pebbles. It is difficult to know when you have committed them, where you have committed them, who has been harmed by them, and how you can set them straight. As the time of repentance comes each year, we ask forgiveness not only for the large sins that we can recall so well, but for all the little sins, too. Not just for the large stone, but for the little pebbles."

[adapted from *Yalkut*]

Rabbi Judah the Pious said, "At times the sin is large though the lusting for it was a trifle; while at times the lusting for a sin is large and the sin itself is small" (*Sefer Chasidim*).

4. Teshuvah

As it happened, a Jewish man once converted and became a Christian. He was so convinced by his new faith that he constantly tempted other Jews to follow his lead. For many years, this behavior annoyed Rabbi Judah the Pious. Then, one day, out of the blue, the convert spied Rabbi Judah out walking and approached him. "I wish to do *teshuvah*," the man said, "to repent and return to my Jewish roots." The rabbi raised his walking stick and said, "See here: This is a staff of dead wood. Do you really imagine that you can repent after all your awful deeds? You are about as likely to be forgiven as this staff is to sprout branches and leaves."

Lo and behold! Only a few days passed before Rabbi Judah was walking again and the staff suddenly shivered. The rabbi was so startled that he dropped the staff from his hand. He stared in awe as branches sprouted on the staff one after another; and he fell to his knees as he saw green leaves appear on every branch. It was a message from heaven! The rabbi felt humbled and repented himself for castigating the convert. Picking up the staff, he went in search of the former Jew.

He found the man sitting beneath a tree. Rabbi Judah showed him the staff, told him how it sprouted, and apologized for his unkindly remarks. The convert was equally astonished, saying, "I myself agreed with you, rabbi. I too thought Heaven might not accept my repentance."

"Nevertheless," Rabbi Judah said, "Heaven has taken notice of you. But how shall we account for this miracle? Have you done something extraordinary?"

The convert sat in thought. "There is only one thing I can recall," he said at last. "I once stopped in a small town where the Jews were greatly agitated. The mayor had accused them of a ritual murder—saying they had killed a Christian child to use its blood in the baking of *matzah*. I knew the people of the town and they knew that I had been a Jew, so I was called to the courtroom to give testimony regarding Jewish customs. Of course, I could not stand before the judges and swear falsely. So I told the court what I knew: that no Jew would ever use human blood in any ritual. And that, in fact, Jewish practice demanded that all blood be drained from meat before eating it. In that way, I explained that ritual murder was an absurd myth. The judges believed me, the townspeople were calmed, and the persecution of the Jews was put to an end."

When Rabbi Judah heard the story, he understood the reason for the miracle. "Come and rejoin your people," he said to the fellow. "Do *teshuvah* through prayers and good deeds. For Heaven itself is ready to accept your repentance."

[adapted from Rappoport, *Folklore of the Jews*, pp. 206-207]

5. Thieves Confess

Before the High Holy Days, on one *Selichot* ("Petitions") night when Jews should be turning their thoughts to repentance, Rabbi Levi Yitzchak and his *gabbai* ("assistant") were walking to the synagogue. Their path took them past a tavern with its doors and windows open to allow the cool night air to circulate.

The open window also allowed the *gabbai* to look in. He was surprised to see a group of Jews drinking and reveling together. "Look at those sinners," he said to Rabbi Levi Yitzchak, "they are drinking and carrying on when they should be joining us at the synagogue to repent their sins."

The rabbi was of a kinder turn of thought. "We are forbidden to think ill of our people," he said to his *gabbai*. "Perhaps they are together to recite the blessing over wine. And, if so, they are fulfilling a command of God."

But just then, as the rabbi and his *gabbai* stood beside the window, they overheard two of the Jews inside speaking of the success of the thefts they had committed that day. The *gabbai* turned to the rabbi with much agitation, saying, "Woe to us that our Jews are confessing to thievery!"

"Ah," said Rabbi Levi Yitzchak, "if they are confessing, then they are truly observant. After all, we ourselves are headed for the synagogue to confess and make our own petitions for forgiveness. And who is more righteous than a Jew who confesses?"

[Newman, *The Hasidic Anthology*, p. 518]

6. Heaven Calls Them Rabbi

Rabbi Elazar ben Durdaya was a great sinner, much addicted to sexual offenses. Once, hearing the glories of an expensive courtesan in a distant land described, he crossed seven rivers to reach her. Whatever offense he committed with her, it was truly grievous, for afterwards she confided to him, "Now, you shall never be received in repentance by God." Leaving her, he went to sit between two hills.

He spoke aloud, saying, "O, hills and mountains, pray for compassion upon me." But they echoed back, "We must first seek compassion for ourselves."

Then he spoke again, saying, "O, earth and heaven, seek mercy for me." But the sky thundered and the earth rumbled, saying, "We must first seek mercy for ourselves."

He then addressed the sun and moon, saying, "Seek mercy for me." But the sun dimmed and the moon winced, as their words reached his ears: "First we must seek mercy for ourselves."

He called to the stars and the planets and received the same reply.

Finally, he whispered to himself, "The matter rests solely on me." So he placed his head between his knees and wailed and wept until his soul passed out of his body.

At that moment, a heavenly voice spoke, saying, "Rabbi Elazar ben Durdaya is appointed for the world to come."

Far away in the city, Rabbi Judah the Prince heard this voice and wept, saying, "There are people for whom many years of prayer do not suffice to attain for them the world to come; and there are people who attain the world to come in but a single hour! Pay attention to the voice of heaven, for it is not enough that the repentant are received into the life to come, but they are even called Rabbis."

[B. Talmud *Avodah Zarah* 17a]

7. *Baal Teshuvah*

🕮 Through the grace of God, when we turn thirteen years old, two angels are appointed over us—one at our right hand and one at our left.

When we choose paths of righteousness these angels rejoice over us and are glad. They cling to us joyfully, calling out as we go: "Give honor to God's image!" But if we veer away from righteousness and walk crooked paths, our angels mourn over us and turn away from us.

For this reason, the Holy One grants sinners the grace to repent and the strength to accomplish their return to righteousness, The person who repents is truly and perfectly alive, joined to Torah, "the Tree of Life." And, being united with the Tree of Life, we call the one who repents. a *baal teshuvah*, "a master of repentance." The *baal teshuvah* is joined to the community of Israel, which is called by the name *Teshuvah* ("Repentance").

So it is said: "Repentant sinners can enter even where the perfectly righteous are not admitted."

[Zohar *Shemot*, §2, 106b]

8. Far and Near

🕮 Rabbi Chiya ben Abba quoted his teacher, Rabbi Yochanan who said, "All the prophets have prophesied only about the rewards to be given those who repent; but concerning the perfectly righteous, no eye has yet beheld their rewards. The rewards of the righteous will be plentiful and they are stored up in heaven awaiting the arrival of the righteous."

Rabbi Abbahu disagreed. He quoted Rav, who said: "In the place where those who repent stand, the righteous do not stand. For it is written: 'Peace, peace to the far and the near' (Isaiah 57:19). First, 'the far' (the sinner who repents), next 'the near' (the righteous). The far is the person who was originally far, the near is the person who was ever close."

But Rabbi Yochanan understood this verse in just the opposite way. He taught: "The far is the person far from sin; the near is the person who was close to sin and turned away from it."

[B. Talmud *Sanhedrin* 99a]

9. The Angel Who Repented

A story is told of an angel who caused God anguish. When the angel came forward, God said, "I will not punish you, but you must prove to Me that you know what I truly desire. Find me the most precious thing on earth."

For many days, the angel searched without finding anything that could be called "the most precious thing." But one day, on a field where a terrible battle had been fought, the angel found a soldier dying. Then he came to God saying, "Here is the most precious thing. It is the last drop of blood from a man who died to save his country from a tyrant."

"That is very precious," said God, "for that soldier died in order that others might live in freedom. But it is not the most precious thing on earth."

So the angel returned to earth and searched again. By chance, he saw a nurse who had saved the lives of many children. Exhausted from her years of labor, she was dying of a fever. The angel took the last breath of this kindly nurse and brought it to God.

Seeing the breath, God said, "That is indeed a very wonderful thing; but even the dying breath of a woman who gave her whole life for others is not the most precious thing to Me."

The angel returned to earth. And as he wandered from one city to the next, he passed through a deep woods and saw a man riding on horseback.

"Where are you going?" asked the angel.

"I am going to kill a man," said the rider. "He cheated me badly when he sold me a farm. Now, I am going to kill him." The rider pulled hard on his horse's reins and rode on.

The angel followed horse and rider through the woods and soon they came to a small house at the edge of town. The rider took a gun from his holster and crept up to a window of the house. The angel followed close behind. Through the window the two watched as the man kissed his children goodnight and put them to bed, tucking the covers under their chins. Suddenly the rider thought of his own family and tears sprang to his eyes.

He put the gun back into its holster and cried, "O God, forgive me for what I almost did."

Now the angel understood what was "the most precious thing." He took one of the rider's tears and brought it to God.

"Yes," God said, "that is the most precious thing to Me. To turn away from the wrong and choose instead to do what is good, that is the finest thing a person can do. And this tear, which shows that he meant it, is the most precious thing on earth. I forgive the man. And now, I forgive you, too, my angel."

[Rossel, *When a Jew Prays*; based on a folktale collected by I.L. Peretz]

10. *Shofar* and Drums

A Jew from a small *shtetl* in Poland heard about the primitive islanders of the South Pacific from his son who was a sailor. One day, he accepted his son's invitation and he traveled to a distant island where the natives received him with great courtesy. A chieftain gave the Jew a hut beside his own. But in the middle of the night the Jew was abruptly awakened by loud drumming. He ran out of his hut and asked his host what was going on. The chieftain reassured him. "Do not worry," he said. "There is a fire on the other side of the island. But now that the drummers have been alerted, the fire will soon be extinguished."

The simple Jew was amazed by the idea of drums that could extinguish fires. For the rest of the night, he tossed and turned and thought of nothing else. There were many fires in his *shtetl*. Everything there was made of wood; everything there was heated with wood; everything there was cooked with wood. In the morning, he purchased a few sets of the native drums and, with the help of his mystified son, he loaded them on the ship for his return home. Eventually, he *shlepped* those drums all the way home to his *shtetl*.

The day after he returned, he gathered his neighbors and told them how the island natives used the drums to extinguish fires. Now the people of the *shtetl* would have nothing to worry about when the next fire occurred. And, with that, he distributed the drum sets.

It was not long before the watchman came running, yelling, "Fire! Fire!" Immediately, the Jew and his neighbors got out their drums and beat out a loud and long tattoo. The whole time, he kept telling everyone, "Have no fear. Everything will be all right." But things went from bad to worse. One ramshackle shack after another burned to the ground. The drums were worthless.

Furious and ashamed, he forced his son to take him back to the island, where he confronted the chieftain who had been his host. He angrily described all that had transpired and claimed that the islanders had somehow cheated him. The drums they sold him had not put out the fires.

"You foolish man," the chieftain answered, "did you really imagine that the beating of the drums put out fires? The drums only signal our fire brigade to douse the fire with water."

When the Maggid of Dubno told this story, he always added, "Many of us are like that fellow from the *shtetl*. We foolishly believe that blowing the *shofar*, beating our breasts, and raising our voices in prayer will extinguish the raging fires of sin and evil that burn in us. How mistaken we are! All these are only alarms meant to rouse us from our spiritual slumber. Once aroused, we must actuate our repentance by rallying to the study of Torah and the obligations of the *mitzvot*. These are the waters that can truly extinguish the fires of sin!"

[adapted from *Parables of the Preacher of Dubno* (Yiddish)]

11. String

When first we are created, we are each tied to God by a string. With every sin we commit, the string is broken. If we repent, the angel Gabriel makes a knot in our string. In the course of a human lifetime, each string becomes full of knots. All this is in accordance with God's plan. For, you see, a string with knots is shorter than one with no knots, and a string with a great many knots is still shorter. In this way, repentance brings us ever closer to God.

[Internet anecdote]

12. Return to Me

A king had a son who had gone astray from his father a journey of a hundred days. His friends advised him, "You should return to your father." The son said, "I cannot." Then the king sent a message saying, "Return as far as you can and I will come to you the rest of the way." So God says, "Return to me, and I will return to you."

[*Pesikta Rabbati* 184b–185a]

6

Messiah

1. The Face of the Messiah

🙾 Once the Baal Shem Tov was leading his community in prayer when his own meditation so carried him away that he seemed to be lifted to a new level of being. He was in a huge hall. At the end of the hall there was a table with people seated all around. The Baal Shem Tov felt compelled to approach the table and when he drew near he saw that there was one empty chair. He knew it was for him.

He sat down and considered his surroundings. Somehow, he recognized the beings there. Some were from his own tradition—one he supposed was Abraham, while another he knew was Moses. There were people from other traditions there, too, sharing that holy space. And there was one seated at the table whose face was veiled.

The Baal Shem Tov sat and the discussion turned to the way in which he was leading his community of Chasidim. All he heard were words of confirmation, support, and encouragement. He was heartened, of course, but he found it difficult to take his eyes off the silent figure with the veil. Finally, he drew up his courage and asked, "Pray tell, who is this one with his face covered?"

They answered, "That's the Messiah."

The Baal Shem Tov nodded. "In that case," he said, "I know why his face is veiled."

"And why is that?" they asked.

The Baal Shem Tov said: "Because the face of the Messiah reflects the face of the one who gazes on it. Before one is ready, that sight would be too much to bear. Until one is ready, the face must remain veiled. In each human being, that anointed one is waiting to be born."

Suddenly, the Baal Shem Tov recalled that, on another level, he was still leading the community in prayer. He realized that the time had come for him to leave. Many of those at the table blessed him, then he stood and turned and found himself in the presence of his community.

The prayers continued, but as he looked into the faces of his congregation, he knew that he was seeing the faces of the Messiah. And the Baal Shem Tov wondered, "How do I tell them? How do I let them know who they are? How do I help them remember?"

[Rossel adapted from *Shivchei HaBesht* (Yiddish)]

2. Before the Messiah Comes

🐍 It is the opinion of many sages that there will be telltale signs in the seven years preceding the coming of the Messiah, the descendant of David.

The first year rain will be scarce and sporadic. The second year the world will experience pangs of hunger. The third year will bring a severe famine in which many will die (so many sages will perish that the study of the Torah will teeter on the edge of neglect).

The fourth year will prove a mixed blessing: famine will not be removed, nor will the harvest be plentiful. Nevertheless, people will perceive that the world is in transition.

The fifth year will bring prosperity with the earth bringing forth its blessings in abundance. Joy will return throughout the earth. The study and knowledge of the Torah will revive and remarkable new scholars will appear in the ranks of Israel.

All through the sixth year, there will be rumors and rumblings of war, but the seventh year the war will descend upon us like a dread visitation.

Only after all these signs have come to pass, at the end of the seventh year, will the Messiah appear.

But other opinions also exist: that prior to the coming of Messiah the world will be as corrupt as it was before the great flood of Noah; that, just as in the days of Sodom and Gomorrah, there will be strife and envy and lack of compassion; that, just as in the days of the accursed Hadrian, contempt for the Torah and for piety will be universal and truth will go unrecognized. Then, humans will be as shameless of their evil ways as wild beasts, and the handful of the righteous who still exist will be in exceeding great distress. Also, persecution will be rife throughout the nations, nor will the young respect the aged, but they will force the aged to rise in the presence of the young. In those days, daughters will rebel against mothers and our worst enemies will live in our own homes. Also, the rulers of the many nations will be infidels, nor will any be found courageous enough to raise an outcry against them, so that humanity will seem to merit northing more than extermination. Those who hold this opinion maintain that if we behold the generations becoming ever more corrupt, we should steel ourselves and take heart, for this can only be proof that soon the Messiah will be revealed.

[Midrash Song of Songs 2]

3. The Messiah among the Beggars

Rabbi Joshua ben Levi was visiting the grave of Rabbi Simeon ben Yochai. As he stood by the entrance to the cave where Simeon was buried, a stranger approached him.

"Peace unto you, Rabbi Joshua ben Levi," the stranger said.

"You must be the prophet Elijah!" said Rabbi Joshua. "What other stranger would know me by name?"

The stranger shrugged. "You have decided," he replied.

"I know you roam the world awaiting the day when you can announce the arrival of the Messiah," Rabbi Joshua said. "By your life, there is something I must know. Tell me, when will the Messiah come?"

The stranger smiled and said, "Why not go and ask the Messiah yourself?"

"Where shall I find him?" asked Rabbi Joshua.

"He is sitting among the beggars at the entrance to the city of Rome."

"And how shall I know him?" asked Rabbi Joshua.

"He is easy to find," said the stranger. "Like the other beggars, his body is covered with sores and wrapped with bandages. Every morning, the other beggars unwrap all their bandages to allow the sun and air to heal their sores. But the Messiah unwraps only one bandage at a time. In that way, when God calls for the Messiah to appear, he will not be delayed, for he will have only one bandage to bind up. You see, Rabbi Joshua, the Messiah is not difficult to identify."

Rabbi Joshua set forth on the long journey to Rome. He traveled to the shore and across the sea. When he came to the gate of the city of Rome, he saw the Messiah, the only beggar with just one bandage untied. As he came close, he raised one hand to greet the Messiah. But, before he could speak, the Messiah greeted him. "Peace be with you, Joshua ben Levi."

"The Jews have suffered much," said Rabbi Joshua. "Our Temple has been destroyed by Rome and our heroes have been defeated. The Romans do not permit us to study the Torah in peace. We long for an end to our suffering."

"I know the suffering of the Jewish people," said the Messiah. "Every sore on my body is a sign of Jewish troubles. And every sore on the bodies of the other beggars is a sign of the troubles of all the other nations of God's world. Even the Romans suffer. Yet God is ready to put an end to the troubles of the world."

Rabbi Joshua sought an answer he could understand. "O master, tell me truly. When will you come and end our suffering?"

The Messiah answered, "Today."

Rabbi Joshua did not tarry. He went down to the sea and set out by ship for the Land of Israel. A storm came up; and waves tossed the ship from side to side. That day came and went, and so did the next, and the storm blew fiercely. Even the sailors sickened; and Rabbi Joshua saw that suffering continued all around him. When, at last, he reached Israel, he made his way by foot to the cave where Rabbi Simeon was buried. Many days had passed, and still the Messiah had not appeared.

The same stranger was waiting for Rabbi Joshua by the cave. "Did the Messiah give you an answer?" the stranger asked.

"The Messiah said, 'Peace be with you, Joshua ben Levi.'"

The stranger nodded. "This means that you and your family will have peace in the days of the Messiah."

Rabbi Joshua shrugged. "How can I believe this is true when the Messiah also lied to me?"

"What did the Messiah say that you did not believe?" the stranger demanded.

"I asked the Messiah when he would come to put an end to the suffering of the world, and the Messiah told me it would be today. Yet he did not appear on that day, or on any day since."

The stranger smiled. "The Messiah spoke the truth. He gave you the beginning of a verse from the Bible. It is written there, 'Today—if you would only listen to God's voice'" (Psalms 95:7).

"Teach me what this means," Rabbi Joshua said.

"It means that the Messiah can come any day, even this very day, if only people hearken to the voice of God, who commanded us to live in peace."

"I still do not understand," Rabbi Joshua said. "If we bring peace to the world, we have no need of the Messiah."

The stranger nodded. "You do understand," he replied. "As soon as human beings no longer stand in need of the Messiah, the time of the Messiah will come. Teach peace and pursue peace, and the day of the Messiah can be today."

[B. Talmud *Sanhedrin* 98a; also in *Sefer HaAggadah*]

REFERENCES

🜂 NOTES 🜂
Early and Rabbinic
Sources

🜂 The Hebrew Bible or "Holy Scriptures" is called the *Tanach*, an acronym for its three units: *Torah* (the Five Books of Moses), *Nevi'im* (the Prophets), and *Ketuvim* (the Writings). The Bible was called the *Torah she-bich'tav*, "Written Law" by the Pharisees and their heirs, the sages and rabbis of Israel.

Oral traditions and teachings concerning the Written Law were called the *Torah she-b'al peh*, usually translated as the "Oral Torah." In the wake of the destruction of the Temple (70) and the disastrous Bar Kochba Revolt (132-135), the sages reversed their original intention to keep the "Oral Torah" fluid and in process by not committing it to writing. Based on earlier textbooks used in the academies of teachers of the Oral Law, and under the aegis of (and relying on the authority of) Rabbi Judah HaNasi, the first compilation of rabbinic law, the *Mishnah* ("Repetition"), was completed around 200.

The *Tosefta* ("Supplement"), completed around the same time, included additional discussions arranged in parallel to the *Mishnah*.

The Talmuds

🜂 Teaching and discussion of the *Mishnah* and the Oral Law continued to flourish in academies in Palestine and in the larger Jewish community in exile in Babylonia.

By the fourth century, a compilation called the *Talmud* (from the Hebrew root for "learning" and "teaching") was issued in the Holy Land. It consisted of the Mishnah and an extended commentary and elaboration called the *Gemara* (from the word for "completion"). It is called by various names: "The Talmud of the Land

of Israel," "The Palestinian Talmud," or "The Jerusalem Talmud."
The abbreviation used to distinguish it throughout this work is "J.
Talmud."

Around the year 500, the rabbinic academies in the Diaspora
promulgated the Babylonian Talmud, a larger and ultimately
more authoritative compilation which included the original *Mishnah* and the Babylonian *Gemara*. The abbreviation used to distinguish it throughout this work is "B. Talmud."

The two *Talmud*s included both law (*halachah*) and lore
(*aggadah*), arranged according to the six units ("orders") and the
chapters ("tractates") of the *Mishnah*. So-called "Minor Tractates" were also composed, commentaries and extended essays
which generally had no corresponding tractate within the *Mishnah*.

The Midrash

🐾 Alongside the development of the *Talmud*s, and extending for
hundreds of years thereafter, two forms of literature collectively
called *Midrash* (from the Hebrew root for "investigation") flourished. The more prevalent form was termed *Midrash Aggadah* or
"Homiletic Midrash." The second form was termed *Midrash Halachah* or "Legal Midrash." A list of some representative works (of
both kinds) and the approximate dates of their compilation gives
some idea of the complexity of this literary outpouring:

> *The Alphabet of Ben Sira* (8th-11th cent.)
> *Avot deRabbi Natan* (8th-10th cent.)
> *Mechilta* (probably 9th cent.)
> *Midrash Proverbs* (8th to 11th cent.)
> *Midrash Psalms* (10th-11th cent.)
> *Midrash Samuel* (7th-10th cent.)
> *Pesikta Rabbati* (mid-9th cent.)
> *Pirke deRabbi Eliezer* (before mid-9th cent.)
> *Pseudo-Philo* (Latin, 1st cent.)
> *Sifra Leviticus* (possibly early 3rd cent.)
> *Sifre Numbers* (3rd-6th cent.)
> *Sifre Deuteronomy* (3rd-6th cent.)
> *Tanna devei Eliyahu* (10th cent.)
> *Tanchuma* (before the end of the 11th cent.)

Tanchuma Buber (compiled by Solomon Buber in 1885 from original manuscripts dating as early as the 5th cent.)

Yalkut (also called *Yalkut Shimoni*, probably 13th cent.)

Midrash Rabbah

🐫 One collection of *Midrash* was termed the *Midrash Rabbot*, since all the works in it had the word *Rabbah* ("great") in their title. Obviously collected for study in the synagogue, it consists of ten volumes which expand and comment on the Five Books of Moses (*Genesis Rabbah, Exodus Rabbah, Leviticus Rabbah, Numbers Rabbah,* and *Deuteronomy Rabbah*) and the Five Scrolls read on Festivals and Holy Days: *Song of Songs* (or *Canticles*) *Rabbah, Ruth Rabbah, Esther Rabbah, Lamentations Rabbah,* and *Ecclesiastes Rabbah.* The earliest of these ten may date from before the third century, while the latest may date as late as the fourteenth century. Their existence as a "set" began in the sixteenth century, no doubt as a result of the spread of printing and the desire of publishers to produce multi-volume works. Throughout this work, each volume within the collection is referred to individually.

Bibliography

Abrahams, Israel, *Chapters on Jewish Literature*, Jewish Publication Society, Philadelphia, 1899.

Agnon, S. Y., *Days of Awe*, Schocken Books, New York, 1948.

Ausubel, Nathan, *A Treasury of Jewish Folklore*, Crown, New York, 1975.

Bialik, Hayyim Nachman. *And It Came to Pass: Legends and Stories about King David and King Solomon*, Hebrew Publishing Company, New York, 1938.

Bialik, Hayim Nahman and Ravnitzky, Yehoshua Hana, eds., *Sefer HaAggadah*, Moriah, Odessa, 1908-11; Dvir, Tel Aviv, 1936. (English translation by William Braude).

Boccaccio, Giovanni. *The Decameron*, Boni & Liveright, New York, 1925.

Braude, William G., *The Book of Legends: Sefer Ha-Aggadah*, Schocken Books, New York, 1992.

——, *The Midrash on Psalms*, Yale University Press, New Haven, 1959.

——, *Pesikta Rabbati: Discourses for Feasts, Fasts, and Special Sabbaths* (2 vols.), Yale University Press, New Haven, 1968.

——, *Tanna Debe Eliyyahu - The Lore of the School of Elijah*, Jewish Publication Society, Philadelphia, 1981.

Bunim, Irving M., *Ethics from Sinai*, Feldheim Publishers, New York, 2000.

Buber, Martin, *Tales of the Hasidim: Early Masters*, Schocken Books, New York, 1947.

——, *Tales of the Hasidim: Later Masters*, Schocken Books, New York, 1948.

Certner, Simon, *101 Jewish Stories: A Treasury of Folk Tales from Midrash and Other Sources*, Jewish Education Committee, New York, 1961.

Cohen, A., *Everyman's Talmud*, E. P. Dutton & Co., New York, 1949.

Danby, Herbert, *The Mishnah*, Oxford University Press, London, 1933.

Davis, Avraham, *Metsudah Midrash Tanchuma* (8 vols.), Metsudah Publications, Boston, 2007.

Eliach, Yaffa, *Hasidic Tales of the Holocaust*, Oxford University Press, New York, 1982.

Epstein, I., ed., *The Babylonian Talmud* (35 vols.), Soncino Press, London, 1935.

Freedman, H. and Simon, Maurice, eds., *Midrash Rabbah* (10 vols.), Soncino Press, 1939.

Friedlander, Gerald, trans., *Pirke De Rabbi Eliezer: (The Chapters of Rabbi Eliezer The Great) According to the Text of the Manuscript Belonging to Abraham Epstein of Vienna*, Sepher Hermon Press, New York 1970.

Friedman, Edwin H., *Friedman's Fables*, The Guilford Press, New York, 1990.

Ganzfried, Solomon, *Code of Jewish Law (Kitzur Shulchan Aruch) A Compilation of Jewish Laws and Customs* (4 vols.), translated by Hyman E. Goldin, The Star Hebrew Book Co., New York, 1928.

Gaster, Moses, ed., *Sefer Ha-Maasiyot, The Exempla of the Rabbis*, (orig. pub. 1924, reprint) Ktav, New York, 1968.

Ginzberg, Louis, *The Legends of the Jews* (7 vols.), Jewish Publication Society, Philadelphia, 1909-38.

Goldin, Judah, trans., *The Fathers According to Rabbi Nathan*, Yale University Press, New Haven, 1955.

Goodman, Philip, *The Rosh HaShanah Anthology*, Jewish Publication Society, Philadelphia, 1970.

Graetz, Heinrich, *History of the Jews* (5 vols.), Jewish Publication Society, Philadelphia, 1891-98.

Hanauer, J. E., *Folk Lore of the Holy Land: Moslem, Christian and Jewish*, Kessinger Publishing, London, 1907.

Hertz, J. H., *Sayings of the Fathers (Pirkey Avot)*, Behrman House, New York, 1945.

Jacobs, Louis, *Jewish Prayer*, Jewish Chronicle Publications. London, 1962.

Jellinek, Adolf, ed., *Bet ha-Midrash*, (originally published 1853-78, reprint: Wahrmann, Jerusalem, 1967.)

Josephus, Flavius, *The Antiquities of the Jews*, G. Routledge, London, 1900.

Kafka, Franz, *Parables and Paradoxes (Parabeln und Paradoxe)*, ed. by Nahum N. Glatzer (bilingual edition), Schocken Books, New York, 1961.

Langer, Jiri, *Nine Gates to the Chasidic Mysteries*, David McKay Company, New York, 1961.

Lauterbach, Jacob Z., trans., *Mekhilta De-Rabbi Ishmael: A Critical Edition* (2 vols.), Jewish Publication Society, Philadelphia, 2004.

Levin, Meyer, *The Golden Mountain*, Behrman House, New York, 1932.

Longfellow, Henry Wadsworth, *Tales of a Wayside Inn*, The MacMillan Co, London & New York, 1919.

Millgram, Abraham, *Jerusalem Curiosities*, Jewish Publication Society, Philadelphia, 1990.

Montefiore, C. G. and Loewe, H., *A Rabbinic Anthology*, Schocken Books, New York, 1974.

Nelson, W. David, *Mekhilta de-Rabbi Shimon bar Yohai*, Jewish Publication Society, Philadelphia, 2006.

Neusner, Jacob, ed., *The Talmud of the Land of Israel* (projected 35 vols., 16 vols. extant), University of Chicago Press, Chicago, 1983-1994.

Newman, Louis I., *The Hasidic Anthology*, Scribner, New York, 1935.

———, *The Talmudic Anthology: Tales and Teachings of the Rabbis*, Behrman House, New York, 1945.

Ramsay, Allan and McCullagh, Francis, *Tales from Turkey*, Simpkin, Marshall, Hamilton, and Kent, London, 1914.

Rappoport, Angelo S., *The Folklore of the Jews*, Soncino Press, London, 1937.

Rossel, Seymour, *Bible Dreams: The Spiritual Quest*, Rossel Books, New York, 2011.

———, *Israel: Covenant People, Covenant Land*, UAHC Press, New York, 1985.

———, *Lessons from Our Living Past*, Behrman House, New York, 1972.

——, *The Storybook Haggadah*, Pitspopany Press, Jerusalem, 2006.

——, *When a Jew Prays*, Behrman House, New York, 1973.

——, *When a Jew Seeks Wisdom: The Sayings of the Fathers*, Behrman House, New York, 1975.

Schwartz, Howard, *Tree of Souls: The Mythology of Judaism*, Oxford University Press, New York, 2004.

Shah, Idries, *The Pleasantries of the Incredible Mulla Nasrudin*, E. P. Dutton & Co., New York, 1971.

Simon, Maurice and Sperling, Harry, translators, *The Zohar* (5 vols.), Soncino Press, 1931.

Simon, Solomon. *The Wise Men of Helm and Their Merry Tales*, Behrman House, New York, 1965.

Singer, Isaac Bashevis, *The Slave: A Novel*, Farrar, Straus, Giroux, New York, 1970.

Swynnerton, Charles, *Indian Nights' Entertainment; or, Folk-Tales from the Upper Indus* Elliot Stock, London, 1892.

Tanakh: A New Translation of The Holy Scriptures According to the Traditional Hebrew Text, Jewish Publication Society, Philadelphia, 1985.

Vermes, Geza, *The Complete Dead Sea Scrolls in English*, Penguin Classics, New York, 2004.

Visotzky, Burton L., *The Midrash on Proverbs* (Yale Judaica Series), Yale University Press, New Haven, 1992.

Weiner, Herbert, *"Ani V'atah"* in Oesterreicher, John M., *The Bridge: A Yearbook of Judaeo-Christian Studies, Volume III*, Pantheon, New York, 1958.

Weizmann, Chaim, *Trial and Error, The Autobiography of Chaim Weizmann*, Harper and Brothers, New York, 1949.

Wiesel, Elie, *Souls on Fire: Portraits and Legends of Hasidic Masters*, Random House, New York, 1972.

✦ INDEX A ✦
Festivals and Holy Days

Shabbat

🐾 Perfect Lesson, 94; Three Sabbaths, 99; How Should We Serve God?, 187; Ready to Receive, 206; Honored Garment, 217; Giving Charity, 243; Puddings, 260; Ox that Kept the Sabbath, 273; Gem from Heaven, 295; Beruriah and Rabbi Meir, 311; Hillel on the Roof, 316; First Sabbath, 322; Sabbath Angels, 322; Remember the Sabbath Day, 323; Joseph-Who-Honors-the-Sabbath, 325; Light a Candle, 326; Sabbath Miracle, 327; Sabbath Spice, 328; Flying with the Torah, 356; Twelve Loaves, 359

Shavuot

🐾 Rabbi Simeon's Recipe, 24; Not a Bird Twittered, 49; Torah Dance, 49; Who Will Be My Surety?, 53; Fox and the Fish, 56; Space Between, 64; Six Hundred and Thirteen to One, 70; Moses and Akiva, 73; Place of Torah, 132; Six Days, 201

Simchat Torah

🐾 Every Four Generations, 19; Not a Bird Twittered, 49; Torah Dance, 49; Who Will Be My Surety?, 53; Fox and the Fish, 56; Space Between, 64; Six Hundred and Thirteen to One, 70; Moses and Akiva, 73; Place of Torah, 132; Six Days, 201

Sukkot

🐾 Dragon of Jerusalem, 223; Visit, 230

Tisha BeAv

🐾 Nazirites, 132; Jeremiah and Moses, 143; Temple in Ruins, 238; Yochanan and Vespasian, 329

Tu BiShevat

🐾 Parable of the Bountiful Tree, 36; Seventy Years Was But a Dream, 101; Secret of the Seedling, 179; How Shall I Bless You?, 344

Yom Kippur (see High Holy Days)

.ঔ INDEX B ঙ.
Notable Characters

Abbreviations: "**b**" = biblical; "**Ch**" = Chasidic; "**s**" =sage or rabbi of Israel (before 600 CE).
Dates: BCE = "Before the Common Era." All dates not cited as BCE are CE = "Common Era."

Aaron (b)
ঙ. Where Is Paradise?, 21; Let My People Go, 30; Who Will Be My Surety?, 53; Visit, 230; Loving Peace and Pursuing Peace, 330

Abbahu (s)
ঙ. Not a Bird Twittered, 49; Far and Near, 375

Abraham (b)
ঙ. What Shall I Worship?, 25; Jeremiah and Moses, 143; Abraham and the Old Man, 220; Visit, 230; Sanctified Before Birth, 358; Face of the Messiah, 380

Adam (b)
ঙ. Adam's Heritage, 3; Comforting the Mourner, 312; First Sabbath, 322; Sanctified Before Birth, 358

Agnon, S.Y. (1887-1970)
ঙ. Wind and I, 233

Acha (bar Chanina?, s)
ঙ. *Minyan*, 131

Akiva (s)
ঙ. Where Is Paradise?, 21; Fox and the Fish, 56; Akiva Studies Torah, 58; All Your Heart, All Your Soul, and All Your Might, 65; Moses and Akiva, 73; Study or Doing?, 82; Like This Day..., 101; It Could Be You, 186; Buy Me a Town, 239; Freedom of Choice, 267; Rachel and Akiva, 289; Harlot Who Went to Heaven, 298; Medicine, 318; Whose Life Should Be Saved?, 319

Alexander the Great (356-323 BCE)
Alexander and the Rabbis, 104; For the Sake of the Cattle, 162

Ammi (s)
City Guards, 57

Amos (b)
Six Hundred and Thirteen to One, 70

Antoninus (Roman emperor, Antonine dynasty)
Body and Soul, 156; Sabbath Spice, 328; Praying Every Hour, 341

Ardavan (king of Parthia, 3rd cent.)
Most Precious Gift, 157

Ashi (s)
Mystery of Manasseh, 158; It Could Be You, 186

Assi (s)
City Guards, 57

Avilmerodach (king of Babylonia, 6th cent. BCE)
Placing God First, 34

Avin the Levite (s)
Temple Windows, 74

Avtalyon (s)
Hillel on the Roof, 316

Baal Shem Tov (Ch, 18th cent.)
Baal Shem Tov at the Curtain, 21; We Are All Travelers, 22; Learning to Walk, 37; Memory—The Forest, 72; Perfect Lesson, 94; New Rabbi, 147; Satan and Israel, 151; Cooperation, 186; Power of the Broken Heart, 357; Need to Whistle, 362; Full Shul, 364; Tightrope, 364; Face of the Messiah, 380

Baer, Dov (also called Maggid of Mezeritch, Ch, 18th cent.)
We Are All Travelers, 22; Memory—The Forest, 72; New Rabbi, 147; Suffering, 208

Balfour, Arthur (1885-1963)
Jerusalem, 78

Barbuchin (sometimes given as Bar Bochin)
Barbuchin, 164

Chiya (bar Abba or ben Abba, s)
📖 Let My People Go, 30; City Guards, 57; Six Days, 201; Far and Near, 375

Chmielnicki, Bogdan (Cossack Hetman, c. 1595-1675)
📖 Visit, 230

Choni (s)
📖 Seventy Years Was But a Dream, 101; Choni the Circle Maker, 193

Dama ben Netinah
📖 Honor Your Father, 191

Daniel (b)
📖 Every Four Generations, 19; Daniel Prays, 264

David (b)
📖 Lowly Spider, 6; Six Hundred and Thirteen to One, 70; Visit, 230; King David and the Frog, 248; Comforting the Mourner, 312

Deborah (b)
📖 Can a Woman Be a Judge?, 288

Durer, Albrecht (1471-1528)
📖 Praying Hands, 211

Einstein, Albert (1879-1955)
📖 Messiah in Your Classroom, 93; What to Wear, 254

Elazar ben Durdaya (s)
📖 Heaven Calls Them Rabbi, 374

Eleazar ben Arach (s)
📖 Comforting the Mourner, 312

Eleazar ben Azariah (s)
📖 Hannah's Prayer, 288

Eleazar ben Charsom (s)
📖 Whoever Would Teach Him, 82

Eleazar ben Shammua (s)
📖 Shipwrecked, 240

Eleazar ben Simeon (s)
📖 Who Is the Ugly One?, 209

Eleazar HaKappar Berebi (s)
📖 Enjoying Life, 369

Monobazus (Jewish king of Adiabene, 1st cent.)
Treasures for the World to Come, 293

Mordecai (b)
Foolish Haman, 111

Moses (b)
Every Four Generations, 19; Where Is Paradise?, 21; Why Moses Stuttered, 29; Let My People Go, 30; God's Power, 31; Your People, Good or Evil, 32; Torah Dance, 49; Who Will Be My Surety?, 53; Why Moses Dropped the Tablets of the Law, 55; God Gives the Law Again, 56; Moses and Akiva, 73; Jeremiah and Moses, 143; Like Zusya, 192; Visit, 230; Little Sheep and the Lowly Bush, 246; Thorn Bush, 247; Zelophehad's Daughters, 286; Loving Peace and Pursuing Peace, 330; Sanctified Before Birth, 358; Fragments of the Broken Tablets, 365; Face of the Messiah, 380

Nachmias (Joseph ben Joseph, fl. c. 1400)
Ruling Powers, 143

Naftali (Zvi Horowitz) of Ropschitz (Ch, 18th-19th cent.)
Reb Naftali's Secret, 106; Ready to Receive, 206; Silence and Interruption, 212

Nachman (ben Jacob, s)
Parables, 86

Nachman ben Isaac (s)
Six Hundred and Thirteen to One, 70; Students, 120

Nachman of Bratslav (Ch, 18th-19th cent.)
Doubtful Message, 41

Nachum of Gamzo (s)
This Too Is for Good, 346

Nachum of Stepinesht (Ch, 19th cent.)
Pegfuls of Troubles, 213

Nazirites
Nazirites, 132; Enjoying Life, 369

Nebuchadnezzar (king of Babylon, 7th-6th cent. BCE)
Israel and the Nations, 33; Placing God First, 34

Noah (b)
Sanctified Before Birth, 358

✿ INDEX C ✿
Concepts and Values

Asceticism
✿ Cave and the World, 82; Nazirites, 132; Barbuchin, 164; *Matzah* Is a Reminder, 201; Get a Fair Price, 242; Enjoying Life, 369

Atonement
✿ God Gives the Law Again, 56; *Minyan*, 131; Nazirites, 132; Jeremiah and Moses, 143; Body and Soul, 156; Who Is the Ugly One?, 209; Temple in Ruins, 238; All God's Creatures, 272; Repaired Souls, 279; Blemish on the Diamond, 280; Harlot Who Went to Heaven, 298; Heaven Knows Her Children, 336; Three Gifts, 350; Power of the Broken Heart, 357; Alphabet, 362; Need to Whistle, 362; Fragments of the Broken Tablets, 365; Berel Forgives God, 366; Enjoying Life, 369; Praying Once a Year, 369; Little Stones and Big Stone, 371; *Teshuvah*, 372; Thieves Confess, 373; Heaven Calls Them Rabbi, 374; *Baal Teshuvah*, 375; Far and Near, 375; Angel Who Repented, 376; *Shofar* and Drums, 377; String, 378; Return to Me, 379

Avodah (see Labor/Service)

Body
✿ Hillel's Image, 27; Body and Soul, 156; Princess and Rabbi Joshua, 209; *Neshamah*, 214; Tongue for Good and Evil, 265; Soap Maker and the Rabbi, 284; Shadow of God's Image, 285; Medicine, 318

Brit (see Covenant)

B'Tzelem Elohim (see God's Image)

Charity/Righteousness
✿ Early and Late, 85; God Provides, 111; What Justice Requires, 154; Hillel's Wife, 159; Barbuchin, 164; Rothschild's Fortune, 190; Heaven Knocking, 192; Reb Yechiel's Candlesticks, 202; Making *Aliyah*, 203; How It Feels to Be Poor, 205; Ready to Receive, 206; Solomon the Poor, 215; Two Brothers, 237; Temple in Ruins, 238; Buy Me a Town, 239; Shipwrecked, 240; Glass and the Mirror, 241; Get a Fair Price, 242; Giving Charity, 243; Hit Him Again, 244; Laws of Sodom,

Friendship

Blind, 135; Singing Stories, 136; Stone Soup, 139; Ruling Powers, 143; Most Precious Gift, 157; Benefit of the Doubt, 161; How Should We Serve God?, 187; Solomon the Poor, 215; Friends, 216; Magic Ring (Version 2), 222; Dragon of Jerusalem, 223; Third Friend, 228; Visit, 230; Wind and I, 233; Two Brothers, 237; Shipwrecked, 240; Remember the Sabbath Day, 323; Golda and the Arab Nations, 330; Loving Peace and Pursuing Peace, 330; Baseless Love, 365

Gentiles/Non-Jews

Emperor and the Sun, 2; Why Moses Stuttered, 29; God's Power, 31; Israel and the Nations, 33; Placing God First, 34; Making Marriages, 35; Not a Bird Twittered, 49; All Your Heart, All Your Soul, and All Your Might, 65; Lost Bracelet, 67; Magic Ring (Version 1), 76; Jerusalem, 78; Treasure, 80; Alexander and the Rabbis, 104; Foolish Haman, 111; Maimonides and the Blind Man, 114; Wisdom Brightens the Face, 124; Hillel and Shammai, 145; Buying a Donkey, 155; Most Precious Gift, 157; Dowdy Dress, 159; For the Sake of the Cattle, 162; Giving Wisdom to Fools, 190; Honor Your Father, 191; Praying Hands, 211; Shipwrecked, 240; Tower of Babel, 245; Daniel Prays, 264; Ox that Kept the Sabbath, 273; Can a Woman Be a Judge?, 288; Good Investment, 296; Harlot Who Went to Heaven, 298; Sabbath Spice, 328; Yochanan and Vespasian, 329; Golda and the Arab Nations, 330; Praying Every Hour, 341; This Too Is for Good, 346; Commissar, 354; *Teshuvah*, 372

God

Blueprint, 1; Creation and the Watch, 1; Emperor and the Sun, 2; I Have Designed a Palace, 4; How God Protected the Sheep, 7; Reflections, 12; What Shall I Worship?, 25; Where Is God's Dwelling?, 25; Seeing God, 26; *Shechinah*, 27; Let My People Go, 30; Making Marriages, 35; Not a Bird Twittered, 49; Torah Dance, 49; Trees and Iron, 133; God's Slaves, 185; God and Beauty, 185; Thorn Bush, 247; Before This World, 268; Shadow of God's Image, 285; Three Gifts, 350; Angel Who Repented, 376

God and Humanity

Emperor and the Sun, 2; Adam's Heritage, 3; I Have Designed a Palace, 4; One Life, 4; Shamir, 5; Torah Is Not in Heaven, 17; Rabbi Simeon's Recipe, 24; What Shall I Worship?, 25; Where Is God's Dwelling?, 25; Seeing God, 26; Hillel's Image, 27; *Shechinah*, 27; Bargain, 28; Why Moses Stuttered, 29; Let My People Go, 30; God's Power, 31; Enough for Just a Day, 31; Your People, Good or Evil, 32; Israel and the Nations, 33; Martin Elbingrod, 33; Placing God First, 34; Making

Marriages, 35; Parable of the Bountiful Tree, 36; Golem, 37; Learning to Walk, 37; Someone Always Sees, 39; Doubtful Message, 41; Imperial Message, 44; Two *Yods,* 45; Torah Dance, 49; Who Will Be My Surety?, 53; God Gives the Law Again, 56; Solomon and the Snake, 59; Lost Bracelet, 67; Magic Ring (Version 1), 76; Cave and the World, 82; Full Barrel, 94; Like This Day..., 101; Mercy and Justice, 105; Foolish Haman, 111; God Provides, 111; *Minyan,* 131; Serving Me, 131; Jeremiah and Moses, 143; Tending the Fields, 183; God's Slaves, 185; God and Beauty, 185; How Should We Serve God?, 187; Testing the Righteous, 189; Giving Wisdom to Fools, 190; Choni the Circle Maker, 193; Suffering, 208; Pegfuls of Troubles, 213; *Neshamah,* 214; Friends, 216; Abraham and the Old Man, 220; Tower of Babel, 245; Little Sheep and the Lowly Bush, 246; Freedom of Choice, 267; Beruriah's Advice, 276; Hidden Blessings, 281; Boulder, 282; Shadow of God's Image, 285; Zelophehad's Daughters, 286; Hannah's Prayer, 288; Can a Woman Be a Judge?, 288; One Golden Leg, 294; Beruriah and Rabbi Meir, 311; First Sabbath, 322; Sabbath Angels, 322; Who to Thank, 335; You And I, 335; Heaven Knows Her Children, 336; Horses Can Pray?, 337; Service of the Heart, 340; Praying Every Hour, 341; Dancing with the Bear, 342; Three Gifts, 350; Flying with the Torah, 356; Sanctified Before Birth, 358; Alphabet, 362; Need to Whistle, 362; Fragments of the Broken Tablets, 365; Berel Forgives God, 366; Defiance, 366; Denying God, 368; Praying Once a Year, 369; Heaven Calls Them Rabbi, 374; Angel Who Repented, 376; String, 378; Return to Me, 379

God's Image

Seeing God, 26; Hillel's Image, 27; Your People, Good or Evil, 32; Martin Elbingrod, 33; Parable of the Bountiful Tree, 36; Golem, 37; Cave and the World, 82; Rooster Prince, 89; Two Pockets, 106; Hillel and Shammai, 145; Body and Soul, 156; Tending the Fields, 183; God and Beauty, 185; Princess and Rabbi Joshua, 209; Who Is the Ugly One?, 209; *Neshamah,* 214; Abraham and the Old Man, 220; Hidden Blessings, 281; Shadow of God's Image, 285; Hillel on the Roof, 316; Remember the Sabbath Day, 323; Twelve Loaves, 359

Gossip (*see* Slander/Gossip)

Happiness

Clowns, 16; Madness or Dancing?, 165; Hidden Treasure, 184; Making *Aliyah,* 203; Wind and I, 233; Choose One Thing, 256; Puddings, 260; Boulder, 282; Rachel and Akiva, 289; One Golden Leg, 294; How Shall I Bless You?, 344; Enjoying Life, 369

Heaven and Earth

Heritage/Tradition

Holiness

Humor

Image of God (*see* God's Image)

Impulses/Inclinations (*Yetzer Tov/Yezter HaRa*)

Intention (*Kavanah*)

Judgment, Final

Whoever Would Teach Him, 82; Body and Soul, 156; Like Zusya, 192; Eighty Witches, 276; Birth and Death, 313

Justice (see also Judging)

Elijah and Rabbi Joshua, 14; Two *Yods*, 45; Solomon and the Snake, 59; Cave and the World, 82; Mercy and Justice, 105; Sharing the Cheese, 119; Justice in Chelm, 138; Fisherman and King, 141; What Justice Requires, 154; Buying a Donkey, 155; Helping Hand, 155; Body and Soul, 156; Two Witnesses, 158; For the Sake of the Cattle, 162; Barrel of Justice, 165; Young Judge, 168; Bell of Justice, 170 & 172; Hole in the Wall, 173; Too Clever, 177; Secret of the Seedling, 179; Treachery, 219; Tower of Babel, 245; Wooden Bowl, 260; Removing an Evil Tongue, 263; Daniel Prays, 264; Laws of Sodom, 268; Zelophehad's Daughters, 286; As Many as You Want, 300; Marvelous Clock, 302; Widow and the Wind, 305; This Too Is for Good, 346; Berel Forgives God, 366; Defiance, 366

Kavanah (see Intention)

Kedushah (see Holiness)

Kiddush Hashem (see Martyrdom)

Kindness to Animals

Shamir, 5; Lowly Spider, 6; How God Protected the Sheep, 7; Solomon and the Snake, 59; Good Advice, 96; Three Pieces of Knowledge, 98; For the Sake of the Cattle, 162; Bell of Justice, 170 & 172; Dragon of Jerusalem, 223; Little Sheep and the Lowly Bush, 246; King David and the Frog, 248; All God's Creatures, 272; Beating a Donkey, 272; Ox that Kept the Sabbath, 273; As Kind as Rebecca, 297; Donkey, 318

Labor/Service (*Avodah*)

In Praise of God, 4; Shamir, 5; Israel and the Nations, 33; Golem, 37; Why Moses Dropped the Tablets of the Law, 55; Akiva Studies Torah, 58; Keeping the Commandments, 68; Show Bread Secrets, 74; Whoever Would Teach Him, 82; Yochanan and the Digger of Wells, 85; Seventy Years Was But a Dream, 101; Motivation, 118; Sharpening the Axe, 120; *Minyan*, 131; Serving Me, 131; Benefit of the Doubt, 161; Tending the Fields, 183; Hidden Treasure, 184; God's Slaves, 185; God and Beauty, 185; It Could Be You, 186; Cooperation, 186; Goat that Made the Stars Sing, 186; How Should We Serve God?, 187; Good Name, 189; Rothschild's Fortune, 190; Heaven Knocking, 192; Suffering, 208; Friends, 216; Little Sheep and the Lowly Bush, 246; King David and the Frog, 248; Boulder, 282; Soap Maker and the Rabbi, 284;

Women
🔖 Hillel's Wife, 159; Beruriah's Advice, 276; Zelophehad's Daughters, 286; Hannah's Prayer, 288; Can a Woman Be a Judge?, 288; Rachel and Akiva, 289; One Golden Leg, 294; As Kind as Rebecca, 297; Widow and the Wind, 305; Beruriah and Rabbi Meir, 311; Golda and the Arab Nations, 330

World to Come
🔖 Clowns, 16; Where Is Paradise?, 21; Gold or Torah, 62; Space Between, 64; Like This Day..., 101; Place of Torah, 132; Treasures for the World to Come, 293; One Golden Leg, 294; Gem from Heaven, 295; Harlot Who Went to Heaven, 298; Twins in the Womb, 313; Heaven Calls Them Rabbi, 374; Far and Near, 375; Messiah among the Beggars, 382

Yetzer HaRa/Yetzer Tov (*see* Impulses/Inclinations)

Zionism (*see* Israel, Love for)

About the Author

Rabbi Seymour Rossel is the author of *The Wise Folk of Chelm; Bible Dreams; The Holocaust: An End to Innocence, The Torah: Portion-by-Portion, A Child's Bible*, and dozens of other books.

Rabbi Rossel is President of RCC, Inc., a former member of the faculty at the Women's Institute of Houston, and founding director of Pathways Foundation. He served the North American Jewish Reform movement in a number of national positions: as Director of the URJ Press, Director of the URJ Department of Education, Director of the Commission on Reform Jewish Education, and Dean of the School of Education of Hebrew Union College-Jewish Institute of Religion, NY. He was Rabbi of Congregation Jewish Community North of Spring, TX; Headmaster of the Solomon Schechter Academy of Dallas, TX; President of Rossel Books; Executive Vice President of Behrman House; and Director of Education for Temple Shalom of Dallas, TX, and Temple Beth El of Chappaqua, NY.

For many years, he sat on the national boards of the Jewish Book Council, the Coalition for the Advancement of Jewish Education, and the National Association of Temple Educators (now the Association of Reform Jewish Educators). In 1988 and again in 1996, Rabbi Rossel was Chairperson of international conferences on Jewish education convened at the Hebrew University in Jerusalem.

As speaker, author, and editor, Rabbi Rossel is listed in *Who's Who in the Eastern States, Contemporary Authors*, and *Who's Who in World Jewry*. He holds several awards for excellence in Jewish Education and was honored by being inducted as an ex-officio member of the Central Conference of American Rabbis.

Rabbi Rossel lectures widely on Jewish legend and lore, Bible, archaeology, mysticism, Jewish history, education, and values; and offers scholar-in-residence engagements, congregational and educational workshops; and retreats in communities throughout North America. His books, workshops, and articles are featured on the web at *http://www.Rossel,net*.

Made in the USA
Las Vegas, NV
06 December 2024